More Advance Acclaim for
Self-Awareness Deficits in Psychiatric Patients

"What does neurology have to teach us about self-awareness? A lot, it turns out. By studying fascinating pathological syndromes resulting from brain dysfunction, the editors of and contributors to this volume help us understand how the brain shapes and maintains our sense of who we are. This is interesting reading, not just for clinicians but also for all those who want to understand more about human consciousness."
> —Andrew Weil, M.D., Clinical Professor of Medicine and Director
> of the Program in Integrative Medicine, University of Arizona

"A remarkable book! Readers will find the thought-provoking argument that deficits in self-awareness cut across many mental disorders. The distinguished contributors to this collection provide lucid descriptions of the neural systems that appear to be related to behavioral deficits in self-awareness and they extend the central thesis to address the specific behavioral and, when appropriate, biological deficits in self-awareness observed in a wide spectrum of common psychiatric disorders. *Self-Awareness Deficits in Psychiatric Patients* is must reading for psychiatrists and other mental health professional interested in expanding their concepts of the fundamental deficits involved in mental disorders."
> — Robert O. Friedel, M.D., Distinguished Clinical Professor of Psychiatry,
> Virginia Commonwealth University, author of *Borderline Personality Disorder
> Demystified* and founding editor of *Current Psychiatry Reports*

"Beitman, Nair, and contributors have gone 'big-game' hunting in their search for the relationship between self-awareness, the evolution of the human brain, and the development of a stable sense of self and human adaptation. In this challenging quest, they have blazed some new trails and widened preexisting ones. The clinical discussions shed new light on self-awareness as an important dimension of psychiatric illness."
> — Barry F. Chaitin, M.D., Professor and Co-Chair, Department
> of Psychiatry and Human Behavior, University of California, Irvine.

Self-Awareness Deficits in Psychiatric Patients

Also by Bernard D. Beitman from W. W. Norton

Integrating Psychotherapy and Pharmacotherapy: Dissolving the Mind-Brain Barrier
(with Barton J. Blinder, Michael E. Thase, Michelle Riba,
and Debra L. Safer)

*Learning Psychotherapy: A Time-Efficient, Research-Based, and Outcome-Measured
Psychotherapy Training Program, Second Edition*
(with Dongmei Yue)

Learning Psychotherapy: Seminar Leader's Manual, Second Edition
(with Dongmei Yue)

A Norton Professional Book

Self-Awareness Deficits in Psychiatric Patients

NEUROBIOLOGY, ASSESSMENT, AND TREATMENT

Edited by

Bernard D. Beitman, M.D.
Jyotsna Nair, M.D.

W. W. Norton & Company
New York • London

For information about permission to reproduce
selections from this book, write to
Permissions, W. W. Norton & Company, Inc.,
500 Fifth Avenue, New York, NY 10110

Production Manager: Leeann Graham
Manufacturing by Quebecor World Fairfield Graphics

Library of Congress Cataloging-in-Publication Data
Self-awareness deficits in psychiatric patients : neurobiology, assessment, and
treatment / edited by Bernard D. Beitman, Jyotsna Nair.
p.   cm.—(A Norton professional book)
Includes bibliographical references and index.
ISBN 0-393-70435-1 (pbk.)
1. Self.   2. Self-perception.   3. Mentally ill.   4. Clinical neuropsychology.
5.   Neuropsychological tests.   I. Beitman, Bernard D.   II. Nair, Jyotsna.   III. Series.

RC489.S43S436   2004
616.89′14—dc22   2004049259

W. W. Norton & Company, Inc., 500 Fifth Avenue, New York, N.Y. 10110
www.wwnorton.com

W. W. Norton & Company Ltd., Castle House, 75/76 Wells St., London W1T 3QT

1   3   5   7   9   0   8   6   4   2

To

Paula Levine with love (BB)

My parents, you let me go
Satish, you helped me grow (JN)

Contents

Contributors

ALARIK T. ARENANDER, PH.D., Director, Brain Research Institute, Institute of Science, Technology and Public Policy, Maharishi University of Management, Fairfield, Iowa

BERNARD D. BEITMAN, M.D., Professor and Chairman, Department of Psychiatry, University of Missouri-Columbia, School of Medicine, Columbia, Missouri

RICHARD J. BURCH, M.D., Assistant Professor of Psychiatry, Department of Psychiatry, University of Missouri-Columbia, Columbia, Missouri

AMEE JO EPLER, B.A., National Institute on Alcohol Abuse and Alcoholism Predoctoral Trainee, Department of Psychological Sciences, University of Missouri-Columbia, Columbia, Missouri

LAURA A. FLASHMAN, PH.D., Associate Professor, Department of Psychiatry, Dartmouth Medical School, Lebanon, New Hampshire

Neuropsychology and Brain Imaging Laboratory, Neuropsychiatry Section, New Hampshire Hospital, Concord, New Hampshire

GLEN O. GABBARD, M.D., Professor of Psychiatry and Director, Baylor Psychiatry Clinic, Baylor College of Medicine

Supervising Analyst, Houston-Galveston, Psychoanalytic Institute, Houston, Texas

ZAC E. IMEL, M.A., Doctoral Student, Department of Counseling Psychology, University of Wisconsin-Madison, Madison, Wisconsin

Jyotsna Nair, M.D., Associate Professor, Department of Psychiatry, University of Missouri-Columbia, School of Medicine, Columbia, Missouri

Robert G. Robinson, M.D., The Paul W. Penningroth Professor and Chairman, Department of Psychiatry, Roy J. and Lucille A. Carver College of Medicine, The University of Iowa, Iowa City, Iowa

Kenneth J. Sher, Ph.D., Curator Professor of Psychology, Department of Psychological Sciences, University of Missouri-Columbia, Columbia, Missouri

James R. Slaughter, M.D., Clinical Associate Professor, Family and Community Medicine, University of Missouri-Columbia, Columbia, Missouri

Frederick T. Travis, Ph.D., Associate Professor and Dean of the Graduate School, Director, EEG/Consciousness and Cognition Lab, Co-Director, Institute for Research on Higher States of Consciousness, Maharishi University of Management, Fairfield, Iowa

Claudia T. Viamontes, M.D., Ph.D., Regional Medical Director, Mental Health Network, Inc., Saint Louis, Missouri

George I. Viamontes, M.D., Ph.D., Regional Medical Director, United Behavioral Health, Inc., St. Louis, Missouri

Assistant Clinical Professor, Department of Psychiatry, University of Missouri-Columbia, School of Medicine, Columbia, Missouri

Jorge A. Viamontes, M.D., Associate Clinical Professor, Department of Psychiatry, Saint Louis University, Saint Louis, Missouri

Preface

AN EMERGING UNDERSTANDING of how self-awareness influences the integrity of the human organism may make its further study one of the defining characteristics of twenty-first-century medical science. With innately resilient and adaptable brains, human beings have adjusted themselves, over the course of several hundred millenia, to ever-changing ecological conditions. Our capacity for self-awareness, as individuals, as groups, and as a species, has endowed us with a sense of our history's meaning, the implications of our present, and the prospects for our future. Among the creatures of the Earth, we seem to be unique in our ability to project our self-awareness across all three of these dimensions. We are further self-aware in possessing the understanding that the fate of the planet is in our stewardship. Though we are seldom conscious of it, we continue to evolve ourselves, and our growing consciousness of our selves and our capacities is foremost among those traits likely to affect the future nature of the human organism.

Like all psychological functions, the human ability to "step back," observe oneself, and to understand the inner workings of another mind, requires some formatting within the brain. By defining those parts of the brain that subserve self-awareness, we may become better able to clearly define *self-awareness*. Once defined, we may then be able to find within our extraordinary brains further abilities and capacities yet to be recognized or even intuited. Neuroscientists tell us that we utilize only a small fraction of our brains; the expansion of our self-awareness may lead us to knowledge of what that unused capacity can do, and what we can do with it. Self-awareness can become that significant.

This book addresses unresolved questions about the neurobiological basis of self-awareness. In order to do so, we used the time-honored medical approach of studying pathological functioning to understand normal functioning. By identifying the anatomical and physiological malfunctions that precipitate specific dysfunctions, we can often illuminate unrecognized elements of normal function. Deficits of self-awareness are seen in nearly all psychiatric disorders. By studying malfunctioning self-awareness in each of the major categories of mental illness, we have clarified those features which the deficits seem to share whenever they manifest as symptoms of mental illness, as well as those characteristics of disordered self-awareness that appear to be specific to individual psychiatric diagnoses. The shared and distinct features of these deficits may be viewed from both neurobiological and psychological bases. We concentrated our studies on disorders that display prominent deficits rather than distortions of self-awareness. Many patients with schizophrenia and patients with profound organic brain syndromes simply lack awareness of how they are affected by the diseases; they may appear to display a benign indifference to something the rest of us find terribly troubling. People with body dysmorphic disorders, on the other hand, suffer from a hyperawareness of themselves that manifests in a distorted sense of their own body images.

These manifestations of disturbed self-awareness deserve concerted attention beyond what they receive in this book. Here we concentrate on those major mental illnesses whose characteristic symptomatology deprives their sufferers of any real sense of themselves in relationship to their environment and the people around them. These deficits can become so all-encompassing that they threaten the individual's ability to function independently in the world, to perform activities of daily living, form meaningful relationships, or survive without significant support from others. In these respects, psychiatric diseases which manifest in significant deficits of self awareness can become as life-threatening as dangerous infections or severe physical traumas. Furthermore they can be highly resistant to treatment, and as such they require the most urgent attention of the medical community.

I come to this task as a psychotherapist intrigued by the ability of my patients to change the way they think about themselves and their relationships within the world. Can I help them any more effectively by knowing more about how the brain supports their ability to observe themselves? The wisdom of the assembled thinkers whose work you are about to read convinces me that I can.

Bernard D. Beitman, M.D.
Columbia, Missouri
March, 2004

Acknowledgments

THE EDITORS THANK several people who contributed to the creation of this book. Bruce Richman edited the chapters with precision and efficiency. Debby Burnley transformed diffusively edited manuscripts into clear typescripts. Barb Klund managed the communications among and between the editors and chapter authors with grace and charm. Pat Connolly copyedited with patience and persistence. The process of going from manuscript to print was carefully overseen by Michael McGandy. Deborah Malmud, our editor at Norton, provided much needed support and encouragement. She believes in us! Thank-you all.

Self-Awareness Deficits in Psychiatric Patients

Part 1

TOWARD A NEUROBIOLOGY
OF SELF-AWARENESS

1

Why Self-Awareness?

Bernard D. Beitman
Jyotsna Nair
George I. Viamontes

EXPANDING HUMAN consciousness provides us with ever increasing knowledge of our inner and outer worlds. Optimal use of this knowledge can inspire idealistic human beings to synthesize visions and plans directed at reducing human suffering and finding ways to create the groundwork for improving the quality of human existence and furthering spiritual evolution. Increasing self-awareness increases our options and choices as human beings.

The study of self-awareness is complicated by the inherent constraints created by the need to use human self-awareness to study self-awareness. The means by which to make useful observations about self-awareness require that some distance be achieved by the observer of self-awareness phenomena. This distance may be accomplished in many different ways including: (1) through the study of evolution; (2) the study of human development; (3) neuroimaging; (4) the study of pathological disease processes; (5) self-report (e.g., by psychotherapists and novelists); (6) questionnaires; and (7) standardized interviewing (Main & Goldwyn, 1993). For this text, in order to define normal self-awareness, we have selected the study of pathological processes and their effect on self-awareness either by its distortion or absence.

3

The study of self-awareness takes place in at least two apparently different verbal realms: the realm of *thought* words and the realm of neurobiology. The *cognitive* words must in some way be mapped onto the *brain* words in a way that merges the two languages. At this time in our evolution, we remain with the confusion created by this increasingly inaccurate dichotomy of mind and brain.

The Internet, with its capability for instantly messaging almost anyone in the world, has created a conceptually much smaller world for us than we had before the advent of radio and telephones. Simultaneously, we are seeing expansions in human consciousness. There is no reason to think that the development of human consciousness stops with each one of us now, but rather that this most recent evolutionary advance has a long way to go. Our new information processing tools, these extracranial memory boxes and computer links and cell phone connectors, have made our brains much more extensively interconnected and more powerful. Children are being born into a world in which instant messaging already existed, and where they can contact their friends by cell phone at any time. Their minds are transported rapidly to distant places, into the minds of others, in ways never conceived 100 years ago. These mind-expanding experiences have the potential to take human self-awareness beyond the levels familiar to readers of this book.

In 2003, Pearl, age 4, and I (BB) were walking away from her parents as they staffed their booth of her father's paintings at the Columbia, Missouri Art in the Park Festival. Pearl wanted to follow the colorful peacock advertising of the local NBC TV affiliate, but I wanted to be sure that Pearl's parents approved and suggested that it might be better to go back. Pearl paused briefly and then said, "When my mommy starts to worry, we will come back." She knew her mother's mind. She knew that if her mother worried, there was a problem, and that her mother would do something about it.

A few months later, Pearl's parents accepted positions in another part of the country, and invited my wife and I to a farewell dinner. After dinner, my wife and I joined her to play tea party with her stuffed animals. We each told Pearl that we would miss her. She drew a picture of a girl, put her name on it, and handed it to us. "Put it on the wall. When you miss me, you can look at it. If you need to, you can look at it all day." How did Pearl know our minds well enough to make this self-assured suggestion?

Pearl likes to report her dreams to her mother. How is it that she remembers them well enough to report them? What made her think they might be interesting? Pearl knows her mind, knows the minds of others, and has some idea about how others imagine her. Pearl is quite self-aware.

Toward a Definition of Self-Awareness

So how do we define self-awareness? The problem is quite complex and at present not well understood. The confusion comes from the need to have accurate definitions of its two root words: *self* and *awareness*. The definition of self is quite perplexing and difficult. Philosophers, religious writers, neuroscientists, psychiatrists, and psychologists have struggled with defining the term and have often failed to do so (Wolfe, 2002). Again, we are confronted with the problem of using ourselves to define what we mean by a self, with each one of us being an individual example of the idea we are trying to define. Perhaps we should think of self as what others would see when they look at me if they were inside of me looking at me. So, self is the person as an object from an intrasubjective perspective. There is something appealing here about the self as an object of self-observation, but it becomes difficult to imagine how someone else could actually enter objectively into our own experience unless we presented ourselves to them fully, and we never could present even a substantial fraction of what is within each of us. We are limited in part because we are unaware of so much of what constitutes our selves.

Developmental Aspects of Self-Awareness

The development of self-awareness in children starts with the development of a sense of self. The first step for the infant is to be able to distinguish between him- or herself and the environment. This is the *mine/not-mine* concept. The timeline of the development of this concept and how this understanding comes about is the focus of this section.

Infants learn about their bodies and the environment. With maturation they develop motility, learning in the process that motor activity can affect a change in the stimuli experienced. For example, an infant in the crib has a foot touching the rail and moves his foot, resulting in the loss of the sensation of touch. This sensation is in the *not-mine* category while internal sensations that are unaffected by movement are in the *mine* group. Infants gradually develop a sense of self and seem to be wired to start connecting with other individuals while learning about themselves. The processes described in this section include empathy, joint attention, mirror self-recognition, and reading the facial expressions of others. For greater detail see Chapter 5 on autism.

The development of a sense of self and others begins gradually in infancy. Neonates 42 minutes old will imitate facial expressions of adults, by, for example, opening their mouths or sticking their tongues out (Meltzoff & Moore, 1977, 1983). Newborns do not see their own facial gestures, of course, and rely on proprioception to make the expressions, and simultaneously convert the visual input from the adult into proprioception to achieve the right gesture. This phenomenon shows that the infant brain is hard wired for gestural imitation, so infants are born ready to learn about themselves and the world.

Older infants, 9 to 12 months old, will look at mirror images and make gestures and watch the image move. They locate objects seen in the mirror. As they grow, infants recognize when an adult is imitating their gestures and will respond. In the process, they are learning actively about their own body and also about others. The physical manipulations and mastery enable the child to make the leap from *acts like me* to *thinks like me*. In other words, other individuals experience their bodies in the same way as the infant does.

Nine-month-old infants can read expressions and respond. They will point to objects of interest or point to a desired object. At this age, if they hear another baby crying they will also cry, but they cannot yet console another child. Eighteen-month-old infants recognize their own image in the mirror, and can tell their image apart from those of others. Thus, they not only recognize themselves, but also recognize the *not-mine*.

These activities demonstrate the development of a physical sense of self. Along with Mirror Self Recognition they are increasingly using the word *I* when they refer to themselves and use *mine* when referring to their toys. At this age, shyness and embarrassment, signs of a developing sense of self, are also seen.

By the age of 3 there is more information available to the toddler. The rule of "seeing leads to believing" develops, and given a choice, the rule will be applied. Pretend games translate into acquiring and becoming proficient at social skills. Connolly and Doyle (1984) measured the capacity for pretend play in 2-, 3-, and 4-year-olds and found that the ones who got into the spirit of the play were the ones who had the greatest social skills.

Children at the age of 4 make a big cognitive leap, understanding for the first time that other people can have ideas or beliefs that are wrong, because they are based on outdated knowledge. This is called false belief. Three-year-olds do not make this connection. In one common experiment, the child is presented with a box of candy and is asked what he or she thinks is in the box. The child will say candies. When the box is opened it reveals pencils. When the child is asked again what he or she thought was in the box a 3-year-old will say pencils while a 4-year-old will say candies. There is a leap in the reasoning ability in this age and unlike the 3-year-old, the 4-year-old can go back and recall that he or she had a mistaken belief about the content (Perner, Leekam, & Wimmer, 1987; Perner, Frith, Leslie, & Leekam, 1989). Here the 4-year-old is going back and thinking of his or her mental state prior to the new knowledge about the contents of the box. Thus, with development children are acquiring the tools of self-awareness; that is, a sense of self, language, memory, bodily awareness, and understanding of others.

Language and Self-Awareness

Is it necessary to have a formal system of language to be self-aware? Is language also the key to understanding self and others? Language, as a means of communication, is unique to humans. It frees us from the present and represents ideas in symbols that can be shared. Thus we can participate in the meeting of the minds.

There is some evidence that animals can communicate via language. Some great apes and dolphins can learn language but the complexity of ideas seen in human language are not there. Human languages vary in complexity and some do not have the kinds of words for feeling and mental states, like many Western languages. The importance of the core vocabulary of the language was demonstrated in experiments that tested for false belief in children.

Testing for false belief has been a way to determine the ability of children to have a concept of the mental state of others. The manner of testing involves arranging a setup where the child observes an adult put an object (say a ball) in one place and then leave. Another person comes in and moves it. The child is asked where the first person would look for the ball when they came back. By age 4, most children know that the person will look in the place where they first placed the object. Avis and Harris (1991) tested Baka children of Cameroon and noted that they could pass false belief tasks at the age of 4 and 5 and could also predict the emotional state of the person with the mistaken idea. Similar results were reported from industrialized literate areas in Japan and China (Flavell, Zhang, Zou, Dong, & Qi, 1983; Gardner, Harris, Ohomoto, & Hamazaki, 1988).

Quechua children from Peru were also tested for their ability to understand false belief. In the Quechua language there are no words to describe many mental states. The closest one would come to the concept of "he thinks" in Quechua would be "he would say." Thus, in the absence of words to express mental status would children have a concept of false belief based on the thoughts of others? The Quechua language is rich in words that describe the appearance of objects. One experiment involved distinguishing the dichotomy of appearance and reality when shown a sponge that looked like a rock. In this experiment the children had no problems. But the same children found it difficult to understand the questions relating to the thought process of another person. They did not demonstrate conclusively their ability to know how another person would act when participating in a false belief experiment (Vinden, 1996).

Closer to home it has been noted that deaf children raised by hearing parents who are not fluent signers, have deficits in the false belief and appearance reality tasks and develop an understanding of these concepts when they become older. This is possibly due to lack of exposure early in life to words and concepts relating to feelings and thoughts, because these deficits are not seen in deaf children raised by parents who are fluent signers (Petersen & Siegal, 1995, 1997; Gale, deVilliers, deVilliers, & Pyers, 1996).

Thus, language is a key element of abstraction: it lets us form mental representations and manipulate them; it lets our imagination roam free without leaving our chairs; it presents a symbolic medium for thoughts and experiences; it supports thinking; is a means of communication and meetings of the minds; it provides us with the ability to navigate past, present, and future and monitor ourselves. These are all important aspects of self-awareness.

Self-Awareness and Inner Speech

Do self-aware individuals participate in more self-talk? One would think so. Encouraging self-talk by patients has been used as a tool by therapists. Some groups seem to favor this view of the functions of self-talk (Siegrist, 1995). PET scans of subjects engaged in self-talk showed increased activity in the left inferior frontal area (McGuire et al., 1996). Levine, Calvanio, and Popovics (1982) reported a case with complete loss of inner speech following a stroke in the same area.

It is not clear whether self-awareness deficits would result from damage in the same area. Orbitofrontal area damage has been associated with disturbance in self-awareness (Leduc, Herron, Greenberg, Eslinger, & Grattan, 1999). One study by Craik and colleagues (1999) showed activation in the left inferior frontal gyrus on PET scan when the subjects were engaged in tasks that referred to self. At this point, it can be said that the left inferior frontal area has a role to play in both self-talk and processing ideas that refer to the self. Other connections remain to be clarified.

Body Awareness

We are aware of our body and the fact that we are in it. The body is our "Earth Suit." We move around, negotiate obstacles, turn if we need to, and have a sense of where our body is in space. We are aware of the body and are also aware of the space the body is in.

The patient suffering spatial hemineglect following injury or stroke lesion to the region of the right posterior parietal lobe, one loses awareness of the left half of bodily space. Mesulam (2000) associated the right posterior parietal lobe with spatial awareness and the ability to judge angles, mental rotations, drawing, and spatial attention. He described the posterior parietal cortex as a "critical gateway for accessing and integrating information related to attention related representation and exploration of the extra personal space" (p. 40). This observation gives some clues to the way one perceives the body and the space around it.

Newberg and colleagues also suggested that the right posterior parietal lobe provides the spatial coordinates to orient the body—*Why God Won't Go Away: Brain Science and the Biology of Belief* (Newburg, d'Aquili, & Rause, 2002). The authors also hypothesized that the left side gives the "mental sense of a limited defined body." The authors call these areas the *right* and the *left orientation awareness* areas. They observed that the left orientation awareness area shows a decreased activity during meditation when the meditator feels the sense of self is merging with a higher power. The explanation for the decreased activity lies in the decrease and later a block in inputs from the sensory modalities due to intense concentration and the consequent sensation of selflessness (Newburg, Alavi, Baime, Mozley, & Aquili, 1997).

Processes that Diminish Self-Awareness

The Viamontes group as well as Arenander and Travis (see Chapters 2 & 3) extensively detail how processes of self-awareness originate as functions of the brain's architecture and neurocircuitry. Their descriptions of normal and pathological brain function and their behavioral manifestations illuminate the interface between mind and brain. Some of these processes are:

1. Genetic and developmental abnormalities
2. Destruction of map areas and their connections
3. Excessive pruning of connections or other reductions in connectivity
4. Excessive amplification of signals
5. Diminished amplification
6. Adaptive simplification
7. Toxic damage
8. Active Suppression

Genetic and Developmental Abnormalities

The definition of reality is, in the final analysis, a central process. If mapping areas don't exist, are improperly structured, or improperly connected, the image of the self that results will not reflect the same reality that others perceive. Dyslexia, for example, has been linked to aberrant alignment of neurons in mapping areas of the cortex; specifically, the left planum temporale (Dronkers, Pinker, & Damasio, 2003)

Autism is a disorder that appears to involve aberrant mapping in the context of emotions, language, symbolic reasoning, and modeling. It presents as a series of incapacitating deficits in emotional integration, social interactions, verbal communication, the selection of objects of interest and activities, and the ability to deal with new situations. Autistic individuals do not appear able to process their own emotional experiences, and are thus unable to infer emotional reactions in others. Not surprisingly, social bonding, which is based in great part on emotional exchanges, is deficient in autistic individuals. In addition, the inability to use language effectively limits symbolic analysis and therefore restricts an important level of self-awareness. The autistic individual is not aware of the deficit in emotional integration. Because the brain circuitry for accessing and integrating emotions never developed, these processes are wholly nonexistent for the autistic person, and therefore outside the reach of conscious awareness.

In addition to genetic factors, appropriate inputs during early life are essential to the development and connection of mapping areas. Newborn kittens that have one eye patched at birth, for example, never develop appropriate connections from the patched eye to the visual cortex, and will be permanently unable to see out of that eye. In addition, kittens that are shown only vertical patterns during early development are later unable to detect horizontal patterns due to vertically biased alignment of neurons in the visual cortex (see review in Cotterill, 1998).

Destruction of Map Areas or Their Connections

Reality is all about brain maps; without a map, nothing can exist. With a map, even nonexistent things can be experienced as real. Phantom limb pain is an example of a central reality without an external correlate. The central map of the missing limb still exists within the brain, even though the limb itself no longer exists.

Conversely, the wholesale destruction of an existing cortical map can obliterate the reality of an object (even a part of the self). Strokes and traumatic brain injuries can be particularly devastating because they destroy both mapping areas and their connections. Capgras syndrome, in which there is a fixed belief that significant others are "doubles" and not the actual individuals, can be a sequela of closed head injury, and is frequently co-morbid with schizophrenia (Tamam, Karatas, Zeren, & Ozpoyraz, 2003). Capgras syndrome involves a significant deficit in self-awareness. The mechanism of this disorder appears to be a change in mapping or associative capacity that makes the *current* experience of significant others different from the *remembered* experience. The individual is unable to appreciate that the deficit is internal, and therefore through projection attributes the discrepancy to changes in others rather than changes in the individual's ability to perceive.

Excessive Pruning of Connections or Reductions of Connectivity

Acquired deficits in connectivity can severely alter the composition and integration of brain maps. One of the primary deficits in schizophrenia appears to be reduced connectivity in the dorsolateral prefrontal cortex (Lewis, 2002). The dorsolateral prefrontal cortex is involved in the potentiation of executive function. Executive function refers to the ability to organize and apply resources to solve complex behavioral problems. This includes setting and maintaining self-direction, learning new information, searching memory systematically, changing behavioral strategies to reflect changing contingencies, implementing motor programs, and using verbal skills and logic to guide behavior.

Although several lines of analysis point to the reduction of neuronal connections within the dorsolateral prefrontal cortex, the exact nature of the deficit is not known. One hypothesis is that connections are excessively pruned during adolescence. Up to 50% of excitatory (not inhibitory) connections are normally broken during the adolescent years to reduce redundancy and improve neural network efficiency. Several lines of evidence have suggested that in schizophrenia, the pruning may continue to an excessive level (see review in Lewis, 2002). Another hypothesis postulates that a developmental problem may promote abnormal connectivity.

Animal models of dorsolateral prefrontal cortex damage have been created by damaging the hippocampus neonatally. This results in abnormal organization of the dorsolateral prefrontal region, and is a reflection of the critical role that the hippocampus plays in wiring the higher cortices. Recent evidence points to a connectivity problem between the medial dorsal thalamic nucleus and the dorsolateral prefrontal region. Lack of prefrontal control can also account for increased dopaminergic stimulation of limbic circuits, which can induce psychotic phenomena (Kapur, 2003).

The deficits in cortical connectivity limit the quality and detail of the maps that the schizophrenic brain can contain. Schizophrenic individuals are not aware of the extent of their problems, because the realities that the individual can represent lack complexity in the first place.

Excessive Amplification of Signals

Amplification can significantly alter information processing in the brain, excessively focusing attention to the exclusion of other relevant information. It can create and perpetuate maladaptive states, such as the anxiety disorders, chemical dependence, body dysmorphic disorder, and many features of the personality disorders. Excessive amplification can cause severe distortions in self-perception, such as the ones that characterize body dysmorphic disorder. In addition, it can magnify maladaptive responses, including aggression and impulsivity, which characterize some of the personality disorders. Amplification in the brain is primarily accomplished by regulatory neurotransmitters, such as dopamine (salience), norepinephrine (enhanced signal-to-noise ratio), and serotonin (normally reduces amplification in brain areas responsible for aggression, impulsivity, and anxiety).

Chemical dependence offers another example of a behavioral deficit precipitated by abnormally focused attention. In this class of disorders, the reward system of the brain has precipitated the storage of powerfully salient memories related to drug or alcohol use. Whenever environmental or internal cues are perceived that indicate the possibility of obtaining and using the individual's drug of choice, glutamatergic excitatory signals from the hippocampus trigger the spiny neurons of the nucleus accumbens into an activated state (Heimer et al., 1997). Concomitantly, dopamine from the ventral tegmental area floods the nucleus accumbens, enhancing the depolarization of activated neurons and causing inactive neurons to hyperpolarize further. The active neurons eventually fire as they receive more excitatory inputs related to the imminence of alcohol or drug use. As the GABAergic accumbens neurons fire, they diminish the tonic inhibition of the thalamus by neurons in the ventral pallidum, and enhance the thalamocortical transfer of the alcohol- or drug-related cues, thus increasing the amplification of their representations in the brain.

The nucleus accumbens is an area of confluence that integrates a variety of inputs from sensory and limbic regions, and focuses attention on potentially rewarding objects and situations. (Heimer et al., 1997). In the face of anticipatory cues, dopamine, in concert with glutamate, activates accumbens circuitry and confers tremendous motivational salience to the next steps in making drug or alcohol use a reality. Awareness of the problems associated with the response to continued addictive behavior is frequently drowned by the intensity of the alcohol- and drug-related representations. In summary, the overwhelming degree of salience that is given to cues associated with alcohol and drug consumption overrides cortical inhibition and leads to the automatic behaviors that culminate in continued, uncontrolled substance use.

Diminished Amplification

Diminished amplification of information can lead to significant deficits in self-awareness. The brain has limited processing capacity, and relies on selective amplification of what it determines to be the most important stimuli at any given time in order to focus processing resources. Attention deficit/hyperactivity disorder (ADHD) is a classical example of diminished, ineffective amplification.

Selective amplification in this regard is thought to be mediated by a series of parallel thalamocorticostriatal loops (McFarland & Haber, 2002). The thalamus sends excitatory information about the environment and internal milieu to various parts of the cortex. At any moment, those stimuli selected as being most important are selectively amplified. Specific mechanisms for selective stimulus amplification are thought to be implemented at the thalamic level. Selective inhibition by the internal segment of the globus pallidus, which is topographically mapped onto the thalamus, is thought to be an important mechanism for signal filtering. The selection of which stimuli to filter out is driven by cortical inputs to the striatum, as well as by dopamine levels. Without dopamine, the filtering process loses some of its selectivity, and a larger proportion of irrelevant stimuli can filter through.

The thalamus is almost completely surrounded by a net of inhibitory neurons called the thalamic reticular nucleus. The thalamic reticular nucleus is an intricate net of inhibitory, GABAergic neurons. Crick (1984) hypothesized that the thalamic reticular nucleus acts as an "attentional spotlight," allowing only signals of interest to pass without attenuation. Signals that don't receive full attention are not completely suppressed, and they constitute the "environmental background" that allows us to perceive a continuous environmental reality and to be ready to discern other possibly interesting signals that might emerge.

The selection of "salient" or important signals depends on whether the signal is signifying a threat, a possible reward, an unusual or novel condition, something that differentiates itself from the background, or an object of cognitive interest. The cingulate gyrus is important in the assignation of motivational salience to objects and situations. Bilateral damage to the cingulate results in a condition of apathy known as *akinetic mutism*. Individuals with unilateral damage may suffer some degree of akinetic mutism, but usually recover. One such recovered patient was asked why she said nothing during her illness. She replied, "Because nothing ever came to mind" (Damasio, 1994).

Individuals with self-awareness deficits related to ineffective amplification tend to have problems with the implementation of effective behavioral strategies, since they are not able to isolate prospective organizing principles. Individuals with akinetic mutism are not aware of their deficit, because the loss of salience prevents most objects or situations from being processed at higher levels.

Individuals with ADHD often know in general terms that they have problems, but are not aware of the precise nature of their deficit. They cannot selectively amplify relevant information from their environment so they miss important clues, especially nonverbal feedback from others; for example, when the person with ADHD is speaking. They then wonder why people may not wish to talk with them.

Alzheimer's disease, at least in the earlier stages, may also be considered to be a disordered amplification. Acetylcholine activates cells in memory pathways and it is deficient in those with Alzheimer's disease. Therefore, memory is not recorded in the present, and maps for recent events and experiences are not developed. Tragically, some early Alzheimer's patients recognize their memory deficits, but as the disease progresses, their ability to compare what they should remember and what they can remember diminishes. They lose awareness of their deficits.

Adaptive Simplification

There is significant evidence indicating that in times of protracted stress, the brain actually simplifies some of the networks that orchestrate behavioral responses to the environment. This can be adaptive in a variety of ways: first, it conserves processing energy; second, it speeds processing; third, it limits possible responses, shortening response time, and making it simpler to choose among behavioral possibilities. Chronic stress, for example, causes dearborization of hippocampal cells, as well as the cessation of the production of new hippocampal neurons (Sapolsky, Krey, & McEwen, 1985). In certain pathological states, such as borderline personality disorder, oversimplification of context can lead to some of the disorder's characteristic symptoms. Interestingly, one of the aims of dialectical behavioral therapy for borderline personality disorder is to expand the patient's ability to integrate context into his or her view of the self and immediate surroundings (Linehan, 1993). Adaptive simplification results in self-awareness deficits because map detail has been simplified. This leads to a "coarser" view of reality, with more generalization when faced with similar situations and diminished ability to distinguish the uniqueness of specific situations. The individual with simplified brain maps is unaware of his or her self-awareness deficit because the missing map information simply does not exist in the brain, and therefore is not known to be missing.

Toxic Damage

Toxic damage of specific brain regions will cause a variety of deficits whose specific nature depends on the location of the injuries. The toxic effects of chronic alcoholism on the brain are thought to be mediated by three distinct mechanisms: (1) direct neurotoxicity of alcohol; (2) nutritional deficiencies secondary to alcohol use; (3) neurotoxic effects of alcohol withdrawal. In rats, chronic alcohol consumption per se has not been associated with specific neuroanatomical defects. Alcohol withdrawal, on the other hand, has been associated with neuronal dearborization and neuronal loss (Lewis, 2002). Humans who drink large amounts of alcohol chronically show evidence of neuronal loss in both cortical and limbic regions. In the cortex, pyramidal neurons appear to be involved (Lewis, 2002).

Individuals who show clinical symptoms of Korsakoff's dementia also have more significant signs of neuropathology. For example, abnormalities have been reported in the frontal cortex as well as in the thalamus, hippocampus, mammillary bodies, and amygdala. Imaging studies in Korsakoff's patients show hypometabolism in prefrontal, parietal, and temporal cortices.

Progressive toxic injury to the brain leads to a decline in cognitive and memory functions. As the disorder progresses, there is a gradual coarsening of cognitive and representational capabilities, and the quality of the individual's self-image, cognitive, and adaptive capacities gradually declines. Damage to brain maps and to their connectivity dampen the alcoholic's ability to notice problems sufficiently to act upon them.

Active Suppression

The active suppression of information is a final mechanism that can cause an impairment in self-awareness. Signal suppression is thought to mediate the symptoms of conversion disorder (also known as hysterical paralysis). Clinically, conversion disorder presents as one or more symptoms or deficits in voluntary motor or sensory function that suggests a neurological or other general medical condition (American Psychiatric Association, 2000). The etiology of the disorder, however, is not neurological but rather neuropsychiatric. Imaging of the brains of individuals with conversion disorders has yielded interesting results.

A study of a woman with complete left hemiplegia of hysterical origin, as well as a study of a man with hypnotically induced left hemiplegia, both showed increased activity in the right anterior cingulate and right medial orbitofrontal cortex. However, there was no activation of right premotor or sensorimotor cortices (Halligan, Athwal, Oakley, & Frackowiak, 2000). These observations seem to suggest possible frontal inhibition of movement. Another PET scanning study compared three men with severe hysterical weakness of one or both arms with individuals who were instructed to feign arm weakness. In this case, the conversion disorder patients showed hypofunction of the left dorsolateral prefrontal cortex, whereas the "feigners" showed hypofunction of the dorsolateral prefrontal cortex (Spence, Crimlisk, Cope, Ron, & Grasby, 2000). A third, more recent PET scanning study of 7 individuals with conversion disorder revealed hypofunction in the contralateral basal ganglia and thalamus. These deficits resolved after the individuals recovered (Vuilleumier et al., 2001).

Although the specific neurocircuitry for conversion disorder has not been fully elucidated, the above hints at a mechanism whereby higher cortical regions inhibit the implementation of specific motor programs. The inhibition most likely takes place at the level of the basal ganglia and thalamus.

Conversion reaction is hypothesized to occur as a subconscious response to an anxiety-provoking situation. The movement deficit removes the anxiety-provoking condition from awareness by blocking motor movements that are symbolically or realistically associated with the anxiety-provoking situation. Individuals with conversion disorders frequently show emotional indifference to their paralysis ("la belle indifference"). Deficits in self-awareness are a hallmark of conversion reactions, because the very point of the reaction is to remove an anxiety-provoking situation from consciousness. This might be accomplished by diminishing the situation's emotional salience ("la belle indifference"), which in turn would tend to shield it from conscious scrutiny.

Defining Self-Awareness

First, how do we define awareness? The easiest part of this question lies in the relationship between consciousness and awareness. One must be conscious in order to be aware. Consciousness requires basic brain functioning to be intact, including such involuntary the functions of breathing, heart beating, an operative autonomic nervous system, and digestion (the protoself). Consciousness can sometimes generate awareness. Awareness generally implies consciousness of a content, so that one becomes aware of a cloud or aware of a building or of a person or of a pain or a pleasant experience. In this book, we are interested in a particular kind of content for consciousness; namely, the self. However, defining the self can be problematic. So here we will define self-awareness by using the terms *self* and *awareness*, each of which we have some general difficulty in defining; nevertheless, we proceed onward. What then can we mean by self-awareness? In its simplest form, self-awareness is the self being aware of itself—I am aware of me. An aspect of the self, which we might call the *observing self* (Deikman, 1982) breaks free of the content of the self to then *observe* the content of the self. The observations are made dispassionately without criticism or evaluation. However, most of us confuse the pure awareness of an aspect of the self with evaluative, judgmental, and action-connected activities. Psychotherapists and some

spiritual leaders try to free us from these judgments and help us to understand self-awareness as uncritical self-consciousness.

Definition of self-awareness is not limited to awareness of the self, but
includes the ability of the self to be aware of the minds of others. This
aspect of self-awareness is often called *theory of mind* (TOM), or less commonly, *mentalization*. A neurobiology for TOM has been postulated which
incorporates our understanding of mind and brain (Calarge, Andreasen, &
O'Leary, 2003). Psychoanalytic research consistent with its emphasis on unconscious functioning has also introduced the term, *reflective self-functioning*,
which is to be distinguished from *self-awareness* and *mentalization*. Reflective
self-functioning refers to automatic processes by which people take note of
their internal experiences and the possibilities going on in the mind of another person, and come to a conclusion about how to respond. With a little
reflection, it becomes apparent that we can not always monitor our internal
and external perspectives when making a decision, but rather must put most
of these operations on automatic pilot so they can respond immediately to
current environmental demands. So, here we have unconscious self-awareness
(Fonagy & Target, 1997).

And so there was one more step that Pearl seemed to be aware of when
she bestowed her self-portrait. Pearl was aware of how we thought of her.
Pearl was not only self-aware, and was not only aware of our experiences,
but was also aware of how we felt about her. This expanded view of self-
awareness can be summarized by the statement: What do you think I think
of you? Consciously or not, Pearl had in one way or another enacted an
expanded form of self-awareness by asking and answering the question,
"What do you think I think of you?"

Aspects of Self-Awareness

Flashman (see Chapter 4) has studied how psychotic patients process information, using self-awareness as one of the defining features in her taxonomy. As readers will find in this volume and elsewhere, there are many
forms of deficient self-awareness but an inadequate vocabulary with which
to describe them, so the same words are used to refer to very different
psychological events. We need a more precise vocabulary for structures
within both the mind and the brain, but we will not have one until we
understand the operation of both more clearly. Sher and Eppler's study of
alcoholic patients (see Chapter 6) demonstrates how the psychological process of denial common among alcoholics, and the delusional processes of

Flashman's schizophrenic patients, share terminology and symptomatology in their distortion of self-awareness, but reflect entirely different major manifestations of distinct mental illnesses.

INSIGHT

The word *insight* means peering in, and it is the first step in understanding what's there; becoming self-aware is noticing an aspect of oneself. Many schizophrenic people do not notice dysfunctions in their thinking or in their behavior. Some may call it denial, and perhaps there is in both alcoholism and schizophrenia an element of denial, but in autism, which often demonstrates a pervasive absence of self-awareness, there does not appear to be a psychological process of denial so much as a disorder of the brain's neurocircuitry of self-awareness. The same may be said for the poststroke syndrome the unconcerned insensibility to the loss of key brain functions. The cerebral hemorrhage has damaged the brain's circuitry in such a way that the brain is unable to recognize its own injury. The news that the lines are down can not get through because the lines are down. The anosognosia described by Robinson (see Chapter 9) may look like what we call *denial* in the alcoholic, and we are quite clear that the one is entirely the result of a profound organic brain syndrome, while the other is a psychological defense mechanism. We are, in fact, probably too clear in our belief in an either–or dichotomy. Although some influences necessarily predominate in individual disease systems, the deficits in self-awareness seen following cerebrovascular accidents and long-term alcohol abuse are both very likely the outcomes of a complex interaction of neurobiological, intrapsychic, social, and genetic factors. Specifically, because we find some manner of distorted self-awareness in so many psychiatric disorders, with so many etiologies, it is an ideal laboratory in which to study psychiatry's most fascinating unsolved puzzle, the interface between mind and brain.

MOTIVATION

Disappointed expectations often elicit negative emotions like fear, anxiety, or anger, responses biologically programmed to stimulate action. Some patients with schizophrenia, right parietal stroke, and hysterical paralysis may be able to demonstrate insight by acknowledging the problem, but are indifferent to the discrepancy between their dysfunction and normality. They recognize that something is wrong, but feel no need to actively respond. The absence of emotional drive limits the possibilities for improving their conditions.

CAUSE

Schizophrenics may blame the conspirators. Alcoholics may blame their wives or the whiskey. Most autistic people have little sense of past and future, however, and have no sense of blame. Whether it is accurately placed or not, blame suggests recognition of a problem and offers hope for leverage to change. Without the causal attribution apparatus embedded in our sense of time, change through self-awareness is restricted.

CLINICAL IMPLICATIONS

Insight, motivation, and proper causal attribution can stimulate people to develop plans for what should be done. The consequences of a discrepancy between what one expects and what actually occurs are dependent upon one's ability to project a sense of the self into the future. Without this ability, there is limited capacity to assess the impact of one's own deficits upon others, to think about what "you" think of "me."

While stroke, autism, schizophrenia, and hysterical paralysis tend to isolate, alcoholism, attention deficit disorder, and borderline personality disorder almost always distribute consequences across the sufferer's social network. Alcoholics can ignore the impact of their behavior on significant others, on their jobs, and social environments. As described by Burch (see Chapter 8), patients with attention deficit disorder (ADD) are moving so quickly they can't catch either their inner experiences or their impact on others. Often socially isolated, children with ADD can't focus long enough to recognize the impact of their rapid speech and behavior on other people and allow themselves to accommodate their responses to those reactions. They can't visualize the mind of the other as the other looks at them. As noted by Gabbard (see Chapter 7), borderline personality disorder patients have learned to disconnect their capacity for empathy to save themselves from intolerable emotional reactions. To be both hated and loved, to be the victim of disgust, apathy, fear, or lust may be too frightening to experience, and the borderline patient protects himself from these feelings by blunting his self-awareness.

Treatment

Some patients cannot be helped by our therapeutic efforts to improve their self-awareness; many schizophrenics with deficits in self-awareness respond fairly well to treatment without becoming more self-aware. As Flashman notes (see Chapter 4), schizophrenic patients who lack awareness are notoriously unwilling to comply with treatment, and have poorer prognoses, though clozapine may help increase self-awareness in some schizophrenics. Autistic children can improve their awareness of themselves and others if they start treatment early in life. Robinson (see Chapter 9) reports that antidepressant treatment seems to increase awareness of the poststroke deficit. Slaughter (see Chapter 10) notes his clinical success in using hypnotic suggestion to mobilize patients suffering from hysterical paralysis. The movement of alcoholics from lack of insight into action is a long struggle with many social, psychological, genetic, and neurobiological barriers, and usually requires that each be addressed. For patients with ADHD, pharmacotherapy can be successful in slowing down their actions and giving them an opportunity to "stop and think." Part of what they learn to think about is the minds of others and their own impact upon the minds of others. In his case examples, Gabbard displays the value of creating a therapeutic environment in which the patient can feel safe in confronting the mind of another and from there expand the safety zone, daring to look inward and confront a sense of self. No one clinician has found the ideal formula for titrating medications and psychotherapy to achieve this condition for all patients and all the kinds of psychopathology that manifest wholly or in part as deficient self-awareness.

Likewise, no one who has studied or treated the conditions collectively described in the American Psychiatric Association's successive editions of the *Diagnostic and Statistical Manual of Mental Disorders* (2000) has yet been able to build a durable, reliable bridge between the mind and the brain. In some cases, the distance to be crossed looks narrow, only a step or two in just the right direction and we'll be there. Sometimes the fog is so thick the other side can hardly be seen. We look for clues on both shores, common elements, the signs of trouble shared by traumatized brains and troubled minds. We'll pick up a thread like self-awareness and try to follow it, hand over hand, to see if it will braid in upon itself and thicken until it becomes strong enough to carry us to the other side. We haven't found the thread that will bear all this weight yet, but when we do we will have embarked upon a path that will not only change the course of medicine, but the course of humanity. The psychiatrists and psychologists whose work you will read here are still testing the thread of self-awareness to see if it will reveal itself as a mighty span.

References

American Psychiatric Association. *Diagnostic and Statistical Manual of Mental Disorders*. 4th ed. rev. Washington, DC: American Psychiatric Press; 2000.

Avis J, Harris PL. Belief-desire, reasoning among Baka children: evidence for a universal conception of mind. *Child Dev.* 1991; 62:460–467.

Carlarge C, Andreasen NC, O'Leary DS. Visualizing how one brain understands another: a PET study of theory of mind. *Am J Psychiatry.* 2003; 160:1954–1964.

Connolly JA, Doyle A. Relation of social fantasy play to social competence in preschoolers. *Dev Psychol.* 1984; 20:797–806.

Cotterill R. *Enchanted Looms: Conscious Networks in Brains and Computers.* Cambridge, U.K.: Cambridge University Press; 1998.

Craik F, Moroz T, Moscovitch M et al. In search of the self: a positron tomography study. *Psychol Sci.* 1999; 10(1):26–34.

Crick FHC. The function of the thalamic reticular complex: The searchlight hypothesis. *PNAS.* 1984; 81:4586–4590.

Damasio AR. *Descartes' Error: Emotion, Reason, and the Human Brain.* New York: Grosset/Putnam; 1994.

Deikman A. *The Observing Self.* Boston: Beacon Press; 1982.

Dronkers N, Pinker S, Damasio A. Language and the aphasias. In: Kandel ER, Schwartz JH, Jessell TM, eds. *Principles of Neural Science.* 4th ed. New York: McGraw-Hill; 2003:1169–1187.

Flavell JJ, Zhang X-D, Zou H, Dong Q, Qi S. A comparison between the development of appearance reality distinction in the People's Republic of China and the United States. *Cog Psychol.* 1983; 15:459–466.

Fonagy P, Target M. Attachment and reflective function: their role in self-organization. *Dev & Psychopath.* 1997; 9:679–700.

Gale E, deVilliers P, deVilliers J, Pyers. *Language and theory of mind in oral deaf children.* Paper presented at: Boston University Conference on Language Development; November 1996; Boston.

Gardner D, Harris PL, Ohomoto M, Hamazaki T. Understanding the difference between real and apparent emotion by Japanese children. *Internat J Beh Dev.* 1988; 11(2): 203–218.

Halligan PW, Athwal BS, Oakley PA, Frackowiak RS. Imaging hypnotic paralysis: implications for conversion hysteria. *Lancet.* 2000; 355:986–987.

Heimer L, Alheid GF, de Olmos et al. The accumbens beyond the core-shell dichotomy. In: Salloway S, Malloy P, Cummings JL, eds. *The Neuropsychiatry of Limbic and Subcortical Disorders.* Washington, DC: American Psychiatric Press; 1997:43–70.

Kapur S. Psychosis as a state of aberrant salience: a framework linking biology, phonomenology, and pharmacology in schizophrenia. *Am J Psychiatry.* 2003; 160(1):13–23.

Leduc M, Herron JE, Greenberg DR, Eslinger PJ, Grattan LM. Impaired awareness of social and emotional competencies following orbital frontal lobe damage. *Brain & Cog.* 1999; 49(1):174–177.

Levine DN, Calvanio R, Popovics A. Language in the absence of inner speech. *Neuropsychologia.* 1982; 20:391–409.

Lewis DA. Neural circuitry approaches to understanding the pathophysiology of schizophrenia. In: Davis KL, Charney D, Coyle JT, Nemeroff C, eds. *Neuropsychopharmacology: The Fifth Generation of Progress.* Philadelphia: Lippincott, Williams & Wilkins; 2002: 730–744.

Linehan M. *Cognitive-Behavior Therapy for Borderline Personality Disorder.* New York: Guilford; 1993.

Main M, Goldwyn R. *Adult attachment scoring and classification system.* Unpublished manuscript. Department of Psychology, University of California. Berkeley: 1993.

McFarland NR, Haber SN. Thalamic relay nuclei of the basal ganglia from both reciprocal and nonreciprocal cortical connections, linking multiple frontal areas. *J Neurosci.* 2002; 22(18):8117–8132.

Mcguire PK, Silbersweig DA, Murray RM et al. Functional anatomy of inner speech and auditory visual imagery. *Psycholog Med.* 1996; 26:29–38.

Meltzoff AN, Moore MK. Imitation of facial and manual gestures by human neonates. *Science.* 1977; 198:75–78.

Meltzoff AN, Moore MK. Newborn infants imitate adult facial gestures. *Child Dev.* 1983; 54:702–719.

Mesulam MM. *Principles of Behavioral and Cognitive Neurology* (2nd Ed.). Oxford, U.K.: Oxford University Press; 2000.

Newberg A, Alavi A, Baime M, Mozley PD, d'Aquili E. The measurement of cerebral blood flow during the complex cognitive task of meditation using HMPAO–SPECT imaging. *J Nuc Med.* 1997; 38:55.

Newberg A, d'Aquili E, Rause V. *Why God won't go away: Brain science and the biology of belief.* New York: Ballantine; 2002.

Perner J, Leekam S, Wimmer J. Three year olds' difficulty with false belief: the case for a conceptual deficit. *Br J Dev Psychol.* 1987; 5:125–137.

Perner J, Frith U, Leslie AM, Leekam SR. Exploration of the autistic child's theory of mind: knowledge, belief and communication. *Child Dev.* 1989; 60:689–700.

Petersen CC, Siegal M. Deafness, conversation and theory of mind. *J Child Psychol & Psychiatry.* 1995; 36:450–474.

Petersen CC, Siegal M. Domain specificity and everyday biological, physical and psychological thinking in normal, autistic and deaf children. *New Dir Child Dev.* 1997; 75: 55–70.

Sapolsky RM, Krey LC, Mc Ewen BS. Prolonged glucocorticoid exposure reduces hippocampal neuron number: implications for aging. *J. Neurosci.*1985; 5(5):1222–1227.

Siegrist M. Inner speech as a cognitive process mediating self-consciousness and inhibiting self-deception. *Psycholog Rep.* 1995; 76:259–265.

Spence SA, Crimlisk HL, Cope H, Ron MA, Grasby PM. Discrete neurophysiological correlates in prefrontal cortex during hysterical and feigned disorder of movement [letter]. *Lancet.* 2000; 355:1243–1244.

Tanam L, Karatas G, Zeren T, Ozpoyraz N. The prevalence of Capgras syndrome in a university hospital setting. *Acta Neuropsychiatrica.* 2003; 15(5):290–296.

Vinden PG. Junin Quechua children's understanding of the mind. *Child Dev.* 1996; 67: 1701–1716.

Vuilleumier P, Chicherio C, Assal F, Schwartz S, Slosmen D, Landis T. Functional neuroanatomical correlates of hysterical sensorimotor loss. *Brain.* 2001; 124:1077–1090.

Wolfe B. The role of lived experience in self- and relational observation: a commentary on Horowitz (2002). *Journal of Psychotherapy Integration* 2002; 12:147–153.

2

Neural Circuits for Self-Awareness

Evolutionary Origins and Implementation in the Human Brain

George I. Viamontes
Bernard D. Beitman
Claudia T. Viamontes
Jorge A. Viamontes

SELF-AWARENESS IS AN emergent property of healthy human brains. The implementation of this adaptive function is spontaneous, and usually transparent to the individual who is self-aware. The brain circuits that generate knowledge about the self are multidimensional, and their connections complex. However, the integration of the multiple streams of knowledge that define the self is accomplished with such efficiency that the fabric of who we are, which in truth is a patchwork quilt, appears seamless.

The study of self-awareness is a systematic search for seams in the fabric of the self. Basic information about the mechanisms that create the self has been obtained from analysis of brain malfunction secondary to accident or

The authors would like to thank Dr. Linda Spollen for her expert assistance with the photography of human brains. We would also like to thank Mr. Matthew Daues for his assistance with the human brain MRIs.

disease, as well as from animal experimentation and imaging studies. This chapter will investigate the brain circuits that generate self-awareness by following four main threads: evolution, neurobiology, development, and dysfunction. These lines of inquiry should provide a balanced foundation for understanding how self-awareness originated and how it is implemented in the human brain.

Evolutionary change in the brain, as in any physiological system, is driven by differential reproduction. To the extent that a modified brain increases the generation of offspring, the modification (provided it can be transmitted genetically) will spread through a population of organisms. Behavioral modifications that enhance reproductive success range from devouring one's mate after fertilization to the development of creative and social skills that can be used to attract desirable partners.

An important theme in brain evolution is the acquisition and conservation of energy. Without adequate supplies of energy, reproduction is not possible. The devouring of male insects after mating, as practiced by spiders and praying mantises, is an extreme way to increase the energy endowment of offspring. In higher species, males tend to survive mating encounters and often support the energy needs of offspring in a sustained manner during the latter's development.

Self-awareness has evolved to a sophisticated level because it is a versatile tool that can enhance both reproduction and energy management. Self-awareness became possible when the size and complexity of organisms warranted the inclusion of internal states as one of the controlling variables in the regulation of directed movement.

Success in securing energy and optimizing its utilization supported the cortical expansion that led to advanced brains. From a neural circuitry perspective, brain evolution shifted the balance of power from the thalamus (which is characterized by a limited number of rapid, automatic responses) to the cortex (which supports a large behavioral repertoire). Cortical function gives rise to the phenomenon of *choice*, and requires the resolution of conflict among competing value-risk assessments (e.g., "I'm hungry, and that dessert looks wonderful! But what about my diet?"). The brains of higher animals take advantage of the many internal and external streams of information that they capture by dedicating large portions of the cortex to integration. The integration of multiple data streams generates a rich, multidimensional experience of physical reality, and makes possible the complex representation of the self that characterizes humans.

An important characteristic of advanced brains is *plasticity*. This term refers to the brain's ability to reorganize its circuitry. Plasticity facilitates the customization of brains to address important challenges in the environment with speed and efficiency. Brains with high levels of plasticity are exceptional in terms of adaptability, but require special inputs during development to function properly.

Dysfunctions of self-awareness are caused by innate or acquired deficits in brain structure. These deficits can be induced by genetic misinformation, developmental problems, disease, or physical injury. Analysis of abnormal states is an important tool for unravelling the mechanisms of self-awareness, and is a major focus of this book.

The Evolutionary Foundation of Self-Awareness

From an evolutionary perspective, the human brain was a serious gamble. It is entrusted with our lives, yet it is fragile, consumes large amounts of energy, and requires years of nurturing before it rewards its owner with an independent capacity for survival. Despite these relative shortcomings, the brain has made humans the most successful complex organism on the planet. The primary reason for this success is a high level of adaptability. The human brain facilitates heightened awareness of the complexities of the self's environment, and generates an abundance of behavioral options at key decision points.

If we examine living species, we can discern two main paths to evolutionary success: simplicity and complexity. The path of simplicity emphasizes frugality and replication: keep things simple, use few resources, and multiply prolifically. This strategy has brought success to diverse phyla ranging from bacteria to insects. Within this scheme, individuals are not "built to last," and have relatively short life spans. Despite rapid turnover of members, the species survives through high reproductive rates and a modest need for resources.

At the opposite end of the organizational continuum is complexity. This evolutionary strategy addresses environmental challenges by maximizing adaptive flexibility and acquisitive power. When implemented successfully, complexity not only underwrites its own cost, but provides many resources beyond. It does represent a long-term investment, however, because individuals must survive through long developmental periods before they can reproduce. Higher animals that utilize this strategy tend to have longer life spans, and often require parental care to survive into adulthood. The evolutionary path to complexity involves the orchestration of many subsystems, and therefore requires a control center to coordinate interactions with the environment. This role has been filled by the brain.

WHY DO WE NEED BRAINS?

The power of the human brain, which is the product of millions of years of evolutionary adaptation, can sometimes obscure its humble origins. The phylogenetic path to the brain, with its 10 billion neurons and an estimated 10^{15} synaptic connections (Mesulam, 2000), has not been, as some might imagine, either direct or purposeful. The forces of evolution simply promote incremental adaptation to the challenges of the environment. To complicate matters, many solutions to problems of adaptation are possible. Humans are no more successful from an evolutionary perspective than insects, plants, or bacteria.

Unlike processes designed through engineering, evolutionary advances are not goal-directed attempts to solve a specific problem. Instead, evolution occurs as selective pressures redirect existing components to new purposes, with gradual refinement of the novel functional capacity over many generations. At any point in development, evolving systems like the human brain contain significant redundancy and inefficiency. Natural selection does bring about functional improvements over time, but only when these improvements, directly or indirectly, result in higher reproductive rates. Complex systems with the ability to acquire a large excess of energy can afford to host more suboptimal, evolving processes than simple systems. In the latter, which tend to have smaller supplies of excess energy, even tiny inefficiencies can tip the balance toward extinction.

The human brain, despite its considerable processing power, is not a finished work from an evolutionary perspective. The best way to describe it is as a collection of interacting subsystems in various developmental stages. Phylogenetically older processes will tend to be better optimized than more recently evolved functions. As we examine these neural functions in detail, it is important to establish a vantage point by addressing the fundamental question that is the title of this section: "Why do we need brains?"

The human brain represents only 2% of an adult's body mass, yet it consumes 20% of the body's oxygen and 25% of its glucose (Magistretti, Pellerin, & Martin, 2000). How can such a disproportionate consumption of resources be sustainable in highly competitive environments? The answer, which might at first seem surprising, is that the brain's cost-effectiveness is highest in environments with intense competition. Simpler systems are sufficient when resources are plentiful, but complex brains increase the chances for survival when resources are difficult to obtain. The biological viability of a brain depends on a simple equation: will the energy that the brain obtains offset its own consumption and provide a surplus to support the organism's other functions?

From the viewpoint of natural selection, it was the development of directed movement that made brains not only viable, but necessary. Simple reactive systems based on nerve nets are present in primitive organisms such as the cnidarians, of which jellyfish are an example. These systems are passive, and depend on the abundance of potential prey for success. Once a fish becomes entangled in a jellyfish's tentacles, reactive systems trigger the firing of poisoned needles. The tentacles then "reel in" the captured prey to the jellyfish's digestive pouch. This system is highly efficient because it requires little energy to maintain and can acquire significant resources. It has a serious limitation, however, in that its passivity limits its adaptive potential. If fish become scarce and don't run into the jellyfish's tentacles, the cnidarian has no capacity to generate alternatives, and will starve.

Directed movement provides a significant advance over simple reactive systems for food acquisition. However, its implementation requires additional complexity. The pathway to efficient directed movement has four steps. First, a sensory representation of the environment must be created. This should have enough sophistication to permit the identification of potential resources at a distance. Second, a system that can assess relative value and risk must be implemented. This system should answer questions of ambiguity and possible cost. If more than one potential resource is available, which one should the organism pursue? Third, since patterns of environmental risk and opportunity are likely to be repeated, a learning system that can facilitate rapid responses to previously encountered situations needs to be developed. Fourth, movement should be directed whenever possible toward acquisition of the specific resources that fulfill internal needs. If an organism became dehydrated, for example, water would be the most critical resource to seek. The identification of the organism's special needs requires the development of a comprehensive array of internal sensors.

Solutions to the four requirements for optimized movement are well implemented in the human brain. Humans have evolved sophisticated cortical maps that can provide detailed representations of physical "reality." These advanced maps have many more components than those of lower animals. Much as the first video games had limited resolution and represented reality as a series of "stick figures" with simple interactive parameters, lower organisms have limited representations of the environment mapped in their nervous systems. Human brains, in contrast, contain elaborate maps of external reality with many levels of integration. Through use of these brain maps, humans are able to define abstract concepts like *meaning*, *responsibility*, and *purpose*. Humans can also discern causality, and make adaptive behavioral choices.

Some of the most important factors that human brains consider relate to questions of risk and reward. Optimal behavior should maximize benefits to the individual while incurring a minimum of risk. Dedicated circuits in the brain manage this important optimization function. The phenomenon of fear exemplifies the complex, multidimensional reactions that can be triggered by the brain to regulate risk. Fear can be literally paralyzing in its effects, and can keep an individual safe by forcing the avoidance of dangerous situations. Conversely, perceptions of potential reward can induce mobilization. When a reward that is consistent with internal needs appears obtainable, special circuits in the brain focus attention and organize behavior to ensure attainment of the potential prize. A sufficiently valuable reward has the power to cause the temporary exclusion of competing motivational variables from consideration. This exclusionary "blackout" can include potential risk, external organizing principles, and prediction of future consequences. The ability of brain reward systems to exclude competing motivational circuits when a valuable reward is at stake underlies the maladaptive phenomenon that we know as chemical dependence.

Risk and reward systems are interwoven with the brain circuits that support memory and learning. It is adaptive to remember frightening situations to ensure avoidance of them in the future. Conversely, the memory of rewarding circumstances facilitates their repetition. The capacity of humans to learn, and to use memory to drive behavior, is unparalleled among living organisms. The memory systems of humans support many forms of remembered information, including conditioned reflexes, complex motor programs, emotional associations, physical locations, symbolic representations, sensory images, and verbal descriptions of objects and events. Without learning and memory, there would be no self other than the transient representation of moment-to-moment interactions with the environment. In fact, we witness a tragic dissolution of the self as memory fails in degenerative disorders such as Alzheimer's disease.

Humans derive adaptive advantages not only from the ability to learn de novo, but from the transmission of knowledge to offspring as the latter develop. For instance, while the language areas of the brain are present at birth, their full development is not achievable without educational input from caretakers and social contacts. Children who are not taught language during the first few years of their lives may never be able to attain full language function. Such individuals are often able to learn rudimentary language skills when they are older, but may not develop the capacity to use language for symbolic reasoning. As this example illustrates, one of the costs of expanded learning is dependence on specific types of inputs during development to guide brain organization. The genes define tentative mapping areas, but these designated regions and their matrices of integrative connections require environmental stimuli to organize properly. Ideally, this arrangement yields organisms that are specifically adapted to the environment in which they developed. Of necessity, it also creates dependence on environmental inputs to guide development. Adverse or impoverished environments during critical developmental periods can impair subsequent function and adaptability.

The evolution of sensory systems that can signal internal needs is not only a requirement for the optimization of directed movement, but the first step in the creation of the self. The dawn of self-awareness cast a tentative glimmer on living organisms with the incorporation of internal sensors into the behavioral equation. Prior to this, there was no representation of internal events, and hence no possibility of a self. Internal sensors are critical to the optimization of directed movement because they can provide a behavioral focus that maximizes the impact of adaptive actions. In animals, internal sensors signal the need to forage for food, to search for mates, or to prepare for hibernation. In humans, internal sensors are just as important; however, they provide only one of many signals that compete to control behavior. Humans do not always eat when they are hungry, sleep when they are tired, or eliminate bodily wastes when they feel the urge. In fact, human society is built on the ability to postpone gratification and implement actions that may run counter to internal desires and fears.

The power to postpone the automatic satisfaction of internal urges creates the ability to control behavior on the basis of external principles, such as social rules. Whereas the emergence of the self is based on the streaming of internal signals into consciousness, the success of the human species has depended on the ability to suppress the fulfillment of internal drives to accommodate external circumstances. This power can energize creativity and maximize adaptability, but it can also engender psychopathology. In fact, maladaptive behavior can occur at both ends of the equation. From a psychological perspective, excessive suppression of internal drives can be just as detrimental as unrestrained satisfaction of internal urges. However, the latter would be more problematic in a social environment.

Social order underlies much of the power of the human race. The relative safety of individuals, family structure, and what predictability exists in life, depend on social controls. Most of us do not personally grow food, yet we can obtain even exotic culinary items at the grocery store. We use computers, cell phones, and televisions without knowing how to make them, and obtain care for our children while we fulfill other duties. The self that each of us knows is rooted in a complex, supportive, and occasionally frustrating social milieu. As might be expected, social complexity closely parallels brain size, since large brains are required to implement advanced social functions. Conversely, social structures support some of the demands of increased brain size. These include protected development time for the young and the acquisition of stable, energy-rich food supplies.

Social structures are present in many insect species, although at the lower end of the complexity scale, they are not supported by large brains. In the social insects, specialized functions are preprogrammed, and each member of a functional class (e.g., worker, drone, soldier, queen) has a very limited behavioral repertoire. Social insects do not recognize each other as individuals, and have very simple methods of communication. Social order is maintained by the limited behavioral repertoires of individuals. Insects have no capacity to change the social order for their own advantage, or to profit unfairly from social structures. In addition, most social insects never reproduce. Therefore, mutations that might benefit an individual at the expense of the group cannot be transmitted to offspring or serve as substrates for natural selection. In a sense, individual social insects are tools generated by a single reproductive "queen" to further her own production of offspring, although all insects in a colony share a common genetic inheritance.

From an evolutionary perspective, self-awareness is an emergent phenomenon made possible by exponential growth in areas of the brain that support effective movement. Specifically, this growth had four major consequences: First, it allowed the consideration of larger numbers of variables before the initiation of nonemergent actions. This capacity is supported by expanded brain maps and by discriminatory functions that assess value, risk, internal relevance, and external propriety. Second, it dictated an expanded role for environmental variables in the determination of brain organization and function. Third, it resulted in expansion of the neural infrastructures that support social interactions. Fourth, it facilitated complex methods of communication that culminated in the emergence of language and symbolic reasoning.

Self-awareness emerged as these functional gains coalesced into coherent behavioral programs for adaptation. Self-awareness requires an integrative synthesis of data from the many brain maps that record information about internal and external environments. If any of these maps or their connections fails, deficits in self-awareness become evident.

THE EXPANSION OF BRAIN MAPS

The expansion of internal brain maps is a defining characteristic of higher species. A simple way to visualize the consequences of expanded mapping is to compare the earliest video game, *Pong*, with today's highly detailed computer games. *Pong* was nothing more than two lines that represented paddles and a dot that represented a ball. It relied on the processing power and imagination of the human player for its effectiveness, and was not a compelling model of the physical world. In contrast, our current computer games contain highly detailed, 4-dimensional virtual worlds that can be explored and manipulated from physical and temporal perspectives. This level of representational detail is made possible by the exponential growth in the processing power, or mapping resolution, of computers.

The phylogenetic expansion of brain maps increased the number of objects and processes that could be represented in the brain, as well as the quality of the representations. The cost of brain expansion, however, was significant. The ultimate size of the human brain has a steep developmental price that must be paid by each baby's parents. Human brains are far from developed at birth, and are only about ¼ of their final size. By contrast, the brains of newborn great apes are already half the adult size at birth (Barrett, Dunbar, & Lycett, 2002). The brains of newborn humans cannot be larger at birth because of the limitations of female pelvic size. The wider hips of females already impose subtle but measurable limitations on locomotion (Barrett et al., 2002). Any further increase in pelvic size would result in unacceptable impairments in walking and running. Consequently, babies are born with immature brains, and human parents must provide extended care for their children. The prolonged nurturance of infants not only makes possible the large size of the human brain, but also contributes to brain development by facilitating cultural transmission and social training.

As we explore the implications of increased brain size, it is important to analyze the specific neural structures that underwent phylogenetic expansion, and to speculate on the possible adaptive advantages of the dramatic, yet biologically costly evolutionary changes that culminated in the human brain. The evolution of the brain has not only yielded an ever-increasing capacity for information processing, but has resulted in the creation of new functions. Many of the traits that define human individuals, for example, are unique to our species. The capacity for language and for advanced symbolic reasoning are prime examples. In addition, a number of evolutionary developments serve specialized functions that support the human lifestyle. For example, contrary to the general expansionary theme, human olfactory maps decreased in size as the brain evolved, reflecting an increased reliance on visual rather than olfactory cues. There are specific, adaptively relevant reasons for this change. A comparison of nocturnal and diurnal primates suggests that the shift to increased activity during the daylight hours strongly influenced the development of enhanced visual perception. Nocturnal apes, in contrast to humans and other diurnal primates, have retained olfactory perception as their primary sensory modality (Barton & Aggleton, 2000). In addition, humans developed a sophisticated repertoire of facial expressions to support complex social structures and processes. The display, recognition, and reactive mechanisms that underlie facial expressions placed special demands on the visual system and its supporting neural structures.

The six facial expressions that are thought to be "universal" across human cultures were first described by Darwin (1872/1998). They are fear, joy, disgust, surprise, sadness, and anger. In addition to the basic expressions, other nonverbal facial displays with social importance have been described. These include: yawning, startle, the "eyebrow flash," the "coy" display, embarrassment, and shame (Schmidt & Cohn, 2001). Humans who are born deaf and blind still demonstrate the basic facial expressions (Eibl-Eibesfeldt, 1989), suggesting that these are part of our phylogenetic inheritance and not a learned component of our behavioral repertoire. Not surprisingly, humans with facial paralysis suffer serious social consequences as a result of their inability to generate appropriate facial displays (VanSwearingen, Cohn, & Bajaj-Luthra, 1999).

The emergence of vision as the dominant sensory modality in humans precipitated concomitant growth in the complexity of the neural systems that translate visual information into behavior. An important example is the amygdala. One of the primary functions of the amygdala is to facilitate fearful, avoidant, and aversive responses in the face of danger. Since these functions are critical for survival, it is not surprising that the amygdala, and in particular its basolateral division, increased in size and developed extensive connections with the ventral stream of visual information in the temporal lobe of primates. This information stream contains detailed data about the identity and properties of environmental objects. In contrast, the amygdala is not connected to the dorsal visual information stream in the parietal lobe (Barton & Aggleton, 2000). The dorsal information stream contains low-level maps that track the movement and spatial orientation of objects. As expected, the basolateral amygdala is disproportionately larger in social, diurnal primates that rely on visual information as the dominant method of assessing the environment. The size of the basolateral amygdalar region also correlates positively with the size of social groups, in keeping with the importance of visual signals in social interactions (Barton & Aggleton, 2000).

The most important evolutionary trend in the primate brain involved expansion of the neocortex. After adjusting for body size, the neocortex is more than three times larger in humans than in the pongid apes (e.g., chimpanzees and gorillas), and more than 100 times larger than in insectivorous mammals (Eccles, 1989). In fact, expansion of the neocortex is responsible for most of the increase in brain size that characterizes higher primates, including humans.

The human cortex contains approximately 20 billion neurons packed into an area of 2,000 sq cm (Mesulam, 2000). The cortex has five distinct functional subtypes: limbic, paralimbic, heteromodal association, unimodal association, and primary sensory-motor. The anatomical details of the following discussion are based on Mesulam (2000).

The limbic zones are the most primitive cortical regions of the brain in terms of organization, with at most one or two layers of neurons. Limbic cortex includes corticoid areas, such as the amygdala and the septum, and allocortical areas such as the hippocampal complex. Corticoid, or "cortex-like" regions, have a cytoarchitecture that is intermediate between nuclear and cortical regions. Nuclear regions do not exhibit neuronal lamination, whereas cortical regions are characterized by distinct neuronal layers and spatially organized dendritic projections. In corticoid regions, there is some rudimentary lamination of neurons, as is characteristic of cortical organization, but the lamination is not uniform, and dendritic orientation is not symmetrically organized.

Allocortex is more highly organized than corticoid areas. Typically, allocortical regions exhibit one to three distinct layers of neurons. These neurons have well-developed apical dendrites with uniform spatial orientations. Two regions in the human brain exhibit allocortical organization. These are the hippocampal formation (also known as *archicortex*), and the primary olfactory cortex (also known as *piriform cortex* or *paleocortex*). The names *archicortex* and *paleocortex* are given to allocortical regions to reflect their primitive organization. The cortical regions of reptiles, for example, like the archicortex and paleocortex, have no more than three layers.

Phylogenetically, paleocortex and archicortex expanded as brains grew in complexity, and assumed enhanced processing functions. Olfactory paleocortex spread ventrolaterally from the orbitofrontal region through the subgenual cingulate, the insula, the temporal pole, and the anterior parahippocampal gyrus. The primary function of paleocortex is the integration of appetitive drives with considerations of risk and reward (Mega, Cummings, Salloway, & Malloy, 1997). Hippocampal archicortex spread posteriorly through the entorhinal and posterior parahippocampal regions, around the corpus callosum, and then anteriorly to form the posterior portion of the cingulate gyrus. Archicortex is primarily concerned with the integration of sensory and spatial information (Mega et al., 1977). The parahippocampal cortex and the cingulate, by virtue of their dual paleocortical and archicortical components, have powerful integrative capabilities that encompass the organism's spatial surroundings, environmental objects, internal drives, and considerations of risk and reward.

An understanding of cortical layering is important to the study of brain organization because cortical layering is correlated with function. Limbic regions, for example, have, at most, simple layering. These regions are fast-acting feature detectors that sound alarms if anything is amiss. For instance, if the amygdala senses danger, it immediately unleashes an endocrine and autonomic barrage, and lets other regions ask questions later. Multiple layers and extended processing are not required for the amygdala's function. In fact, such features would reduce its survival value, since they would delay emergency responses. The amygdala does eventually obtain more highly processed information that helps it decide whether to continue the alarm. It receives this through its connections with higher-level processors (the orbitofrontal and medial prefrontal cortices) that can signal an "all-clear" and diminish amygdalar firing should the perceived danger prove to be false. Reptilian brains consider a very limited number of variables before they trigger behavior. They also provide very sparse sensory integration. As a result, reptilian brains are characterized by very limited cortical connectivity, and hence have no need for more than three cortical layers.

Paralimbic cortex, also known as *mesocortex*, is intermediate in both organization and position because it forms a transition between the more primitive allocortex and the more highly organized, six-layered neocortex (described below). Paralimbic cortex has distinct neuronal layers, which tend to be diffuse in areas adjacent to limbic regions and more sharply defined in areas where it abuts neocortex. There are five principal paralimbic zones (Figures 2.1 & 2.2), including the orbitofrontal cortex, the temporal pole, the insula, the parahippocampal complex (including the entorhinal and perirhinal cortices), and the cingulate gyrus (Mesulam, 2000).

The paralimbic regions are among the most phylogenetically ancient association cortices in the brain. The orbitofrontal cortex is an important integrative center that receives projections from many limbic areas, including the amygdala, the anterior cingulate, the insula, the temporal pole, the entorhinal and perirhinal cortices, the hippocampus, the primary olfactory cortex, and the superior and inferior temporal gyri (Salloway, Malloy, & Duffy, 2001). In addition, the orbitofrontal cortex receives inputs from every sen-

FIGURE 2.1
APPROXIMATE LOCATIONS OF FUNCTIONAL
CORTICAL REGIONS OF THE HUMAN BRAIN

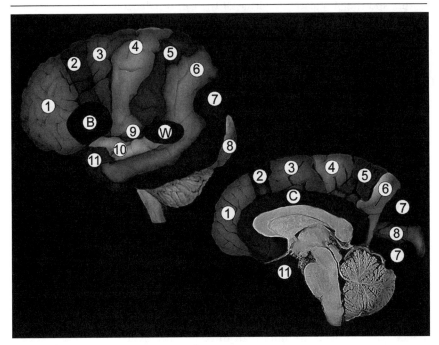

*1) Prefrontal cortex (multimodal). 2) Unimodal motor cortex. 3) Primary motor cortex.
4) Primary somatosensory cortex. 5) Unimodal somatosensory cortex. 6) Parietal and
temporal association cortices (multimodal). 7) Unimodal visual cortex. 8) Primary visual
cortex. 9) Primary auditory cortex. 10) Unimodal auditory cortex. 11) Paralimbic cortex.
B) Broca's area. W) Wernicke's area. C) Cingulate gyrus (paralimbic). (Based on Mesulam, 2000)*

sory modality as well as from the dorsolateral prefrontal cortex (Salloway et
al., 2001). The reciprocal connections between the orbitofrontal cortex and
the amygdala play an important role in the modulation of amygdalar responses on the basis of expanded information processing. The orbitofrontal
cortex can quiet fears and reduce emotional reactivity by decreasing amygdalar activation (Salloway et al., 2001). The orbitofrontal cortex is also critical in the suppression of internal drives on the basis of external principles.
It is tempting to speculate that the connections with dorsolateral prefrontal
cortex may provide access to abstract organizing principles. The temporal

pole integrates representations of physical objects with perceived value (Rolls, 1999). The insula, which in lower animals integrates represented objects with aversive tastes, has an expanded function in higher animals, and integrates generally "distasteful" or "disgusting" experiences with the objects and circumstances that precipitate them. In addition, the insula also integrates both somatic and emotional information to generate representations of emotional states that are accessible to consciousness (Phillips, Drevets, Rauch, & Lane, 2003). The parahippocampal complex is an important locus of convergence for highly processed sensory, spatial, and limbic information. This information is integrated and eventually relayed to the hippocampus to serve as the raw materials for the creation of memories. The cingulate gyrus is an important conduit and integrative center for limbic information. Its paleocortical and archicortical origins link the cingulate to highly processed information about internal states and external objects. The cingulate can therefore integrate data about objects with their "meaning," which reflects risk and value with respect to internal states and needs.

Most of the surface of the human brain is covered with the six-layered cortex known as neocortex. Cortical layer I, the *molecular layer*, is closest to the brain surface and contains mostly axons and dendrites. Layers II and IV, the external and internal granular layers, are primarily afferent and receive sensory inputs. Layer III, the external pyramidal layer, is primarily efferent. Its medium-sized pyramidal cells send axons to other cortical areas. Layer V, the internal pyramidal area, contains the largest pyramidal cells, which send axons to subcortical nuclei. Layer VI, the multiform layer, is an efferent layer that projects to the thalamus.

Cortical afferent connections are of four types (Nolte, 1999):

1. Topographically organized projections from thalamic nuclei
2. Diffuse projections from subcortical nuclei (e.g., serotonergic projections from raphe nuclei, noradrenergic projections from locus ceruleus, dopaminergic projections from mesencephalic nuclei, histaminergic projections from hypothalamic nuclei, cholinergic projections from basal forebrain, and glutamatergic projections from the amygdala)
3. Association fibers that link cortical areas in the same hemisphere
4. Commissural fibers that link cortical areas in opposite hemispheres

Cortical efferent projections are either subcortical (to thalamus, amygdala, and other nuclei) or corticocortical (to regions in the same or opposite hemisphere). Most cortical neurons act as coincidence detectors because ex-

citatory inputs from many neurons are required to trigger an action potential
(Kandel & Siegelbaum, 2000). Routine cortical transmission is excitatory and
glutamatergic (via activation of AMPA receptors). In addition, a variety of
interneurons modulate cortical signaling. The most abundant interneurons,
which comprise 20% to 25% of cortical neurons, are inhibitory GABAergic
neurons. GABA receptors are ion channels that can hyperpolarize neurons
through influx of chloride ions (GABA A) or outflow of potassium ions
(GABA B; Kandel & Siegelbaum, 2000).

The neocortex is subdivided into two distinct types: unimodal association
cortex and heteromodal, or high-order association cortex. Unimodal association cortex (Figure 2.1) performs advanced processing of information related
to a single sensory modality, such as sight, touch, or hearing. Unimodal
cortices receive inputs directly from the appropriate primary sensory cortex
as well as from other unimodal regions that serve the same sensory modality.
Unimodal association cortices, for example, map the various properties of
objects that are perceived by sight, such as shape, color, and movement.
Each sense has its own unimodal association cortices, and damage to such
cortices affects only a single sensory modality. From the perspective of self-
awareness, the expansion of unimodal association cortices has interesting
implications. Such expansion has increased the complexity of the sensory
maps that can be created. The visual unimodal association cortices, for example, are highly developed in humans, with the result that visual experiences
have a wide spectrum of components that can be appreciated. Our olfactory
experiences, by contrast, are very rudimentary, and represent only a fraction
of what a dog experiences. The processing of sensory signals first involves
signal expansion to reveal discreet informational components. Professional
wine tasters, for example, have well-developed taste and olfactory cortices,
and earn a living by describing in great detail all the nuances that combine
into a particular wine's characteristic flavor and aroma. Larger mapping areas
permit the appreciation of more distinct parameters within the sensory experience. After the signal is expanded, it is reintegrated, combined with signals
from other sensory modalities, and, in humans, collapsed into the compact,
symbolic representation known as a name. Simple lookup tables in the brain
hold lists of names for familiar persons and common objects.

Unimodal association cortices make possible the powerful processes of
classification and abstraction. When an object is perceived by the senses, a
basic map of its qualities is created in the primary sensory cortices. If the
object arouses interest, its sensory map is further expanded into the unimodal
and heteromodal association cortices. In the unimodal association cortices,
the object's properties are actually separated from the object itself. There is

a defined area in visual unimodal association cortex, for example, that is activated by all red objects, another that is activated by all round objects, and one that is activated by moving objects (Wurtz & Kandel, 2000). These qualities can be perceived as special categories that have an existence beyond the individual objects that embody them because they exist as independent mapping areas in unimodal association cortex. If every red object didn't excite a unique area in the visual unimodal association cortex, then the color red would not exist as an independent concept. The "concreteness" that can be detected in some patients (e.g., an apple and an orange are alike because they are round) can be explained in terms of brain maps. In these patients, object representation maps may not be routinely expanded to the higher heteromodal association cortices. The concept of "fruit," and other similar categorical abstractions, requires a more advanced mapping level in heteromodal association cortex than the concept of "round."

Heteromodal, or high-order association cortex, has a six-layer architecture; however, it is not as highly organized as unimodal association cortex. Actually, it is closer in structure to paralimbic cortex (Mesulam, 2000). On the basis of cytoarchitecture, therefore, heteromodal association cortex, despite the fact that it carries out some of the most advanced mental processes, is less rigidly structured than unimodal association cortex. What might be the reason for this? Heteromodal association cortex is a more recent evolutionary development than unimodal cortices. In contrast to the unimodal cortices, which organize in concert with sensory stimuli during early development, heteromodal cortices retain significant plasticity, and organize throughout an individual's lifetime to reflect perceived relationships within the environment, rather than simply the sensory properties of the physical world. The unimodal cortices, which are designed to map primary sensory perceptions, have well-defined layers that can encode sensory data effectively. Sensory data must be strictly mapped, and fall within a specific range of parameters (e.g., visual and auditory spectra, primary tastes, thermal and tactile stimuli). In contrast, heteromodal cortices often map nonlinear relationships, and reflect a lifetime of connective rearrangements. These rearrangements do not take place in an orderly fashion, as is the case with the time-limited, linearly ordered organization of sensory systems during development. In short, the heteromodal cortices are dynamic mapping areas whose connections reflect an individual's current understanding (as opposed to simple representation) of his or her world. In keeping with the function of heteromodal cortices, their structure is in continuous flux. It is tempting to speculate that for this reason, the human observer will perceive their cytoarchitecture to be less rigidly organized than that of the unimodal cortices.

Functionally, heteromodal association cortex (Figure 2.1) is distinguished by the fact that neurons within it can respond to each of the sensory modalities, and there are individual neurons that respond to more than one type of sensory signal. Heteromodal association cortex also responds to motor information and to motivational relevance (Lynch, 1980). It is clear that heteromodal association cortex serves an integrative purpose, and is able to blend multisensory, motor, and motivational information into a coherent, multidimensional experience of reality. Damage to heteromodal association cortex results in multidimensional deficits that involve more than one functional modality.

It is within the heteromodal association cortices that the final patchwork quilt of the self is assembled. The integration of the various informational modalities is performed with such efficiency that the seams in the fabric of the self are seldom noticed. In humans, the prefrontal cortex, the posterior parietal cortex, the lateral temporal cortex, and parts of the hippocampal complex are constructed from heteromodal association cortex (Mesulam, 2000).

The prefrontal cortex, which is the region of the frontal lobe rostral to the motor and premotor areas (Figure 2.1), contains the tools for fashioning an expanded self. It facilitates multidimensional associations, and provides the means to "navigate" through time. While many parts of the brain function to define the "now," the prefrontal cortex tempers the present moment with an autobiographical, analytic synthesis of the past, as well as a projection of the self into the future. The prefrontal cortices add important options to behavior, and facilitate the transcendence of reactive here-and-now responses. This ability to inhibit impulsive, internally driven behavior is essential for social order. For example, in a pride of lions, the lower-ranking animals must suppress the urge to gorge themselves on a fresh kill until the more dominant members of the pride have been sated.

The ability of the prefrontal cortices to suppress simple reactivity and provide other behavioral options is the foundation of the concepts of choice and "free will." If behavioral responses to environmental situations were simply preprogrammed, then there would be no such thing as free will. It is the ability to transcend automatic responses that makes humans both "free" to act and responsible for their actions. The frontal cortices provide the means to direct behavior on the basis of internalized principles and a projected vision of the future.

The prefrontal cortices play a critical role in the process of self-awareness because they generate an expanded sense of the self. This expanded conceptualization represents the self as an independent agent with a personal history, principles, choices, and plans. The impairment of prefrontal cortical function diminishes this expanded self-awareness, decreases the sense of the self as an independent agent, magnifies the effect of the present on behavior, and increases impulsivity, which is the implementation of action without reflective thought.

The second of the main heteromodal cortices, namely the posterior parietal area, is an essential component of the brain's circuitry for spatial awareness and attention. The posterior parietal region integrates sensorimotor, cognitive, and limbic information to support the adaptive mechanism of spatial attention (Mesulam, 2000). The posterior parietal cortex is a critical epicenter of a distributed network that maps the environment and its objects, including the self, and defines viable movement strategies for escaping danger and obtaining objects of interest. The posterior parietal cortex has access to a rich array of sensory information, including visual, auditory, somatosensory, and vestibular inputs (Mesulam, 2000). In addition, the posterior parietal cortex has 2-way connections with the cingulate gyrus, the orbitofrontal cortex, the insula, the premotor cortex, the frontal eye fields, the superior colliculus, and the parahippocampal gyrus (Mesulam, 2000). The connections with the cingulate gyrus are particularly strong, and provide the cingulate gyrus direct access to a continuously updated inventory of all the objects that are available in the environment. Connections with the superior colliculus and the frontal eye fields support the ocular saccades by which we continuously "foveate," or visually explore the environment. Ocular saccades occur automatically, and usually without conscious awareness. They facilitate continuous visual surveillance of our surroundings. Connections with the parahippocampal gyrus may facilitate the formation of new memories if an object or situation proves worthy of remembrance. The orbitofrontal cortex and insula may provide information regarding the "meaning" of perceived objects with respect to the current needs of the self. For example, orbitofrontal neurons fire in response to food if an individual is hungry; however, they stop firing once the individual is sated (Rolls, 1999). The orbitofrontal cortex also functions in reducing behavioral impulsivity, and in the selection of behaviors that are socially and cognitively appropriate (Zald & Kim, 2001).

The lateral temporal cortex is the third of the major heteromodal cortices. It serves to correlate the many sensory and cognitive streams associated with faces and objects into a coherent, multimodal experience. Without the integrative contributions of temporal heteromodal cortex, the physical characteristics of objects or faces may be perceived, but the object or face will not be recognized. In humans, for example, both familiar and unfamiliar faces trigger neurons in the unimodal regions of the fusiform gyrus, but only familiar faces activate heteromodal association regions in the temporal cortex (Mesulam, 2000). In a sense, only familiar faces and objects have a "history," and their representation in heteromodal temporal cortex most likely provides access to special linkages that lead to the neural networks of which they have become a part. The recognition of voices and familiar sounds also depends on the actions of temporal heteromodal cortex.

The fourth heteromodal association cortex is contained within the hippocampal complex. The hippocampus itself is a structure that forms in the embryo on the medial walls of each hemisphere along the hippocampal fissure. The hippocampus derives its name from the fact that it resembles the outline of a sea horse in cross-section (Figures 2.2 & 2.15). The following discussion of hippocampal structures is derived from Carpenter (1985). Initially, the hippocampal formation forms a large arch that extends from the interventricular foramen to the inferior horn of the lateral ventricle. The upper parts of the hippocampal formation do not develop, because they are invaded by fibers of the corpus callosum. In the adult, the only trace of the upper portion of the hippocampal arch is a vestige known as the *indusium griseum*.

The temporal portion of the original arch differentiates into the hippocampus, which bulges into the lateral ventricle's inferior horn. The lips of the hippocampal fissure differentiate into the dentate gyrus above and the parahippocampal gyrus below. If we consider that the hippocampal formation has an "S" shape in cross-section, the bottom of the S forms the entorhinal cortex, while the ascending portion of the S is the subiculum and related areas (presubiculum and parasubiculum). The upper portion of the S is the hippocampus (Carpenter, 1985). The hippocampus is essential for the storage of memories, and also for the use of memories in the modulation of behavior.

The six-layered heteromodal association cortex in the hippocampal complex is contained in the lateral entorhinal cortex. This region is highly ordered laterally, but as it transitions medially into the subiculum, the layers become less distinct. As the subiculum transitions into the hippocampus proper, only three layers (polymorphic, pyramidal, and molecular) can be distinguished (Carpenter, 1985).

The entorhinal cortex is located below the hippocampal formation, and it receives a rich array of afferent inputs that represent the entire spectrum of experience (some arrive indirectly via the parahippocampal and perirhinal

FIGURE 2.2
CORONAL SECTION THROUGH A HUMAN BRAIN

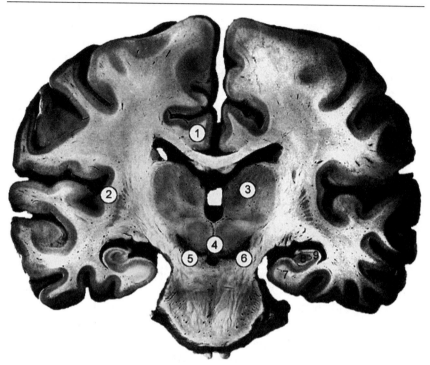

1) Cingulate gyrus. 2) Insula. 3) Thalamus. 4) Ventral tegmental area. 5 and 6) Left and right substantia nigra. 7) Entorhinal cortex. 8) Dentate gyrus. 9) Hippocampus (CA1-CA3).

cortices). These include projections from the prefrontal cortex, the cingulate gyrus, the occipital lobe, the superior and inferior temporal gyri, the temporal pole, the amygdala, and the insula (Woolsey, Hanaway, & Mokhtar, 2003). These inputs are integrated and transmitted to the hippocampus by way of the perforant pathway. This pathway projects from the entorhinal cortex to the dentate gyrus, and from the dentate gyrus, information flows into the CA3 region of the hippocampus. The wide spectrum of integrated information that converges on the hippocampal complex is consistent with the function of this region in the creation of multidimensional memories.

From the perspective of self-awareness, the heteromodal association cortices are essential to the creation of an integrated, multidimensional self.

Without heteromodal association cortices, the self that can be represented is coarse, simple, and far more reactive than reflective. The scientific literature demonstrates that damage to heteromodal association cortices can make entire dimensions of the self vanish. This occurs because the maps for the vanished dimensions of the self have been destroyed. Damage to the right posterior parietal cortex, for example, can make the entire left side of the body seem nonexistent. Damage to the prefrontal cortices can destroy social restraints, empathy for others, and the ability to solve complex problems. Damage to the lateral temporal cortex leads to a variety of agnosias, including the inability to recognize once familiar faces, objects, and voices (Mesulam, 2000). Damage to the hippocampus can impair the formation of new memories and the retrieval of memories that are less than 2 to 3 years old. Lack of awareness of neurologic deficits appears to result not only from damage to integrative cortices, but from loss of the memory of how previous functionality "felt." The affected individual has no capacity to use the damaged cortex and no memory of how it felt to use it in the past; therefore, there is no frame of reference for defining functional changes, and no awareness that anything has been "lost."

The final type of cortex is primary sensory-motor cortex, also known as *idiotypic cortex* (Figure 2.1). Idiotypic cortex is the most highly organized of the cortices, with at least six very distinct cell bands. Idiotypic cortex serves primary sensory and motor processes. In the human brain, primary sensory-motor cortex supports either sensory functions or movement, and is present in occipital striate cortex (visual), Heschl's gyrus (auditory), postcentral gyrus (primary somatosensory cortex), and the precentral gyrus (motor cortex) (Mesulam, 2000).

Only idiotypic cortex and limbic cortex (the amygdala) are connected to internal and external environments, either directly or through a thalamic relay. The other cortices are not directly connected to internal or external inputs, but rather serve as processors of the information that is acquired by the limbic and primary sensory cortices. The limbic and primary sensory cortices therefore contain first order maps of the internal and external environments. The other cortices expand the maps, facilitate abstraction, and eventually extract meaning from the information. *Meaning* is a relative term that represents the implications of primary information to the self. The meaning of primary information is developed as the information is expanded and linked in the association cortices. This information is used to further the primary interests of the self: survival, avoidance of pain, pursuit of pleasure, creative expression, and expansion through intellectual, artistic, and social means.

In summary, most of the growth of the human brain was devoted to expansion of the neocortex, a powerful integrative tool that facilitated advanced information processing. The neocortex made possible abstraction and categorization, generated a sense of connectedness among sensory representations, and ultimately resulted in the birth of meaning.

Paralleling the development of the cortex, complimentary processing structures also grew in size and complexity as the brain evolved. For example, the striatum, which provides advanced signal selection and filtering, is proportionately twice as big in humans as in the pongid apes, and 10 times larger than in insectivores (Eccles, 1989). The striatum works in concert with the cortex to regulate movement as well as signal selection, and expansion of information into the advanced association cortices. In order to facilitate this process, the sensory, motor, and association cortices are somatotopically mapped onto the striatum. Of necessity, therefore, as the human cortex grew in complexity, the striatum, which contains a compressed map of cortical regions, had to grow also. The expansion of a signal means that the signal is connected to memories, concepts, associated ideas, and relevant data in other parts of the brain. This facilitates comprehension of the signal's meaning, definition of its context, and utilization of its information in an optimal manner. Creativity depends on the ability to expand perceptive signals and integrate the information they contain in novel ways.

Given the biological cost of larger brains, what adaptive advantages does a larger brain provide? A variety of hypotheses have been developed in this regard. One of the most interesting and compelling is the social brain hypothesis (also known as the Machiavellian brain hypothesis) proposed by Byrne and Whiten (1988; Barrett et al., 2002). The social brain hypothesis states that the most important adaptive value of a large brain is that it affords an increased capacity to obtain survival-enhancing benefits through the manipulation of other members of one's species. Research has demonstrated that the relative size of the neocortex of a particular species is directly correlated with the species' social complexity (Dunbar, 1992). A large brain is necessary not only to track complex social relationships through time, but to facilitate the derivation of maximum survival and reproductive advantages from the social milieu.

Two other physical adaptations have maximized the functionality of increased brain size. These are the folding of the brain surface and the differential specialization of brain hemispheres. Folding of the brain increases surface area significantly without increasing outer volume. Hemispheric specialization is another simple way of making maximal use of existing resources. Such specialization increases functional capacity at the expense of redundancy, and has important implications in the understanding of both normal and dysfunctional brain states.

ORIGINS OF FREE WILL

The expanded brain, with its enlarged neocortex, can consider an increased number of variables before the initiation of nonemergent actions. Humans are unique in the large numbers of factors that they can consider before they act. Human social order is based, in great part, on the ability to inhibit automatic impulses and act on the basis of abstract principles or rules. Many psychiatric disorders, in fact, are associated with a decrease in the number of variables that are considered before initiating actions.

Mesulam (2002) described a "default" brain mode that is driven primarily by automatic responses based on the internal milieu, "impervious to modification by context or experience." The default brain mode, which is present to varying degrees in lower species, is characterized by automatic actions and a drive toward immediate gratification with little regard for consequences. In humans, the frontal lobes represent the major alternative to the default mode of the basal brain. The presence of functional frontal lobes results in the insertion of a pause before the initiation of nonemergent actions. After that, the choice of an action hinges not only on internal motivation, but also on learned rules, modeling, and other considerations. It is the frontal lobes that endow us with social graces, and make it possible for us to diet. Our sense of having choices in daily life is in great part dependent on the function of the frontal lobes.

An important problem that accompanies expansion of the variables that drive behavior is conflict resolution. When two or more courses of action are possible, which one should be chosen? Phylogenetically, humans have moved away from the behavioral inflexibility and reactivity of thalamic control into the realm of flexible behaviors with many determinants that characterizes neocortical control. This requires both a way of integrating relevant variables and a mechanism for conflict resolution when the variables don't agree.

In lower animals, the thalamus is an important tool for resolving simple conflicts. The thalamus is a set of nuclei that serves to coordinate transmission of sensory information to the cerebral cortex and to regulate of a variety of low-level processes that are of critical importance to the organism. The main functions of the thalamus include (Scheibel, 1997):

- Basic processing of information from internal and external sources, and selective transmission of data to the cerebral cortex
- Representation and maintenance of a dynamic body image

- Control over environmental engagement through selective maintenance of wakefulness, attentiveness, and sleep
- Modulation of physiological and chemical states in specific areas of the brain

The thalamus consists of two symmetrical lobes that form the dorsal portion of the diencephalon (Figure 2.3). As many as 50 individual thalamic nuclei have been identified, although most of the nuclei are usually classified into

---

FIGURE 2.3
SELECTED THALAMIC NUCLEI AND ADJACENT STRUCTURES
IN CORONAL SECTION

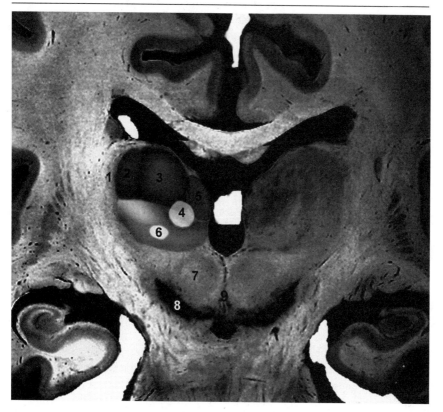

1) *Reticular nucleus.* 2) *Ventral lateral nucleus.* 3) *Lateral posterior nucleus.* 4) *Centromedian nucleus.* 5) *Dorsomedial nucleus.* 6) *Ventral posterolateral nucleus.* 7) *Red nucleus.* 8) *Substantia nigra. (Based on Nolte, 1999)*

one of four main groups: anterior, medial, ventrolateral, and posterior. The nuclei in these groups are called *relay* nuclei, because they transfer information to defined cortical areas. The following discussion of the anatomy and function of the thalamus is based on the reviews by Amaral (2000) and Carpenter (1985).

In humans, the anterior thalamic group consists of one nucleus, which receives inputs from the presubiculum (part of the hippocampal complex) and from the mammillary nuclei of the hypothalamus (which mark the termination of the fornix, one of the primary output pathways of the hippocampus). The anterior thalamic nucleus is also connected with the cingulate gyrus and frontal cortices, and is thought to play a role in the modulation of emotion and memory (Amaral, 2000). The medial thalamic group has one main nucleus, namely the mediodorsal nucleus. Each of the three divisions of this nucleus is linked with a specific region of the frontal cortex. The mediodorsal nucleus is also connected to the amygdala, basal ganglia, and midbrain, and is thought to facilitate memory processes. The ventral thalamic nuclei contain compressed motor and sensory homunculi because they relay motor and sensory information to specific areas of the cortex. Specifically, the ventral anterior and lateral nuclei transmit motor information from the cerebellum and basal ganglia to the cortex, while the ventral posterior lateral nucleus transmits somatosensory information to discrete cortical processing areas. The posterior group of thalamic nuclei contains the pulvinar, and the lateral posterior nucleus. The pulvinar is particularly large in humans, and is connected with association cortices in the temporal, parietal, and occipital lobes, as well as with the superior colliculus, which functions in the coordination of eye movements. The pulvinar is thought to function in the distribution of information to extrastriate visual processing centers (striate processing centers are the main visual processing centers in the occipital lobe) for use in the identification of objects and situations. The medial geniculate nucleus transmits auditory information to the superior temporal gyrus for advanced processing. The lateral geniculate nucleus transmits highly organized information from the retina to the primary visual cortices in the occipital lobe.

In addition to the four main functional groups, the thalamus contains an array of important regulatory nuclei referred to as *diffusely projecting* or *nonspecific* nuclei. These nuclei receive projections from various regions in the brainstem, cerebellum, and spinal cord, and transmit processed information to limbic areas. They are believed to function in arousal, in the transmission of internal state information to the limbic system, and in the modulation of sensory information processing (Amaral, 2000).

The thalamus is covered by a unique, netlike structure called the reticular nucleus. Most of the neurons of the reticular nucleus are inhibitory, GABA-ergic neurons. The reticular nucleus does not project to the cortex. Instead of transmitting information beyond the thalamus, this nucleus serves to modulate the outputs of other thalamic nuclei. Strong outputs can activate the reticular nucleus and suppress weaker signals. This arrangement provides a basic system for signal selection.

In reptiles, the thalamus is the main control center of the brain. It can perform basic signal selection, and can help to amplify signals most relevant to current internal states and needs. The reptilian thalamus does have reciprocal cortical connections; however, these can be thought of as small "scratch-pads" which hold a limited amount of information that can be used to fine-tune thalamic processes. The thalamocorticostriatal loops of reptiles have, in fact, very limited cortical inputs. Action selection is therefore automatic, with the largest external stimuli that fit current internal needs receiving priority. In humans, the reciprocal connections from cortical regions back to the thalamus are orders of magnitude more numerous than the projections from the thalamus to the cortex. Rather than act as a scratch pad to fine-tune thalamically regulated information flow, the human cortex has taken over the control of information transmission by regulating thalamic function. Lamina VI of the human cortex is, in fact, dedicated to communication with the thalamus, and contains the axonal projections from the cortex to the thalamic nuclei.

The evolution from thalamic to cortical control has increased dramatically the number of variables that can be considered before the initiation of non-emergent actions. Instead of simply augmenting thalamic modulation through the use of small cortical scratchpads, the human cortex can bring entire libraries of information to bear on the selection of responses to environmental challenges. The survival benefits of considering many variables before acting, as well as the difficulties inherent in this process, are vividly illustrated by Mesulam (2002) in his description of the maternal behavior of female turkeys.

A human observer of a turkey hen protecting her hatchlings would likely be impressed with the turkey's fierceness and dedication to the safety of her offspring. Because of the limited processing power of the turkey brain, however, the turkey hen's apparent dedication is actually quite tenuous. In general, the turkey hen's brain directs her to attack anything in the vicinity of her nest with the exception of her hatchlings. In keeping with the limited processing power of its brain, however, the turkey hen knows its hatchlings only by virtue of a single variable, namely their chirping. If a turkey hen becomes deaf, either naturally or experimentally, it will actually kill its own chicks!

The ability to consider multiple variables before undertaking actions can clearly enhance adaptive flexibility, and makes an individual's behavioral responses less dependent on any single circumstance. On the other hand, the added complexity may hinder rapid responses in hostile environments. Thus, the consideration of multiple factors before initiating actions may be most beneficial in relatively safe, socially complex environments. In the wild, reactivity and simplicity may be preferable. For example, domesticated animals, which are taught to consider more variables before they act, often don't fare well if they are released into natural, more hostile environments.

The mechanics of considering multiple variables before initiating actions are far from simple. The first task that must be accomplished is identification, integration, and evaluation of the relevant variables. One of the most difficult challenges in this context is the exclusion of irrelevant variables from consideration. Next, the most compelling variable or set of variables must be chosen. Finally, appropriate actions based on the chosen variables must be undertaken. In a very real sense, this process is equivalent to creating a "to do" list and addressing the list's items in order of importance.

In primates, the region that appears to coordinate the generation of the brain's "to do" list is the cingulate gyrus. The cingulate gyrus is a C-shaped band of paralimbic cortex that borders the corpus callosum above its upper edge on the medial surface of each brain hemisphere (Figures 2.1 & 2.4). From an evolutionary perspective, the cingulate gyrus arose from two different waves of cortical development. Mesulam (1985) described the regions that resulted from these developmental waves as *paralimbic belts*. Specifically, the first developmental wave originated in the orbitofrontal region of the olfactory paleocortex. This wave progressed ventrolaterally through the insula, temporal pole, and parahippocampal region (Mega & Cummings, 2001). All of these structures are involved in the integration of appetitive drives with the desirability (attraction or aversion) of specific objects and situations. The olfactory paleocortex is also closely associated with the amygdala, and therefore contains information about potentially threatening conditions.

The second developmental wave originated in the hippocampal archicortex and spread posteriorly through the entorhinal cortex, the posterior parahippocampal region, and the cingulate gyrus (Mega & Cummings, 2001). These regions are involved in the integration of the various sensory modalities, and represent a significant evolutionary development away from the thalamic control characteristic of reptiles and toward the cortical control of mammals (Mega & Cummings, 2001).

FIGURE 2.4
MID-SAGITTAL VIEW OF HUMAN BRAIN

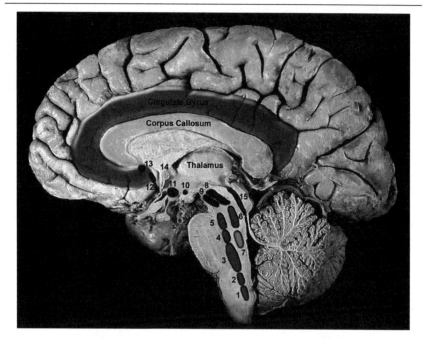

1–6: Serotonergic nuclei—1) Nucleus raphe obscuris. 2) Nucleus raphe pallidus. 3) Nucleus raphe magnus. 4) Nucleus raphe periolivarius. 5) Nucleus raphe medianus. 6) Nucleus raphe dorsalis. 7) Locus ceruleus (norepinephrine). 8) Substantia nigra (dopamine). 9) Ventral tegmental area (dopamine). 10) Tuberomammillary nucleus of hypothalamus (histamine). 11) Nucleus basalis of Meynert (acetylcholine). 12) Diagonal band of Broca (acetylcholine). 13) Septal nuclei (acetylcholine). 14) Anterior commissure. 15) Periaqueductal gray to left of number; superior and inferior colliculi to right of number. (Based on Carpenter [1985] and Nolte [1999])

By virtue of its paleocortical and archicortical components and connections, the cingulate gyrus contains both spatial information and value judgments about perceived objects and situations. In addition, it contains data about the motivational tendencies imposed by internal appetitive drives. Specific cells in the cingulate react to the prospect of impending reward, and focus attention and behavior on assuring the latter's attainment. This function of the cingulate ensures that the organism focuses behavioral resources on what is most attainable and valuable among a list of competing possibilities, while postponing attention to alternative activities (Shidara & Richmond, 2002). A lion chasing a herd of gazelles, for example, focuses its attention on the closest of the animals, and not on the rest of the herd as it speeds away in the distance. In humans, the cingulate gyrus detects and tracks potential objects of interest, links reward values with these targets, anticipates events related to acquiring the targets, signals procedural errors, and motivates the motor processes related to acquisition of the targeted objects (Bush et al., 2002).

The representation of available objects and their value in the cingulate gyrus, together with information about which one should be addressed first, generates a very efficient "to do" list, and serves to focus behavior toward those actions most likely to obtain resources. As the cortex develops, the "to do" list generated with the help of the cingulate becomes more refined. Damage to the cingulate gyrus is consistent with the loss of the brain's "to do" list, and causes the disappearance of the all-important motivational dimension of the self. Bilateral damage to the cingulate results in a condition known as *akinetic mutism*. Individuals with this problem don't speak spontaneously, don't respond to pain, are apathetic, and have severely impaired decision making, especially when presented with go/no-go problems (Mega & Cummings, 2001). Patients with unilateral damage to the cingulate cortex can also experience akinetic mutism, but in many cases are able to recover. One such patient later stated that during the period of akinetic mutism, she was inactive and mute because "nothing ever came to mind" (Damasio, 1994).

A possible neurobiological correlate of the cingulate's ability to integrate information of diverse origins is the finding of large, spindle-shaped neurons in layer Vb of the cingulate cortex (Nimchinsky, 1999). The density of these cells correlates remarkably with phylogeny: the highest density is found in human brains, next highest in chimpanzees, then in orangutans and gorillas. They are not present at all in nonprimate species. It has been hypothesized that these cells connect spatially distant regions in large brains, and that they participate in the integration of motivational, sensory, and cognitive information that characterizes cingulate function.

PLASTICITY AND ADAPTATION: ENVIRONMENTAL VARIABLES
ORGANIZE THE BRAIN

The next evolutionary theme to consider is the expanded role for environmental variables in the determination of brain organization and function. This trend makes the best possible use of the increased computational capacity of the human brain because it focuses that capacity on the most common challenges encountered during development, with enough plasticity for post-developmental learning. Evolutionary progress has a significant lag from the time a stimulus that triggers natural selection is encountered to the time an evolutionary response to the stimulus spreads throughout a species. The explosive cultural development in humans over the past 10,000 years has been too rapid to allow natural selection to optimize the hard-wiring of our brains to meet the demands of an advanced technological society (Bowlby, 1973).

Our brain's high level of functionality in a world far different from the one in which it evolved is due in great part to its ability to organize around developmental stimuli. In other words, our brains are designed to complete their wiring under the influence of the environment in which they will eventually function. This arrangement bestows on the brain dramatic powers of adaptability, especially if appropriate environmental challenges are encountered during the brain's developmental phases. The lengthy periods of schooling that many individuals in our culture undertake are designed to create brains that are superbly adapted to the demands of a technological society. Unfortunately, this arrangement also has disadvantages. The brain's plasticity renders it vulnerable to problems during development. In fact, some of the consequences of developmental trauma can be difficult, if not impossible to reverse, because they are structurally encoded. From the perspective of self-awareness, developmental deficits result in a lack of first-hand knowledge of what is considered "normal." The developmentally impaired individual is unaware of the nature of his or her specific deficit because the deficit state is all that person has ever known.

Carter (2000) discussed the tragic case of a child in Los Angeles who had been locked in a small room from birth until she was discovered in 1970, at the age of 13. Her eyes were unable to focus any further than the length of the room in which she had lived, and she could say only two words, *stopit* and *nomore*. After the child was liberated from her prison, she expanded her vocabulary considerably. However, she could never learn correct grammar. Functional imaging studies of her brain revealed that when she spoke, she used the right side of her brain, rather than the usual left. While this nominal arrangement is found in up to 5% of the population (mostly left-handed persons), in these individuals, normal language areas have developed on the right rather than the left. In the imprisoned child, normal language areas never developed at all, atrophying irreversibly for lack of environmental inputs that could guide developmental wiring. From a functional perspective, the child was never fully liberated from her prison.

She was able to learn to make word sounds and attach them to objects. However, she was not able to use grammar or symbolic reasoning because her entire speech capacity was centered on the use of a brain area that normally functions in the processing of environmental noises.

This dramatic example illustrates the downside of the developmental plasticity of the human brain. Many examples of psychopathology related to early trauma and neglect can be found in any clinician's caseload. While therapeutic rewiring may not be possible in these cases, the task of the clinician is to discover what adaptive capacities the patient may still have and develop strategies for organizing behavioral responses around these adaptive resources. Individuals who never developed specific dimensions of the self as a result of developmental problems are not aware that anything is missing, although they may realize that they "don't fit" into many social situations. It is important for clinicians who treat developmentally impaired individuals to gauge the extent of their patients' self-awareness deficits and structure therapeutic interventions appropriately.

Evolution of the Social Brain

The next evolutionary theme to consider is the expansion of brain infrastructures that support social interaction. We have already discussed the social brain hypothesis, which postulates that expansion in brain size was driven by natural selection in connection with obtaining maximum survival and reproductive benefits from social contacts. In a sense, social development was essential to the development of large brains, because only through social cooperation in hunting and gathering could there be a rich enough diet to support large brains. Human brain metabolism consumes 20% to 25% of daily calories. This compares to 8% to 10% for nonhuman primates, and 3% to 5% for other mammals (Leonard, 2003). Clearly, without appropriate means of securing a consistent, high-energy diet, such metabolic math would be a path to extinction.

The human brain has many specialized structures that facilitate social interactions. For example, critical steps in the initial phases of the visual aspects of a social encounter and the brain regions involved in each step include:

1. Processing of initial information about the individual in the visual cortices
2. Activation of the face region in the fusiform gyrus with subsequent special processing of the face as a special object
3. Recognition of the expression on the face through processing by the superior temporal sulcus and amygdala

4. If the face is familiar, processing in heteromodal temporal cortices to connect the face with its remembered "history"
5. Generation of emotional meaning through limbic processing
6. Generation of cognitive meaning through prefrontal processing
7. Coordination of an appropriate response through the integration of emotional and cognitive aspects of the experience in the prefrontal cortices

Unlike humans, lower mammals utilize olfaction as a primary means of social recognition. In higher primates, social recognition has become increasingly visual. Recording studies of the inferior temporal cortices of monkeys have demonstrated specific cells that are selective for faces, direction of gaze, body orientation, and perceived intended action (Adolphs, 2001). In humans, a distributed system for the processing of facial information has been hypothesized, based on imaging studies. The fusiform gyrus appears to be critical for the identification of static features of faces, such as the identity and general characteristics. The fusiform gyrus identifies the face as a special object and directs subsequent information flow to the appropriate processing modules. Changeable features, such as emotional expression and direction of gaze, are processed in the superior temporal sulcus (Haxby et al., 2000).

In addition to these feature-detecting regions, the "meaning" of what is perceived is developed in other brain regions. The amygdala, together with closely associated structures such as the temporal pole, the perirhinal cortex, and the retrosplenial region are important processing centers for social cues. In particular, these regions extract value signals from facial expression and body postures, especially when the latter represent a threat (Adolphs, 2001). The right hemisphere also participates in the processing of nonthreatening social cues. Damage to the neocortex of the right hemisphere impairs performance in "theory of mind" tasks, in which an individual must make inferences about the mental states of others (Happe et al., 1996). Damage to the right somatosensory cortices, the right insula, or the right supramarginal gyrus impaired the ability to infer the emotional states of others by evaluating the expressions on their faces or their tone of voice (Adolphs, 2001).

The recognition of social cues is complemented by the ability to react appropriately. In this regard, the orbitofrontal cortex has great importance. Humans with orbitofrontal damage exhibit socially inappropriate behavior, have a diminished capacity for empathy, and an impaired ability to adjust behavior in response to punishment (Damasio, 1994). Without orbitofrontal influence, socially appropriate behavioral restraints cannot be implemented, and significant dysfunction in social and possibly legal settings results.

Individuals with damage to the fusiform gyrus (usually bilateral) are un-able to recognize even familiar faces (Mesulam, 2002). However, they are usually aware of the deficit and make arrangements to manage the problem (e.g., having their spouse wear a characteristic article of clothing). Individu-als with amygdalar or orbitofrontal damage, in contrast, are not usually aware of their deficit. The reason individuals with fusiform gyrus damage can appreciate their deficit is that while they lack the specific maps that permit the identification of faces, they possess other maps that suggest that the individual they can't identify actually exists. For example, many cues would demonstrate that one's spouse is present at a party, even though one may not be able to recognize the spouse's face. This would include the fact that the individual drove with his or her spouse to the party.

The loss of amygdalar function, on the other hand, completely erases fear-related brain maps, and makes it impossible to experience fear. There are no sweaty palms, no sinking feeling at the pit of the stomach, and no rapid heartbeat. In the absence of the ability to generate the physiological state of fear, no internal reference is available to show what one might be missing. If someone who previously had amygdalar function were to lose it, she might realize that she no longer experiences fear in certain situations as she did in the past. For example, she might realize that watching a horror movie is no longer uncomfortable. However, in many novel situations that would induce fear in intact individuals, the person with an amygdalar defi-cit would not be aware that she was "missing" the fear response.

Damage to the orbitofrontal cortex is another condition that can cause deficits in self-awareness. Such damage can completely destroy maps related to social propriety. Because the maps that define social protocols are missing, individuals with orbitofrontal damage don't know any of the rules that they are violating, and therefore are unaware of their deficit.

Orbitofrontal damage is associated with significant social dysfunction, since it results in socially inappropriate behavior that is threatening or offen-sive to others. Unfortunately, the lack of orbitofrontal inhibition makes this behavior very difficult to control, even with professional treatment.

LANGUAGE AND SYMBOLIC REASONING
The final evolutionary theme to consider is the development of language and symbolic reasoning. The discussion that follows is based on the review by Barrett and associates (2002). Fossil and neurobiological evidence indi-cates that speech probably arose about half a million years ago. This is the age of the oldest *homo sapiens* fossils. These fossils, but none of the earlier hominid fossils, show expansion of the spinal cord's gray matter in the tho-

racic region. This expansion innervates the muscles that control breathing, and fine control of breathing is essential for the production of speech. Likewise, the hypoglossal canal, which is a conduit for the innervation of the tongue, shows expansion in the earliest *homo sapiens* fossils, but not in apes or more primitive hominids such as *homo erectus* (Barrett et al., 2002). Another approach to the problem (Aiello & Dunbar, 1993) used specialized equations that consider relationships between brain size, grooming time, and social group size that predict at what point grooming alone would have been insufficient to sustain bonding within social groups. The answer obtained with this method also pointed to the time of the earliest *homo sapiens* fossils half a million years ago.

Several theories have been proposed to account for the evolutionary origins of language. We will discuss three of them briefly, namely the gossip hypothesis, the social contract hypothesis, and the Scheherazade effect (Barrett et al., 2002). In addition, there is the hypothesis proposed by Chomsky (1975) that language has no specific adaptive function, and developed largely by accident. The social gossip hypothesis proposes that as the social environment grew in complexity, an informational exchange system became necessary to remain informed about the dynamic and often rapidly changing conditions in an individual's social milieu. The ability to exchange social information would be critical in maintaining alliances, surviving the attacks of enemies, and policing the social network for "freeriders" who sought to derive social benefits but were not prepared to contribute. Language would also facilitate the division of labor among the social group, and would serve to inform members who had been absent (e.g., on a hunting expedition) what had occurred while they had been gone. A study of conversations by both men and women found that men spend about 63% of the time discussing social topics, while women discuss social topics almost 70% of the time (Dunbar, Duncan, & Nettle, 1997).

The social contract hypothesis postulates that language developed as a necessary tool for social contracting. Such contracting would be important for pair bonding, especially if males had to be absent from their mates while hunting. The absence of social contracts under such conditions would have made the maintenance of large social groups very difficult. Other contracts, for example, related to the sharing of shelter and resources, would also be greatly facilitated by language.

A final hypothesis is the so-called Scheherazade effect (Miller, 1999). This suggests that language may have enabled humans to attract and keep mates. Like the Scheherazade of myth, verbally skilled individuals could use their talents to great advantage. An interesting study that seems to support this hypothesis was conducted by Miller (1999). He hypothesized that intellectual creativity may be a male advertising strategy to attract potential mates. His study found that the outputs of male jazz musicians, novelists, and painters peaked at around the age of 30 (which is a peak time of sexual competition in humans), and was as much as 10 times higher than the output of women in comparable professions. The above hypotheses are not, of course, mutually exclusive. While it is not known for certain what caused language to evolve, these hypotheses provide some thought-provoking possibilities.

The evolution of language gave rise to another powerful and uniquely human function, namely symbolic reasoning. The first tentative representations of objects by sounds in a primitive social group half a million years ago began the symbolic revolution that eventually resulted in written language, technology, philosophy, and culture. From the simple representation of objects by sounds, linguistic development progressed to the representation of the properties of objects, and the relationships between objects. Important concepts like purpose and causality could for the first time be articulated, and the ability to manipulate language eventually translated into the ability to manipulate a virtual copy of the environment and its objects within the brain.

Symbolic reasoning gave humans the ability to construct detailed models of the world that could be used to make predictions. The survival value of this ability is incalculable. The key to symbolic reasoning is not only that a sound can be made that represents an object, but also that the sound is linked to all the brain maps associated with that object. In a sense, words, and other symbols, are a type of shorthand. They stand for much more than simple physical objects. In fact, they represent the entire history of objects, including their emotional impact, with respect to human perceivers. Language made possible a more refined type of self-awareness than could be attained in its absence. The ability to articulate feelings, emotions, and dreams, revolutionized the human view of the self, and transformed the elements of social bonding. In addition, the ability to represent the self within neural models of the environment facilitated problem solving and planning for the future.

Language processing in the brain utilizes the classical Broca's and Wernicke's areas, but it also makes use of a variety of additional resources, such as the higher order left prefrontal, temporal, and premotor cortices, the left basal ganglia, thalamus, and supplementary motor area (Damasio & Damasio, 2000). Broca's area provides the motor control necessary to articulate words, whereas Wernicke's area provides the processing power necessary to understand them. The loss of language functions is frustrating, disabling, and disconcerting. Individuals with Wernicke's aphasia, for example, can develop paranoia and agitation (Damasio & Damasio, 2000).

Language and symbolic reasoning are fundamental to human self-awareness. The ability to manipulate ideas in "psychological space" within the brain provides the ability to map the self in relation to the environment in exquisite detail. This level of detail allows humans to see themselves in the present, the future, and the past. Some mystics even claim the ability to see themselves outside the ordinary space–time continuum.

Parallel Selves: From Primitive Representations To Integrated Maps

The development of self-awareness is a complex process that involves the integration of information from many sources. Defects in self-awareness are caused by a lack of necessary information, deficits in integration, or both. The first prerequisite for self-awareness is mapping. *Every aspect of personal reality must first exist as a brain map. If it can't be mapped, it doesn't exist.* Self-awareness therefore begins with integration of brain maps to develop a comprehensive picture of the state of the body and the body's surroundings. From this dynamic image, actionable views of "reality" are continuously developed. These images, which are constantly changing, facilitate the use of knowledge about the self and the self's environment to drive behavior. As a result of this process, the self contained within the human brain is by no means a simple, unidimensional construct. In fact, it has many dimensions, and we shift among them without conscious effort. At a single moment in time, only some of the "selves" at our disposal are being used. Low-level representations are always at the core of the self; however, at higher levels, one or more specialized sets of self-representations come into play. These representations include:

- The Protoself
- The Emotional Self
- The Spatial Self
- The Automatic Self
- The Appetitive Self
- The Social Self
- The Remembered Self
- The Neocortical Observing Self

This set of critical representations, their neural circuitry, and the dimensions they create are the raw materials from which the images, feelings, and perceptions that underlie self-awareness are constructed.

THE PROTOSELF

The acquisition of information with which to develop a vision of the self begins with the mapping of data from internal sensors. The most primitive form of such mapping has been described by Damasio (1999) and called the *protoself*. The protoself is the foundation on which the entire edifice of self-knowledge rests. It contains comprehensive, nonverbal information about the state of the organism. Protoself information is not usually accessible to consciousness, yet it sets the tone for all conscious constructs and interactions. Moment to moment, the protoself depicts the state of the organism with respect to the body's musculoskeletal frame, as well as internal emotional and arousal states. These states have a profound influence on the eventual quality and intensity of interactions with the environment.

The maps that define the protoself are contained in a variety of phylogenetically ancient sites. These include the secondary somatosensory cortices, especially in the right hemisphere, which contain basic internal and external sensory maps, the hypothalamus, which maps information about homeostatic and drive-related functions (e.g., autonomic responses, temperature regulation, hunger, thirst, and aggressiveness), and the brainstem nuclei, such as the locus ceruleus (vigilance, level of curiosity), dorsal raphe (satiety, aggressiveness, impulsivity, sociability), the ventral tegmental area (motivational salience), the periaqueductal gray (nociceptive information, emotional integration), and the insula (somatic and emotional integration). Figure 2.4 shows the anatomical location of many of these important areas. According to Damasio, the protoself is "the something-to-which-knowing is attributed," the organism's basic physical infrastructure that forms the foundation for all advanced representational processes. As internal events and external objects change the protoself, the changes are represented in heteromodal associative cortices, and the individual becomes aware of the self through appreciation of its constantly changing attributes. The confusional states that can be precipitated by sensory deprivation can be explained by this model as the inhibition of dynamic, second-order mapping involving the protoself and its interactions with external objects. In the absence of external stimuli, only internal processes are available to interact with protoself representations. This limited type of interaction is unable to sustain a stable self-representation in heteromodal cortices, and hallucinatory experiences result. The model suggests that a key component of the self-representations that are required to sustain self-awareness is change. Without the continuous changes brought about by environmental stimuli, a clear representation of the self that can be brought into consciousness may simply not emerge.

INTERNAL SIGNALS

The perception of internal states provides a critical focus for the adaptive process of selective energy expenditure that we call behavior. Hunger and thirst are obvious examples of internal signals that clamor for behavioral attention. The urge to eliminate internal wastes, somnolence, sexual urges, and the sensation of being hot or cold are other important instances of the continuous stream of internal signals that vie for behavioral attention. Many of our daily routines are structured around the demands of these powerful internal attractors. In addition to the types of signals just discussed, which signify specific internal needs, two other types of internal signals are also critical in the implementation of adaptive, energy-efficient behavior: these are, signals that convey internal states of readiness, and signals that echo recent environmental interactions, with special regard for successes, failures, dangers, opportunities, gains, and losses.

Signals that convey internal states of readiness play an important role in shaping self-awareness and determining behavior. These signals include such bodily sensations as pain, fatigue, nausea, and malaise. Pain is an important signal that can prevent serious injury. Individuals with defective pain transmission often suffer injuries to their extremities of which they are unaware. Fatigue is an important indicator that tells us that our muscles need to recover before they are ready for further extensive action. The "sickness response" is another important behavioral modulator. When we are ill, internal signals conspire to limit our physical activities. This can be highly adaptive because an ill animal is not likely to be effective in obtaining food, and would be at greater risk of suffering injury. In order to maximize our safety while we are fighting infections, our brains are receptive to the chemical signals, or cytokines, which are disseminated by our immune systems. These signals diminish urges to move about, and also conveniently suppress appetite.

The neurobiology of cytokine-induced sickness behavior (Figure 2.5) has been defined (Dantzer, 2001). Normally, the inflammatory cytokines, interleukin-1 (IL-1), interleukin-6 (IL-6), tumor necrosis factor-α (TNFα), and the interferons (IFNs), are released by monocytes and macrophages as a response to local infection by pathogens. These cytokines influence the brain in two stages. First, afferent vagal nerve endings are triggered by the cytokines, and activate the nucleus tractus solitarius (NTS), which is the primary

FIGURE 2.5
NEUROBIOLOGICAL SUBSTRATES OF SICKNESS BEHAVIOR

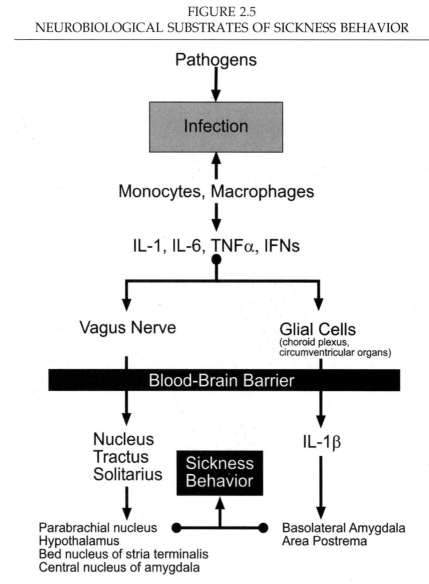

Monocytes and macrophages migrate to infection sites and secrete a variety of leukins, including interleukin-1 (IL-1), interleukin 6 (IL-6), tumor necrosis factor α (TNF α), and interferons (IFNs). These leukins not only modulate the immune system, but also the brain. First they stimulate vagus nerve endings near the infection site. These nerve endings converge on the nucleus tractus solitarius in the brain, which in turn activates the parabrachial nucleus, the hypothalamus, the bed nucleus of the stria terminalis, and the central nucleus of the amygdala. At the same time, glial cells outside the blood–brain barrier in the choroid plexus and circumventricular organs become activated by leukins and secrete IL-1. The IL-1 diffuses into the brain and activates the basolateral amygdala and the area postrema. The action of all the activated brain areas generates the phenomenon that we know as sickness behavior. (Based on Dantzer, 2001)

vagal projection site in the brain. Excitation of the NTS secondarily activates the parabrachial nucleus, the paraventricular and supraoptic hypothalamic nuclei, the bed nucleus of the stria terminalis, and the central nucleus of the amygdala. These regions trigger the motivational, psychomotor, and autonomic changes that are associated with the experience of feeling ill. The induction of a high level of sickness behavior by pharyngeal infections, for example, is consistent with the extensive vagal innervation of the pharynx.

The second stage of cytokine activation involves production of interleukin-1β (IL-1β) by glial cells in the brain's choroid plexus and circumventricular organs. These areas are not shielded from cytokines in the peripheral circulation by the blood–brain barrier. Production of IL-1β in the circumventricular organs and choroid plexus causes slow diffusion of this cytokine into the brain parenchyma. IL-1β directly stimulates neurons in the basolateral amygdala, promoting social withdrawal and inactivity, and in the area postrema, promoting activation of the hypothalamic-pituitary-adrenal (HPA) axis (Konsman, Kelley, & Dantzer, 1999). The full sickness response includes lethargy, social withdrawal, anorexia, anhedonia, and feelings of anergia. It is an adaptive mechanism that protects organisms with an active infection by decreasing their engagement with the external environment, limiting their appetitive needs, and encouraging rest until the infection subsides. The sickness response is a dramatic and ubiquitous example of an induced motivational state. It illustrates how brain circuits can alter behavior on the basis of internal information. In this case, the stimuli that triggered the widespread responses associated with sickness actually originated at the cellular level.

The final category of internal signals involves those that convey a perception of our current situation in the environment. These signals are, of course, emotional states. In an important sense, emotions provide a type of behavioral and perceptive continuity because they allow the effects of important experiences to persist and influence subsequent perceptions and behaviors. For example, if we win an award or achieve occupational successes, emotions can make the positive feelings permeate subsequent interactions for some time. Conversely, adverse events can cause difficulties with subsequent interactions. As we know only too well, emotional signals can malfunction and limit both enjoyment of life and behavioral repertoires.

Internal signals are the substrate on which the experience of self-awareness is built because they give substance to the "self," whose properties are being made conscious. Internal signals can color and limit self-awareness, especially if they malfunction. Mood disorders can cause severe distortions or limitations in what is possible to know about the self.

THE EMOTIONAL SELF

Emotions are complex mind–body representations that reflect the subjective meaning of experience and prepare the individual to take action on the basis of perceived meaning. *Meaning* in this context is the calculated value or threat of the experience in relation to internal signals. For example, rain could elicit a positive emotion if one had just planted a garden, but a negative one if it came right before a planned outdoor wedding. In other settings, rain might be entirely neutral. Phillips and colleagues (2003) reviewed neuroimaging studies of emotional states. They identified three stages in the generation of an emotional response. First, the emotion-producing stimulus is identified and evaluated. Second, an affective state is produced in response to the stimulus. This state includes neuroendocrine and autonomic activation, changes in facial expression, vocalizations, gestures, and specific behavioral responses. In light of all these changes, the individual becomes conscious of the emotional response that has just occurred. Third, the emotion is modulated with respect to perceived appropriateness and context. For example, if one has just scored a touchdown in a football game, the elation of the crowd and one's teammates will amplify the ensuing emotional state. On the other hand, the successful closing of a business deal would probably call for subdued expressions of emotionality, no matter how high the personal gain.

Phillips and associates (2003) also defined the brain regions responsible for the generation of emotions and their subsequent regulation. First, stimuli are evaluated and emotional responses are generated by a ventral processing system with epicenters in the amygdala, the insula, the ventral striatum (including the nucleus accumbens), ventral regions of the anterior cingulate gyrus, and ventral regions of the prefrontal cortex (Figure 2.6).

The amygdala is important for coordinating responses to objects and situations that elicit a sense of risk or fear. The amygdala also functions in the recognition of facial expressions (particularly angry, threatening, or fearful expressions), and participates in the brain's reward system. The insula generates specific representations of *disgusting* or *distasteful* experiences (Penfield & Faulk, 1955). It also functions more widely in the generation of emotional states that are accessible to consciousness, during the perception of sadness, pain, or anticipatory anxiety, in the experience of guilt, and during the recall of emotional states. Both the amygdala and the insula appear to be important in the identification of the emotional value of stimuli and in the coordination of an appropriate emotional response (see review in Phillips et al., 2003). The ventral striatum, and in particular the nucleus accumbens, is the centerpiece of the brain's reward system. It functions in the identification of objects

FIGURE 2.6
THE VENTRAL EMOTIONAL SYSTEM

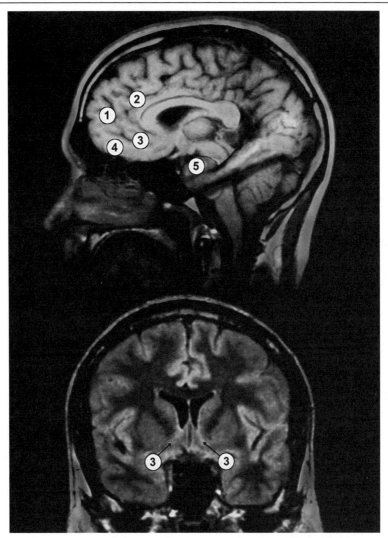

The top half of the figure contains a composited MRI that includes a mid-sagittal view of the brain as well as a more lateral portion that shows the hippocampus and amygdala. The bottom half is a coronal view. Key components of the ventral emotional system include the following regions: 1) Ventromedial prefrontal cortex; 2) Anterior cingulate gyrus; 3) Nucleus accumbens. The accumbens, or recumbent nucleus, forms the ventral striatum, and is clearly visible in the coronal section. Its location is actually lateral to the mid-sagittal view at the top of the figure, and the number 3 is used only to mark its general location; 4) Orbitofrontal cortex; 5) Amygdala. The ventral emotional system functions in the generation of the physical and psychological components of emotional responses. (As described by Phillips, Drevets, Rauch, & Lane, 2003)

of potential value, and in motivating the organism to pursue the acquisition of these objects. The anterior cingulate gyrus appears to function in the generation of affective states, and in the connection of objects with appropriate motivation. It focuses attention on activities likely to yield high reward, and helps to generate mood-related affective states, whether happy or sad (see review in Phillips et al., 2003).

The dorsal emotional system appears to function in the modulation of emotions with respect to contextual constraints. The dorsal system (Figure 2.7) includes the hippocampus, the dorsal anterior cingulate, and the dorsal regions of the prefrontal cortex (Phillips et al., 2003). These areas are able to modulate emotional states with respect to contextual cues, memory, and internalized rules. An imaging study (Ochsner, Bunge, Gross, & Gabrieli, 2002) examined whether rational reappraisal of negative emotions could result in attenuation of the negative emotional state. The study found that reframing emotional events in unemotional terms did reduce affective intensity. The neural correlates of this phenomenon began with activation of the dorsal and ventral regions of the left lateral prefrontal cortex, as well as the dorsomedial prefrontal cortex during the reappraisal procedure. Activation of the right anterior cingulate and the right supramarginal gyrus was correlated with success in mitigation of negative emotion. The specific neural correlates of successful emotional reappraisal involved increased activation of lateral and medial prefrontal cortices combined with decreased activation of the amygdala and medial orbitofrontal cortex.

Emotions play an important role in self-awareness. While the causes of emotions are often not conscious, the arousal and autonomic states that they generate bring to consciousness the knowledge that a noteworthy change (the one that triggered the emotion) has occurred. The emotional self is a highly aware and energized representation, because emotions evolved specifically to affect arousal, motivation, and behavior. Rolls (1999) identified 10 specific functions of emotions, and these are paraphrased and explained below:

1. Modulation of autonomic and endocrine functions (e.g., tachycardia, sweaty palms, release of adrenaline) in response to noteworthy environmental stimuli.
2. Promotion of flexible behavioral responses. The generation of emotional states rather than fixed behavioral responses enhances the ability to customize end behaviors. It also facilitates the generalizability of behavioral responses to situations that have not been specifically encountered before, but which arouse a particular emotion.

FIGURE 2.7
THE DORSAL EMOTIONAL SYSTEM

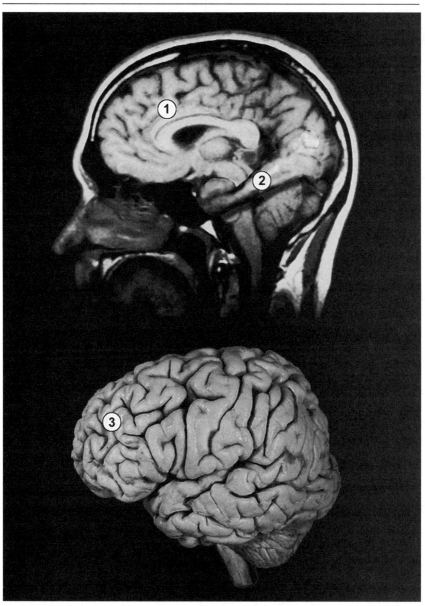

The top half of the figure contains a composited MRI as described in Figure 2.6. Key components of the dorsal emotional system include the following regions: 1) Dorsal anterior cingulate gyrus; 2) Hippocampus; 3) Dorsolateral prefrontal cortex. The dorsal emotional system functions in the regulation of emotional responses. (As described by Phillips, Drevets, Rauch, & Lane, 2003)

3. The generation of a motivational state likely to promote a behavior that successfully addresses the cause of the emotion.
4. Social bonding. Higher primates are very sensitive to emotional expressions. Emotional displays that are shared promote social bonding (e.g., laughing together at a party, expressing elation during a sports contest, or expressing sadness at a wake). The attachment of parents and offspring is also solidified by emotional expression.
5. Communication. Emotional displays can convey important messages to others, such as fear, anger, and joy.
6. The promotion of activities that have survival value through positive emotion.
7. Facilitation of memory storage. Events that have high emotional content are more likely to be remembered than neutral events. This is believed to be mediated by activation of ascending cholinergic and noradrenergic pathways.
8. The modulation of the cognitive and emotional processing of events and memories during the time the emotion lasts. This can provide a sense of continuity to experience, since proximal sequences of events are processed and interpreted under a similar emotional context.
9. The persistence of emotion makes important events influence subsequent interactions with the environment for a period of time. This can have survival value in dangerous situations, and can maximize the ability to exploit favorable conditions.
10. Emotions trigger relevant memories. This can either be adaptive, by making important information accessible, or maladaptive, by triggering dysfunctional recollections that result in problematic behavior.

Fear is a type of emotional response that is particularly important for survival. Fear impacts self-awareness by causing marked arousal, while at the same time creating a narrow and urgent behavioral focus designed to escape or avoid the cause of the fear. Pathological states centered on fear can be incapacitating, because the fear representation blots out other organizing principles while the emotional state lasts. The cause of the fear may not be accessible to consciousness (e.g., in panic disorder), but the fear state assumes control of conscious processes. Fearful states are mediated by the amygdala, and a discussion of amygdalar function follows below.

THE AMYGDALA AND THE FEARFUL SELF
The amygdalae (Figure 2.8) are bilateral, almond-shaped structures located at the medial edges of the temporal lobes. Each amygdala is composed of

FIGURE 2.8
CORONAL MRI AT THE LEVEL OF THE AMYGDALA

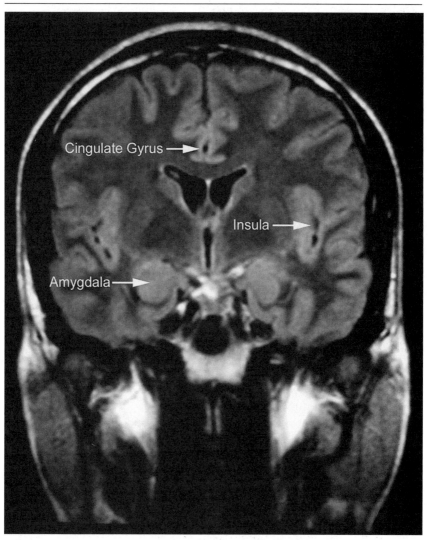

The cingulate gyrus, amygdala, and insula, each of which is involved with the generation of emotion. The primary emotion associated with the amygdala is fear.

13 nuclei that function in a variety of processes related to the generation of emotion, arousal, autonomic and hormonal responses, and recognition of facial expressions (Sah, Faber, Lopes de Armentia, & Power, 2003). The amygdala is one of the brain's fastest integrators of sensory information, and when circumstances dictate, it generates the adaptive function of fear. Fear is an abstract concept that describes the changes in the body and brain in response to circumstances that are perceived to be threatening. Fear has both physiological and motor components, and generates strong memories that decrease the chances of a repetition of the fear-provoking situation. The major amygdalar nuclei are usually divided into three groups (Sah et al., 2003): (1) The basolateral, or deep group, which includes the basal nucleus, the lateral nucleus, and the accessory basal nucleus. (2) The corticomedial or superficial group, which includes the cortical nuclei and the nucleus of the lateral olfactory tract. (3) The centromedial group, which includes the central and medial nuclei.

The basolateral nuclei receive inputs from a wide variety of regions, including the sensory cortices, the perirhinal and entorhinal cortices, the hippocampal formation, the thalamus, hypothalamus, and frontal cortex. This provides the amygdala with a wide range of processed sensory information. Basolateral nuclei project to the prefrontal cortex, hippocampal formation, and adjacent medial temporal lobe regions, the nucleus accumbens, and the striatum. The corticomedial group has dense reciprocal connections with olfactory cortices. Amygdalar inputs are for the most part ipsilateral, and cortical inputs usually originate in lamina V of the cortex (Sah et al., 2003). The central nucleus receives inputs from the midbrain, pons, and medulla, as well as from the thalamus, hypothalamus, sensory cortices, subiculum, perirhinal, and entorhinal cortices. It sends outputs to many important targets from the viewpoint of the generation of emotional states, arousal, and autonomic modulation. These include the bed nucleus of the stria terminalis, the hypothalamus, midbrain, pons, medulla, and the ascending cholinergic, dopaminergic (substantia nigra and ventral tegmental area), serotonergic, and noradrenergic systems (Sah et al., 2003). The medial nucleus receives inputs from the frontal cortex, perirhinal, entorhinal, and piriform cortices, subiculum, and hypothalamus. It sends outputs to the olfactory system, bed nucleus of the stria terminalis, and the thalamus (Sah et al., 2003). The concept of the *extended amygdala* (Alheid & Heimer, 1988) involves the suggestion that the centromedial amygdala should be extended rostrally and medially into the bed nucleus of the stria terminalis and the substantia inominata (ventral pallidum). The rationale for this suggestion is that the amygdala innervates both regions, and the latter are also connected to the descending, efferent projections of the amygdala.

The amygdala mediates fear responses, and helps to manage risk by limiting behaviors that elicit fear. It is the amygdala that keeps us from going into dark alleys, both literally and within the mind. Under normal circumstances, fear-provoking behaviors usually constitute actions that place the self at risk; therefore it is adaptive to limit them. In pathological states, on the other hand, inappropriate assignation of fear can stifle behavioral adaptability. The amygdala is connected to key brainstem nuclei, including the ventral tegmental area, the periaqueductal gray, the locus ceruleus, and the dorsal raphe (Sah et al., 2003). It also receives inputs from the sensory cortices (Figure 2.9). In a sense, the amygdala is a gateway to the possible. For most individuals, it functions as an appropriate moderator of risk. For others, with high amygdalar responsivity, fear can severely constrain the

FIGURE 2.9
NEURAL TARGETS OF THE EFFERENT TRACTS
OF THE AMYGDALA

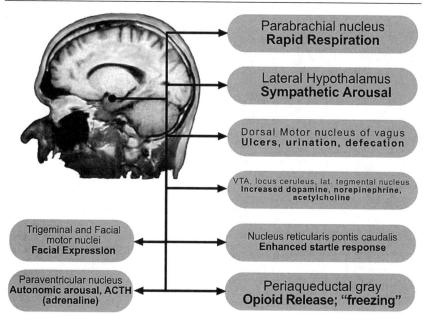

The amygdala coordinates all the physical aspects of fear responses, including the initial "freezing" reaction and startle response, facial expression, loss of sphincter control, sympathetic arousal, rapid breathing, and release of adrenaline and excitatory neurotransmitters. (Based on Davism, 1992)

limits of the possible. Conversely, lack of amygdalar tone can facilitate risk taking through creating a deficit in self-awareness. For the hypoamygdalar individual, risky situations "feel" no different from safe ones.

The amygdala can implement rapid emergency responses to threatening situations by virtue of direct input from the auditory thalamus (LeDoux, 1996). The startle reaction when someone approaches from behind and shouts is an amygdalar response. The subsequent attenuation of the startle response when it becomes obvious that it is just a practical-joking friend is mediated by subsequent cortical processing of sensory signals and amygdalar inhibition.

The amygdala is important for the integration of emotional experiences into a vision of the self. In particular, the amygdala is essential for precipitating the experience of fear within appropriate contexts, as well as for enabling the recognition of fear or threat in the facial expressions of others. Damasio (1999) described a female patient with Urbach-Wiethe disease whose amygdalae had calcified bilaterally. While she was able to function for the most part, she tended to be overly familiar with others and was uninhibited with regards to touching. She was also unable to experience fear, either in herself, or in the faces of others. In the absence of a personal capacity for fear, she was also unable to distinguish menacing facial expressions in others. While she had clear deficits in self-awareness, she could not tell that she had these deficits. Fear, which was never mapped in her brain, was simply nonexistent in subjective terms. In other words, in the absence of a self-referential experience, the concept of fear itself had no meaning. This phenomenon is important to note as a general concept. If an individual is missing a core map that is critical for building a complete image of the self, the fact that an entire map is missing will make it difficult for the individual to be aware of the deficit. Incompleteness of a brain representation may signal that something is wrong, but complete absence of a brain map at a low level can remove the involved function from subjective existence.

In addition to mediating immediate fear-driven responses to threats, the amygdala is responsible for fear conditioning. That is, an individual may come to associate fear with objects or situations which have been connected with personal risk. Fear-driven memories may be subconscious, but they emerge as an unpleasant body state when the individual is exposed to the feared object or situation. Fear conditioning, which is classified as a type of procedural memory, occurs independently of declarative memory (remembering facts or events), which is mediated by the hippocampus (Figure 2.10).

Individuals with bilateral hippocampal damage cannot remember facts or events, but will remember fear-causing situations subconsciously and will

FIGURE 2.10
SELECTED MEMORY SYSTEMS IN THE BRAIN

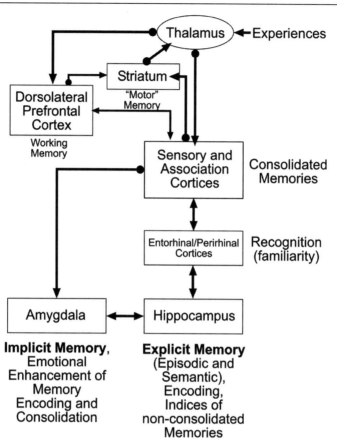

The dorsolateral prefrontal cortex coordinates the functions of working memory. Control sequences for well-rehearsed, automatic movements (e.g., throwing a ball, driving a car) are stored in the striatum. The amygdala coordinates the formation of implicit memories (see text), although the amygdala does not store the actual information that constitutes the memories. The amygdala also enhances the effectiveness of memory storage under highly emotional circumstances and promotes consolidation (i.e., long-term retention) of emotionally charged memories. The hippocampus functions in the encoding and consolidation of explicit memory. The right hippocampus is more involved in the encoding and consolidation of episodic, or event-based memories, while the left hippocampus is more involved in semantic or verbal memories. The sense of rapid recognition (i.e., familiarity) with regard to objects or situations is thought to depend on the function of the perirhinal cortex. For a period of time (years), retrieval of memories requires an intact hippocampus and its surrounding cortices. Memories that have persisted for several years become consolidated, and at some point no longer require the hippocampus for retrieval. Consolidated memories are thought to be stored in distributed fashion within the higher cortices.

avoid them in the future. LeDoux (1996), a leading amygdala researcher, recounted a story about a woman who had suffered bilateral damage to her temporal lobes and lost all ability to store episodic or semantic memories. A French psychologist named Edouard Claparede cared for this patient. The patient never remembered Claparede after they parted company, even if he left the examining room for only a few minutes and then returned. Because the patient never remembered the psychologist, she normally shook hands with him each time they met. One day, Claparede conducted an experiment. He concealed a thumbtack in his hand and pricked the patient during their handshake. He left the room, and returned a few minutes later. The patient did not recognize him, but refused to shake hands with him.

This experiment demonstrated the existence of a system for the storage of emotional memories that is independent of the hippocampus. It is now known to be amygdala-driven, although the amygdala itself is not the site of memory storage. Normally, experiences with high emotional content will be stored preferentially in memory. This is not the case, however, for individuals with bilateral amygdalar damage, who show no preferential storage of emotionally laden memories (LeDoux, 1996). The amygdala has important reciprocal connections with the hippocampus, from which it receives context, and with orbitofrontal cortex, which can attenuate amygdalar responses. Amygdalar outputs allow it to control all the experiential components of fear. Specifically, the central nucleus of the amygdala projects to a variety of anatomical targets that mediate each of the elements of fear. These include (Davis, 1992, p. 364):

- The parabrachial nucleus, which induces rapid respiration
- The lateral hypothalamus, which causes sympathetic arousal with tachycardia, pupil dilation, pallor, and blood pressure elevation
- The dorsal motor nucleus of the vagus, which mediates gastric ulcer formation, as well as fear-induced urination and defecation (the counting of fecal pellets is often used to assess fear responses in rodents)
- The ventral tegmental area, locus ceruleus, and dorsal lateral tegmental nucleus, which increase levels of dopamine, norepinephrine, and acetylcholine. These neurotransmitters generate arousal, sharpen attention, heighten motivation, and promote memory storage
- The nucleus reticularis pontis caudalis, which mediates the startle response
- The periaqueductal gray region, which mediates release of endogenous opioids and causes fear-induced "freezing"

- The trigeminal and facial motor nuclei, which mediate facial expression
- The paraventricular nucleus of the hypothalamus, which causes autonomic arousal and induces the pituitary to release adrenocorticotrophic hormone (ACTH). ACTH in turn influences the adrenal to release corticosteroids

As might be expected, the amygdala also plays a central role in anxiety responses, which are mediated by fear of a present condition or an imagined future situation.

The Automatic Self

Many of the important actions that we perform daily require very little, if any, conscious intervention. The ability to walk and to climb stairs automatically, for example, falls under this category. Numerous other simple and complex actions, such as riding a bicycle, driving a car, hitting a tennis ball, or throwing a football, are also automatic sequences of movements that have been learned through practice and do not require conscious coordination for their implementation. Research has shown that complex sequences of movements such as the ones described are encoded through interactions of the basal ganglia and the cortex, with subsequent modification of specific thalamocorticostriatal loops (Graybiel, 1998). Automatic movement sequences, once learned, can be triggered on demand simply by exposure to the appropriate context. For example, the sight of a red traffic light will induce most individuals to step on the brake of their automobile.

From the perspective of self-awareness, the automatic actions that we have learned throughout our lifetimes are very important to the definition of who we are. We define ourselves by the unconscious actions that we can perform as much as by any other criteria. Someone might say, for instance, "I played tennis in college. I am now a secretary and type 80 words a minute. I drive a new sports car, and my hobbies are tennis, knitting, and dancing." All of these activities, of course, involve automatic actions.

Sports figures become famous because of their ability to perform complex movement sequences at just the appropriate moment. Automatic actions are essential for the basic conduct of our lives. They also support leisure activities such as sports, and may be critical for the implementation of our chosen occupations, particularly if these demand specialized sequences of movements. It would not be wise to solicit the services of a surgeon who has to coordinate her fingers consciously as she ties surgical knots. The hallmark of automatic actions is that they require a great deal of practice to learn, and their performance is worsened by conscious attempts to control the movements. Once automatic actions have been learned, they are retained for long periods within the behavioral repertoire.

Zen swordsmanship and other Zen-based martial disciplines rely on harnessing the functions of the basal ganglia. Zen-inspired martial arts training begins with long periods of highly disciplined practice to encode proper sequences of movements. Once the movements have been encoded, the individual is taught to resist any desire to control them consciously. Rather, the practitioner of Zen allows his or her actions to be generated through the unconscious activation of movement by perceived cues. Suzuki (1959) described this process:

> However well a man may be trained in the art, the swordsman can never be the master of his technical knowledge unless all his psychic hindrances are removed and he can keep the mind in the state of emptiness, even purged of whatever technique he has obtained. The entire body together with the four limbs will then be capable of displaying for the first time and to its full extent all the art acquired by the training of several years. They will move as if automatically, with no conscious efforts on the part of the swordsman. (p. 152)

These are, of course, very difficult processes to master, since the conscious self likes to supervise behavior, especially in times of stress.

The Spatial Self

The human cerebral hemispheres are not functionally symmetrical. Specifically, the right hemisphere (which is generally the nondominant hemisphere) is specialized for spatial perception. Language and symbolic functions are localized in the left, or dominant hemisphere. The left hemisphere exerts its influence through logic and detailed descriptions. The right hemisphere, in contrast, exerts its influence by inducing a sense of "intuitive" understanding, or by triggering body states of comfort or unease. Novel objects and events are initially processed within the right hemisphere. After they become "routine," processing moves to the left hemisphere (Goldberg, 2001). The network that represents the body in *object space*, that is, as a 3-dimensional entity among the various objects in the environment, has been well defined. It has epicenters in the posterior parietal cortex, the frontal eye field region, the superior colliculus, and the cingulate gyrus (Mesulam, 2000). In addition, the frontal cortex and the basal ganglia participate in the circuit. The posterior parietal cortex contains detailed sensory information about the space in which we find ourselves. The superior colliculus and the frontal eye fields contain spatial coordinates of the self, and control exploration of the surrounding space, particularly exploration through visual saccades. The cingulate gyrus contributes salience to specific objects, and the basal ganglia, in conjunction with the cortex, facilitate differential gating of information at the level of the thalamus. Information gating refers to the amplification of specific inputs that have aroused attentional focus and attenuation of the rest. The complete circuit just described contains not only spatial information, but also information about the salience of specific objects and the behavioral strategies to acquire them. Damage to the right posterior parietal cortex can result in the profound deficit in self-awareness called *anosognosia* (see below). Figure 2.11 contains conceptual and schematic information about this important circuit.

Awareness of the body in space is enhanced by the simultaneous representation of the body and environmental objects in the associational cortices, with emphasis on the continuous changes in body-object relationships. The ability of second and higher order representations to emphasize changes as the body interacts with objects generates the dynamic stream of consciousness that we experience as self-awareness. The brain is designed to accommodate to unchanging conditions. For example, we can tune out certain levels of background noise, and attenuate our responsiveness to many other continuous stimuli. Low-level, repetitive background noises can even be used to induce sleep, and commercial sound machines that emulate repetitive, low-level sounds such as ocean waves and rain exploit this principle. The representation of changing relationships between the self and the self's environment in associational regions such as the cingulate gyrus and prefrontal cortices is therefore an important mechanism for bringing the representation of the self as an independent agent into consciousness. In humans, the symbolic, verbal representations of the self and environmental objects that exist in the left brain are also critical components of the mechanisms that generate conscious self-awareness. These symbolic representations are updated continuously as their relationships change. Verbal representations are especially powerful because they can be manipulated logically to clarify relationships and implications, and to construct models of the future. The availability of these verbal representations of the self and the self's surroundings contribute significantly to the conscious phenomenon of human self-awareness.

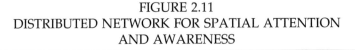

FIGURE 2.11
DISTRIBUTED NETWORK FOR SPATIAL ATTENTION
AND AWARENESS

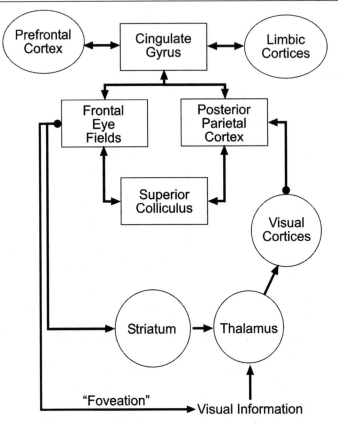

Major epicenters of this network include the posterior parietal cortex, cingulate gyrus, frontal eye fields, and superior colliculus. The superior colliculus, in conjunction with mesencephalic and pontine reticular formations, controls saccadic movements of the eyes and therefore foveation or visual exploration of targeted objects with the fovea (i.e., the most sensitive part of the retina). The posterior parietal cortex contains spatial informa- tion about the environment and its objects. The cingulate gyrus, through its inputs from the limbic cortices, contains information about perceived value and risk of potential tar- gets. The dorsolateral prefrontal cortex contains cognitive information about potential targets, as well as information that allows the eyes to refocus on a remembered target. The frontal eye field integrates the various types of targeting information and modulates the superior colliculus to trigger targeted saccades. The superior colliculus is normally inhibited by the substantia nigra. When they generate targeted saccadic movements, the frontal eye fields activate the superior colliculus directly and also activate the caudate, which in turn inhibits the substantia nigra, releasing the superior colliculus from inhibi- tion. (Based on Mesulam, 2000)

Faces and Objects

The distributed network for the recognition of faces and objects (Figure 2.12) is centered in the fusiform gyrus and the temporal region. The fusiform gyrus appears to be an important switching station that receives basic visual information, recognizes the type of object that is being perceived, and directs subsequent processing to the appropriate set of specialized circuits. In keeping with this function, the fusiform gyrus has a specific face region, a region for objects other than faces, and a region for letter-strings that have been identified as words (Mesulam, 2000). Each of these requires specialized processing, and its recognition as a specialized object in the fusiform gyrus ensures that the appropriate type of processing is applied. For example, a face requires processing for expression, familiarity, and signs of age. A letter string, in contrast, must be sent through the processing system centered in Wernicke's area, in order to determine its meaning. Bilateral loss of the fusiform gyri leads to the inability to recognize once familiar faces simply from visual cues, since the sensory signals are not sent to the appropriate processing centers. Even the faces of one's spouse or children are not recognized. If the temporal region remains intact, other cues (such as hearing the person speak) can bring about recognition. The inferior temporal gyrus contains a representation of environmental contents as invariant objects that can be mentally manipulated (earlier representations of objects are fragmented). Objects are fully imbued with value in the temporal pole (Rolls, 1999). This area receives inputs from the amygdala and hippocampus, and has extensive connections with the cingulate gyrus. Imaging studies have indicated that autistic individuals are not able to use the "face area" of the fusiform gyrus, like normal individuals, to recognize human faces as specialized objects and organize appropriate processing. Instead, human faces activate idiosyncratically aberrant regions in the autistic subjects' brains. These include the frontal cortex, the primary visual cortex, and the cerebellum (Pierce, Muller, Ambrose, Allen, & Courchesne, 2001). Proper recognition of faces and objects is critical to the development of an accurate and stable self-image. Individuals with damage to recognition areas find themselves in an alien land, with no hope of ever attaining the sense of comfort that comes from familiar surroundings.

The emergence of a comprehensive view of the self depends on the definition of a *personal space* (Cotterill, 1998). This personal space contains a representation of the self as well as a representation of the environment and its objects. The self-representation includes low-level sensory information, a sense of position in space, and a sense of internal appetitive and emotional

FIGURE 2.12
BASIC NEURAL CIRCUITRY FOR FACE RECOGNITION

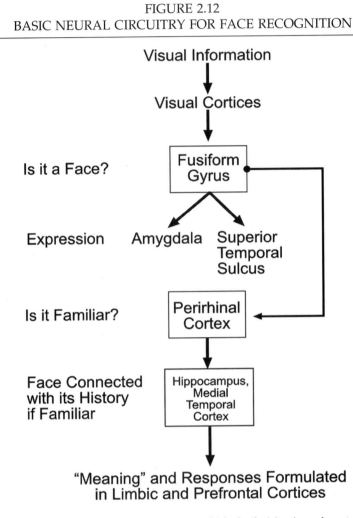

The fusiform gyrus appears to be a gateway at which the decision is made as to whether a perceived object is a face. It is activated by familiar and unfamiliar faces, cartoon faces, incomplete faces, and face-like abstract designs. If an object is perceived to be a face, information is directed to the appropriate processing streams. Facial expression is evaluated in the amygdala and superior temporal sulcus. Rough familiarity is perceived in the perirhinal cortex. If a face is familiar, further processing by the hippocampus and adjacent medial temporal cortex connects the face with its history. Finally, the meaning of the perceived face and expression, as well as appropriate responses, are formulated in limbic and prefrontal cortices.

states. As mentioned previously, Damasio (1999) called the most primitive representation of the self the protoself. The protoself, according to Damasio, is generated by information flowing out of the brainstem nuclei, hypothalamus, and secondary somatosensory cortices. In addition, there is a second-order representation of the self that emerges as soon as the protoself interacts with an object. Damasio believes that second-order mapping, in which protoself information is integrated with information about external objects, takes place in a processing network with epicenters in the superior colliculus, the cingulate gyrus, the thalamus, and the frontal cortices. The accuracy with which the personal space models the internal and external environments influences the quality of the self-image that emerges. The main difference between primitive brains and more highly evolved brains is that primitive brains define a less detailed personal space and take fewer variables into account before they cause the organism to move. Some of the disorders that impair the definition of personal space or decrease the number of variables considered before the initiation of movement reduce the brain to a more "primitive" functional state.

Within the personal space, certain objects are imbued with *salience,* that is, they emerge from the sensory background and their representations are sent through the associative cortices for further processing. These are, of course, objects deemed worthy of attention. Salience can imbue an object for a variety of reasons, including risk, potential reward, novelty, or simple physical properties (e.g., movement) that make it stand out from the background. In other words, unique, dangerous, or rewarding objects capture attention. In addition, the cortex can also impose salience on otherwise uninteresting objects or tasks (e.g., reading a dull book in preparation for an exam).

The activation of memory by an object's representation can also trigger attention. Dopamine is an important neurochemical in this context because it can imbue attention-worthy objects with salience (Kapur, 2003) by amplifying their representations and suppressing signals from other objects (see "The Appetitive Self," below). Important components of the attention network include the ventral tegmental area (dopamine production), the cingulate gyrus (executive attention center and generation of the "to do" list), the thalamus (selective transmission of information), the thalamic reticular nucleus (signal filtering), and the posterior parietal cortex (spatial representation, disengaging from one spatial stimulus to attend to another). The prefrontal cortex is also essential for the perception of complex phenomena, especially when the attention task involves integration of multiple information streams.

Attention first involves signal expansion, then symbolic representation, and finally analysis of the implications of the symbolic representation through modeling. When an object is deemed worthy of attention, its representation in the brain undergoes expansion. Signals about its shape, color, position, and other properties are allowed to project beyond the simple sensory cortices and into the more complex heteromodal cortices. These signals are eventually compressed back into a whole object (in the inferior temporal cortex). Finally, the object is described in symbolic (verbal) terms in the left hemisphere. Symbols, as discussed above, are a powerful type of shorthand, because even though they are a highly compressed representation of an object, they trigger arrays of *pointers* (to use a programming term) that indicate links to other elements within the brain's labyrinth of memories, objects, emotions, and internal signals. The symbolic representation of the latest pen obtained from a pharmaceutical representative, for example, would have much different "pointers" than the representation of the pen given by one's spouse as a Valentine's Day present.

Deficits in attention, as we know from observing individuals with ADHD, can impair the ability to focus energy and organize behavior adaptively. Stimulants that increase dopamine and norepinephrine can restore the ability of ADHD patients to focus attention. Dopamine is critical to the neural representation of salience. Without dopamine, objects and events lose individual importance, because they do not emerge from the perceptual background, and the organism has difficulty generating a motivational state related to the perceived objects. With too much dopamine, the opposite occurs, and objects and events can be imbued with excessive salience. In a sense, chemical dependence and ADHD are at opposite ends of the attentional spectrum. In one case, it is not possible to focus, while in the other, it is difficult to shift attention from the highly salient environmental and internal cues that signal the possibility of using the substance to which the individual has become addicted.

The Appetitive Self

The reward system of the brain evolved to facilitate the exploitation of environmental resources. In higher animals with extensive behavioral repertoires, the reward system provides an important behavioral focus because it encourages the repetition of special activities, from eating to sexual interactions, which are essential for reproduction and survival (Kalivas, 2002).

The feeling of *reward* is a body state that the brain interprets as pleasant. When pleasurable stimuli are experienced, the reward system of the brain promotes the formation of memories that store details of the circumstances that led to the experience. This causes the individual, in the future, to try to repeat the same circumstances that led to the pleasurable experience, a phenomenon known as reinforcement.

Naturally rewarding experiences (e.g., genetically preprogrammed pleasures such as eating certain foods or sexual contact) activate the reward system and produce reinforcement of the actions that led to the pleasurable experience. Drugs of abuse short-circuit reward pathways by activating specific components of the system directly. This causes strong reinforcement of the events that led to drug use through accumulation of larger amounts of reinforcing neurotransmitters than are released in response to normal stimuli.

The neural circuitry of reward is implemented by a distributed network with epicenters in the nucleus accumbens, the ventral tegmental area, the hippocampus, the amygdala, the prefrontal cortex, and the ventral pallidum (see Figure 2.13). The nucleus accumbens is an area of confluence where diverse streams of information flow together, and as they blend, potentially rewarding objects and situations are given attentional and behavioral focus. The accumbens, along with the extended amygdala, is part of a distributed network that functions in the linkage of motivation to action (Heimer et al., 1997). The nucleus accumbens receives a broad spectrum of inputs that carry information about available objects and their potential value. Key afferents include projections from the hippocampus, entorhinal and perirhinal cortices, olfactory cortex, anterior cingulate, orbitofrontal cortex, inferior temporal gyrus, the insula, the basal amygdala, and the midline thalamic nuclei (Heimer et al., 1997). The nucleus accumbens also receives dense dopaminergic afferents from the ventral tegmental area.

Anatomically, the nucleus accumbens is part of the ventral striatum. It consists of a central core surrounded by a "shell," medially, ventrally, and laterally. The caudate and putamen, which form the dorsal striatum, border the nucleus accumbens core dorsally and are continuous with it (Heimer et al., 1997). The core of the nucleus accumbens receives dopaminergic inputs from the substantia nigra, serotonergic inputs from the dorsal raphe, and glutamatergic inputs from the motor cortex. The shell of the accumbens receives dopaminergic inputs form the ventral tegmental area, serotonergic inputs from the medial raphe, and glutamatergic inputs from the cingulate gyrus, orbitofrontal cortex, and inferior temporal gyrus. Both shell and core receive glutamatergic inputs from the hippocampus and associated cortices,

FIGURE 2.13
THALAMOCORTICOSTRIATAL LOOP THROUGH
THE NUCLEUS ACCUMBENS

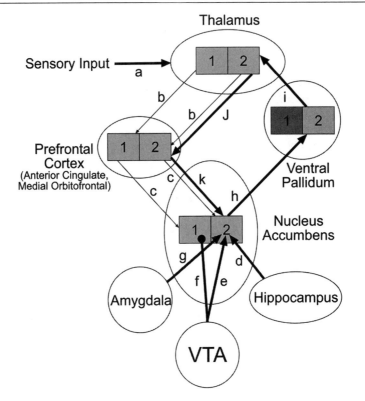

The nucleus accumbens is a region of confluence in which inputs from the prefrontal cortex, amygdala, and hippocampus are integrated to emphasize specific actions or events and de-emphasize others. Two channels (1 and 2) are represented by shaded rectangles. a) Sensory input arrives at the thalamus (a) and baseline level representations of the data are projected (b) to the appropriate cortical areas. Representations are segregated within distinct tracts, or channels. From the prefrontal cortex, baseline representations are projected (c) to the nucleus accumbens. Within the nucleus accumbens, representations that are recognized through hippocampal processing and considered noteworthy receive an activating (depolarizing) signal (d). The amygdala can also contribute a value/risk-related modulatory signal (g). The ventral tegmental area (VTA) releases dopamine whenever noteworthy objects or events are noticed. Dopamine (see text), through voltage-sensitive mechanisms, further suppresses channels that are not receiving additional activation (channel 1) and amplifies activated channels (channel 2). When a channel is activated in the nucleus accumbens, the corresponding channel is inhibited in the ventral pallidum (h). This in turn disinhibits the appropriate tract in the thalamus (i), leading to enhanced representation of the object or event in the prefrontal cortex (j). Cortical stimulation of neurons in the nucleus accumbens that represent the object of interest (k) close the circuit and enhance the strength of the representation.

basal amygdala, and thalamus. The inputs from the last three sources are somatotopically organized (Heimer et al., 1997). The somatotopic organization creates channels that are functionally related, on a one-to-one basis, to each of the many inputs that are evaluated continuously within the nucleus accumbens. Through this arrangement, the nucleus accumbens is able to generate amplified cortical and limbic representations of specific stimuli with high-perceived value, while simultaneously attenuating the rest. This allows the accumbens to focus attention and behavioral resources on objects and situations expected to yield high levels of reward, while excluding less valuable possibilities from attentional focus.

In humans, about 70% of the accumbens neurons are medium-sized spiny neurons with high densities of synaptic spines. This is consistent with their role as coincidence indicators (Heimer et al., 1997). The accumbens spiny neurons are GABAergic and inhibitory, and project to the ventral pallidum. These projections, in turn, give the accumbens the capacity to modulate thalamoprefrontal circuits. Neurons from the accumbens shell also project to the central amygdala, lateral hypothalamus, cholinergic and dopaminergic regions, and a variety of other autonomic and somatomotor targets (Heimer et al., 1997). These projections give the accumbens the ability to modulate arousal, autonomic tone, emotionality, and the amplification or suppression of cortical representations. Accumbens neurons are normally quiescent, and will not fire unless activated by multiple stimuli. Ventral pallidal neurons, on the other hand, are tonically active, and normally inhibit portions of the thalamus (Nolte, 1999). When an accumbens neuron fires, it inhibits target neurons in the ventral pallidum, and disinhibits specific channels within the thalamus, thus transmitting an amplified representation of the object that triggered the accumbens to the cortex (Figures 2.13 & 2.14).

The spiny neurons within the accumbens have two possible states, an "up" state with a resting membrane potential of about −55 mV (close to the threshold for the generation of an action potential) and a "down" or hyperpolarized state, with a resting membrane potential of −80 to −90 mV (Heimer et al., 1997). Neurons in the down state must be brought into the up state before they can fire. The main excitatory inputs to the accumbens originate in the hippocampus, the amygdala, the cingulate and orbitofrontal cortices, and other association cortices. Conceivably, these inputs could also exert inhibitory influences on accumbens neurons through the activation of GABAergic interneurons. Accumbens neurons can be "gated" into the up state by excitatory inputs from the hippocampus. This is a practical arrangement, since it allows the hippocampus, and therefore remembered environmental cues, to trigger transition of accumbens neurons into an excitable

FIGURE 2.14
SCHEMATIC REPRESENTATION OF A SPINY NEURON
IN THE NUCLEUS ACCUMBENS

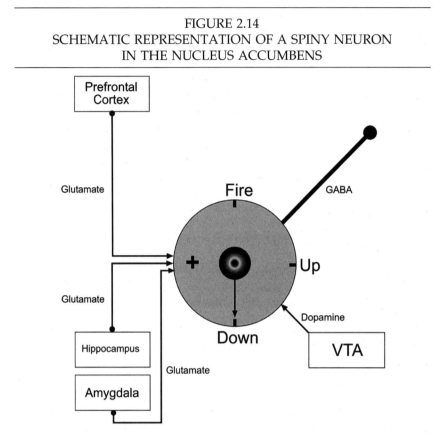

These neurons are bistable, with an excited (i.e., "up") state and a hyperpolarized (i.e., "down") state. Neurons in the down state must be brought into the up state through stimulation before they can fire. Stimulation from more than one source is usually necessary for triggering accumbens neurons. Modulatory inputs converge on the spiny neurons from the prefrontal cortex (glutamate), hippocampus (glutamate), amygdala (glutamate), and ventral tegmental area (VTA—dopamine). The summation of these inputs, as well as putative inputs from inhibitory (GABA) interneurons, determines the spiny neuron's state as well as its firing rate.

state in which any additional excitatory input will trigger an action potential (Heimer et al., 1997).

The actions of dopamine on accumbens neurons have important functional implications. Striatal (including accumbens) dopamine levels modulate the "reactivity" of the organism (Berke & Hyman, 2000). For example, mice that have genetically engineered dopamine deficits are motorically hypoactive and stop eating a few weeks after birth. They starve to death unless treated with dopamine agonists (Berke & Hyman, 2000). Accumbens neurons possess both D1 and D2 dopamine receptors. D2 receptors are inhibitory, and hyperpolarize neurons that are in the down state even further through the opening of potassium channels (Berke & Hyman, 2000). In contrast, D1 dopamine receptors can exert opposing effects depending on the activation state of the neuron. Neurons in the up state are further depolarized by activation of D1 receptors. This is mediated through the opening of voltage-sensitive calcium L channels. Conversely, activation of D1 receptors on neurons in the down state results in hyperpolarization through the inhibition of sodium channels and the potentiation of voltage-sensitive potassium channels (Hernandez-Lopez, 1997). Dopamine, which is frequently secreted into brain areas where selections among inputs and channels must be made (e.g., dorsal striatum, nucleus accumbens, prefrontal cortex, cingulate gyrus), therefore enhances the distinction between active and inactive neurons. In other words, it makes inactive neurons even more hyperpolarized while at the same time increasing the depolarization of activated neurons. In this manner, dopamine is able to aid in the amplification of a single, powerful input while suppressing weaker signals. In the presence of dopamine, a very strong impulse can dominate behavior, while weaker impulses will tend to be ignored.

The amygdala plays an important role in positive reinforcement because it mediates the emotional memory component of the reward circuit. The circuit from the nucleus accumbens to the ventral pallidum also serves to integrate limbic and motor systems. Neurons in the accumbens core actually fire to motivate movement sequences designed to secure known rewards, such as addictive drugs (Chang, Sawyer, Lee, & Woodward, 1994). The prefrontal cortex can exert an inhibitory influence on dopaminergic release both at the ventral tegmental area and in the nucleus accumbens itself through activation of inhibitory interneurons. This provides cortical modulation of limbically driven activities ("look before you jump"). The system can be overwhelmed, for practical purposes, by release of large amounts of dopamine into the nucleus accumbens combined with at least one strong, reward-signaling cue. This promotes a limbic override of behavioral directions proposed by the cortex and amplification of reward-seeking behaviors, and is an important component of drug addiction. The individual who falls into this state has difficulty shifting attention from the highly salient object or situation that has caused the dopamine release. The concerns of the cortical self are thus drowned in a flood of dopamine.

From the perspective of self-awareness, the operation of the brain's reward system can be both satisfying and problematic. The accumbens circuitry is designed not only to cause amplification of a particular signal and attenuation of the rest, but also to trigger arousal, autonomic and hormonal activation, and the generation of an appropriate emotional state. This ensures that the individual is consciously aware of the pleasurable experience that is expected. On the other hand, the attenuation of competing inputs in the face of a particularly strong one can cause the lapses in self-awareness that characterize addictive states. During these lapses, the appetitive self, powered by the expectation of reward, emerges triumphant and suppresses other self-representations. There is no consideration of consequences, internalized rules, or intimations of the future when the appetitive self is in ascendancy. The treatment for addictive behaviors includes decreasing exposure to reward cues, and strengthening the rational aspects of the self to motivate behavior not by the expectation of immediate reward, but by a vision of a productive present and a promising future.

The Social Self

Many technical elements of the social self have already been discussed above. From the perspective of self-awareness, the social self is a ubiquitous representation that modulates other views of the self. Social interactions can either be powerful reinforcers or instant destroyers of the prevailing self-image. Validation of an individual's self-view through social interactions is a lifelong pursuit. The construction of a satisfying self-image begins at a young age, and is either aided or hindered by the actions of the infant's caregivers. As the individual reaches adolescence and eventually adulthood, relationships intensify, and their modulation of self-representations becomes extremely powerful.

Social settings in our culture are punctuated by competition, and the individual's self-image will also be molded by his or her level of success in competitive endeavors. The successful individual is likely to approach new situations with confidence and expectations of continued success. Repeated failures, on the other hand, can engender a vicious cycle in which expectations of failure become a self-fulfilling prophecy.

The neurobiology of social cooperation has been studied. Imaging experiments have shown that mutually satisfying episodes of social cooperation involved activation of brain areas that function in reward processing. These include the nucleus accumbens, the caudate nucleus, the ventromedial prefrontal cortex, the orbitofrontal cortex, and the rostral anterior cingulate cortex (Rilling et al., 2002). The presence of accumbens activation during reciprocal social interactions provides an interesting perspective on one possible mechanism of social bonding. Satisfying social interactions lead to activation of reward pathways, which in turn promotes repetition of the interactions. In addition, the specific individuals involved will serve as cues that elicit positive emotions and make future social interactions with those particular persons more likely.

The Remembered Self

Memories are the raw materials with which we build the present and weave dreams of the future. Without memories, the self has no continuity and no clear vision beyond the now, since there is nothing on which to base that vision. The memory systems that support human selves are multifaceted and complex. Memory functions can be divided into two main categories: implicit and explicit (Kandel, Kupfermann, & Iversen, 2000). Implicit memory includes the learning of habits and motor skills as mediated by the striatum (discussed in "The Automatic Self" above), various types of reflexive learning, such as operant conditioning (mediated by the striatum and cerebellum), and fear conditioning, a process mediated by the amygdala that links fear responses to previously neutral objects. Explicit memory, which involves the recollection of locations, objects, and events, as well as their verbal descriptions, is mediated by the actions of the hippocampus. More specifically, the right hippocampus functions in the generation of episodic, nonverbal aspects of memory, including memories of the characteristics of physical spaces, while the left hippocampus elaborates semantic, or verbal memories, that involve the encoding of experience into the powerful symbolic representations facilitated by language (Kandel et al., 2000).

The left–right dichotomy of episodic and semantic memory provides a rich array of tools for creating detailed representations of the self and the self's environment. Left-brain memory representations are, by nature, symbolic because they are based on language. This facilitates logical and quantitative manipulations of the representations, and permits the definition of complex interactions among the representations, including such concepts as intentionality, causality, meaning, and purpose. Right-brain memory representations are more holistic and experiential, and recalling them provides a less intense but qualitatively similar replay of how the experience "felt" originally in terms of emotions, arousal, autonomic tone, and hormonal release.

In some cases, the recalled right-brain memories can be too real, and are experienced as "flashbacks" and the other symptoms associated with post-traumatic stress disorder (PTSD).

A functional imaging study has compared brain activity in the recall of traumatic memories between individuals with and without PTSD (Lanius et al., 2004). Individuals without PTSD activated left brain regions as they recounted traumatic experiences. These regions included the left superior frontal gyrus, the left anterior cingulate gyrus, the left striatum, the left parietal lobe, and the left insula. These areas, as discussed above, are important epicenters for the representation of objects and their subjective value. Within the brain's left hemisphere, however, the representations involved are symbolic rather than experiential.

In contrast, individuals with PTSD activated their right brains when they recounted traumatic memories. Specifically the right posterior cingulate gyrus, the right caudate, the right parietal lobe, and the right occipital lobe were activated (Lanius et al., 2004). These areas are again epicenters for the representation of objects and their subjective value; however, the right-sided representations have more of an experiential than a verbal nature, and actually included a visual component in the occipital lobe.

The process of creating memories can be divided into four distinct steps (see review in Kandel et al., 2000):

1. Encoding, or the process by which the elements of a potentially new memory are first translated into neural processes. Encoding is the result of differential activation of specific brain regions and changes in neuronal amplification that can bind the memory components into a coherent whole for a limited period of time.

2. Consolidation, or the processes that stabilize information for longer term retention. Consolidation involves the synthesis of new proteins that bring about structural changes in neuronal connectivity. In essence, memories are stabilized through the translation of chemical representations of information into structural representations.

3. Storage, or the process by which memories are retained over long periods of time. The major difference between consolidation and storage has to do with location. Consolidation takes place within the memory encoding regions of the brain in the hippocampal complex. For a time, these regions hold a record of the integrated memory and the addresses of the individual memory components (e.g., olfactory, visual, tactile) in the higher cortices. Eventually, if the memory is deemed worthy of permanent storage (through frequent reactivation and perceived importance), recurrent connections from

hippocampal regions to the higher cortices direct rewiring of the higher cortices to represent the memory at that level.

4. Retrieval, or the process by which encoded, consolidated, or stored memories are recalled and possibly recombined with other materials. Successful retrieval of explicit memories requires a functional working memory, which is a temporary, chemically sustained representational space that can hold recalled materials short-term for processing. Working memory consists of 3 components: First, a central executive, or attentional control system, which is implemented in the lateral prefrontal cortex (see Knight & Stuss, 2002, for review). This system can focus attention on specific items and events and facilitate their integration with each other and with other internal representations. The system is thought to have a capacity of only about 12 items. The central executive controls access to two other temporary storage spaces that can hold memory representations for processing. The first temporary storage space is the articulatory loop, in which words and numbers can be stored for a very short time and maintained through vocal or subvocal speech (e.g., when we mentally repeat a number that we must recall for a short time). The second temporary storage space is the visuospatial sketchpad, which can store the spatial location and visual attributes of objects for a short time. The spatial portion of this storage space is implemented in the parietal cortex, while the visual portion is implemented in extrastriate cortices (Kandel et al., 2000). Working memory provides much of the continuity that we take for granted in daily experience, and facilitates the integration of internal representations in novel ways.

For practical reasons, it is beneficial to separate the consolidation and storage processes of memory formation. First, it is not possible to rewire the higher cortices rapidly enough to support memory storage without an intermediate holding process. Second, many memories need to be stored for a moderate period of time, but are not important enough to induce higher cortical rewiring. These memories can be held for the required period within the hippocampal complex, and then allowed to fade when they are no longer needed. Such a process is energy efficient and ensures that only important events and recollections are allowed to influence the connectivity of the higher cortices.

The structure of the hippocampus and its associated cortices is well suited to their function in the encoding and consolidation of memories as well as in the coordination of long-term memory storage in the higher cortices. The hippocampal complex receives most of its inputs at three main regions—the parahippocampal, perirhinal, and entorhinal cortices. The perirhinal and parahippocampal cortices also project to the entorhinal cortex, which therefore contains the widest representation of incoming information within the hippocampal complex. The array of inputs that converge on the entorhinal cortex includes projections from the prefrontal cortex, cingulate gyrus, occipital lobe, superior and inferior temporal gyri, temporal pole, amygdala, and insula (Woolsey, Hanaway, & Mokhtar, 2003). These inputs contain a comprehensive summary of experience, from properties of objects and their value to perceived risk, associated emotions, and cognitive factors.

From the entorhinal cortex, the information flows to the dentate gyrus via the perforant pathway. The dentate gyrus contains sparsely connected neurons, and is thought to function in the orthogonalization of informational patterns (Kemperman, 2002). Orthogonalization is a process through which the representations of individual data sets are made as different as possible to enhance later separability and minimize interference. From the dentate gyrus, the information is conveyed to the CA3 region of the hippocampus. This region also receives direct inputs from the entorhinal cortex. Neurons in the CA3 region are extensively connected, and are thought to implement the actual memory encoding that is eventually consolidated for medium-range storage (Rolls, 2000).

From the CA3 region, information flows through the Schaffer collaterals to another area within the hippocampus, the CA1 region. This step marks the transition from the consolidation of information to long-term storage. From the CA1 region, information flows backward through the subiculum to the entorhinal cortices. Information flows are somatotopically mapped, to allow the same entorhinal cells that originated a particular signal to receive the appropriate backprojections. From the entorhinal cortex, information flows back to the parahippocampal and perirhinal cortices, and then to the unimodal and polymodal cortices where the information originated (Figure 2.15). As the backprojections travel from the hippocampus to the higher unimodal and polymodal cortices, larger numbers of neurons participate in the process at each level, to the point that, while the number of inputs to the CA3 region is much lower than the numbers of inputs to parahippocampal, perirhinal, and entorhinal cortices, by the time backprojections reach higher cortical areas, the numbers of axons that reach these areas are roughly equal to the numbers of axons that project to the hippocampal complex (Rolls, 2000).

Through this arrangement, projections from the higher cortices are consolidated as they travel toward the hippocampus, and reexpanded as they travel back to the cortices of origin. Memory formation, in this context, represents far more than a simple method of information storage. It is, in

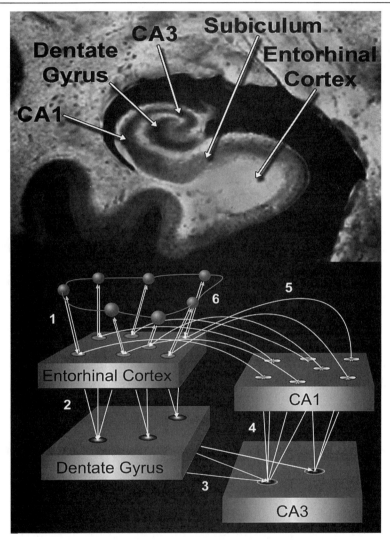

Information flows from the sensory and association cortices to the entorhinal cortex (1). From the entorhinal cortex, compressed information is conveyed via the perforant pathway to the dentate gyrus (2). The dentate gyrus is believed to function in orthogonalization, or the maintenance of separation among encoded memory patterns. From the dentate gyrus, the information is conveyed to the CA3 region (3), which has the highest level of compression. From the CA3 region, information travels along the Schaffer collaterals to the CA1 region (4). Decompression of information begins here. From CA1, information flows along the subiculum back to the entorhinal cortex (5). Recurrent feedback from the entorhinal cortex to the higher cortices (6) may be important in memory consolidation, presumably by directing cortical reconnection.

fact, a method for wiring the higher cortices on the basis of important experiences. The experiences used to direct cortical rewiring must have persisted within the hippocampal complex for at least 2 or 3 years. This eliminates the incorporation of relatively trivial organizing principles into the cortex. The influence of memory systems on the elaboration of a stable and comprehensive self-image is therefore twofold. First, memory systems provide continuous access to many levels of information acquired by the individual during his or her lifetime. Second, and perhaps most importantly, the brain's memory system directs the creation of facilitated paths through the cortex as it binds the elements of memory into special networks during the transition from consolidation to long-term storage. Who we are and how we process information is determined, to a large extent, by the memories that we have transferred to long-term storage.

The consolidation of memories is facilitated by emotional arousal. Memories that have a high emotional content are encoded and consolidated more efficiently than those that are neutral from an emotional perspective (Pare, 2003). This is facilitated by the actions of the basolateral amygdala, which can enhance memory processes by promoting the release of facilitatory neurochemicals such as norepinephrine and acetylcholine (Pare, 2003). In pathological states such as depression, sustained activity of the amygdala can maintain the flow of negative emotions (Siegle, Steinhauer, Thase, Stenger, & Carter, 2002), and can adversely influence memory systems if the dysfunction is sustained. In addition to the paths that connect it to the higher cortices, the hippocampus has another important projective pathway, the fornix, which carries information to limbic system components that include the amygdala, the cingulate gyrus, and the nucleus accumbens (Figure 2.16). The fornix, which follows a semicircular path between the thalamus and the corpus callosum, is a prominent component of the historically famous circuit of Papez.

The Neocortical Observing Self

The neocortical associative areas are powerful integrators that correlate inputs from many other cortices, as well as subcortical regions. In the process of extracting meaning and developing behavioral determinants from this information, the neocortex assumes the role of observer. Anything that can be represented, including aspects of the self, can be "observed." Moving information into working memory engages observational and integrative processes in the dorsolateral prefrontal cortex, and any information that is

FIGURE 2.16
THE HIPPOCAMPUS AND SURROUNDING STRUCTURES

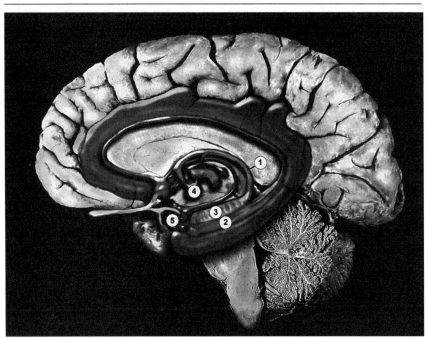

The main outflow tract of the hippocampus (3) to the limbic system is the fornix (1), which loops around the thalamus and terminates at the mammillary bodies (4). Neighboring structures include the entorhinal cortex (2) and the amygdala (5).

relevant to the generation of behavior or movement will be brought to consciousness as it is integrated with protoself representations.

The neocortex also functions, together with the temporal lobe, in the generation and use of symbols. Symbolic representation of objects and the use of these representations in modeling, before deciding on a course of action, is one of the highest levels of processing available to the brain. Modeling expands self-awareness into a projected future, and plays a critical role in the development of a comprehensive vision of the self and the self's relations with the environment. Logical embedding is another critical component of self-awareness. It recognizes that other individuals are also able to use logic, and therefore attempts to guide behavior based on an inference of what a person believes other logic-using individuals will do. Cotterill (1998) described a chimpanzee that was eating bananas under a tree. Another, more powerful chimpanzee approached. The first chimpanzee quickly moved away from the bananas to hide their location, inferring that the larger monkey would take them away. The larger chimpanzee seemed to leave, but actually hid behind a tree. When the first chimpanzee returned to the bananas, the larger animal rushed in and indeed took them away. This is presented as an example of second-order logical embedding. Humans are said to be capable of fourth-order embedding (Cotterill, 1998). The capacity for logical embedding is essential to having a theory of mind, and is therefore critical to the development of a sophisticated view of the self in relation to others.

The neurological substrates for symbolic representation and modeling include, first of all, the brain's language centers (Damasio & Damasio, 2000). Traditionally, these have been identified as Broca's area, in the left frontal operculum (language is usually implemented in the left, or dominant hemisphere), and Wernicke's area, which straddles the left lateral and posterior cortex and the supramarginal gyrus (Figure 2.1). In general, Broca's area supplies the motor components of language, whereas Wernicke's area functions in language comprehension. An individual with extensive damage to Broca's area can understand speech but cannot produce it fluently. The converse is true with damage to Wernicke's area. In these cases, the individual can produce fluent words, but they do not make sense. In addition to Broca's and Wernicke's areas, as discussed above, a variety of other brain regions contribute to the implementation of language. Language is a powerful tool for symbolic representation and analysis, and its loss leads to a significant reduction in the capacity for self-awareness, because it limits the most sophisticated type of symbolic representation of which humans are capable.

The neocortical regions, by virtue of their representation of diverse aspects of the self, are able to facilitate a high level of observational introspection. The power of the human cortex has led to the ascendancy of the higher brain functions in both practical and conceptual terms. We certainly do not define ourselves in terms of the excellence of our autonomic functions or our ability to regulate temperature. Instead, we define who we are in terms of intelligence, creativity, and even the capacity to execute complex, symbolic motor programs such as the ones that define our sports.

The primacy of the cortex in defining our humanity has led to a tacit sense that the higher brain functions are somehow primary, and that the rest of the brain exists to support them. In reality, nothing could be further from the truth. The higher brain functions, including the faculty of self-awareness, evolved as enhancements to the basic behavioral repertoires of lower life forms. Initially, cortical regions were simply "scratch-pads" that held small amounts of information that could be used to modulate thalamic functions. As the brain evolved, however, cortical regions expanded into libraries, and ultimately, were transformed into control centers.

The generation of behavior starts with a simple representation of internal and external milieus. The identification of critical events is then coupled to specific motor programs that serve vital functions such as energy acquisition, reproduction, and the management of threats. Freud would have approved of this concept. The edifice of humanity, with its defining phenomena of free will, culture, and the lofty aspirations of the spirit, is built on a foundation of automatic behavioral programs that seek to maximize acquisition, reproduction, and self-defense.

When the frontal cortices fail, humans, in a practical sense, revert to a less sophisticated type of behavioral control by a more primitive, more automatic brain. Success in the prevailing sociocultural milieu, on the other hand, is based, with few exceptions (e.g., a handful of athletes and entertainers) on the application of cortical power. Social organizing principles demand control over primal drives through the use of higher cortical circuits. Nevertheless, the limitations of the cortex are tacitly acknowledged. Limbic crimes, for example, are not considered as serious as cortical, or "premeditated" infractions. Legal culpability quickly dissolves, together with behavioral restraints, in the flood of neurotransmitters that generates "the heat of passion."

The frontal subcortical circuits play a critical role in self-awareness, in perception, and in the implementation of movements that are responsive to environmental challenges. By definition, frontal subcortical circuits loop through the frontal lobe, striatum, and thalamus (Figure 2.17), and are also called thalamocorticostriatal loops. Five such circuits have been identified (Mega & Cummings, 2001). They are: (1) the motor circuit, which originates in the supplementary motor area; (2) the oculomotor circuit, which originates in the frontal eye fields; (3) the dorsal prefrontal circuit, which originates in dorsal prefrontal cortex; (4) the lateral orbitofrontal circuit; and (5) the anterior cingulate circuit.

The motor circuit facilitates the implementation of movement. Cortical organization related to movement, which is a behavioral output, is inversely structured with respect to the cortical arrangement for the integration of sensory inputs. In sensory processing, the starting point is one of the primary sensory cortices, and information moves progressively into higher order, heteromodal association cortices. In the case of movement, by contrast, the

FIGURE 2.17
MAIN THALAMOCORTICOSTRIATAL CIRCUITS
IN THE HUMAN BRAIN

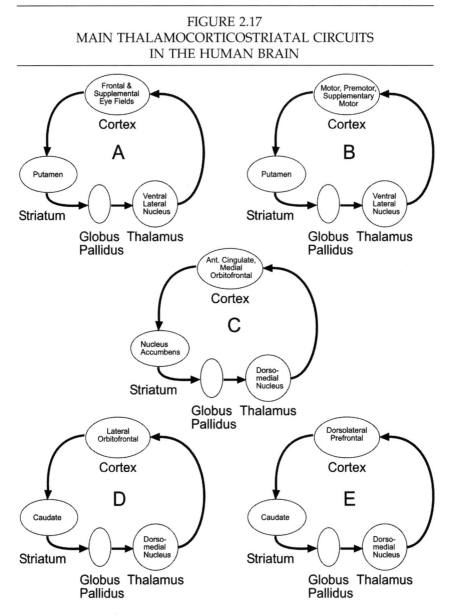

In general, these loops function in the processes of attention and action selection. The globus pallidus tonically inhibits the thalamus, and establishes a baseline for the intensity of stimuli that have not been identified as noteworthy. The striatum, globus pallidus, thalamus, and cortical regions involved in the loops, contain a large array of separate tracts, or "channels," that can represent individual objects or events as distinguished from competing stimuli. The representation of a particular object or event can therefore be selectively enhanced or suppressed (see Figure 2.13 for a detailed description of Loop C). A) Oculomotor Circuit; B) Motor Circuit; C) Anterior Cingulate Circuit; D) Lateral Orbitofrontal Circuit; E) Dorsal Prefrontal Circuit.

starting point is a set of complex heteromodal regions, the premotor and supplementary motor cortices, which integrate the determinants of movement. Once a movement has been selected, information flows to the primary motor cortex, and the movement is executed.

The oculomotor circuit controls the critically important function of eye-movement coordination. Normally, the eyes move fluidly across environmental spaces, exploring objects of interest without conscious effort. Conscious control of gaze is possible, but would be inefficient as the primary controller of visual exploration. The primary oculomotor circuit facilitates the automatic movement of the eyes that is essential for efficient scanning of the environment.

The anterior cingulate circuit facilitates the execution of motivated behavior, and appears to generate the "to do" list of the brain. Damage to this circuit can result in apathy, or, in other words, loss of the brain's "to do" list. The highest degree of apathy is manifested in a condition known as akinetic mutism, which can be a consequence of cingulate damage. Individuals with this disorder rarely move or speak, are incontinent, and eat and drink only when fed. They do not display emotions, do not react to pain, and are indifferent to objects and events in the environment (Mega & Cummings, 2001). As these clinical findings indicate, the cingulate gyrus, which is a multifunctional associative cortex, is essential for advanced self-awareness. Without cingulate function, the entire motivational dimension of the self will be nonfunctional. Individuals with cingulate damage are not aware that anything is missing because they lack the ability to assemble the higher order cortical maps that represent object value and provide the motivation for action. Without the cingulate, no thought of potential actions related to internal needs or external stimuli ever enters consciousness.

The dorsolateral prefrontal cortex is essential for the implementation of executive function. This behavioral capacity encompasses such important functions as the ability to organize internal and external resources to solve complex problems, the ability to define a viable self-direction, the ability to implement motor programs, the ability to retrieve memories, and the ability to use language to guide behavior (Mega & Cummings, 2001).

Individuals who suffer damage to this cortical region are unable to organize behavior around internal or external demands, have difficulty retrieving memories, perseverate in their thoughts and speech, and have difficulty adjusting behavior to changing environmental circumstances. Decision making (especially making go/no-go decisions) is impaired, and there is a strong tendency to be drawn indiscriminately toward objects and situations with high salience, even if this is inappropriate in the current context. Individuals with dorsolateral prefrontal damage often engage in *utilization behavior*, a technical term for the indiscriminate and frequently inappropriate handling of any salient objects that they encounter (Mega & Cummings, 2001).

Self-awareness deficits are a common result of lesions of the dorsolateral prefrontal circuits. Individuals with such lesions have a limited and fragmented view of the self, determined only by day-to-day activities, and not by external organizing principles, memories of the past, or visualizations of the future. They have limited capacity for logical reasoning, and are unable to appreciate the complexity of many situations. Much of their behavior involves simple reaction to external objects and internal appetitive signals, because they have lost the ability to drive behavior on the basis of internalized principles. Individuals with damage to dorsolateral prefrontal circuits are not aware of their deficits because they lack the ability to integrate behavioral determinants with internalized principles of order, and thus are not aware of alternative options prior to the initiation of a particular behavior. These individuals have lost all memory of having functioned differently in the past, and therefore have no point of reference on which to base the knowledge that something has changed.

The medial orbitofrontal cortex is involved in the regulation of mood and neurovegetative functions. Both the medial and lateral orbitofrontal cortices are connected to the amygdala and provide inhibitory inputs to the latter. Individuals with medial orbitofrontal damage generally feel low on energy, are often depressed or dysphoric, and can develop symptoms of obsessive–compulsive disorder (OCD; Mega & Cummings, 2001).

The lateral orbitofrontal cortex is critical to the mediation of empathy, and of socially appropriate behavior. Individuals with lateral orbitofrontal lesions can demonstrate physical aggression and high impulsivity. This can be complicated by low serotonin levels. These individuals can also develop OCD, as well as symptoms of severe mood lability and mania (Zald & Kim, 2001). They frequently show utilization behavior and tend to imitate others. From a social perspective, these individuals have severe deficits. They simply lack the tools necessary for appropriate social interactions. They tend to be irritable, impulsive, intrusive, and tactless, and tend to treat others in a coarse manner and with undue familiarity. From the perspective of self-awareness, individuals with orbitofrontal damage are not usually aware of their deficits. The maps that once supported orbitofrontal functions have been destroyed, as have the memories of the previous, more functional state.

The neocortical self is capable of introspection; that is, it is able to observe the self as an object. This capacity is made possible by the ability to integrate neural self-representations with representations of environmental objects, and with internalized principles. Such a level of integration permits comparative and evaluative assessments, and leads to a critical view of the self. The neocortical, observing self can assess personal strengths, define areas of deficit, and generate strategies for improvement. All of the frontal lobe syndromes impair neocortical observing functions because they involve destruction of critical sets of integrative cortical maps.

The right dorsomedial prefrontal cortex seems to play a critical role in the development of models of the self (Mega & Cummings, 2001). This has been confirmed by several imaging studies, including a recent study of self-evaluation, in which individuals made self-referential inferences by determining whether positive or negative descriptions applied to them (Fossati et al., 2003). Without self-models, it is difficult to plan for the future, muster resources for problem solving, or perform complex adaptive actions.

In general terms, the frontal cortices provide many important integrative functions, and exert regulatory control over behavior. They reduce impulsivity, facilitate compliance with social norms, and promote contemplative analysis before the initiation of nonemergent actions. In addition, the frontal cortices ensure that behavior is compatible with existing internal models of the self. The prefrontal cortices, although not essential for life or for basic consciousness, are nevertheless repositories of much of our humanity. Without the prefrontal cortices, self-awareness, and the ability to use critical observations to improve the self, will be profoundly impaired.

In Search of the Self

Somewhere in the very distant past, the evolving brain assumed a central role in the quest for effective movement, and generated the elements of the self. The self is a complex, dynamic representation that integrates multiple brain maps, and uses them to coordinate behavioral sequences of adaptive movements. The movements generated by the brain not only react to environmental challenges and opportunities, but address potential "calls to action" in relation to emotional and appetitive states, memories, internalized principles, and a projected view of the future.

The incorporation of internal maps into the pathways that generate movement had three critical consequences. First, it increased the efficiency of movement by making it contingent on both internal and external variables. Thus, a lion that has just eaten does not automatically chase a gazelle that wanders into its field of view. Similarly, a human with an intestinal virus is not motivated (or "induced to move") by food during the course of the illness.

Second, the introduction of a self-representation with both inner and outer components as joint determinants of physical action generated the phenomenon of *meaning*. The raw materials for the generation of meaning include the inner components of the self, namely, the emotional, appetitive, autonomic, and sensory spheres, as well as a representation of external reality. The integration of these raw elements yields a dynamic view of the body in *object space*, and places value on objects based on their ability to satisfy internal drives or needs. Under these circumstances, external events have *meaning*, which is defined in terms of their ability to affect internal states. A meal, for example, can be either delightful or disappointing depending on how it moves the senses and activates the emotions.

Third, the monitoring of changes in internal signals as the organism interacts with the environment creates a primitive sense of self. This monitoring is essential for optimizing the effectiveness of interactions with the environment in light of the organism's needs. Damasio's concept of a primitive self-representation, the protoself, which generates a dynamic self-image as it changes through interactions with external objects, is a powerful starting point for understanding how self-awareness evolved.

Practically, the process of self-awareness is based on a core sense of the body, complete with internal signals and explicit knowledge of the body's location with respect to external objects. The self is constantly redefined as it interacts with objects and implements adaptive behaviors. The dynamic signals generated by these interactions are the raw materials from which the most basic representations of the self are constructed. As I interact with the environment, I define a self that is distinct from the external world.

Advanced dimensions of self-awareness integrate basic representations of the self and the self's environment, and assess the meaning of these representations with respect to present and future needs. Meaning is generated through the interaction of distributed processing systems that define perceived risk, estimate potential reward with respect to internal needs, and integrate cognitive elements such as contextual constraints, internalized rules, and consideration of future consequences. What we know about our environment and ourselves can be summarized succinctly in motivational (risk and reward) and cognitive terms. Risk and reward considerations generate motivation, and create powerful attractors that command our attention and shape our actions. Cognitive considerations temper and modulate raw motivational drives. Moreover, our cognitive functions allow us to interpret the meaning of situations in terms of a set of organizing principles. Ideally, these incorporate memory, learning, reasoning, symbolic analysis, and socio-cultural norms.

In humans, many parallel selves exist in terms of neural circuitry that facilitate optimal functioning in specific settings. At primitive levels, the protoself and the spatial self provide a basic representation of the organism in the environment, and permit navigation and exploration within environmental space, as well as the basic identification of objects that hold potential interest. The appetitive self integrates internal drives with environmental opportunities, and motivates behaviors most likely to satisfy the organism's primary needs. The brain's reward system is exquisitely sensitive to environmental clues that signal the availability of environmental resources that have generated pleasure in the past. This powerful motivational system can be short-circuited by substances of abuse. These substances, which activate components of the reward system directly, create strong memories of themselves that engage attention and motivation whenever cues related to the agents' availability and use are encountered. The appetitive self is forever competing with the neocortical, observing self, which is the reason-driven, future-oriented self generated in the prefrontal cortices. It is the appetitive self that makes it difficult to diet, motivates gambling and encourages sexual indiscretions. On the other hand, the appetitive self also facilitates and motivates the many pleasurable experiences that bring joy and meaning to our lives.

The emotional self adds an important behavioral refinement. It represents the meaning of objects and situations with respect to the interests of the self, and creates motivational and arousal states designed to influence behavior on the basis of the perceived meaning. The automatic self is a ubiquitous manifestation of our past experiences that takes over whenever routine tasks must be performed. The handling of routine movement sequences by mechanisms inaccessible to consciousness ensures that the tasks will be performed accurately and with a minimum of energy expenditure or conscious effort. The automatic self is the sum of our learned motor behaviors. This aspect of the self allows us to ride a bicycle, drive a car, throw a football, and type rapidly on a computer keyboard. Attempts to supervise automatic behaviors through conscious processes usually result in less effective performance of the behaviors.

The social self is an important representation that can deeply influence our ultimate self-image. We often become in our own eyes what others see when they look at us. The establishment of a successful social self is a critical foundation for the maintenance of a stable and satisfying self-image. In order to establish a successful social self, bonding with important others must take place, and a healthy orbitofrontal cortex, which ensures the propriety of social behavior, must guide the individual's actions. Emotional and facial expressiveness, as well as language, are among the critical tools that facilitate social processes.

The remembered self is a multifaceted collection of representations that not only provides continuity to experience, but also directs how the cortex is wired. As experiences are transferred to long-term memory, they take the form of enhanced cortical connectivity among the various areas that represent individual aspects of the remembered experience. The cortex therefore develops facilitated connections based on experiences that have been deemed *memorable*. Episodic and semantic memories are accessible to consciousness; however, procedural memories are normally not. Memory space is divided into episodic memories, which are stored in the right hemisphere, and verbal, semantic memories, which reside in the left hemisphere. The ability to use language and logic to manipulate the components of experience clarifies their meaning and facilitates projection into the future.

One of the most remarkable features of the remembered self is that memories not only provide temporal continuity, but also play a determinative role in the wiring of cortical regions. Memories that are stored long-term cause specific changes in the connections of the cortex. In a sense, the remembered self also defines the hardware on which all self-representations will subsequently be based. Many therapeutic challenges in the treatment of individuals with traumatic memories are rooted in the fact that a very deep level of organization is involved that includes hard-wiring.

From the perspective of self-awareness, the individual with a dysfunctional remembered self is usually aware of the superficial aspects of the problem. He or she can probably recall the traumatic events that led to the current situation. Unfortunately, affected individuals have no way of knowing that memory-directed rewiring is affecting the function of their brains at a very basic level. These individuals process new situations maladaptively because their brain's hardware is not optimally connected. In some cases, the individual has defined his or her personal reality around a central organizing principle that is maladaptive. In other cases, there is inappropriate affective intensity, or maladaptive overgeneralization. Part of the power of the remembered self is that it never disappears, even when the memories have been put away. It is a permanent component of the brain's representation of the self because it has shaped the substrate on which the representation is defined.

The neocortical, observing self is a high-level self-representation created through the integrative power of the neocortex. Through a synthesis that encompasses many levels of brain maps, it is possible to create models of the self and the self's environment and make predictions about the anticipated future. The neocortical self can actually "observe" in self-referential fashion because a virtual self-representation exists in the brain. This representation not only incorporates the "feel" of what it means to be oneself, but can be manipulated in abstract, verbal terms in the left hemisphere. The ability to apply logical operations to an internal representation of the self, and to integrate this representation with other internalized objects and relationships, creates a powerful simulation engine that allows us to rehearse difficult encounters and avoid potential disasters through prediction and preparation. The powerful simulation engine in our brains even permits us to glimpse the future, and creates the motivational drive to actualize our dreams.

Self-awareness is ultimately built on an interacting framework of parallel selves. Each of these selves is a set of functions that represent solutions to common problems. They are encoded by specific, distributed neural networks with epicenters in the various functional regions of the brain. For example, self-representations that require a verbal component will have epicenters in the left hemisphere; those that require fearful responses will have an epicenter in the amygdala, and those that require the use of previously learned, automatic movements, will have prominent epicenters in the basal ganglia. The range and depth of the self therefore ebbs and flows with the situations in which we find ourselves. We have the capacity to be many things in different contexts, from cook to philosopher, from physician to athlete, from gardener to parent.

A powerful way to visualize the self is as a dynamic organizing principle that correlates the most relevant functions available through neural circuitry with whatever task is at hand. Thus, in a football game, emotion, neocortical strategy, and automatic movements might be incorporated into the "self" that emerges at kickoff. In a game of chess, attention, prefrontal strategy, memory, and some emotion will predominate. In poker, the ability to disconnect emotional centers from the emergent self that deals the cards would be a distinct advantage. We construct who we are one situation at a time, bringing to bear relevant neural circuits, sensing, integrating, and frequently improvising. Ultimately, we solve problems by abstracting the environment into our neural circuits, processing the representations, and defining a set of movements, or actions, that change the environment adaptively.

We have discussed how the self, the environment, and objects are mapped in the brain. We have also described several circuits (e.g., the reward circuit, the amygdalar fear circuit, and the basal ganglia circuit for automatic movement generation) whose function is to serve as feature detectors and to execute predefined programs if a feature of interest is detected. In lower animals, predetermined hierarchies of circuits exist. For example, if an animal is eating, but a serious threat is perceived, the animal will generally stop eating and automatically take evasive action. In other words, if a circuit is active, but another circuit with a higher priority is suddenly engaged, behavior will change abruptly and automatically, driven by the higher priority circuit.

Interestingly, circuitry hierarchies are not equivalent among life forms, as a simple example will illustrate. If a fly lands on one's dinner, it is difficult to swat it with one's hand, because flies have strong evasive programs that are activated at the first sight of danger. A mosquito, in contrast, is easy to swat, since it attempts to finish its meal at all costs. For a female mosquito (male mosquitoes do not feed on blood), one blood meal is sufficient to facilitate egg laying, and it pursues that meal tenaciously. One of the authors, deep in thought about neural circuitry, actually encountered two flies mating on a leaf. To the author's surprise, the flies did not move at the sense of approaching danger, and even allowed themselves to be picked up. With this information, we can construct a simple hierarchy for the fly's behavioral circuitry: mating, danger, feeding. Flies are willing to interrupt a meal at any sign of danger, but will not interrupt an act of mating regardless of the risk. Risk perception circuits are probably disengaged during mating. The author left the flies alone and rushed to record his observations.

Humans are highly responsive to threat, both through reflex movements and through amygdalar arousal. The complexity of the human behavioral repertoire, however, does not permit simple hierarchies to control all behavior (although in children, simple need hierarchies are definitely in control). The first level of conflict resolution in the human brain is handled by a circuit with the cingulate gyrus as a prominent epicenter. If the cingulate-centered circuitry cannot resolve the conflict, or if the resolution involves complex, internalized rules rather than simple risk–reward–need considerations, then the problem is referred to the prefrontal cortices for resolution.

Self-awareness is created as the questions whose answers determine behavior are posed at various levels. The most primitive self-awareness involves relatively trivial questions that may not even rise into consciousness; namely, interactions of the protoself with the most mundane demands of the environment. The feelings generated by changes in the sensory cortices and internal signaling circuits define the core self. As the questions become more complicated, higher levels of integration are engaged, and a more complex self emerges. At the highest levels, critical introspection by the neocortical observing self can define a complex, comprehensive, and sophisticated vision. Damage to brain circuits reduces the possible levels of questioning, until the higher cortices are no longer engaged (e.g., in the case of an advanced Alzheimer's patient), and the individual reverts to simple behavioral hierarchies. We redefine the self continuously as we integrate the functional circuits of the brain to answer daily challenges. Our successes and failures gradually shape a self-image-in-context that provides an instant sense of the likely outcome of novel or routine situations. For instance, a skilled neurosurgeon who has no fear of repairing the most convoluted aneurysm may also be a dismal plumber, and will cringe at the thought of repairing a leaky faucet. Who we are is determined as much by context as by internal circumstances and skills. The self that we know is a harmonious blend of internal and external representations, central organizing principles, emotions, determinations of need, value, and risk, application of appropriate automatic movements, and visions of past and future. The success of this integrated self in answering the questions of daily life and the consistency with which self-representations organize adaptive behavior will determine, in great part, what we find when we turn our gaze inward.

References

Adolphs R. The neurobiology of social cognition. *Curr Opin Neurobiol.* 2001; 11:231–239.

Aiello LC, Dunbar RI. Neocortex size, group size, and the evolution of language. *Curr Anthro.* 1993; 34:184–193.

Alheid GF, Heimer L. New perspectives in basal forebrain organization of special relevance for neuropsychiatric disorders: the striatopallidal, amygdaloid, and corticopetal components of substantia inominata. *Neurosci.* 1988; 27:1–39.

Amaral DG. The functional organization of perception and movement. In: Kandel ER, Schwartz JH, Jessell TM, eds. *Principles of Neural Science.* 4th ed. New York: McGraw-Hill; 2000: 337–348.

American Psychological Association. *Diagnostic and Statistical Manual of Mental Disorders.* 4th Edition, Text Revision. Washington, DC: American Psychiatric Association; 2000.

Barrett L, Dunbar R, Lycett J. *Human Evolutionary Psychology.* Princeton, NJ: Princeton University Press; 2002.

Barton RA, Aggleton JP. Primate evolution and the amygdala. In: Aggleton JP, ed. *The Amygdala: A Functional Analysis.* Oxford, UK: Oxford University Press; 2000: 479–508.

Berke JD, Hyman SE. Addiction, dopamine, and the molecular mechanisms of memory. *Neuron.* 2000; 25:515–532.

Bowlby J. *Attachment and Loss.* Vol. 2. New York: Basic Books; 1973.

Bush G, Vogt BA, Holmes J, et al. Dorsal anterior cingulate cortex: a role in reward-based decision-making. *PNAS.* 2000; 99(1):523–528.

Byrne RW, Whiten A. *Machiavellian Intelligence: Social Expertise and the Evolution of Intellect in Monkeys, Apes, and Humans.* Oxford, UK: Oxford University Press; 1988.

Carpenter MB. *Core Text of Neuroanatomy.* 3rd ed. Baltimore, Md: Williams & Wilkins; 1985.

Carter R. *Mapping the Mind.* Los Angeles: University of California Press; 2000.

Chang JY, Sawyer SF, Lee RS, Woodward DJ. Electrophysiological and pharmacological evidence for the role of the nucleus accumbens in cocaine self-administration in freely moving rats. *J Neurosci.* 1994; 14:1224–1244.

Chomsky N. *Reflections on Language.* New York: Pantheon Press; 1975.

Cotterill R. *Enchanted Looms: Conscious Networks in Brains and Computers.* Cambridge, UK: Cambridge University Press; 1998.

Crick FHC. The function of the thalamic reticular complex: the searchlight hypothesis. *PNAS.* 1984; 81:4586–4590.

Damasio AR. *Descartes' Error: Emotion, Reason, and the Human Brain.* New York: Grosset/Putnam; 1994.

Damasio AR. *The Feeling of What Happens: Body and Emotion in the Making of Consciousness.* New York: Harcourt Brace; 1999.

Damasio AR, Damasio H. Aphasia and the neural basis of language. In: Mesulam MM, ed. *Principles of Behavioral and Cognitive Neurology.* 2nd ed. Oxford, UK: Oxford University Press; 2000: 294–315.

Dantzer R. Cytokine-induced sickness behavior: where do we stand? *Brain, Beh, & Immun.* 2001; 15:7–24.

Darwin C. *The Expression of the Emotions in Man and Animals.* 3rd ed. New York: Oxford University Press; 1872/1998.

Davis M. The role of the amygdala in fear and anxiety. *Ann Rev Neurosci.* 1992; 15: 353–375.

Dronkers N, Pinker S, Damasio A. Language and the aphasias. In: Kandel ER, Schwartz JH, Jessell TM, eds., *Principles of Neural Science, Fourth Edition.* New York: McGraw-Hill; 2003: 1169–1187.

Dunbar RIM. Neocortex size as a constraint on group size in primates. *J Hum Evol.* 1992; 20:469–493.

Dunbar RIM, Duncan NDC, Nettle D. Size and structure of freely forming conversational groups. *Hum Nat.* 1997; 6:67–78.

Eccles J. *Evolution of the Brain: Creation of the Self.* London: Routledge; 1989.

Eibl-Eibesfeldt I. *Human Ethology.* New York: Aldine de Gruyter; 1989.

Fossati P, Hevenor SJ, Graham SJ, et al. In search of the emotional self: An fMRI study using positive and negative emotional words. *Am J Psychiatry.* 2003; 160:1938–1945.

Goldberg E. *The Executive Brain.* New York: Oxford University Press; 2001.

Graybiel AM. The basal ganglia and chunking of action repertoires. *Neurobiol Learn Mem.* 1998; 70:119–136.

Happe F, Ehler S, Fletcher P et al. Theory of mind in the brain: Evidence from a PET scan study of Asperger's Syndrome. *Neuroreport.* 1996; 8(1):197–201.

Haxby JV, Martin A, Clark VP, Hoffman EA, Schouten J, Ungerleier LG. The processing of faces, inverted faces and other objects in the ventral object vision pathway. *Neuroimage.* 1997; 5:54–65.

Heimer L, Alheid GF, de Olmos JS et al. The accumbens beyond the core-shell dichotomy. In: Salloway S, Malloy P, Cummings JL, eds. *The Neuropsychiatry of Limbic and Subcortical Disorders.* Washington, DC: American Psychiatric Press; 1997: 43–70.

Hernandez-Lopez S. D1 receptor activation enhances evoked discharge in neostriatal medium spiny neurons by modulating an L-type C2+ conductance. *J Neurosci.* 1997; 17: 3334–3342.

Kalivas PW. Neurocircuitry of addiction. In: Davis KL, Charney D, Coyle JT, Nemeroff C, eds. *Neuropsychopharmacology: The Fifth Generation of Progress.* New York: Lippincott, Williams & Wilkins; 2002: 1358–1367.

Kandel ER, Kupfermann I, Iversen S. Learning and memory. In: Kandel ER, Schwartz JH, Jessell TM, eds. *Principles of Neural Science.* 4th ed. New York: McGraw-Hill; 2000: 1227–1245.

Kandel ER, Siegelbaum SA. Synaptic integration. In: Kandel ER, Schwartz JH, Jessell TM, eds. *Principles of Neural Science.* 4th ed. New York: McGraw-Hill; 2000: 207–218.

Kapur S. Psychosis as a state of aberrant salience: a framework linking biology, phenomenology, and pharmacology in schizophrenia. *Am J Psychiatry.* 2003; 160(1):13–23.

Kempermann G. Why new neurons? Possible functions for adult hippocampal neurogenesis. *J Neurosci.* 2002; 22:635–638.

Knight RT, Stuss DT. Prefrontal cortex: the present and future. In: Stuss DT, Knight RT, eds. *Principles of Frontal Lobe Function,* New York: Oxford University Press; 2002: 573–597.

Konsman JP, Kelley K, Dantzer R. Temporal and spatial relationships between lipopolysaccharide-induced expression of Fos, interleukin-1 beta and inducible nitric oxide synthase in rat brain. *Neurosci.* 1999; 89(2):535–548.

Lanius RA, Williamson PC, Densmore et al. The nature of traumatic memories: a 4-T fMRI functional connectivity analysis. *Am J Psychiatry.* 2004; 161:36–44.

LeDoux J. *The Emotional Brain.* New York: Simon & Schuster; 1996.

Leonard WR. Food for thought. *Sci Am.* 2003; (special issue):62–71.

Lewis DA. Neural circuitry approaches to understanding the pathophysiology of schizophrenia. In: Davis KL, Charney D, Coyle JT, & Nemeroff C, eds., *Neuropsychopharmacology: The Fifth Generation of Progress.* New York: Lippincott, Williams & Wilkins; 2002: 730–744.

Lynch JC. The functional organization of posterior parietal association cortex. *Behav Brain Sci.* 1980; 3:485–499.

Magistretti PJ, Pellerin L, Martin JL. Brain energy metabolism: an integrated cellular perspective [Internet edition]. In: Davis KL, Charney D, Coyle JT, Nemeroff C. eds. *Neuropsychopharmacology: The Fourth Generation of Progress.* New York: Lippincott, Williams & Wilkins; 2000.

McFarland NR, Haber SN. Thalamic relay nuclei of the basal ganglia form both reciprocal and nonreciprocal cortical connections, linking multiple frontal areas. *J Neurosci.* 2002; 22(18):8117–8132.

Mega MS, Cummings JL. Frontal subcortical circuits: Anatomy and function. In: Salloway SP, Malloy PF, Duffy JD, eds. *The Frontal Lobes and Neuropsychiatric Illness.* Washington, DC: American Psychiatric Publishing; 2001: 15–32.

Mega MS, Cummings JL, Salloway S, Malloy P. The limbic system: an anatomic, phylogenetic, and clinical perspective. In: Salloway SP, Malloy PF, Cummings JL, eds. *The Neuropsychiatry of Limbic and Subcortical Disorders.* Washington, DC: American Psychiatric Publishing; 1997: 3–18.

Mesulam MM. Patterns in behavioral neuroanatomy: association areas, the limbic system, and hemispheric specialization. In: Mesulam MM, ed. *Behavioral Neurology.* Philadelphia: FA Davis; 1985: 1–70.

Mesulam MM. Behavioral neuroanatomy: large-scale networks, association cortex, frontal syndromes, the limbic system, and hemispheric specializations. In: Mesulam MM, ed. *Principles of Behavioral and Cognitive Neurology.* 2nd ed. Oxford, England: Oxford University Press; 2000: 1–200.

Mesulam MM. The human frontal lobes: transcending the default mode through contingent encoding. In: Stuss DT, Knight RT, eds. *Principles of Frontal Lobe Function*. Oxford, U.K.: Oxford University Press; 2002: 8–30.

Miller GF. Sexual selection for cultural displays. In: Dunbar R, Knight C, Power C, eds. *The Evolution of Culture*, Edinburgh, UK: Edinburgh University Press; 1999: 71–91.

Nimchinsky EA. A neuronal morphologic type unique to humans and great apes. *PNAS*. 1999; 96:52–68.

Nolte J. *The Human Brain: An Introduction to Its Functional Anatomy*. St. Louis, MI: Mosby; 1999.

Ochsner KN, Bunge SA, Gross JJ, Gabrieli JD. Rethinking feelings: an fMRI study of the cognitive regulation of emotion. *J Cog Neurosci*. 2002; 14(8):1215–1229.

Pare D. Role of the basolateral amygdala in memory consolidation. *Prog Neurobiol*. 2003; 70:409–420.

Penfield W, Faulk ME. The insula: further observations of its function. *Brain*. 1955; 78:445–470.

Phillips ML, Drevets WC, Rauch SL, Lane R. Neurobiology of emotion perception I: the neural basis of normal emotion perception. *Biol Psychiatry*. 2003; 54:504–514.

Pierce K, Muller RA, Ambrose J, Allen G, Courchesne E. Face processing occurs outside the fusiform "face area" in autism: evidence from functional MRI. *Brain*. 2001; 124(10):2059–2073.

Rilling JK, Gutman DA, Zeh TR et al. A neural basis for social cooperation. *Neuron*. 2002; 35:395–405.

Rolls ET. *The Brain and Emotion*. Oxford, UK: Oxford University Press; 1999.

Rolls ET. Hippocampo-cortical and cortico-cortical backprojections. *Hippocampus*. 2000; 10:380–388.

Sah P, Faber ES, Lopes de Armentia M, Power J. The amygdaloid complex: anatomy and physiology. *Physiol Rev*. 2003; 83:803–834.

Salloway SP, Malloy PF, Duffy JD. The frontal lobes and neuropsychiatric illness. In: Salloway SP, Malloy PF, Duffy JD, eds. *The Frontal Lobes and Neuropsychiatric Illness*. Washington, DC: American Psychiatric Publishing; 2001: 3–6.

Scheibel AB. The thalamus and neuropsychiatric illness. In: Salloway SP, Malloy PF, Cummings JL, eds. *The Neuropsychiatry of Limbic and Subcortical Disorders*. Washington, DC: American Psychiatric Publishing; 1997: 31–42.

Schmidt KL, Cohn JF. Human facial expressions as adaptations: evolutionary questions in facial expression research. *Yearbk Physical Anthro*. 2001; 44:8–24.

Shidara M, Richmond BJ. Anterior cingulate: single neuronal signals related to degree of reward expectancy. *Science*. 296:1709–1711.

Siegle GJ, Steinhauer SR, Thase ME, Stenger A, Carter CS. Can't shake that feeling: event-related fMRI assessment of sustained amygdala activity in response to emotional information in depressed individuals. *Biol Psychiatry*. 2002; 51:693–707.

Spence SA, Crimlisk HL, Cope H, Ron MA, Grasby PM. Discrete neurophysiological correlates in prefrontal cortex during hysterical and feigned disorder of movement [letter]. *Lancet*. 2000; 355:1243–1244.

Suzuki DT. *Zen and Japanese Culture*. Bollingen Series 64. Princeton, NJ: Princeton University Press; 1959.

Tamam L, Karatas G, Zeren T, Ozpoyraz N. The prevalence of Capgras syndrome in a university hospital setting. *Acta Neuropsychiatrica*. 2003; 15(5):290–296.

VanSwearingen JM, Cohn JF, Bajaj-Luthra A. Specific impairment of smiling increases the severity of depressive symptoms in patients with facial neuromuscular disorders. *Anesthet Plast Surg*. 1999; 23:416–423.

Vuilleumier P, Chicherio C, Assal F, Schwartz S, Slosmen D, Landis T. Functional neuroanatomical correlates of hysterical sensorimotor loss. *Brain.* 2001; 124:1077–1090.

Woolsey TA, Hanaway J, Mokhtar GH. *The Brain Atlas: A Visual Guide to the Human Central Nervous System.* 2nd ed. Hoboken, NJ: Wiley & Sons; 2003.

Wurtz RH, Kandel ER. Perception of motion, depth, and form. In: Kandel ER, Schwartz JH, Jessell TM. eds. *Principles of Neural Science.* 4th ed. New York: McGraw-Hill; 2000: 548–571.

Zald DH, Kim SW. The orbitofrontal cortex. In: Salloway SP, Malloy PF, Duffy JD, eds. *The Frontal Lobes and Neuropsychiatric Illness.* Washington, DC: American Psychiatric Publishing; 2001: 33–70.

3

Brain Patterns of Self-Awareness

Alarik T. Arenander
Frederick T. Travis

WHAT IS THE NATURE of self awareness? The *Oxford English Dictionary* (OED) indicates that there are two modes of self-awareness: awareness with and without content. The distinction is evident among the list of six definitions of self-awareness. The first five involve the process of experience: (1) interpersonal cognitive relations; (2) remembering on a first-hand basis one's past actions or experiences; (3) awareness of any object; (4) immediate awareness of one's mental processes; and (5) the totality of mental experiences that constitute our conscious being. Consistent with most chapters in this book, self-awareness thus refers to the content of conscious experience. The sixth definition in the OED offers a broader sense of self-awareness: (6) the general mode of awareness that is distinct from the content that makes up the stream of consciousness.

We suggest that this last definition of self-awareness—as awareness distinct from the content that makes up the stream of consciousness—may be the "ground" of all experiences of self-awareness. As the ground of experience, we suggest that this putative foundational level of self-awareness needs to be appreciated to fully understand both "normal" as well as dysfunctional modes of self-awareness, as presented in other chapters in this book. Thus, this chapter serves to introduce the concept of a foundational state of self-awareness, which is both independent and the source of conscious experiences. This chapter also explores brain states that may differentiate the

foundational state of self-awareness from its derivative, diverse modes represented by the major states of consciousness—waking, dreaming, and sleeping—as well as the various types of waking self-reflective awareness related
to body and environmental awareness.

The prevailing Western view is that an individual cannot be conscious
without particular contents in consciousness (Natsoulas, 1997), that one cannot be aware without being aware of *something*. In this paradigm, no subjective
state can be its own *object* of experience (James, 1902/1961). In contrast, the
subjective traditions of the East—the Vedic tradition of India (Maharishi,
1967), and the Buddhist traditions of China (Chung-Yuan, 1969) and Japan
(Reps, 1955)—include formalized meditation techniques intended to lead to
the direct experience of a state of "pure self-awareness" or "pure consciousness," a foundational state of consciousness devoid of mental content. For
instance, the *Maitri Upanishad* (Maitri Upanishad 6:19, in Upanishads, 1953)
stated:

> When a wise man has withdrawn his mind from all things without, and
> when his spirit of life has peacefully left inner sensations, let him rest in
> peace, free from the movements of will and desire. . . . Let the spirit of life
> surrender itself into what is called *turya*, the fourth condition of conscious-
> ness. For it has been said: There is something beyond our mind which
> abides in silence within our mind. It is the supreme mystery beyond
> thought. Let one's mind . . . rest upon that and not rest on anything else.

Maharishi Mahesh Yogi, responsible for bringing the Transcendental
Meditation (TM)* technique to the West from the Vedic tradition of India,
explained: "When consciousness is flowing out into the field of thoughts and
activity it identifies itself with many things, and this is how experience takes
place. Consciousness coming back onto itself gains an integrated state. . . .
This is pure consciousness" (1967, p. 25).

Pure consciousness is "pure" in the sense that it is free from the processes
and contents of knowing. It is a state of "consciousness" in that the individual
or knower is fully aware or conscious, and can afterwards describe the experience. The content of pure consciousness is awareness itself. In contrast,
the content of normal waking experiences is awareness of outer objects,
inner thoughts and feelings, along with a sense of self-awareness.

Pure consciousness can be a direct experience during some systematic
meditation practices (Maharishi, 1967). This chapter places pure conscious-

* Transcendental Meditation® is registered in the U.S. Patent and Trademark Office as a service
mark of Maharishi Foundation, Ltd., and is used under license by Maharishi University of Management.

TABLE 3.1
Self and Objects in Each State of Consciousness:
An Heuristic Classification for Organizing a Review of the Literature

STATE OF CONSCIOUSNESS	SELF	OBJECTS
Sleep	No	No
Dreaming	No	Yes
Waking	Yes	Yes
Pure Consciousness	Yes	No

ness, experienced during TM practice, in the context of the three ordinary states of consciousness—waking, sleeping, and dreaming. These four states are differentiated in terms of the presence/absence of the two key modes of experience: experience of self and experience of objects.

States of consciousness categorized by experience of self or of objects are presented in Table 3.1. For instance, during deep sleep, neither self nor objects exist. During a good night's sleep, there is no experience from falling asleep to waking up. During dreaming, illusory dream images fill awareness. However, the conscious experience of the self who is having the experience is largely absent. During waking experiences, both self-awareness and objects exist and interact to give rise to ongoing experiences. Lastly, meditation practices are reported to produce the state of the self alone, without the cognitive activity of thoughts, perceptions, and feelings. When self-awareness no longer occurs in relation to the boundaries of experience, it is reported as complete silence, as being unbounded. This level of experience is often written with a capital S—Self—to differentiate it from the experience of self-awareness identified with ongoing experiences, thoughts, and actions. As the predominance of self-awareness and/or objects vary, so brain activation patterns underlying these modes of self-awareness also change. This chapter reviews the literature on each of these four major states of consciousness and identifies brain areas activated and deactivated during each state.

Sleep State: Self and Objects Cease to Be

The dance of perceptual and motor systems during waking changes abruptly with the onset of sleep, which progresses through four stages, each marked by distinct EEG patterns. Stage 1 sleep involves the gradual sliding in and out of awareness. Stage 2 sleep, with its characteristic sleep spindles, is the mark of sleep onset. Stages 3 and 4 sleep are marked by high amplitude, slow (1–3 Hz) synchronized EEG. Delta sleep is homeostatically driven (Feinberg, 1999, 2000) and is reported to be important for restoring frontal executive functions during waking (Anderson & Horne, 2003).

EEG patterns that characterize waking and sleeping are generated in the thalamus and the cortex, regions linked by reciprocal projections. The thalamus is the major gateway and integrator for sensory and arousal information to enter the cortex, and thus is the first stage that is blocked with sleep onset (Steriade, 2001). Sleep onset, marked by the occurrence of sleep spindles (12–15 Hz), is associated with the absence of perception and self-awareness. During Stage 2 sleep, sleep spindles are generated within the thalamus (Steriade, 2003) as a result of rhythmic and prolonged bursts of the GABAnergic nucleus reticularis thalamic (NRT) neurons (Steriade et al., 1993; Steriade 2001). The NRT receives axonal collaterals from both thalamic neurons that project to the cortex and cortical neurons that project to the thalamus. In turn, the NRT projects its axons into the thalamic nuclei, exerting a variety of possible influences over thalamocortical activity. Thus, the NRT is uniquely positioned to influence the flow of information between the cortex and thalamus and exert phasic and tonic control over the mode of thalamic cell activity. The figure below depicts the central position that the NRT plays in guiding traffic in thalamocortical circuits: serving as a fundamental gating mechanism for thalamocortical dynamics, and, therefore, subjective experience.

While Stage 2 sleep is nominally the mark of sleep onset and loss of awareness, 45% of individuals report "being awake" when they are aroused from EEG-defined Stage 2 sleep (Sewitch, 1984). Thus, self-awareness is still intact in many individuals during Stage 2 sleep. As sleep deepens into Stage 3 and 4 (slow wave sleep, SWS), less than 3% of individuals report being awake when their sleep is interrupted (Sewitch, 1984).

During SWS, both the self and objects appear to be absent. The control of sleep onset appears to be related to hypothalamic and basal forebrain circuits that inhibit thalamocortical activity as well as brainstem monoaminergic firing (Pace-Schott & Hobson, 2002). The balance of activity between sleep-active and waking-active neurons represents a switching mechanism for triggering sleep. As sleep deepens, with the active withdrawal of excitatory systems in the hypothalamus and brainstem, thalamocortical cells become further depolarized giving rise to delta frequency EEG, characteristic of SWS (Steriade, 2001; Steriade et al., 1991). The cortex appears to contribute to the thalamic rhythm generating mechanism during SWS. Layer 6

FIGURE 3.1
PIVOTAL ROLE OF NRT ON THALAMOCORTICAL ACTIVITY

Cortical Areas

Thalamic Nuclei

The nucleus reticularis thalami (NRT) is a thin shell of GABAnergic neurons that surrounds the dorsal and lateral aspects of the thalamus. It receives excitatory (+) input from both thalamic and cortical axonal collaterals and sends a powerful inhibitory (−) influence onto most thalamic nuclei. Based on the convergence of thalamocortical as well as basal forebrain and brainstem influences, the NRT is capable of both phasic and tonic control over thalamocortical activity and corresponding states of consciousness.

thalamo cortical pyramidal cells drive NRT neurons that, by virtue of their inhibitory actions and widespread projections to the dorsal thalamus, hyperpolarize thalamocortical neurons and synchronize pools of thalamocortical cells and their projections back to the cortex (Anderson & Horne, 2003; Petsche et al., 1984; Steriade, 2001). This thalamocortical interaction forms a stable, reinforced, slow rhythmic EEG that is considered to disallow normal information processing and thus precludes both self-awareness and mental content of awareness.

SWS seems to reflect nearly complete sensory disengagement, suggesting a more profound resting state of the cortex in general, and the prefrontal cortex (PFC) in particular. Highly synchronous delta EEG is associated with decreased global blood flow as well as significant regional decreases, especially in PFC (Balkin et al., 2002; Marquet, 2000). These SWS thalamocortical dynamics may serve a greater purpose, helping to reorganize cortical circuits highly active during waking experiences, in part by homeostatically regulating ionic currents, as well as energy and enzyme regulation (Anderson & Horne, 2003; Steriade et al., 1993). By virtue of the dramatic shift in the style of neural activity provided by SWS, the PFC may recover its crucial functional role in guiding executive processes during waking (Desteshe & Sejnowski, 2001; Muzur et al., 2002), as supported, for example, by positive correlations between performance on neuropsychological tests of executive functioning and delta EEG during sleep (Anderson & Horne, 2003).

This significant reduction in PFC activity, which continues in dreaming states, may thus correspond to the loss of many aspects of executive function, including a sense of self during sleep. In terms of our table, the near complete absence of self-awareness and awareness of objects in SWS is characterized by the generation of strongly synchronized delta EEG. This contributes to the disconnection of the brain from the outside world, cessation of mentation, and suspension of self-awareness (Llinas & Ribary, 1998).

Dreaming: Illusory Dream Images

The transition between waking and SWS may be characterized by global reduction in brain activity levels. The transition between SWS and dreaming, however, is marked by a general reactivation of some brain areas, such that the early morning dreaming or rapid eye movement (REM) sleep periods can be metabolically more active than the subsequent waking periods. During REM, selective reactivation of the medial portions of the PFC are observed, including medial PFC and the cingulate cortex, in the presence of continued deactivation of anterior and dorsolateral PFC (Balkin, Braun et al., 2002; Muzur et al., 2002).

Our current understanding of the neuronal basis of dreaming is centered on the activation of cholinergic nuclei in the mesopontine tegmental area (pedunculopontine and lateral dorsal tegmental nuclei). These "REM-on" cells are nearby monoaminergic nuclei that are simultaneously turned off, hence referred to as *REM-off cells*. The REM-off cells include the locus coeruleus, the source of cortical norepinephrine, and selected raphe nuclei, the source of cortical serotonin. The REM-on cells gained their name from their relative silence during waking and sleep, and sudden rapid firing at the onset of dreaming, exerting acetylcholine (ACh)-mediated effects on thalamocortical circuits. These ACh cells alter the firing patterns of thalamocortical cells by depolarizing them, and thus inhibiting the burst firing mode necessary for slow wave oscillatory behavior associated with sleep onset and deep sleep. In particular, these cells activate the thalamic nuclei responsible for visual dream images (lateral geniculate body) and motor sequences in dreams plans (ventral anterior and ventral lateral nuclei; Hobson, 1995). We seldom act out our dramatic dream scenarios. This is because during dreaming the mesopontine tegmental nuclei generate a global state of bodily atonia (lack of muscle tone) by organizing a powerful brainstem inhibitory influence on spinal motor neurons.

In dreaming, individuals report experiences of bizarre, fragmented, and improbable mentation. With the onset of dreaming, portions of the ventromedial and medial areas of the PFC are activated, sometimes to levels that exceed those seen during waking (Nofzinger, 1997). As earlier noted, the dorsolateral PFC remains deactivated in REM sleep, probably because it is inhibited by acetylcholine, and because monoaminergic tone has been lost (Muzur et al., 2002). Ventromedial PFC is closely tied to limbic areas and emotions, whereas dorsolateral PFC subserves executive processing functions like self-awareness, working memory, planning, and decision making (Fuster, 2000). Thus, dreaming appears to constitute a generalized state of perceptual and emotional activation—objects of experiences—without the normal participation of executive systems which work on higher order processing like support of self-regulatory processes, reality checking, and monitoring functions of working memory including experiences of self.

Thus, we would suggest that the self is largely absent during dreaming,* due primarily to deactivation of the dorsolateral PFC and consequent off-line status. In terms of our chart, ventral medial and medial PFC, as well as medial parietal areas, appear important in some aspect of the experience of objects, while dorsolateral PFC appears to be important for the experience

* During lucid dreaming, individuals report they are aware that they are dreaming and can manipulate the dream state scenario. We suggest that this is a special case of dream, which is characterized by EEG patterns that differ from those accompanying normal dreaming. As brainstate mechanisms of lucid dreaming are not understood, we focus in our review on normal dreaming (Travis, 1994). "The junction point model: A field model of waking, sleeping, and dreaming relating dream witnessing, the waking/sleeping transition, and Transcendental Meditation in terms of a common psychophysiologic state."

of self-awareness. But perhaps there is more here. Raichle and colleagues (2001) reviewed data from many sensory tasks and concluded that medial PFC (and other midline) regions are preferentially activated in eyes-closed waking states during comparatively more self-referral conditions (passive, undirected flow of attention), than during object-referral, eyes-closed task conditions (demanding directed sensorimotor attention) (Fiset et al., 1999; Paus, 2000). We may tentatively interpret dream neuroimaging patterns in this context: the medial PFC may be related to the identity and emotional value of the "agent" in the dreams, but without the self-monitoring, reality-checking functions of working memory performed by the dorsolateral PFC. A form of experience is thereby available in sleeping dreams that is fundamentally different from waking. In dreams, clear self-awareness is lacking and the suppression of environmental sensory information (Llinas & Ribary, 1998) inhibits the organizing influence of ordinary objects of experience; hence, the often bizarre, fragmented, unremembered quality of dreams.

Waking State: The Integration of the Self and Objects

Waking is characterized by the experience of the outer world and the awareness that you are having the experience, that you are conscious. Both a sense of self and outer objects or inner mentation are available to awareness in waking experience.

Neuroimaging studies suggest that wakening, the initial return to self-awareness that accompanies regaining conscious awareness, is predominantly a function of the activation and return of integrated thalamic activity, while the subsequent values of alertness, executive functions, and a more complete range of self-awareness appear (5–20 minutes after initial waking) dependent upon dorsolateral PFC activation (Balkin et al., 2002). Thus, whereas a fundamental awareness of self would depend upon the thalamic activation (with minimal cortical assistance) supported by midbrain reticular activation, a fuller sense of the self in the world relies on the integrated functioning of the PFC. The PFC would presumably coordinate via the NRT and general thalamic and midbrain activity fully intact experiences of self-awareness supporting normal mental content and executive functions. This coming online of PFC creates a full complement of integrated self-regulatory thalamocortical executive function.

A variety of waking experiences characterized as more self-referential or self-referral and less driven by environment stimuli, are associated with activation of both medial frontal and parietal association areas. Experiences of objects during waking, operationalized as bodily processes contributing to one's point of view, are reported to activate medial parietal cortices, including the precuneus and angular gyrus (Taylor, 2001). Experiences of self-awareness during waking predominately activate a midline frontal–parietal network. For instance, stories containing either 1st or 3rd person pronouns were found to activate the precuneus in a PET study (Ruby et al., 2002), and the anterior cingulate in a fMRI study (Vogeley, Bussfeld et al., 2001). The level of abstractness of 1st person reflection (personality traits vs. physical traits) activated precuneus and angular gyrus, respectively (Kjaer et al., 2001). Action planning also activates these structures (Ruby et al., 2002). Other studies have reported medial frontal activation during self-referential judgments of pictures (Gusnard et al., 2001), and in self-referential judgments of trait adjectives (Kelley et al., 2002). Thus, a distributed system of midline structures appear to be important for predominantly self-referential or self-referral waking experience.

A Meditative State: The Experience of Pure Consciousness without Time, Space, and Body Sense

The meditative state may be unfamiliar to many readers. The prevailing Western view of self-awareness is that an individual cannot be conscious without being conscious of something. However, the last several decades have seen a few authors discussing a state of consciousness that may underlie perceptual and mental experiences. O'Shaughnessy suggested that consciousness itself is "distinct from particular consciousnesses or awareness." He proposed that this level of consciousness may be like an "empty canvas" that cannot be viewed representationally, but "makes possible and is physically necessary to view a painted picture" (1986, p. 50). Woodruff-Smith defined a level of consciousness that is "the inner awareness that makes an experience conscious . . . a constituent and constitutive feature of the experience itself" (1986, p. 150). Baars (1997) offered a theater metaphor which includes an attention director or deep self whose function seems similar to what other writers have described, providing a context (framework) to connect one conscious event with another.

Ancient traditions of meditation are distinguished from prevailing modern concepts in presenting both theoretical and experiential aspects of the experience of pure consciousness or *consciousness itself*. This state of self-awareness is clearly distinct from normal waking experiences. Recently, we conducted a content analysis of descriptions of deep experiences during practice of the TM technique (Travis & Pearson, 2000). Three themes characterized the meditation experience during practice of the TM technique: silence, unboundedness, and the loss of time, space, and body sense (time, space, and body sense being the essential framework for understanding waking experience). Specific qualities (color, shape, size, movement, etc.) are the content of waking experiences. During the experience of consciousness itself, both the fundamental framework and the content of waking experience were reported to be absent. This suggests that pure consciousness is not an "altered" state of waking. This state of self-awareness is not described as a distorted waking experience. Rather, it is described by the absence of the customary qualities and characteristics of waking experience. Subjects report being awake during this state, and can subsequently describe the absence of time, space, and body sense. Thus, the subjective descriptions of consciousness itself portray a state of *self-awareness without waking processing and contents* (Travis & Pearson, 2000): It is the empty canvas aware of its status as an empty canvas. Pure consciousness is not itself a bounded object or experience, but enables and is necessary to any experience.

The experience of pure consciousness during meditation is marked by unique patterns of activity in the dorsolateral PFC and parietal areas. During practice of the visualization form of Tibetan Buddhism, for example, intensely focused attention and experiences reported as "loss of the usual sense of space and time" were associated with increased frontal and decreased parietal cerebral blood flow (Newberg et al., 2001). Similar findings were noted in cerebral blood flow during "verbal" based meditation by Franciscan nuns involving the internal repetition of a particular phrase (Newberg et al., 2003). In contrast, practitioners of TM practice report that the absence of any concentration or effort unfolds experiences of "unboundedness" and the "loss of time, space, and body sense." These experiences of Self-awareness were associated with profound bodily relaxation, marked by spontaneous breath quiescence (10–40 sec periods of essentially no respiratory activity) and global, high amplitude, slow frequency (alpha) EEG patterns which are general highly coherent across frontal leads (for review, see Travis & Pearson, 2000; see also Badawi et al., 1984; Farrow & Hebert, 1982; Mason et al., 1997; Travis & Wallace, 1999).

Thus, the activity of the prefrontal cortex, which became active in the transition from dreaming to waking, also appears to be important for the experience of pure consciousness. The experience of pure consciousness is marked by high levels of frontal EEG coherence, a measure of the stability of phase relationship between scalp leads. Many researchers consider that higher levels of coherence indicate cerebral areas are linked for transitory periods to connect together or "bind" the diverse processing modes in service of the larger cognitive event. While early research on TM practice investigated coherence in narrow EEG bands (theta and alpha), more recent research suggests that reliable markers of TM effects can also be seen with broadband (8-45 Hz) EEG (Levine, 1976; Travis, Tecce et al., 2002). Broadband coherence is theorized to represent large-scale cortical integration necessary for the unity of subjective experience (Varela et al., 2001). Thus, broadband frontal coherence may characterize the large-scale neural integration necessary to unite thalamocortical circuits to support the experience of pure self-awareness, awareness itself.

Neuroimaging studies in our laboratory (Arenander & Travis, research in progress) and others are anticipated to reveal the unique brain state configuration associated with this ground state of self-awareness. In this unique state, we can imagine that global blood flow is reduced, but that, unlike SWS and REM, regional connectivity analysis will find that dorsolateral PFC remains a "player" and is not turned off as it is in sleep and dreaming, thus supporting an intact sense of self. A generalized PFC-mediated, top-down reorganization of brain and bodily processes is hypothesized. This would involve a controlled, partial reduction of monoaminergic and reticular activation and corresponding stabilization of NRT slow oscillatory drive on thalamocortical circuits to maintain settled states of awareness and disallow sleep (Arenander, 1996; Travis & Wallace, 1999).

Recent studies (Mason et al., 1997; Travis, 2002) suggest that repeated alternation of waking, dreaming, and sleeping with twice-daily experience of pure consciousness during meditation practice leads to long-term plastic changes in brain function and a remarkable shift in conscious experience. Amongst long-term practitioners of the TM technique, EEG alpha rhythms are significantly increased during SWS delta oscillations, and broadband coherent frontal EEG is observed to be increased during waking cognitive tasks. These brainstate modifications are found predominantly in individuals who report the experience of the ground state of self-awareness as coexisting throughout waking, sleeping, and dreaming states of consciousness. These brainwave measures of heightened neural synchrony correlate with a significant transformation of personal experience in which the individual reports the continuous, unbroken experience of self-awareness—awareness of the self alone—across the entire 24 hours of each day (Alexander et al., 1990; Travis et al., 2004).

This research indicates the possible existence of an additional, fifth major mode of human self-awareness, an integrated state of self-referral awareness and objects of awareness. This mode of the self would serve as a stable, nonchanging ground for all changing experiences across waking, sleeping, and dreaming states of consciousness. The systematic development of such an integrated state of awareness appears to have advantageous mind–body consequences. Practitioners of the TM technique are found to have greatly reduced mental and physical problems (Herron & Hillis, 2000; Herron, Schneider et al., 1996; Herron et al., 1996; Orme-Johnson, 1987a, 1987b; Orme-Johnson & Herron, 1997). Research shows the coherent cortical activity characteristic of this state is correlated with higher levels of health of mind and body. For example, there is a high correlation between EEG coherence and increased emotional stability, moral reasoning, self-referral orientation, neuromuscular and cognitive efficiency, and intelligence, and decreased negativity and neuroticism (Alexander et al., 1991; Dillbeck & Orme-Johnson, 1987; Eppley et al., 1989; Orme-Johnson & Haynes, 1981; Travis et al., 2004).

These initial studies suggest that ancient meditative techniques can provide insight into the full potential of mind–body health. Future research on brainstate signatures of conscious experience will yield significant and exciting insights into the neural mechanisms of self-awareness as well. In particular, these findings should help clarify the distinction (Searle, 2000) between the neural correlates of consciousness itself (self-referral NCC) and the neural correlates of consciousness of a particular perception (object-referral NCC).

Conclusion

This chapter has introduced the concept of a foundational state of self-awareness, which is posited to be both independent and the source of conscious experiences. Research suggests that high levels of broadband frontal EEG coherence are associated with this ground state of self-awareness. This basic awareness may act as an empty canvas upon which we organize, direct, and experience the ever-changing circumstances of our lives. Intact, highly synchronous prefrontal circuits appear to be critical to the direct experience of this ground state of awareness, as well as the transition from an episodic, meditation-dependent experience of this condition to its gradual development as a coexisting continuum across waking, dreaming, and sleeping states of consciousness. Our review supports the existence of at least two primary modes of self-awareness, one with and one without content, as well as the possibility of a third, integrated mode, in which knower and known, self and objects coexist. Future research should continue to characterize both this putative ground of self-awareness and the consequences of its repeated and systematic experience on brain plasticity and function. Once such a research-based foundation is established, then the various, diverse expressions of self-awareness can be better understood as progressive layers of processing and interaction between the knower (self-awareness) and the known (the inner and outer environment). In turn, we should be in a better position to understand and effectively treat the variety of dysfunctional modes of self-awareness.

References

Alexander C, Rainforth M, Geldeloos P. Transcendental Meditation, self-actualization, and psychological health: a conceptual overview and statistical meta-analysis. *J Soc Beh & Pers.* 1991; 5:189–247.

Alexander CN, Davies JL, Dixon CA et al. Growth of higher stages of consciousness: Maharishi's Vedic psychology of human development. In: Alexander CN, Langer EJ, eds. *Higher Stages of Human Development: Perspectives on Adult Growth.* New York: Oxford University Press; 1990: 286–341.

Anderson C, Horne JA. Prefrontal cortex: links between low frequency delta EEG in sleep and neuropsychological performance in healthy, older people. *Psychophysiol.* 2003; 40:349–357.

Arenander AT. *Global Neural Ground State: Coherent Brain Mechanisms Associated with Transcendental Consciousness.* Paper presented at: *Toward a Science of Consciousness;* 1996. Tucson, AZ.

Baars BJ. *In the Theater of Consciousness: The Workspace of the Mind.* New York: Oxford University Press; 1997.

Badawi K, Wallace RK, Orme-Johnson D, Rouzere AM. Electrophysiologic characteristics of respiratory suspension periods occurring during the practice of the Transcendental Meditation Program. *Psychosom Med.* 1984; 46(3):267–276.

Balkin TJ, Braun AR, Wesemsten NJ et al. The process of awakening: a PET study of regional brain activity patterns mediating the re-establishment of alertness and consciousness. *Brain Res.* 2002; 125:2308–2319.

Chung-Yuan C. *Original Teachings of Ch'an Buddhism.* New York: Vintage; 1969.

Desteshe A, Sejnowski T. *Thalamocortical Assemblies.* New York: Oxford University Press; 2001.

Dillbeck MC, Orme-Johnson DW. Physiological differences between Transcendental Meditation and rest. *Am Psychol.* 1987; 42:879–881.

Eppley KR, Abrams AI, et al. Differential effects of relaxation techniques on trait anxiety: a meta-analysis. *J Clin Psychol.* 1989; 45(6):957–974.

Farrow JT, Hebert JR. Breath suspension during the Transcendental Meditation technique. *Psychosom Med.* 1982; 44(2):133–153.

Feinberg I. Delta homeostasis, stress, and sleep deprivation. *Sleep.* 1999; 22:1021–1030.

Feinberg I. Slow wave sleep and release of growth hormone. *AMA.* 2000; 284:2217–2218.

Fiset P, Paus T, Diloze T et al. Brain mechanisms of propofol-induced loss of consciousness in humans: a positron emission tomographic study. *J Neurosci.* 1999; 19:5506–5513.

Fuster JM. Executive frontal functions. *Exp Brain Res.* 2000; 133(1):66–70.

Gusnard DA, Akbudak E, Shulman GL, Raichle ME. Medial prefrontal cortex and self-referential mental activity: relation to a default mode of brain function. *PNAS.* 2001; 98(7):4259–4264.

Herron RE, Hillis SL. The impact of the Transcendental Meditation program on government payments to physicians in Quebec: an update. *Am J Health Prom.* 2000; 14(5): 284–291.

Herron RE, Hillis SL, Mandarino JV, Orme-Johnson DW, Walton KG. The impact of the Transcendental Meditation program on government payments to physicians in Quebec. *Am J Health Prom.* 1996; 10(3):208–216.

Herron RE, Schneider RH, Mandarino JV, Alexander CN, Walton KG. Cost-effective hypertension management: comparison of drug therapies with an alternative program. *Am J Man Care.* 1996; 2(4):427–437.

Hobson JA. *Sleep.* New York: Scientific American Library; 1995.

James W. *Varieties of Religious Experiences.* New York: Collier Books; 1902/1961.

Kelley WM, Macrae CN, Macrae CN, Wyland CL, Caglar S, Inati S, Heatherton TF. Finding the self? An event-related fMRI study. *J Cog Neurosci.* 2002; 14(5):785–794.

Kjaer TW, Nowak M, Kjaer KW, Lou AR, Lou HC. Precuneus–prefrontal activity during awareness of visual verbal stimuli. *Conscious Cog.* 2001; 10(3):356–365.

Levine P. The coherence spectral array (COSPAR) and its application to the study of spatial ordering in the EEG. *Proc San Diego Bio-Med Symp.* 1976; 15:237–247.

Llinas RR, Ribary U. Temporal conjunction in thalamocortical transactions. *Adv Neurol.* 1998; 77:95–103.

Maharishi (1967). *On the Bhagavad-Gita A New Translation and Commentary.* Baltimore, Md: Penguin; 1967.

Marquet P. Functional neuroimaging of normal human sleep by positron emission tomography. *J Sleep Res.* 2000; 9:207–232.

Mason LI, Alexander CN, Travis FT et al. Electrophysiological correlates of higher states of consciousness during sleep in long-term practitioners of the Transcendental Meditation program. *Sleep.* 1997; 20(2):102–110.

Muzur A, Pace-Schott EF, Hobson JA. The prefrontal cortex in sleep. *Trends in Cog Sci.* 2002; 6:475–481.

Natsonlas T. Consciousness and self-awareness: Part 1. Consciousness 4, consciousness 5, consciousness 6. *J Mind Behav.* 1997; 18:53–74.

Newberg A, Alavi A, Daime M, Pourdehnad M, Santana J, d'Aquili E. The measurement of regional cerebral blood flow during the complex cognitive task of meditation: a preliminary SPECT study. *Psychiatry Res.* 2001; 106(2):113–122.

Newberg A, Pourdehnad M, Alavi A, d'Aquili E. Cerebral blood flow during meditative prayer: Preliminary findings and methodological issues. *Percept Mot Skills.* 2003; 97(2): 625–630.

Nofzinger EA. Forebrain activation in REM sleep: an FDG PET study. *Brain Res,* 70: 192–201.

Orme-Johnson D. Medical care utilization and the Transcendental Meditation program [published erratum appears in *Psychosom Med.* 1987; 49(6):637]. *Psychosom Med.* 1987a; 49(5):493–507.

Orme-Johnson DW. Medical care utilization and the Transcendental Meditation program. *Psychosom Med.* 1987b; 49:493–507.

Orme-Johnson DW, Haynes CT. EEG phase coherence, pure consciousness, creativity, and TM–Sidhi experiences. *Int J Neurosci.* 1981; 13(4):211–217.

Orme-Johnson DW, Herron RE. An innovative approach to reducing medical care utilization and expenditures. *Am J Man Care.* 1997; 3(1):135–144.

O'Shaughnessy B. Consciousness. *Midwest Studies in Philosophy.* 1986; 10:49–62.

Pace-Schott EF, Hobson JA. The neurobiology of sleep: genetics, cellular physiology and subcortical networks. *Nature Rev Neurosci.* 2002; 3:591–605.

Paus T. Functional anatomy of arousal and attention systems in the human brain. *Prog Brain Res.* 2000; 126:65–77.

Petsche H, Pockberger H, Rappolsberger P. On the search for the sources of the electroencephalogram. *Neurosci.* 1984; 11(1):1–27.

Raichle ME, MacLeod AM, Snyde AZ, Powers WJ, Gusnard DA, Shulman GL. A default mode of brain function. *PNAS.* 2001; 98(2):676–682.

Regs P. *Zen Plesh, Zen Dones.* New York: Doubleday Anchor; 1955.

Ruby P, Sirigu A, Decety J. Distinct areas in parietal cortex involved in long-term and short-term action planning: a PET investigation. *Cortex.* 2002; 38(3):321–339.

Searle JR. Consciousness. *Ann Rev Neurosci.* 2002; 23:557–578.

Sewitch DA. NREM sleep continuity and the sense of having slept in normal sleep. *Sleep.* 1984; 7:147–154.

Sewitch DA. The perceptual uncertainty of having slept: the inability to discriminate electroencephalographic sleep from wakefulness. *Psychophysiol.* 1984; 21:243–259.

Steriade M. Active neocortical processes during quiescent sleep. *Arch Ital Biol.* 2001; 139:37–51.

Steriade M. The corticothalamic system in sleep. *Front Biol.* 2003; 1: 878–899.

Steriade M, Curro Dossi R, Nunez A. Network modulation of slow intrinsic oscillation of cat thalamocortical neurons implicated in deep delta waves: cortically induced synchronization and brainstem cholinergic suppression. *J Neurosci.* 1991; 11:3200–3217.

Steriade M, McCormick DA, Sejnowski TJ. Thalamocortical oscillations in the sleeping and aroused brain. *Science.* 1993; 262:679–684.

Taylor JG. The central role of the parietal lobes in consciousness. *Consciousness & Cog.* 2001; 10(3):379–417.

Travis F. Development along an integration scale: longitudinal transformation in brain dynamics with regular Transcendental Meditation practice. *Psychophysiol.* 2002; 39:S81.

Travis F, Arenander A, DuBois D. Psychological and physiological characteristics of a proposed object-referral/self-referral continuum of self-awareness. *Conscious Cog.* 2004; 13:401–420.

Travis F, Pearson C. Pure consciousness: distinct phenomenological and physiological correlates of "consciousness itself". *Int J Neurosci.* 2000; 100(1–4):

Travis F, Wallace RK. Autonomic and EEG patterns during eyes-closed rest and Transcendental Meditation (TM) practice: the basis for a neural model of TM practice. *Consciousness & Cog.* 1999; 8(3):302–318.

Travis FT. The junction point model: a field model of waking, sleeping, and dreaming relating dream witnessing, the waking/sleeping transition, and Transcendental Meditation in terms of a common psychophysiologic state. *Dreaming.* 1994; 4(2):91–104.

Travis FT, Tecce J, Alexander A, Wallace RK. Patterns of EEG coherence, power, and contingent negative variation characterize the integration of transcendental and waking states. *Biol Psychol.* 2002; 61:293–319.

Varela F, Lachaux JP, Rodriguez E, Martinerie J. The brainweb: phase synchronization and large-scale integration. *Nat Rev Neurosci.* 2001; 2(4):229–239.

Vogeley K, Bussfeld P, Newen A et al. Mind reading: neural mechanisms of theory of mind and self-perspective. *Neuroimage.* 2001; 14(1 Pt 1):170–181.

Part 2

SELF-AWARENESS
IN PSYCHIATRIC PATIENTS

4

Disorders of Insight, Self-Awareness, and Attribution in Schizophrenia

Laura A. Flashman

SCHIZOPHRENIA IS A psychiatric disorder characterized by psychotic symptoms, including (American Psychiatric Association, 1994) delusions, prominent hallucinations, disorganized speech, or disorganized and catatonic behavior. Negative symptoms (i.e., alogia, affective blunting, avolition/asociality, anhedonia) are also considered part of the clinical presentation. Positive (both psychotic and disorganized) symptoms appear to reflect an excess or distortion of normal functions; in contrast, negative symptoms appear to reflect a diminution or loss of normal functions. The most typical symptoms of schizophrenia involve a range of cognitive and emotional dysfunctions, including alterations in perception, inferential thinking, language and communication, behavioral monitoring (including awareness), affect, fluency, and productivity of thought and speech, hedonic capacity, volition, and attention. No single symptom is pathognomonic of schizophrenia. Instead, the diagnosis involves the recognition of a constellation of signs and symptoms associated with impaired occupational and social functioning.

The Diagnostic and Statistical Manual of Mental Disorders (DSM-IV; American Psychiatric Association, 1994), criteria for a diagnosis of schizophrenia, in-

Some of the research presented in this chapter was supported by a Young Investigator Award from the National Alliance on Research on Schizophrenia and Depression (NARSAD), as well as by New Hampshire Hospital and the Ira DeCamp Foundation.

clude persistence of symptoms for at least 6 months, with at least one month of 2 or more active-phase symptoms. Prodromal symptoms are often present prior to the active phase, and residual symptoms may follow. The signs and symptoms are associated with marked dysfunction in one or more areas of functioning, and might include impairments in interpersonal relations, work, education, or self-care. When distinguishing schizophrenia from similar conditions, observable symptoms should not more closely match those described for schizoaffective disorder or a mood disorder with psychotic features than those characteristic of schizophrenia. Further, the disturbance must not be attributable to the direct physiological effects of an ingested or environmental substance or a general medical condition.

Prevalence rates of schizophrenia vary, but generally range from 0.2% to 2% (e.g., American Psychiatric Association, 1994; Goldner, Hsu, Waraich, & Somers, 2002). The lifetime prevalence rate is estimated at between 0.6% and 1% of the population; this means that approximately 1 in every 100 people suffers from schizophrenia. Because schizophrenia tends to be a chronic disorder, incidence rates are considerably lower than prevalence rates, and are estimated to be approximately 1 per 10,000 per year (American Psychiatric Association, 1994; Goldner et al., 2002).

The onset of schizophrenia typically occurs between the late teens and the mid-30s. The median age at onset for the first psychotic episode of schizophrenia is in the early to mid-20s for men and in the late 20s for women. The age at onset may have both pathophysiological and prognostic significance. Individuals with an early age of onset are more often male and have a poorer premorbid adjustment, lower educational achievement, more evidence of structural brain abnormalities, more prominent negative signs and symptoms, more cognitive impairment, and a worse outcome. In contrast, individuals with a later age of onset are more often female, have less evidence of structural brain abnormalities or cognitive impairment, and experience a better outcome. Other factors associated with a better prognosis include good premorbid adjustment, acute onset, precipitating events, associated mood disturbance, brief duration of active-phase symptoms, good interepisode functioning, a family history of mood disorder, and no family history of schizophrenia.

Although it has often been reported that males and females are affected in approximately equal numbers, estimates of gender ratio in schizophrenia are confounded by issues of ascertainment and definition. While community-based surveys have mostly suggested an equal sex distribution, hospital-based studies generally report a higher rate of schizophrenia in males. Broader definitions of schizophrenia with respect to the boundary of mood disorders will yield a higher female-to-male ratio than the relatively narrow construct of schizophrenia as defined by the *DSM-IV*.

The etiology of schizophrenia remains unclear, but current conceptualizations recognize schizophrenia as a disorder of the brain (e.g., Andreasen, 1997; McCarley et al., 1999; Sawa & Snyder, 2002), although no investigator has yet been able to definitively implicate a specific brain region or structure. Many investigators have studied the gross morphology of the brains of individuals with schizophrenia using postmortem tissue, computerized axial tomography (CT), and magnetic resonance imaging (MRI). Results have been variable, but some relatively consistent findings include smaller brain volumes, enlarged ventricles (e.g., Shenton, Dickey, Frumin, & McCarley, 2001), fewer neurons in the prefrontal cortex (Brown et al., 1986), and reduced hippocampal volume (Nelson, Saykin, Flashman, & Riordan, 1998). Kovelman and Scheibel (1984) found pronounced abnormalities in the orientation of cells in the hippocampi of deceased patients with schizophrenia, with a markedly more disorganized distribution than the parallel orientation found in the brains of healthy controls. Recently, Kozlovsky, Belmaker, and Agam (2002) found abnormal neuronal distribution in schizophrenic patients' brains, suggestive of aberrant programmed cell death. These findings are consistent with a neurodevelopmental concept of schizophrenia.

Lack of Awareness of Illness in Schizophrenia: Introduction

Unawareness of illness has received increasing empirical investigation in psychiatric disorders, including schizophrenia. It has been reported that most patients with schizophrenia (68–89%) demonstrate impaired awareness of their illness, including difficulty identifying their symptoms, recognizing that they have a mental disorder, and misattributing their symptoms to external causes (Amador et al., 1994). Unawareness of illness in patients with schizophrenia is of considerable clinical relevance because it may increase delays in seeking treatment, treatment noncompliance, poor work performance, and impaired social skills (Drake, Holey, Akhtar, & Lewis, 2000; Francis & Penn, 2001; Kampman et al., 2002; Lacro, Dunn, Dolder, Leckband, & Jeste, 2002; Lysaker, Bryson, & Bell, 2002; Novak-Grubic & Tavcar, 2002).

There are several theories about the etiology of impaired awareness of illness in schizophrenia. Until quite recently, most theories proposed that unawareness functions as an unconscious defense or coping mechanism serving to preserve self-esteem and to minimize disability (Birchwood, Mason, Macmillan, & Healy, 1993; Lally, 1989; Lysaker & Bell, 1998; McGlashan &

Carpenter, 1976; McGlashan, Levy, & Carpenter, 1975; Mechanic, McAlpine, Rosenfield, & Davis, 1994; Warner et al., 1989; White et al., 2000). Very little empirical research has directly measured the relationship between unawareness of illness and defense, however, what data is available has indicated that psychological or psychosocial etiologies play a relatively small role in why so many schizophrenic patients are unaware that they are ill (Kasapis, 1995; Nelson, 1997).

Growing attention has been directed to the possibility of a neurobiological basis for schizophrenia patients' difficulty in recognizing their illness (Amador et al., 1993). We will proceed in this chapter to explore the multifactorial nature of the phenomenon, studying evidence for impaired awareness across several of these dimensions. Using the concept of neurological anosognosia as a model for some particular types of unawareness, we will also review studies using neuropsychological assessment and neuroimaging to investigate the neurologic or neuronal mechanisms that cause schizophrenia patients to remain blithely oblivious to an illness that is usually painfully obvious to the people around them.

Definition of Lack of Awareness

Conceptualizations of how one is aware of one's own characteristics or capabilities, or how such awareness might be absent or deficient in some people, or for some features, are neither straightforward nor unitary. Many terms are used in the scientific and lay literature to describe elements of this concept. It is important to keep the variety of available terms, characteristics, and distinctions in mind when considering the literature on unawareness, because imprecision and inconsistency are common in the vocabulary of this discussion. Terms like *agnosia, anosognosia, unawareness,* and *denial* have been used as if they were synonyms, in otherwise learned considerations of unawareness as a sign or symptom of various neurological disorders. Nevertheless, the context of their application in individual articles suggests an ever-moving target, oriented toward particular hypotheses or theoretical formulations. For clarification, we briefly define several prominently seen related terms (Table 4.1).

Dimensions of Awareness

Recognition of several different dimensions may be helpful in understanding the concept of absent awareness. We have previously described a schema

TABLE 4.1
Terms and Definitions Used When Describing Lack of Awareness

Agnosia	Denotes an impairment in recognition that cannot be explained on the basis of primary motor or sensory impairment; failure to recognize the significance of objects (e.g., visual agnosia)
Anosognosia	A lack of knowledge about a deficit. Frequently used to describe an apparent loss of recognition or awareness of left hemiplegia following an abrupt brain insult (Babinski, 1914). Currently used to describe the occurrence of frank denial of a neurological deficit
Denial of illness	Redescription of anosognosia (Weinstein & Kahn, 1955) implies a psychological or psychodynamic level of explanation; that is, patients with anosognosia are believed to be motivated to block distressing symptoms from awareness by using defense mechanism (denial)
Insight	Has been used to describe a spectrum of concepts, ranging from a psychological defense mechanism to lack of cognitive skills which permit understanding of deficits; generally considered to be a multidimensional construct
Anosodiaphoria	The absence of concern, or indifference to an acknowledged deficit or illness.
Lack of Self-awareness	Lack of understanding of how the limitations of an illness *affect* one's functioning (vs. simply a lack of understanding or recognition of one's actual limitations)
Consciousness	Here-and-now perception in relation to the self. This is in contrast to the abstract idea of self-awareness. It has been suggested that one must be conscious to be self-aware (i.e., consciousness is a precursor to self-awareness)

(Flashman, Amador, & McAllister, 1998) proposing three distinct dimensions related to awareness. The first of these is the presence or absence of knowledge of a specific deficit or difficulty in the affected individual. For example, individuals with schizophrenia commonly experience several kinds of difficulties, including psychiatric symptoms (e.g., hallucinations, delusions, alogia, anhedonia), cognition (e.g., memory, attention, executive dysfunction), and social/behavior (e.g., loud outbursts, bizarre behaviors, awkward social interactions). While some people may acknowledge and accurately describe these problems, some others with similar symptoms or deficits may recognize no difference from their preillness state despite dramatic evidence to the contrary. This dimension appears to reflect the definition of *insight* in Table 4.1.

The second dimension represents the affected individuals' emotional response to their symptoms, difficulties, or deficits. In patients aware of a given deficit, responses can range from complete indifference (anosodiaphoria) to bitter complaint. Similarly, patients unaware of their deficits can manifest responses ranging from indifference to angry denial when attempts are made to convince them of their impairment.

The third dimension is the ability to comprehend the impact or consequence(s) of a deficit on daily life. Some individuals are aware of and troubled by such significant deficits as hallucinations or memory impairment, but believe that they can function at their premorbid level without difficulty. This dimension appears to closely correspond to *self-awareness* as described in Table 4.1.

The manner in which an individual accounts for admitted difficulties or deficits is a separate but related issue. Causal attribution of a particular deficit or difficulty first requires that the individual acknowledges a deficit, and then attributes it to his or her illness to a degree sufficient for the diagnosis of schizophrenia to become integrated in that person's self-definition (modified from Gordon et al., 1998). Many patients with schizophrenia will acknowledge certain problems, for example, but then identify the source of these problems as "a fight with my Mom" or a "government conspiracy," rather than their mental illness. Although these individuals have some awareness of a deficit, their inability to attribute the deficit to their illness can interfere with personal commitment to a therapeutic regimen or understanding of why other people react to them the way they do. Patients with schizophrenia show special deficits in insight, self-awareness, and attribution that complicate their treatment and compound the terrible pain imposed by their disease.

Unawareness of Illness in Schizophrenia

Unawareness of illness in schizophrenia has been variously explained as a psychological defense mechanism (motivated denial), a cultural variation, or a kind of neuropsychological impairment (Amador et al., 1993). It is, in fact, quite reasonable to assume that this peculiar response represents a complex tangle of interacting malfunctions within complex psychological, neurological, and environmental systems. For purposes of this discussion, however, we will concentrate for the time being on how neuronal influences in particular contribute to the schizophrenic patient's inability to recognize either the presence of his disease or the manner in which it affects his life.

We will try to demonstrate how the absent awareness of illness seen in patients with acquired brain lesions secondary to insults like stroke or head injury, or in patients with neurodegenerative disorders, can help us understand the neuronal etiology of similar manifestations in schizophrenia and other functional psychoses (Amador, Strauss, Yale, & Gorman, 1991; Flashman, McAllister, Andreasen, & Saykin, 2000; Flashman, McAllister, Saykin, et al., 2001). Unawareness in schizophrenia holds a number in common with the poststroke anosognosia syndrome so well-described by Robinson (see Chapter 9). Resistance to direct evidence or confrontation, delusional explanations for illness-related events like hospitalization, and a continuum of severity are common to the failed awareness seen in poststroke or posttraumatic organic brain syndromes as well as that characteristically affecting schizophrenic patients (Cuesta & Peralta, 1994).

As described by Robinson (see Chapter 9), a dramatic absence or deficit of awareness can be seen in individuals who have sustained hemiplegia and hemianopia following a cerebrovascular accident. Functionally, these individuals are unable to move the contralateral limb, or perceive stimuli in the contralateral hemifield, but say they are well and unimpaired. When the deficits are pointed out, emotional responses can range from denial (anosognosia) to bland acceptance (anosodiaphoria). Most evidence suggests that involvement of the nondominant inferoparietal cortex is required (Critchley, 1953; Gerstmann, 1942); but similarly affected patients with lesions apparently restricted to the frontal lobes have also been described (Zingerle, 1913). More specifically, it has been hypothesized that unawareness of illness results from an interaction between frontal lobe circuitry impairment, which compromises the ability to self-monitor, self-correct, and draw proper inferences, and parietal lobe dysfunction, which affects the complex integration of sensory input (Benson & Stuss, 1990; Ellis & Small, 1993). Anosognosia related to left hemiplegia and left hemianopia, with both corticosubcortical lesions and lesions confined to deep structures, has also been reported (Bisiach, Vallar, Perani, Papagno, & Berti, 1986; Gerstmann, 1942; Healton, Navarro, Bressman, & Brust, 1982; Watson & Heilman, 1979). Furthermore, although the most common examples of anosognosia occur after nondominant hemisphere lesions, the frequent occurrence of severe speech and language deficits associated with analogous lesions in the dominant hemisphere limits the conclusions that can be drawn. Of note, not all hemiplegic and hemianopic patients with large lesions involving the inferoparietal cortex develop anosognosia.

Robinson notes (see Chapter 9) an increased number of lesions in the temporoparietal regions and the basal ganglia, particularly in the right hemisphere, associated with anosognosia. He also reported evidence of a preexisting risk factor in those patients who developed anosognosia, manifested by enlarged ventricles. Robinson again found an increased association between anosognosia and right hemisphere and basal ganglia lesions in a second study sample, as well as an increase in the number of lesions reported in the insula.

Frith (1987) and Frith and Done (1989) have developed a neuropsychological model of schizophrenia in which it is proposed that certain positive psychotic symptoms result from a failure to properly monitor internally generated intentions to act. These can be considered part of the experience of "alien control" (i.e., thought insertion or withdrawal, delusions of control, auditory hallucinations). The theory also suggests that many negative symptoms, including social withdrawal, avolition, anhedonia, and alogia, arise from a failure to initiate spontaneous actions. Frith and Done's model proposes that people constantly (and usually unconsciously) monitor their actions against their intentions. However, should the monitoring system become defective, or should information regarding self-generated actions fail to reach it, then the individual may misassign the motivations for self-generated actions to origins other than themselves.

This becomes particularly interesting when considered in the context of the role frontal cortex dysfunction, possibly in combination with other cortical and subcortical regions, is increasingly seen to play in schizophrenia. While a number of studies have explored relationships between cognitive impairment and neurological disorders with a component of unawareness of illness, only a few studies have investigated this issue in schizophrenia; these will be described shortly.

Methodological Issues in Assessing Unawareness in Schizophrenia

Definitions of insight, measures for quantifying unawareness of illness, and specific characteristics of the subject population have all been variously described, and disagreement about each among investigators has complicated study of the phenomenon and made it difficult to compare conclusions from one study to the next (Markova & Berrios, 1995). The concept of *unawareness* and its components are said by some to include unawareness of illness (lack of recognition that one has an illness), of symptoms, of specific deficits, or of the effects of medication or other treatment. Deficiencies in self-awareness might include an absence of insight into the social consequences of the illness, unawareness of the impact of various symptoms or deficits on general functioning, or inappropriate emotional reactions. Some studies have also examined correct or incorrect attribution of recognized symptoms or deficits.

Methods used to assess unawareness may create apparent variations in estimates of prevalence. Unawareness has been assessed by direct interview, review of medical records, and structured questionnaires. Other studies have looked at prediction and monitoring of performance or symptoms, or compared patient self-ratings with those of a knowledgeable informant (e.g., a family member, a member of the treatment team). Early work identified unawareness based primarily on a single item (number 104) from the Present State Exam (PSE), "Do you think there is anything the matter with you?" The item is scored on a scale from 0 to 3, with 0 described as "full insight . . . able to appreciate the issues involved," and 3 described as "denies nervous condition entirely." More comprehensive questionnaires have been developed to try to address the multidimensional aspects of awareness. The two most popular scales are the Scale to Assess Unawareness of Mental Disorders (SUMD; Amador & Strauss, 1992; Amador et al., 1993) and the Schedule of Assessment of Insight (SAI or SAI-Expanded Version; David, 1990; Kemp & David, 1991). The SUMD is a semistructured interview and scale that assesses present and past awareness. There are both general questions (awareness of having a mental disorder, the effects of medication on the disorder, understanding of the social consequences), and items that pertain to specific symptoms. If the patient demonstrates awareness of a symptom (Rating ≤ 3), he or she is asked about the attribution of that symptom. The SAI measures three separate dimensions, including treatment compliance (0–4), recognition of illness (0–6), and relabeling of psychotic phenomena (0–4), with a supplementary question on response to hypothetical contradiction.

Finally, samples used to assess unawareness have included both acute and chronic patients with schizophrenia, as well as psychotic patients of all types. Carpenter and colleagues (1973) reported that lack of insight, using the single item on the PSE, was one of the 12 signs/symptoms that were "especially discriminating between schizophrenia and other psychiatric disorders." Amador and associates (1994) observed that unawareness of illness was more prevalent in schizophrenia than in other psychiatric disorders, but other investigators have not been able to replicate his conclusion (David et al., 1995; Pini, Cassano, Dell'Osso, & Amador, 2001).

Clinical Correlates of Unawareness of Illness in Schizophrenia

The relationship between the various symptoms of schizophrenia and unawareness of illness remains unclear, but it has been reported in most patients with schizophrenia. In general, these studies have focused on the concept defined here as *insight*, looking at items that assess awareness of illness, symptoms, deficits, and, sometimes, effects of medication or other treatment.

Unawareness in schizophrenia does not appear to be associated with gender, ethnicity, or age at onset of illness. It does not appear to be consistently associated with epidemiological variables, neurological signs, or positive and negative symptoms (Amador et al., 1993; Cuesta & Peralta, 1994; David et al., 1995). Some studies have found a significant relationship between unawareness and positive symptoms (Kemp & Lambert, 1995; Kim et al., 1997; Schwartz, 1998); thought disorder (Pini et al., 2001; Smith, Hull, Israel, & Willson 2000); negative symptoms (Kemp & Lambert, 1995); and disorganization (Cuesta, Peralta, & Zarzuela, 1998; Dickerson, Boronow, Ringel, & Parente, 1996; Kim et al., 1997; Smith, Hull, & Santos, 1998). Lower levels of depression have been reported to be associated with greater unawareness of illness (e.g., Kemp & Lambert, 1995; Smith et al., 1998), and unawareness was found to be associated with excitement and hostility in acute schizophrenic patients as assessed by the PANSS (Cuesta et al., 1998). A meta-analysis (Mintz, Dobson, & Romney, 2003) suggested a small negative relationship between insight and global, positive and negative symptoms, and a small positive relationship between insight and depressive symptoms in patients with schizophrenia (Bartko, Herczog, & Zador, 1988; Kemp & David, 1996).

Some studies suggest that unawareness of illness may correlate with the severity of psychosis (e.g., Markova & Berrios, 1992), but the relationship is rather weak, and possibly nonlinear (David et al., 1992; McEvoy et al., 1989). Others have not found any relationship between unawareness of illness and global severity of psychopathology (David et al., 1995; McGlashan, 1981; McEvoy et al., 1989). It has also been noted that insight does not improve consistently with symptomatic improvement in the illness. Two studies (David et al., 1992; McEvoy et al., 1989) found that frequently hospitalized patients, who might be generally considered more severely ill than those who are able to remain in the community, had the same degree of insight as those requiring fewer hospitalizations.

Of note, deficits of awareness have consistently been associated with poorer medication compliance, poorer prognosis and response to treatment, and poorer social and vocational functioning (Bartko et al., 1988; Kemp & David, 1996; Lysaker & Bell, 1995; Lysaker et al., 2002; Smith, Barzman, & Pristach, 1997).

We have studied a group of 30 patients with *DSM-IV* diagnosed schizophrenia spectrum disorder. Patients were characterized as *aware* or *unaware* based on their average score for current awareness of symptoms, using the SUMD. Demographic information is presented in Table 4.2. Groups differed only in terms of estimated baseline verbal IQ, as assessed by the American National Adult Reading Scale, but both groups performed in the average range for estimated premorbid ability. We also evaluated awareness using the three general questions on the SUMD. As shown in Figure 4.1, 43% of patients denied that they had a mental illness when asked (i.e., received a score of 4 or 5). Of interest, 80% of the remaining subjects, who did acknowledge they had a mental illness, identified their illness as something other than schizophrenia. Figure 4.2 shows the distribution of awareness scores for patients with regard to their understanding of the social consequences of their illness; most patients denied that any of the difficulties they were having in their daily lives were related to having a mental illness.

We found no significant correlations in our patient sample between unawareness of current symptoms and either positive symptoms ($r = 0.20$;

TABLE 4.2
Demographic Characteristics of the Patient Sample

	AWARE GROUP (N = 18)	UNAWARE GROUP (N = 12)	t	$p <$
Age	36.1	33.2	0.65	.50
Gender (M:F)	13:5	9:3	$X^2 = .03$	.87
Handedness (R:L)	16:2	11:1	$X^2 = .06$	.80
Estimated premorbid IQ (ANART)	109.7	99.2	2.63	.02*
FSIQ	97.1	89.8	1.40	.17
SANS	11.1	13.4	1.20	.24
SAPS	10.1	10.6	0.43	.67
BPRS	44.2	48.1	1.03	.31

FIGURE 4.1
AWARENESS OF HAVING A MENTAL DISORDER (INSIGHT)

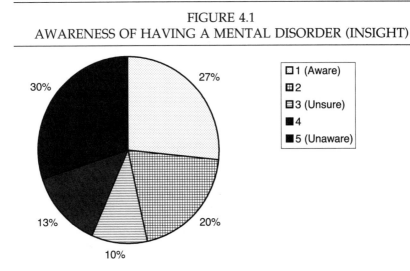

Using the first general item on the SUMD, 43% of patients with schizophrenia spectrum disorder demonstrated a lack of awareness (score of 4 or 5) when asked directly if they believed they had a mental illness. However, it should be noted that of the 57% who did acknowledge having a mental illness, a large proportion (80%) described their illness as "nerves" or depression, rather than as a schizophrenia spectrum disorder.

Schedule for Assessment of Positive Symptoms; [SAPS]) or negative symptoms ($r = -0.20$; Schedule for Assessment of Negative Symptoms [SANS]). We did find a modest but significant positive correlation between the unawareness of symptoms and symptom severity, using the BPRS total score ($r = 0.40$, $p < .04$). That is, greater unawareness was associated with greater current symptom severity.

Neuropsychological Correlates of Unawareness of Illness in Schizophrenia

Several studies have found a modest inverse correlation between unawareness of illness and overall intellectual ability (IQ) (David et al., 1992; David et al., 1995; Lysaker & Bell, 1994; Young, Davila, & Scher, 1993), although the literature does not support the notion that unawareness of illness is simply a function of global cognitive impairment (Cuesta & Peralta, 1994; McEvoy et al., 1993). For example, McEvoy and colleagues (1989) found

FIGURE 4.2
AWARENESS OF SOCIAL CONSEQUENCES/IMPACT
OF ILLNESS (SELF-AWARENESS)

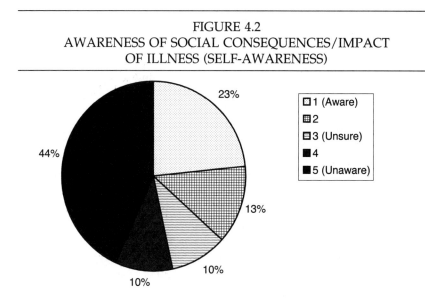

Using the third general item of the SUMD, 54% of patients demonstrated a lack of awareness (score of 4 or 5) regarding the impact of their illness of daily functioning (i.e., needing to be hospitalized, having difficulty maintaining employment).

that neuropsychological scores were not correlated with scores on a questionnaire assessing insight and treatment attitudes for psychotic outpatients. Cuesta and Peralta (1994) also found that items assessing lack of insight were not associated with global cognitive deficits in patients with schizophrenia.

Other studies have specifically examined the hypothesis that dysfunction in frontal-subcortical circuitry is related to unawareness of illness in psychosis. These studies have yielded inconsistent findings, with evidence both supporting (e.g., Buckley, Hasan, Fiedman, & Cerny, 2001; Mohamed, Fleming, Penn, & Spaulding, 1999; Smith et al., 2000; Young et al., 1998) and failing to support (e.g., Amador et al., 1994; Collins, Remington, Coulter, & Birkett, 1997; Cuesta et al., 1995; Kemp & David, 1996; McEvoy, Freter, Merritt, & Apperson, 1993) this hypothesis. Young and colleagues (Young, Davila, et al., 1993; Young, Zakzanis, et al. 1998) examined the relationship between unawareness of illness and frontal lobe performance in patients with chronic schizophrenia and found that poor insight was strongly correlated with the degree of frontal lobe dysfunction (or impairment of working memory) as assessed by the Wisconsin Card Sorting Test (WCST). Rossell, Coakes, Shapleske, Woodruff, and David (2003) also reported a significant correlation between poorer WCST performance and poorer insight. Other frontal lobe measures of executive functioning, including the Trail Making Test and verbal fluency, were not related to unawareness. Lysaker and Bell (1998) found that schizophrenics with poor insight and frontal lobe impairment, unlike those with poor insight but intact frontal lobe functioning, continued to demonstrate unawareness of illness following psychosocial treatment. Further, Lysaker and Bell (1995) reported that subjects with impaired insight demonstrate consistently poorer performance on the WCST over a period of one year than subjects with unimpaired insight. However, Cuesta, Peralta, Caro, and deLeon, (1995) evaluated psychotic patients and did not find any significant correlations between WCST and insight. Some studies (Buckley et al., 2001; Cuesta et al., 1995; Mohamed et al., 1999) have shown a relationship between unawareness, negative symptoms, and deficits in some aspects of executive functioning (fluency, WCST or Trails B). Smith and associates (2000) reported that the WCST was significantly associated with symptom misattribution rather than unawareness of symptoms.

In the very few studies that have reported data on other neuropsychological functions, a significant relationship has been noted between unawareness of illness and performance on tests sensitive to parietal lobe dysfunction (Flashman et al., 1997; McEvoy et al., 1996). As can be seen in Figure 4.3, the patients in our sample who were unaware of their illness were significantly more impaired on tasks assessing parietal lobe function than patients who were aware of their illness.

In contrast, a number of studies have found no significant correlations between awareness and any neurocognitive measures (Collins et al., 1997; Cuesta & Peralta, 1994; Dickerson et al., 1996; Kemp & David, 1996; Sanz, Constable, Lopez-Ibor, Kemp, & David, 1998). Despite the inconsistencies, neuropsychological studies have clearly indicated that further investigation into the neurobiological basis of unawareness of illness in psychosis is warranted.

Neuroanatomy of Unawareness of Illness in Schizophrenia

Evidence about the neural correlates of unawareness is provided by research using both structural and functional neuroimaging. The results are described below.

STRUCTURAL NEUROIMAGING CORRELATES
The relationship between brain anatomy and unawareness of illness in patients with schizophrenia or other psychoses has received less empirical in-

FIGURE 4.3
PERFORMANCE ON NEUROPSYCHOLOGICAL TASKS
ASSESSING PARIETAL LOBE ABILITIES

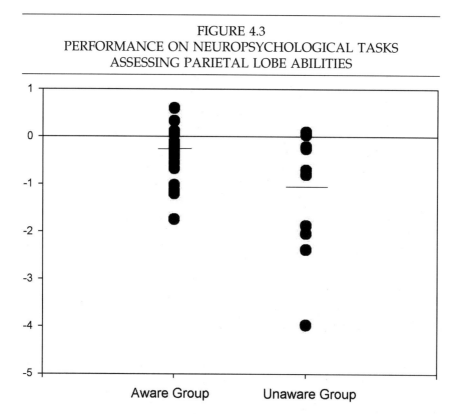

As can be seen, both groups performed significantly more poorly than healthy controls, based on normative data (z-score of 0). In addition, there was a significant group difference for the Parietal Lobe Index, t = 1.87, p < .05, with the unaware group performing significantly more poorly than the aware group. Spearman rank correlations confirmed the relationship between unawareness of symptoms and the Parietal Index (r = −0.42, p = .02).

vestigation. Takai, Uematsu, Ueki, Sone, and Kaiya (1992) measured the area of several brain structures on a midsagittal brain slice acquired using magnetic resonance imaging (MRI) in a sample of 22 male, chronic schizophrenic inpatients and outpatients using the single item which assesses insight on the Present State Examination. The authors reported that greater unawareness of illness was associated with ventricular enlargement, but not in the area of the cingulate gyrus, frontal, parietal, or occipital lobes. David and colleagues (1995) used computerized tomography scans (CT) to assess total volume of the lateral ventricles, calculated by summing area measurements for the body and frontal, anterior, and temporal horns of the lateral ventricle. The single item on the PSE was again used. Subjects were 150 inpatients whose onset of psychosis had occurred within 5 years of the scans. They were unable to replicate the finding of Takai and associates (1992); that is, no significant relationship between insight and ventricular volume was observed in this larger sample.

Laroi and colleagues (2000) examined 20 medicated inpatients and out-patients with schizophrenia using the Scale for Unawareness of Mental Disorders (SUMD), neuropsychological testing, psychiatric ratings, and CT imaging. CT scans were blindly rated by two experienced neuroradiologists for degree of ventricular enlargement and cortical atrophy using a 4-point scale, and atrophy was localized to the frontal, parietal, temporal, or occipital lobes. They reported that five patients (25%) had ventricular enlargement, while seven patients (35%) had cortical atrophy, which was predominately localized to the frontal lobes in all patients. Greater cortical atrophy correlated with less current awareness of illness, based on SUMD ratings. Morgan and colleagues (2002) classified 82 first-presentation psychosis patients as having "low" or "high" awareness of illness, awareness of symptom recognition, and total insight. Differences in grey and white matter volume between "low" and "high" insight groups were calculated. Statistically significant differences were observed in both grey and white matter in the cingulate gyrus for low insight patients; grey matter in the cingulate gyrus and a region including insula and inferior frontal lobes bilaterally for the low symptom recognition patients; and both grey and white matter in the cingulate gyrus, and grey matter in the left insula, for low total insight patients. For the low total insight group, increased grey matter adjacent (superior) to left insula and increased white matter at left insula were also noted. Stepwise linear regression analyses controlling for age, sex, diagnosis, symptoms, social class, ethnicity, IQ, height, and total tissue volume showed cingulate gyrus deficits were predictive of poorer illness awareness and poorer symptom recognition, while cingulate gyrus and left insula grey matter deficits were predictive of poorer total insight. The authors concluded that the cingulate gyrus and the insula may be part of a cortical system involved in self-appraisal of one's psychotic status.

Our group has also used MRI to investigate possible structural correlates of unawareness of illness in psychosis. In our initial study, we examined the relationship between lobar volumes and unawareness of illness in schizophrenia, using several measures of awareness from the SUMD (Flashman et al., 2000). Based on the neurologic model of anosognosia and the neuropsychological literature, we hypothesized that patients with unawareness of illness would show reduced frontal and parietal lobe volumes. Results revealed lower whole brain and bilateral frontal lobe volumes in patients with impaired awareness compared to those with intact awareness of illness. The group difference for frontal lobe volume was no longer significant, however, when intracranial volume was used as a covariate. Because global volumes of any given lobe may not be sensitive to subtle subregion differences, we subsequently measured the volume of eight frontal lobe subdivisions in patients with schizophrenia to further evaluate structural correlates of unawareness (Flashman et al., 2001). Findings indicated a significant relationship between lower SUMD awareness of symptoms (insight) and decreased bilateral middle frontal gyrus volume. In addition, significant inverse correlations were found between unawareness and the right gyrus rectus and the left anterior cingulate gyrus. Furthermore, on the SUMD Misattribution of Current Symptoms subscale (attribution) there was significant negative correlation with bilateral superior frontal gyrus volume, indicating that patients with smaller superior frontal gyri were more likely to attribute their symptoms to causes other than mental illness. These findings remained significant even when intracranial volume was used as a covariate. A dissociation between brain correlates of insight (bilateral middle frontal gyrus, right gyrus rectus, left anterior cingulate) and attribution (superior frontal gyrus) suggests that there are different neural circuits involved in various types of awareness deficits.

Rossell and associates (2003) tried to replicate the finding of a correlation between whole brain volume and impaired insight in a group of 71 male schizophrenics and 31 normal male controls. Awareness was assessed using the expanded SAI (SAI-E; Kemp & David, 1991; Sanz et al., 1998). MRI measures included calculation of whole brain volume, grey and white matter volume, and total CSF volume. Schizophrenic patients had significantly less white matter and total brain volumes than the healthy controls, but the investigators found no significant correlations between total insight scores and grey matter, white matter, CSF, or total brain volume.

In summary, structural neuroimaging studies of schizophrenia have suggested a relationship between unawareness of illness and ventricular enlargement, smaller brain size, and frontal lobe abnormalities, including the cingulate gyrus and insula. Our observation of a relationship between reduced middle and superior frontal lobe volume and greater unawareness of illness is consistent with evidence of dorsolateral prefrontal cortex involvement in schizophrenia in general (Bertolino et al., 2000; Carter et al., 1998; Goldman-Rakic & Selemon, 1997; Manoach et al., 1999; Park, Puschel, Sauter, Rentsch, & Hell, 1999), as well as with theories implicating frontal lobe circuitry dysfunction in unawareness of psychotic illness (e.g., Barr, 1998;

Frith, Blakemore, & Wolpert, 2000; Goldman-Rakic & Selemon, 1997). At the same time, these findings suggest distinct areas of involvement for different dimensions of unawareness. These results indicate that additional structural and novel functional neuroimaging studies of unawareness of psychotic illness will be fruitful in further illuminating the mechanisms of relationship between brain structures and psychotic symptoms.

FUNCTIONAL NEUROIMAGING CORRELATES
No study to date has used functional neuroimaging to evaluate the neuronal correlates of illness unawareness in schizophrenia or other psychoses. The structural neuroimaging literature suggests that functional studies focusing on frontal lobe circuitry mediated cognitive functions may be particularly informative.

HYPOTHESIZED NEUROANATOMY AND NEUROCIRCUITRY OF INSIGHT, SELF-AWARENESS, AND ATTRIBUTION
As described by Viamontes and colleagues (see Chapter 2), many brain regions have been implicated in the complex system required for intact self-awareness. These include the prefrontal and orbitofrontal cortex, right posterior parietal lobe, the amygdala, the nucleus accumbens, the ventral tegmental area, the ventral pallidum, the thalamus and hypothalamus, as well as somatosensory cortices, the brainstem nuclei, and striatum. Neurotransmitters such as dopamine, norephinephrine, glutamate, and GABA, also influence integration of self-awareness.

In considering dimensions of awareness described here, specific brain regions and pathways have been identified which appear crucial to an individual's awareness. Stuss (Stuss, 1991; Stuss & Benson, 1986) has suggested that the frontal lobes, or perhaps frontal systems, play a critical role in the maintenance of full awareness, while the knowledge of function, or conversely the knowledge of specific deficits (dimension one: insight), is associated with posterior brain functions. Patients with these disorders can have knowledge of some of their symptoms or deficits, but not others. This phenomenon contradicts the notion of a central awareness mechanism, and suggests instead that a substrate of dimension one (i.e., knowledge of deficits) may be linked to modality specific posterior (probably nondominant) brain regions; that is, lesions in specific posterior regions lead to specific primary deficits. In such a paradigm, awareness of visual deficits would involve posterior regions, probably in the visual association cortex. Based on the anosognosia associated with hemiplegia findings, awareness of contralateral motor function has been linked to the region of the inferior parietal lobule.

The response to acknowledged deficits likely involves several different brain regions. The response to deficits most closely linked to lack of awareness is anosodiaphoria. An important component of this indifference to an obvious deficit may be selective inattention or neglect. Watson, Valenstein, and Heilman (1981), for example, reported that a patient with a right medial thalamic stroke who demonstrated contralateral neglect and acknowledged his neurological deficits, including hemiparesis, but was quite unconcerned about them. The authors (Watson et al., 1981) suggested that several interconnected regions, including the midbrain reticular formation, selected thalamic nuclei, and the frontal cortex, facilitate attention and preparation of the brain for action (motor intention). Lesions in these areas may result in problems with neglect or the motor intention system, and could cause the affected individual to appear somewhat unconcerned by deficits that are obvious and significant to others. Such an individual with impairment of the motor intention system (an inability of move the upper extremity), may explain that, "I never intended to move my arm," but not acknowledge that "I cannot move my arm." The frontal lobes also may be important, because they play a role in the affective response to a given stimulus. Individuals with dorsolateral frontal injury often display muted, bland, apathetic responses to significant stimuli. This may well be associated with the anosodiaphoria, or indifference, to deficits that are seen in patients with schizophrenia.

The third dimension of awareness, the ability to appreciate the implications of a given deficit for an individual's routine functions, and to recognize the manifestations of those deficits as they are occurring (self-awareness), seems to involve self-monitoring. Stuss (Stuss, 1991; Stuss & Benson, 1986) suggested that frontal systems generate self-awareness, self-reflectiveness, and self-monitoring. Thus, frontal lobe damage can affect either or both the ability to understand the impact of deficits upon daily activities, and the ability to apply knowledge about a deficit or symptom to an immediate situation. Even when individuals affected in this manner admit to some symptoms or areas of impairment, they will often be unable to predict the implications of these deficits in current or future social situations. The man with the impaired motor intention system who cannot move his arm may not realize that as a result he will be unable to carry wood into the house for his fireplace, or understand the need to seek assistance for this routine task.

Little data is available illuminating the neuroanatomical substrate which correctly associates acknowledged deficits to mental illness. Our preliminary

results (Flashman et al., 2001), however, suggest the superior frontal gyrus
may be a factor.

CASE VIGNETTES

Below the cases of two patients with schizophrenia with varying levels of
impaired self-awareness are presented.

Case Vignette 1: RW was a 20-year-old single male with 13 years of education. Neuropsychological testing revealed a low average IQ. He scored a 67
on the Brief Psychiatric Rating Scale (range in our sample 27–67, with an
average of 48), indicating a significant level of symptom severity at the time
of the evaluation. He endorsed a significant number of negative symptoms,
scoring 13 on the Schedule for Assessment of Negative Symptoms (Andreasen, 1984). He received scores of 3 or higher (range 0–5) on items
assessing blunted affect, anhedonia, and apathy. He scored a 9 on the Schedule for Assessment of Positive Symptoms (Andreasen, 1983), endorsing primarily delusions (scored 5 on a scale of 0–5), and bizarre behavior (scored
3 on a scale of 0–5). His primary delusion focused on the notion that college
is evil. He had a past psychiatric history of two relatively brief episodes of
depression, but was doing fairly well until he started college. At that point,
he became convinced that the teachers at his college were "death warriors"
who ripped the skin off their students, and that they were trying to kill him.

On the SUMD (Amador & Strauss, 1992; Amador et al., 1993), he scored
5 (total unawareness) on the three general items, which ask whether the
subject is aware of having a mental disorder, how medication affects the
disorder, and whether the subject understands the social implications of his
illness. RW remained convinced that he did not have a psychiatric illness,
despite the fact that he had been hospitalized many times, did not work or
go to school only because teachers would find and harm him if he went out,
and not because he was committed to a state hospital, and that he felt completely normal, "other than that people want to kill me." He was able to
recognize and acknowledge that his life was not like the lives of other people, that he lived in fear, and was unable to do many things he wanted to
do. However, when asked to explain these difficulties, he vehemently stated,
"college, it's all because of college."

RW manifested poor insight, recognizing neither the presence of his severe mental illness nor many of his symptoms (delusions, bizarre behavior).
There was nevertheless, some insight into other aspects of his illness; he
recognized and acknowledged that he did not get pleasure out of life the
way he had in the past, that he had less interest and energy, that he was
not able to do as much as he had premorbidly. Self-awareness was generally

intact, in that he could recognize many (if not all) of the ways his illness was impacting on his functioning, but he showed major deficits in attribution. Even when he was able to identify limitations imposed by his illness, he could not properly attribute them to his schizophrenia, but insisted that they were the work of the conspiracy developed at his college.

Case Vignette 2: EF was a 27-year-old divorced male with 12 years of education and a low average IQ. He scored a 51 on the Brief Psychiatric Rating Scale, indicating a significant level of symptom severity at the time of the evaluation. He scored a 6 on the Schedule for Assessment of Negative Symptoms (Andreasen, 1984), with scores of only 3 or higher (range 0–5) on items assessing anhedonia. He endorsed a significant number of negative symptoms, scoring 13 on the Schedule for Assessment of Positive Symptoms (Andreasen, 1983), endorsing primarily hallucinations (3 on a scale of 0–5) and delusions (scored 3–4 on a scale of 0–5); bizarre behavior was also noted. His primary delusion involved the belief that he was under state and federal investigation, for unclear reasons. "They" had implanted a device in his ear to monitor his behavior and interfere with his life. He had no psychiatric history prior to this episode, which reportedly began after he was in an automobile accident (which he reported was not his fault) and the state police arrived to investigate.

On the SUMD (Amador & Strauss, 1992; Amador et al., 1993), he scored 5 (total unawareness) on the items assessing awareness of having a mental disorder, the effects of medication, and understanding of the social consequences. He was convinced that he did not have a mental illness, despite the fact that he had lost his job, his wife had left him, and he had been hospitalized several times. He denied that mental illness had any impact on his life.

EF manifested impaired insight and self-awareness. He denied mental illness, limitations, or symptoms related to a mental illness, and showed no understanding of how his limitations/symptoms affected his current level of functioning. Given his total lack of awareness, attribution is difficult to assess, except to note his belief that such social consequences pointed out to him (hospitalization, loss of relationship and job) were the result of a "cover-up" of the accident and the monitoring and control device implanted in his ear.

These case vignettes illustrate the extreme features of illness unawareness often seen in patients with schizophrenia. Our study also examined JR, a 28-year-old married man who falsely believed that he was a famous guitarist. He responded well to treatment with clozapine, showed a decrease in positive symptoms, and an increase in awareness about his mental illness and its consequences. When asked whether he had a mental illness, he responded that although he did not know that he was ill before he was placed on medication, he now realized he had a "chemical imbalance" which caused a mental illness that made him think things that weren't true and made him act in unusual ways. He reported that he was holding down a job in the community, living with his wife, and living a reasonably normal life, but he noted that he would have to remain on medication indefinitely to maintain his current condition. This is a striking example of the intact insight and self-awareness that is less commonly seen in this population. Further research may show us how neurophysiologic and psychologic mechanisms interact to determine why some schizophrenics are entirely aware of their condition and its implications, and others are more deeply compromised by an absence of insight into their illness.

TREATMENT
The various components of unawareness of illness, including the absence of insight, self-awareness, and attribution, often create extra impediments to treatment in schizophrenia. Patients who are unaware of their illness, symptoms, and the resulting effects upon their lives tend to cooperate poorly with treatment plans, medication regimens, or guidance from healthcare providers or concerned family members. Furthermore, patients who are unaware of the limitations imposed by their illness may try to perform impossible, unrealistic, and even dangerous activities. When they fail to achieve these goals, their already weakened self-esteem is further diminished, sometimes resulting in the complications of depression and withdrawal.

Several studies have examined awareness of illness in schizophrenia and its relationship to treatment outcome (Cuffel, Alford, Fischer, & Owen, 1996; Rossi et al., 2000; Yen, Yeh, Chen, & Chung, 2002). For example, Yen and associates (2002) used the SAI or SAI-E at baseline to assess awareness in schizophrenic outpatients in remission or considered to have minimal psychopathology; outcome was assessed at one-year follow-up. Baseline insight into treatment was associated with fewer and shorter hospitalizations and better social adjustment, but an association between baseline level of illness awareness and long-term prognosis could not be made. The authors concluded that some dimension(s) of insight may predict hospitalization and social adjustment, but the prognostic value of insight in schizophrenic patients is otherwise limited. Cuffel and colleagues (1996) found mixed support for the theory that lack of awareness limits treatment compliance and help-seeking behavior. They studied patients with schizophrenia as soon after discharge as possible, and again 6 months later. They found that at the time of hospital discharge, schizophrenic patients with higher awareness perceived a greater need for and complied more closely with treatment recommendations, but at 6-month follow-up, the association could no longer be seen.

These findings suggest that neither a prerequisite level of awareness nor awareness training is necessarily an essential component of treatment compliance or behavioral change (e.g., Sohlberg, Mateer, Penkman, Glang, & Todis, 1998). In a study examining absence of insight in traumatic brain injury patients, Herbert and Powell (1989) reported that optimism and motivation were better predictors of treatment outcome than level of insight. These results suggest that intervention strategies or treatment plans to improve the quality of life, strengthen treatment compliance, or modify aberrant behaviors can all succeed even if illness awareness is limited or lacking. Schizophrenic patients can be taught to make behavioral compensation, comply with medication regimens, or otherwise engage in treatment, even when they don't understand why or don't believe they need assistance.

On the other hand, in contrast, Rossi and colleagues (2000) reported that poor awareness of negative symptoms like blunted affect, anhedonia, and asociality was predictive of poor treatment outcome in 30 patients with schizophrenia. Insight was assessed using an abbreviated version of the SUMD, and outcome using the Strauss-Carpenter Scale (Strauss & Carpenter, 1972). Patients were divided into "poor outcome" and "good outcome" groups using the median score on the outcome scale. The findings suggest that although the presence of insight does not necessarily predict a good outcome in patients with schizophrenia, the absence of insight generally correlates with poorer outcome.

Many approaches have been tried to improve the level of illness awareness among schizophrenics, but there is little empirical evidence that any have been effective. Treatment usually includes assessment, neuropsychological evaluation, development of a therapeutic alliance, patient education, and engagement of the patient's support system. Medication has become increasingly prominent.

Assessment is useful in delineating the extent and profile of the awareness deficit, particularly when it has been unclear whether the problem is based in a knowledge deficit (dimension 1: insight), an inappropriate response to an acknowledged deficit (e.g., dimension 2: anosodiaphoria), or an inability to understand the deficit's effect upon activities of daily living (dimension 3: self-awareness). For patients who acknowledge deficits, it is important to assess whether they accurately attribute those deficits to their mental illness. This clarification process usually helps to inform the treatment process.

Neuropsychological testing can be critical in determining whether the failure of awareness is related to cognitive defects or psychological denial mechanism. The distinction is important in developing treatment plans that the patient can process and understand.

The most important element of the intervention is development of a therapeutic relationship, particularly for a group that doubts the very premise of an illness requiring treatment. The therapist must walk carefully between validation of the individual's self-worth and confirmation of delusional beliefs. There is some evidence of a positive and sustained effect of psychoeducation on insight in patients with schizophrenia (e.g., McEvoy et al., 1993).

Education and supportive therapy for significant others can also contribute to improved awareness in the affected individual. This enables the patient's family, as well as or in addition to the treatment team, to gain a better understanding of schizophrenia and the issues related to awareness. Reconceptualization of the awareness deficit as a part of the schizophrenic disease process is crucial; even staff members who routinely work with mental illness sometimes lose sight of the fact that individuals who demonstrate unawareness of illness are neither stubborn or noncompliant, but actually have neurological and neuropsychological deficits that account for their behavior. Furthermore, it is important to communicate that just because a person can verbalize some or all of his or her deficits, does not mean that this knowledge can be adequately acted on by that person. This facilitates improved coping skills, which in turn enable the providers and family to give better support to the patient. Modeling the process of gentle teaching about deficits can save a well-meaning family member from inadvertently provoking a catastrophic psychotic storm in a schizophrenic patient.

Awareness deficits can be difficult to manage even in the presence of a strong therapeutic relationship. Impairments associated with schizophrenia, especially those in the areas of cognition and social skills, are often long-standing in nature, and do not resolve with relief of psychotic symptoms. Some individuals may accept psychotropic medication or help in certain areas (e.g., job training) but remain resistant to the idea that they need help with interpersonal skills. Treatment modalities intended to improve insight in patients with schizophrenia must recognize distinctions between cognitive and psychological deficits, understand that multiple awareness deficits may be at work simultaneously, and appreciate the self-protective role that denial may hold for the patient. Therapy might target specific awareness deficits with specific treatment goals in mind, but might shift focus at different junctures in the treatment course. Patients may be engaged in psychoeducation, strategic encouragement toward awareness of symptoms or the disease itself, or application of deficit awareness to problems of daily life. Sometimes the therapist and patient can pursue a common goal (e.g., remaining out of the hospital) as the primary focus of work, without ever confronting knowledge of illness, symptoms, or disabilities.

Very little data is available about the effects of traditional neuroleptics on awareness deficits in schizophrenic patients. Pallanti, Quercioli, and Pazzagli (1999) used a crossover design to compare clozapine with older-line neuroleptics in 22 schizophrenic patients. They reported that clozapine patients showed better awareness of illness than patients treated with traditional antipsychotics. Further exploration of the atypical antipsychotics' effectiveness in ameliorating these symptoms will be required with larger study samples and clear distinctions between cognitively impaired and psychologically defensive patients. As more becomes known about the brain circuitry of deficient insight in schizophrenia, studies may be able to target particular neurotransmitter systems for augmentation or desensitization strategies.

Conclusions

The concept of unawareness is clearly multidimensional, and deficits in several distinct aspects of awareness, including insight, self-awareness, and attribution, are commonly seen in schizophrenia. There is clear evidence that unawareness is an autonomous entity, an independent construct to be individually appreciated among the various symptoms of schizophrenia. Although insight may be poorer in patients with more severe psychopathology, degree of insight does not always improve as symptoms resolve. Various aspects of illness unawareness correlate modestly with many clinical features, including positive symptoms, negative symptoms, depression, and global severity; there are also significant correlations between unawareness of illness, medication compliance, and poorer outcome in patients with schizophrenia.

The available neuropsychological and structural neuroimaging evidence suggests that unawareness of illness in schizophrenia may sometimes be associated with abnormalities of prefrontal and parietal cortices and their associated cortical and subcortical neural pathways. Impaired insight, impaired self-awareness, and difficulties with correct attribution of symptoms all appear to have independent, but related, structural neuronal correlates. Future studies examining functional correlates of these dimensions of unawareness are likely to clarify our understanding of the neural circuitry involved in unawareness.

Unawareness of illness has important negative implications for quality of life and treatment efficacy, because patients who are unaware of their illness or of the implications of their illness are far less likely to cooperate with treatment plans, medication regimens, or the guidance and protection of medical professionals and concerned family members. Patients so afflicted are likely to fail in important social relations, gainful employment, and independent living. They depend heavily upon the tenacious good will and resources of others. While there is limited evidence about the effectiveness of treatment interventions, education of the patient and family can improve compliance and understanding. Finally, new atypical antipsychotics may address this significant symptom component of the schizophrenic process.

References

Amador XF, Flaum M, Andreasen NC, et al. Awareness of illness in schizophrenia and schizoaffective and mood disorders. *Arch Gen Psychiatry.* 1994; 51:826–836.

Amador XF, Strauss DH. Poor insight in schizophrenia. *Psychiatric Q.* 1992; 64:305–318.

Amador XF, Strauss DH, Yale SA, et al. Assessment of insight in psychosis. *Am J Psychiatry.* 1993; 150:873–879.

Amador XF, Strauss DH, Yale SA, Gorman JM. Awareness of illness in schizophrenia. *Schiz Bull.* 1991; 17:113–132.

American Psychiatric Association. *Diagnostic and Statistical Manual of Mental Disorders.* 4th ed. Washington, DC: American Psychiatric Press; 1994.

Andreasen NC. *Scale for the Assessment of Positive Symptoms (SAPS).* Iowa City: University of Iowa, Dept of Psychiatry; 1983.

Andreasen NC. *Scale for the Assessment of Negative Symptoms (SANS).* Iowa City: Iowa University, Dept of Psychiatry; 1984.

Andreasen NC. Linking mind and brain in the study of mental illnesses: a project for a scientific psychopathology. *Science.* 1997; 275(5306):1586–1593.

Babinski J. Contribution a l'etude des troubles mentaux dans l'hemiplegie organique cerebrale (anosognosie). *Rev Neurol (Paris).* 1914; 27:845–848.

Barr WB. Neurobehavioral disorders of awareness and their relevance to schizophrenia. In: Amador XF, David AS, eds. *Insight and Psychosis* New York: Oxford University Press; 1998: 107–141.

Bartko G, Herczog I, Zador G. Clinical symptomatology and drug compliance in schizophrenic patients. *Acta Psychiatrica Scand.* 1988; 77:74–76.

Benson DF, Stuss DT. Frontal lobe influences on delusions: a clinical perspective. *Schiz Bull.* 1990; 16:403–411.

Bertolino A, Esposito G, Callicott JH, et al. Specific relationship between prefrontal neuronal n-acetylaspartate and activation of the working memory cortical network in schizophrenia. *Am J Psychiatry.* 2000; 157:26–33.

Birchwood M, Mason R, MacMillan F, Healy J. Depression, demoralization and control over psychotic illness: a comparison of depressed and non-depressed patients with a chronic psychosis. *Psychol Med.* 1993; 23(2):387–395.

Bisiach E, Vallar G, Perani D, Papagno C, Berti A. Unawareness of disease following lesions of the right hemisphere: anosognosia for hemiplegia and anosognosia for hemianopia. *Neuropsychologia.* 1986; 24:471–482.

Brown R, Colter N, Corsellis JA, et al. Postmortem evidence of structural brain changes in schizophrenia. *Arch Gen Psychiatry.* 1986; 43:35–42.

Buckley PF, Hasan S, Fiedman L, Cerny C. Insight and schizophrenia. *Compreh Psychiatry.* 2001; 42(1):39–41.

Carpenter WTJ, Strauss JS, Bartko JJ. Flexible system for the diagnosis of schizophrenia: report from the WHO International Pilot Study of Schizophrenia. *Science.* 1973; 182(118):1275–1278.

Carter CS, Braver TS, Barch DM, Botvinick MM, Noll D, Cohen JD. Anterior cingulate cortex, error detection, and the online monitoring of performance. *Science.* 1998; 280: 747–749.

Collins AA, Remington GJ, Coulter K, Birkett K. Insight, neurocognitive function and symptom clusters in chronic schizophrenia. *Schiz Res.* 1997; 27:37–44.

Critchley M. *The Parietal Lobes.* London: Hafner Press; 1953.

Cuesta MJ, Peralta V. Lack of insight in schizophrenia. *Schiz Bull.* 1994; 20:359–366.

Cuesta MJ, Peralta V, Caro F, deLeon J. Is poor insight in psychotic disorders associated with performance on the Wisconsin Card Sorting Test? *Am J Psychiatry.* 1995; 152: 1380–1382.

Cuesta MJ, Peralta V, Zarzuela A. Psychopathological dimensions and lack of insight in schizophrenia. *Psychol Rep.* 1998; 83(3 Pt 1):895–898.

Cuffel BJ, Alford J, Fischer EP, Owen RR. Awareness of illness in schizophrenia and outpatient treatment adherence. *J Nerv & Men Dis.* 1996; 184:653–659.

David A, Van Os J, Jones P, Harvey I, Foerster A, Fahy T. Insight and psychotic illness: cross-sectional and longitudinal associations. *Br J Psychiatry.* 1995; 167:621–628.

David AS. Insight and psychosis. *Br J Psychiatry.* 1990; 156:798–808.

David AS, Buchanan A, Reed A, et al. The assessment of insight. *Br J Psychiatry.* 1992; 161:599–602.

Dickerson FB, Boronow JJ, Ringel N, Parente F. Illness awareness in outpatients with schizophrenia. *Schiz Res.* 1996; 18(2–3):120.

Drake RJ, Haley CJ, Akhtar S, Lewis SW. Causes and consequences of duration of untreated psychosis in schizophrenia. *Br J Psychiatry.* 2000; 177:511–515.

Ellis SJ, Small M. Denial of illness in stroke. *Stroke.* 1993; 24:757–759.

Flashman LA, Amador X, McAllister TW. Lack of awareness of deficits in traumatic brain injury. *Sem Clin Neuropsychiatry.* 1998; 3(3):201–210.

Flashman LA, McAllister TW, Andreasen NC, Saykin AJ. Smaller brain size associated with unawareness in patients with schizophrenia. *Am J Psychiatry.* 2000; 157:1167–1169.

Flashman LA, McAllister TW, Johnson SC, Miller M, Crampton J, Saykin AJ. Unawareness of illness in schizophrenia: relationship to frontal and parietal lobe structure and cognitive function. *J Neuropsychiatry & Clin Neurosci.* 1997; 9:670.

Flashman LA, McAllister TW, Saykin AJ, Johnson SC, Rick JH, Green RL. Specific frontal lobe regions correlated with unawareness of illness in schizophrenia. *J Neuropsychiatry & Clin Neurosci.* 2001; 13:255–257.

Francis JL, Penn DL. The relationship between insight and social skill in persons with severe mental illness. *J Nerv & Men Dis.* 2001; 189(12): 822–829.

Frith CD. The positive and negative symptoms of schizophrenia reflect impairments in the perception and initiation of action. *Pscyholo Med.* 1987; 17:295–298.

Frith CD, Blakemore S, Wolpert DM. Explaining the symptoms of schizophrenia: abnormalities in the awareness of action. *Brain Res.—Brain Res Rev.* 2003; 31(203):357–363.

Frith CD, Done DJ. Experiences of alien control in schizophrenia reflect a disorder in the central monitoring of action. *Pscyhol Med.* 1989; 19:359–363.

Gerstmann J. Problems of imperception of disease and of impaired body territories with organic lesions. *Arch Neurol & Psychiatry.* 1942; 48:890–913.

Goldman-Rakic PS, Selemon LD. Functional and anatomical aspects of prefrontal pathology in schizophrenia. *Schiz Bull.* 1997; 23:437–458.

Goldner EM, Hsu L, Waraich P, Somers JM. Prevalence and incidence studies of schizophrenic disorders: a systematic review of the literature. *Can J Psychiatry—Rev Can de Psychiatrie.* 2002; 47(9):833–843.

Gordon WA, Brown M, Sliwinski M, et al. The enigma of "hidden" traumatic brain injury. *J Head Trauma Rehab.* 1998; 13(6):39–56.

Healton EB, Navarro C, Bressman S, Brust JC. Subcortical neglect. *Neurology.* 1982; 32:776–778.

Herbert CM, Powell GE. Insight and progress in rehabilitation. *Clin Rehab.* 1989; 3:125–130.

Kampman O, Laippala P, Vaananen J, et al. Indicators of medication compliance in first-episode psychosis. *Psychiatry Res.* 2002; 110(1):39–48.

Kasapis C. *Poor insight in Schizophrenia: Neuropsychological and Defensive Aspects.* New York, NY: New York University, Department of Psychology.

Kemp R, David A. Insight and compliance. In B. Blackwell, ed. *Treatment Compliance and the Therapeutic Alliance in Serios Mental Illness.* Amsterdam, Netherlands: Harwood Academic; 1991: 61–84.

Kemp R, David A. Psychological predictors of insight and compliance in psychotic patients. *Br J Psychiatry.* 1996; 169:444–450.

Kemp R, Lambert T. Insight in schizophrenia and its relationship to psychopathology. *Schiz Res.* 1995; 18:21–28.

Kim Y, Sakamoto K, Kamo T, et al. Insight and clinical correlates in schizophrenia. *Compreh Psychiatry.* 1997; 38:117–123.

Kovelman JA, Scheibel AB. A neurohistologic correlate of schizophrenia. *Biol Psychiatry.* 1984; 19:1601–1621.

Kozlovsky N, Belmaker RH, Agam G. GSK-3 and the neurodevelopmental hypothesis of schizophrenia. *Eur Neuropsychopharmacol.* 2002; 12(1):13–25.

Lacro JP, Dunn LB, Dolder CR, Leckbland SG, Jeste DV. Prevalence of and risk factors for mecication nonadherence in patients with schizophrenia: a comprehensive review of recent literature. *J Clin Psychiatry.* 2002; 63(10):892–909.

Lally SJ. Does being in here mean there is something wrong with me? *Schiz Bull.* 1989; 15:253–265.

Laroi F, Fannemel M, Ronneberg U, et al. Unawareness of illness in chronic schizophrenia and its relationship to structural brain measures and neuropsychological tests. *Psychiatry Res.* 2000; 100:49–58.

Lysaker P, Bell M. Insight and cognitive impairment in schizophrenia: performance on repeated administrations of the Wisconsin Card Sorting Test. *J Nerv & Men Dis.* 1994; 182(11):656–660.

Lysaker P, Bell M. Work rehabilitation and improvements in insight in schizophrenia. *J Nerv & Men Dis.* 1995; 183:103–106.

Lysaker P, Bell M. *Impaired Insight in Schizophrenia: Advances from Psychosocial Treatment Research.* Oxford, UK: Oxford University Press; 1998.

Lysaker PH, Bryson GJ, Bell MD. Insight and work performance in schizophrenia. *J Nerv & Men Dis.* 2002; 190(3):142–146.

Manoach DS, Press DZ, Thangaraj V, et al. Schizophrenic subjects activate dorsolateral prefrontal cortex during a working memory task, as measured by fMRI. *Biol Psychiatry.* 1999; 45:1128–1137.

Markova IS, Berrios GE. The assessment of insight in clinical psychiatry: a new scale. *Acta Psychiatrica Scand.* 1992; 86:159–164.

Markova IS, Berrios GE. Insight in clinical psychiatry: a new model. *J Nerv & Men Dis.* 1995; 183:743–751.

McCarley RW, Wible CG, Frumin M, et al. MRI anatomy of schizophrenia. *Biol Psychiatry.* 1999; 45(9):1099–1119.

McEvoy JP, Freter S, Everett G, et al. Insight and the clinical outcome of schizophrenics. *J Nerv & Men Dis.* 1989; 177:48–51.

McEvoy JP, Freter S, Merritt M, Apperson LJ. Insight about psychosis among outpatients with schizophrenia. *Hosp & Commun Psychiatry.* 1993; 44:883–884.

McEvoy JP, Hartman M, Gottlieb D, Godwin S, Apperson LJ, Wilson W. Common sense, insight, and neuropsychological test performance in schizophrenia patients. *Schiz Bull.* 1996; 22:635–641.

McGlashan T. Does attitude toward psychosis related to outcome? *Am J Psychiatry.* 1981; 138:797–801.

McGlashan TH, Carpenter WTJ. Postpsychotic depression in schizophrenia. *Arch Gen Psychiatry.* 1976; 33:231–239.

McGlashan TH, Levy ST, Carpenter WTJ. Integration and sealing over: clinically distinct recovery styles from schizophrenia. *Arch Gen Psychiatry.* 1975; 32(10):1269–1272.

Mechanic D, McAlpine D, Rosenfield S, Davis D. Effects of illness attribution and depression on the quality of life among persons with serious mental illness. *Soc Sci & Med.* 1994; 39:155–164.

Mintz AR, Dobson KS, Romney DM. Insight in schizophrenia: a meta-analysis. *Schiz Res.* 61:75–88.

Mohamed S, Fleming S, Penn DL, Spaulding W. Insight in schizophrenia: its relationship to measures of executive functions. *J Nerv & Men Dis.* 1999; 187(9):525–531.

Morgan KD, Dazzan P, Suckling J, et al. Neuroanatomic correlates of poor insight: the aesop first-onset psychosis study. Paper presented at: Biennial Winter Workshop on Schizophrenia; Jan. 2002; Davos, Switzerland.

Nelson EA. *"Poor Insight" as a Manifestation of Psychological Defensiveness in Schizophrenia.* Paper presented at New York University, Department of Psychology, New York; 1997.

Nelson MD, Saykin AJ, Flashman LA, Riordan HJ. Hippocampal volume reduction in schizophrenia as assessed by magnetic resonance imaging: a meta-analytic study. *Arch Gen Psychiatry.* 1998; 55:433–440.

Novak-Grubic V, Tavcar R. Predictors of noncompliance in males with first-episode schizophrenia, schizophreniform and schizoaffective disorder. *Eur Psychiatry: J Asso Eur Psychiatrists.* 2002; 17(3):148–154.

Pallanti S, Quercioli L, Pazzagli A. Effects of clozapine on awareness of illness and cognition in schizophrenia. *Psychiatry Res.* 1999; 86(3):239–249.

Park S, Puschel J, Sauter BH, Rentsch M, Hell D. Spatial working memory deficits and clinical symptoms in schizophrenia: a 4-month follow-up study. *Biol Psychiatry.* 46: 392–400.

Pini S, Cassano GB, Dell'Osso L, Amador XF. Insight into illness in schizophrenia, schizoaffective disorder, and mood disorders with psychotic features. *Am J Psychiatry.* 2001; 158:122–125.

Rossell SL, Coakes J, Shapleske J, Woodruff PWR, David AS. Insight: its relationship with cognitive function, brain volume, and symptoms in schizophrenia. *Psychol Med.* 2003; 33:111–119.

Rossi A, Arduini L, Prosperini P, Kalyvoka A, Stratta P, Daneluzzo E. Awareness of illness and outcome in schizophrenia. *Eur Arch Psychiatry & Clin Neurosci.* 2000; 250:73–75.

Sanz M, Constable G, Lopez-Ibor I, Kemp R, David A. A comparative study of insight scales and their relationship to psychopathological and clinical variables. *Psychol Med.* 1998; 28:437–446.

Sawa A, Snyder SH. Schizophrenia: diverse approaches to a complex disease. *Science.* 2002; 296(5568):692–695.

Schwartz RC. Symptomatology and insight in schizophrenia. *Psychol Rep.* 1998; 82: 227–233.

Shenton ME, Dickey CC, Frumin M, McCarley RW. A review of MRI findings in schizophrenia. *Schiz Res.* 2001; 49(1–2):1–52.

Smith CM, Barzman D, Pristach CA. Effect of patient and family insight on compliance of schizophrenia patients. *J Clin Pharmacology.* 1997; 37:147–154.

Smith TE, Hull JW, Israel LM, Willson DF. Insight, symptoms, and neurocognition in schizophrenia and schizoaffective disorder. *Schiz Bull.* 2000; 6(1):193–200.

Smith TE, Hull JW, Santos L. The relationship between symptoms and insight in schizophrenia: a longitudinal perspective. *Schiz Res.* 1998; 33:63–67.

Sohlberg MM, Mateer C, Penkman L, Glang A, Todis B. Awareness intervention: who needs it? *J Head Trauma Rehab.* 1998; 13(5):62–78.

Strauss JS, Carpenter WTJ. The prediction of outcome in schizophrenia, I: characteristics of outcome. *Arch Gen Psychiatry.* 1972; 27:739–746.

Stuss DT. Disturbance of self-awareness after frontal system damage. In Prigatano GP, Schacter DL, eds. *Awareness of Deficit after Brain Injury.* New York: Oxford University Press; 1991: 63–83.

Stuss DT, Benson DF. *The Frontal Lobes.* New York: Raven Press.

Takai A, Uematsu M, Ueki H, Sone K, Kaiya H. Insight and its related factors in chronic schizophrenic patients: a preliminary study. *Eur J Psychiatry.* 1992; 6:159–170.

Warner R, Taylor D, Powers M, Hyman J. Acceptance of the mental illness label by psychotic patients: effects on functioning. *Am J Orthopsychiatry.* 1989; 59:398–409.

Watson RT, Heilman KM. Thalamic neglect. *Neurology.* 1979; 29:690–694.

Watson RT, Valenstein E, Heilman KM. Thalamic neglect: possible role of the medial thalamus and nucleus reticularis in behavior. *Arch Neurology.* 1981; 38:501–506.

Weinstein EA, Kahn RL. *Denial of Illness. Symbolic and Physiological Aspects.* Springfield, Ill: Charles C. Thomas Press, 1955.

White R, Bebbington P, Pearson J, Johnson S, Ellis D. The social context of insight in schizophrenia. *Soc Psychiatry & Psychiatric Epidemi.* 2000; 35:500–507.

Yen CF, Yeh ML, Chen CS, Chung HH. Predictive value of insight for suicide, violence, hospitalization, and social adjustment for outpatients with schizophrenia: a prospective study. *Compreh Psychiatry.* 2002; 43(6):443–447.

Young D, Zakzanis KK, Bailey C, et al. Further parameters of insight and neuropsychological deficit in schizophrenia and other chronic mental disease. *J Nerv & Men Dis.* 1998; 186:44–50.

Young DA, Davila R, Scher H. Unawareness of illness and neuropsychological performance in chronic schizophrenia. *Schiz Res.* 1993; 10:117–124.

Zingerle H. Ueber Stoerungen der Wahrnehmung des eigenen Koerpers bei organischen Gehirnerkrankungen. *Monatsschr Psychiatr Neurol.* 1913; 34:13–36.

5

Knowing Me, Knowing You

Self-Awareness in Asperger's and Autism

Jyotsna Nair

IT IS UNCERTAIN whether the incidence of autism is increasing in the United States, but psychiatrists and general practitioners throughout the country report seeing increasing numbers of autistic children in their practices.

In 1979, Wing and Gould drew attention to the triad of deficits found in autism: socialization, communication, and imagination. Kanner (1943) and Asperger (1944) independently described autism in research done on two different continents. Kanner described autistic aloneness, an obsessive insistence on sameness, and absence of emotional contact with others. The children showed limited facial expression and did not focus their gaze on objects. Wing and Gould (1979) rekindled interest in autism with their triad of deficits.

They reported the incidence of autism at 1 to 2 per 1000 live births, or 1 per 2000 using more restrictive criteria. Less restrictive criteria utilizing the triad of communication, socialization, and imagination deficits would raise the incidence rate to 1 in 500 live births. Asperger's syndrome, a similar condition, is not marked by the significant delays in language, cognitive, and adaptive skills observed in classical autism.

Boys outnumber girls by 4 or 5:1 among the higher functioning autistics and by 2:1 in the most seriously affected group. Approximately two thirds of the children with autism have IQ scores of 70 or less, and about 40% have an IQ of 50 or less. Five to 30% of autistic children have normal or above average IQ (Mitchell, 1997).

159

Kanner and Eisenberg (1956) reported that the parents of the Asperger's syndrome children in their sample also showed evidence of psychiatric disturbance. Fathers had social problems, lacked imagination, and had strange interests. This would reflect a genetic clustering, but Kanner interpreted it to mean that "refrigerator parenting" affected the children's behavior. Kanner's hypothesis was not supported by later research.

Piven and Folstein (1994) reviewed the genetic evidence and found that siblings had a 3% concordance while twins had a concordance varying from 30% to 80%. If it was purely genetic concordance would be close to 100% thus it was concluded that both genetic and environmental factors played a role in autism. About 30% of autistic children's parents showed deficits in such basic social skills as turn taking in conversation, missing the intent of the conversation, and not picking up social cues.

Autism is an inherited, biologically based disorder with a spectrum of presentations, ranging from fairly high function to extreme impairment. Autistic children have restricted pretend play, reflecting their limited imagination. In both autism and Asperger's, children show such profound difficulty interacting with others that the symptoms suggest deficits more deeply seated than a mere misunderstanding of the social norms.

Self-Awareness and Autism

Kanner (1973) observed that autistic children have impaired self-awareness; that is, the ability to maintain a stable concept of self over time, adapt it to different settings by mental manipulations and make inferences affecting future behavior. Most of the process is automatic and occurs at a subconscious level. We see individuals in various circumstances and react to cues we receive from them. We receive data, process it, respond to it, and the other person does likewise. If people repeatedly tell a child that he cannot read, for example, then the child will begin to believe that he cannot read, even if he can. This child has received, processed, and adjusted his sense of self to environmental cues regardless of their accuracy.

Command of some specific concepts and abilities are essential to one's sense of self-awareness. First among these is, of course, the sense of self (I or me), a sense of others (you), and an understanding that *you* are different from *me*. There is an implicit knowledge that I can think, and those thoughts are mine. There is also an understanding that you can think, that your thoughts are different from mine, and that we can communicate an exchange of ideas to one another using language. An individual's self-awareness pro-

motes his awareness of others and enables him to adjust certain of this behaviors to meet the expectations of others.

To know myself, know you, and to develop self-awareness, I require a
theory of another's mind. A theory of mind is an understanding that each
one of us has a mental state, and that these states can differ from one another. Early researchers in autism worked on the premise that autistic children lacked a theory of mind. More recent investigators have modified that
belief to propose only that the autistic's theory of mind is different from
that of nonautistic individuals.

Another way to conceptualize self-awareness is to consider the following
three questions: What do I think of myself? What do I think of you? And
what do I think, you think of me? The questions suggest that there is a me
to know, a you to know, and that something of our identities resides in the
consciousness of others. As we discuss the various aspects of autism and
Asperger's, we will be returning to these three concepts to evaluate the manner in which self-awareness is affected by the two conditions.

Case Example: Harry

I have created a composite model out of the autism and Asperger's patients I have seen. Harry is the result. Harry will guide us through the chapter by providing a picture of what a therapist is likely to encounter in the
clinic. We will discuss clinical, developmental, and neurological components
of the observed impairment in self-awareness characteristics of autism, and
consider their treatment implications.

Harry is an extremely intelligent 12-year-old, who has been an enigma
to his parents. They noticed that Harry was different from the other children
they knew. At first, it was small things, like his habit of turning his plastic
lawnmower over and gazing at the wheel as he spun it with his hands. He
loved to watch the ceiling fan as it went round and round. He could read
at an early age of 3, but he could not understand what he read.

Over time he developed a persistent interest in planes, and could recite
technical details about them without consulting any sources. It started with
building model planes and collecting the details. His room had posters of
planes, and a collection of model airplanes. His shelf was full of books on
aviation, and he could discuss the topic at great length.

Harry's conversations about airplanes sound like a lecture. He seems unaffected when the listener shows signs of disinterest in the topic. He is
oblivious to the other person's fidgeting, attempts to get up, or to change

the subject. He does not read these cues, and continues even if interrupted. His conversation is essentially a monologue, and he does not offer the customary pauses and cues to give his listener a chance to speak.

Despite good command of the language, Harry is unable to use it to communicate and achieve a meeting of minds. He does not take turns in a conversation, and there is no exchange of ideas. There is a flow of ideas from Harry to the person being addressed—until he is interrupted.

Harry's big dream is to run a private airport of his own, but he worries that he may not get the opportunity. He plans to earn $4 billion so that he can afford to build and run this airport. Simply working in an airport will not satisfy his ambition. He knows detailed plans of existing major airports in the country from travel books (he has not actually seen an airport yet!) and can describe them.

His parents have made many attempts to keep Harry connected with other children his age and help him make friends. They have kept him active in Cub Scouts from an early age, but other members of his group tend to leave him alone. His dad described one of Harry's characteristic encounters with the other children. A child who was "rather kind" made overtures to Harry, listening patiently when Harry talked incessantly about airplanes. At the next group meeting, Harry ran to the boy, hugged him very tightly, and squeezed him. From then on the child kept his distance from Harry and would not approach him again.

Harry expressed how this experience hurt his feelings. When it was explained to him that his tight hugging made others uncomfortable, he did not understand. In his mind the child was his friend and you hug friends. He was unable to look at the situation from the perspective of the other child.

Harry experiences similar social difficulties every day, and they extend from his scout troop to home and school. He is not invited to any birthdays and after school activities, and he is aware of that.

Harry thinks of his model collection as just *planes*. He will line them up, describe them, but never gives them personalities of their own. He does not pretend that. They take him to imaginary exotic places, rather, they retain their concrete form as models. He lacks the ability to imagine and pretend as he plays.

Harry has demonstrated all three of the classic Asperger's syndrome deficits in communication, imagination, and socialization. His *DSM IV-TR* diagnosis of Asperger's syndrome is included among the autism spectrum disorders (American Psychiatric Association, 2000).

Sense of Self and Others, Autism and Self-Awareness (Developmental Perspectives)

The first step self-awareness is a sense of self in relation to others. This is a gradually evolving process that develops throughout our lives. In this section, the process of development of self and others from infancy onwards will be described, with Harry's assistance.

Harry Continued

Harry's parents recall him as a rather cute and good-looking baby. They were constantly complimented on how quiet and well behaved he was. He was fairly easy to care for, and did not cry much. This was their first child and neither had much prior experience with children. When they took him to a playgroup, Harry's parents realized that other children looked at their mothers and fathers, but Harry showed no such interest in them. Harry did not interact like the other children.

As Harry grew older, his limited interactions became more pronounced, and he would not approach others. He seemed to be on his own island and functioned without taking into account how others reacted.

The following section describes the differences in the normal and autistic child's sense of self and others.

Development of Sense of Self and Others

The theory of mind is the ability to understand that we have an individual psychological state and that others have mental states different from our own. Infants and babies make tremendous mental progress in understanding themselves in their environment. Most children develop this concept gradually over time, but the timeline of children with autism and Asperger's syndrome is much slower, persisting through adulthood as social deficits in understanding others and themselves.

Significant differences are noted in joint attention, reading parental expression, pretend play, mirror self-recognition, tracking the gaze of others, declarative and imperative pointing, and false belief tasks. Most theory of mind research has studied higher functioning autistic or Asperger's children, using developmentally delayed but age and intelligence matched controls.

INFANCY

The gradual development of a sense of self and others begins in infancy. Infants are hard-wired to pay attention to human faces, and will imitate adult facial gestures (Meltzoff & Moore, 1983). Infants attend to faces preferentially, or like to look at complex, high-contrast stimuli like faces (Johnson & Morton, 1991). Imitation is so important to babies that they get distressed if they cannot imitate the gesture they see, and their eyes brighten when they succeed. They will also attempt gestures that are difficult, like protruding the tongue to the side of the mouth (Meltzoff & Moore, 1997). As infants grow, they actively gather information about themselves and others, and differences can be observed between autistic, developmentally delayed, and normally developing children.

NINE MONTHS TO EIGHTEEN MONTHS

By the age of 9 months, most children point to indicate their needs. A child sitting on the rug points to a colorful toy that is out of reach while checking to see if the adult has noticed the gesture. This is *imperative pointing*, and means that the child wants the object. Children will also point in the direction they want to go while being carried, another manifestation of imperative pointing.

Declarative pointing describes a child's pointing to an object of interest to show it to another person, such as when a child in a stroller points to direct the parent's attention to a puppy playing in a yard. Children with autism show imperative pointing but rarely use declarative pointing, suggesting diminished interest in sharing attention (Baron-Cohen, 1989b).

By 9 months of age, children will follow the pointing finger when asked to look at an object, *sharing* attention and interest with another person as they both look at the same thing. This ability is called *joint attention*. Autistic children have difficulty with joint attention, with sharing their gaze with another (Mundy & Sigman, 1989). They seem disinterested in what others are looking at.

Nine-month-old babies are surprisingly sophisticated in reading and responding to the facial expressions of adults. If an adult has made an unpleasant facial expression upon opening a box, the baby will be reluctant to open the box. The child will play with the box, handle it, but not open it. No such inhibitions are seen if the baby is given a box toward which an adult has made a happy face. Clues are already being found and interpreted in facial expressions, and the babies are on their way to becoming mind readers (Repacholi, 1998).

Continuing to develop their understanding of what others are thinking, 1-year-old babies will check a caregiver's expression to determine whether it is safe to move forward when crossing a visual cliff. If the parent seems fearful, then the child will not advance but is more likely to do so if the parent smiles and encourages him or her. At this young age, the child is already seeking and reacting to the emotional information in the caregiver's expression (Sorce, Emde, Campos, Klinert, 1985).

Thus, in the first year itself the baby has acquired skills to learn about itself and others. These are key steps in the processes of character development and socialization.

EIGHTEEN MONTHS

At 18 months, the child is building on earlier gains. The baby is participating in imaginative pretend play and the first stages of teasing. At this age, babies have also taken a first major step toward self-recognition and self-awareness by becoming able to recognize their own image in the mirror. Mirror self-recognition was one of the early dramatic experiments that demonstrated self-awareness in the baby.

Most children pay attention to mirrors as they grow. Nine-month-old babies look at the mirror and try to peer behind it to find the child that they see, not comprehending that the image is their own. Eighteen-month-old babies know it is their image, and make faces in the mirror. Investigators have covertly placed a harmless mark on the infants' faces and observed them as they looked at mirrors, touching the spot on their faces rather than on the mirror to demonstrate their understanding of the image concept. Autistic children of the same age do not recognize their image in the mirror, but do so at a later age. One study observed autistic children above the age of 5 consistently recognizing themselves in the mirror and showing curiosity about the covert mark made on their faces (Dawson & McKissick, 1984).

Eighteen-month-old normal children show early signs of empathic development, a capacity to appreciate another person's different experience. Most toddlers offered a choice between broccoli and goldfish cheddar crackers, prefer goldfish. The examiner would then taste both items while the children watched. He would either match the children by indicating a preference for goldfish, or mismatch them by saying he liked broccoli better. When the child was asked by the examiner to give him more, the child always offered the item for which the examiner had expressed a preference (Repacholi & Gopnik, 1997). Thus, at this early age the understanding that others may have different preferences could be seen. The seeds of empathy were there.

Children of this age love to imitate, and will do so readily. Children with autism are able to determine object permanence like their nonautistic peers, but do not imitate as well. Investigators have found a correlation between imitative behavior and demonstrated empathy in autistic toddlers. The better able an autistic child was to imitate the more likely he was to demonstrate more empathy (Dawson, Metzloff, Osterling, & Renaldi, 1998).

By the end of 18 months, the baby has a concept of me (mirror self-recognition), a concept of you (empathy, checking gaze, joint attention, reading adult facial expression and acting on it), but has not yet formulated the question, What do you think of me? Autistic children do not demonstrate any of these at this chronological age, and will only understand some of these concepts when they are older.

THREE TO FOUR YEARS

At 3 years of age, there is more information available to the child. The simple concept has developed that one must look in a box to know its contents. This idea is crucial to the understanding of self and others. By now the child knows that touching the box does not tell you what is in there and that to gain such information you have to look in the box. Autistic children are still lacking this concept at age 3 (Baron-Cohen & Goodhart, 1994; Pratt & Bryant, 1990).

Pretend games and the simple understanding of jokes have developed. They are looking at clues in speech and communication that lie beneath the surface of what is being said. If mother said that she liked to eat little children and she would eat them, then the 3-year-old would infer from mom's prior behavior that this was a joke or game (Baron-Cohen, 1997). Autistic children miss this second level of communication and interpret things only in literal terms.

At age 3 the child knows that the brain is used to think, dream, and imagine. A child of this age does not yet associate such functions as speech and movement with the brain; these are exclusively the actions of the mouth and the legs. Autistic children are less able to associate thinking and other mental functions with the brain, and their thought processes are more concrete than their normal age cohorts (Baron-Cohen, 1989).

Unlike other children with developmental delays and not autism, most autistic children at age 4 have difficulty with the dual reality and appearance. An apple made of wax is either a candle or an apple, but not both to autistic 4 year olds. On the other hand, most 3- or 4-year-olds know they cannot pet a dog they are only thinking about, and that the brain has both mental and physical functions (Wellman & Estes, 1986). They are very clear in differentiating a raisin in the tummy from a raisin in the brain. The first one is real and the other one is imagined (Watson, Gelman, & Wellman, 1998).

Four-year-old children can understand that people may have incorrect ideas based on obsolete information: false belief. Three-year-olds do not make this connection. A well-known study presented children with a candy carton and asked what each child thought was in the box. The children say "candy." When the box is opened it reveals pencils. When the child is asked again what he or she thought was in the box the first time, a 3-year-old will say "pencils" and a 4-year-old will say "candy." There is a leap in the reasoning ability in this age. A 4-year-old can recall that he or she had a mistaken belief about the contents, and the 3-year-old cannot make that connection. Autistic children, even those of mental age and verbal ability older than a 4-year-old, will continue to say "candy" and will develop the ability to recognize the mistaken belief only at a much later age (Perner, Frith, Leslie, & Leekam, 1989). Here the 4-year-old is remembering his or her mental state prior to the new knowledge about the contents of the box. The same concept can be reframed around drawing conclusions about the mental state of another person with a mistaken belief.

By the end of the fourth year the imagination has developed, as has the ability to attribute mental states to others. Normal children have gained a knowledge of themselves (brain helps you think, awareness of one's own mental state earlier in the false belief task); have learned a lot about you (mental state of others in false belief, understand jokes, appearance, and reality), but still don't show much evidence of concern for *what you think of me*. Autistic children still demonstrate delays and deficits in learning about both themselves and others.

FOUR TO SIX YEARS
By the age of 4 children know that they have intentions or reasons for why they act the way they do. If they cannot reach an apple on a tree, they may try to aim at it with a stone and try to knock it down. If the stone misses its mark and hits one of their friends, they are quite clear that their intention was not to hit the friend but to get the apple. One study instructed children to hit a target in a video machine. The result was manipulated in such a way that they hit a different target. Nonautistic children said that they missed the intended target, while autistic children of the same age said the wrong target was the one they originally intended to hit. Knowing the reason behind one's actions is an important part of knowing me (Philips, Baron-Cohen, & Rutter, 1998).

Most 4- to 6-year-olds can describe fairly complex reasons to explain their feelings. The explanation could be that they are happy because they got what they wanted or they are excited because they won a game (Harris, Johnson, Hutton, Andrews, & Cooke, 1989). Children with autism, on the other hand, have difficulty with complex emotions like surprise but can identify simple emotions like happy, sad, and angry (Baron-Cohen, Spitz, & Cross, 1993).

Baron-Cohen and Cross (1992) showed that 4-year-old children could guess what a person was thinking by observing the direction of their gaze (i.e., if they were looking to the left or right, or upwards with no object in sight). Autistic children have difficulty understanding the concept and attending to the eyes (Baron-Cohen, Campbell, Karmiloff-Smith, & Grant, 1995). Nonautistic children start paying attention to the direction of other people's gaze from the time they are quite young, and learn about expressions and their relevance.

At age 6, the child has made further gains and understands itself (knows intentions, explains feelings) and others (can read the expression of others), though we do not know whether they have yet constructed the concept of *what you think of me* and can act on it. Autistic children still lag in the development of self (intention and complex emotion recognition) and others (do not read expressions of others and do not attend to gaze).

ADULTS

High-functioning adults with autism continue to have problems picking up social cues. Autism and Asperger's syndrome are more frequent in the families of engineers, mathematicians, and physicists. A more than sixfold occurrence of autism was reported in the families of students who majored in the physics, math, and engineering group as compared to students of literature (Baron-Cohen et al., 1998). Fathers and grandfathers of children with autism and Asperger's syndrome were twice as likely to work with computers or be in engineering as compared to the control group. Almost 29% had fathers or grandfathers in engineering (Baron-Cohen, Wheelwright, & Scott, 1997).

Adults (18–21-year-old college students) were able to read an individual's basic expression and guess the person's current feeling state by looking at a picture of the full face. When complex emotions were to be judged, then a picture of the eyes alone was just as good as the whole face (Baron-Cohen et al., 1996; Baron-Cohen, Wheelwright, & Jolliffe, 1997). The results of these studies contrast sharply with those seen by the same investigators in similar studies of high-achieving academicians in math, physics, or computer science with a diagnosis of high functioning autism or Asperger's syndrome. These subjects had significant difficulty in recognizing the expression of the person from the eyes alone (Baron-Cohen et al., 1999; Baron-Cohen, Wheelwright, & Jolliffe, 1997). The experiment was performed using pictures of actors portraying the basic emotions of happiness, sadness, and anger, followed by the more complex emotions like scheming, admiration, interest, and thoughtfulness. Adults were to judge the emotion from two forced choices, looking at the face, mouth, or the eyes. Eyes alone yielded the same level of accuracy as the face for the control group in both complex and simple emotions, but individuals with Asperger's did poorly when they were asked to infer the emotion from pictures of the eyes alone. The Asperger's group showed improvement when assessing basic emotions from pictures of the full face, and may have used the other features of the face to do so. Complex emotional recognition was also difficult for this group. Interestingly, parents of Asperger's children also did poorly on this task, but had more success when they had to look for embedded figures (Baron-Cohen & Hammer, 1997).

In summary, there are clear developmental differences in social behavior that persist into adulthood. An inability to read the facial expression of others does constitute a clear social deficit. Adults with Asperger's tend to be isolative, work alone, and stay unconnected, even if they are in a group.

"Knowing Me, Knowing You" and the Sense of Self and Others

Regarding the question of *what I think of me*, children with autism and Asperger's syndrome differ from normal children in how they develop a sense of self. Intellectual processes like mirror self-recognition, ability to reason, and understanding of one's own false beliefs and intentions are delayed. More complex false belief tasks are never achieved in adulthood.

The Asperger's and autistic children also show deficits in associating themselves with others, as characterized by the phrase, *what I think of you*. Gaze monitoring, identifying another person's false belief, and reading others' expressions are all negatively affected in individuals with autism and Asperger's syndrome.

The last question of our triad is, *What I think, you think of me*. It necessarily draws from the first two impaired concepts, knowing me and knowing you. We might reasonably expect impairment here also.

Development of Language, Autism, and Self-Awareness

Language development and the presence of language is a key to self-awareness. Animals that do not possess language are unable to convert their experiences into thoughts and free themselves from the present. Thoughts liberate us from the constraints of immediate experience and enable us to navigate time in our imagination.

Language also plays a role in how we understand and interpret the world around us. If our vocabulary did not have words referring to mental states, then we could not think and express those terms and concepts. In studies conducted in a non-Western culture where a particular language lacked psychological terminology, children could not demonstrate any concept of another person's mind (Vinden, 1996). This suggests that the understanding of other minds and self-awareness may not be universal.

Interestingly, deaf children raised by hearing parents have shown deficits similar to those seen in autistic children in studies of imagination and theory of mind. This may be associated with lack of exposure to mental state conversations early in life, because the same deficits are not seen in deaf children raised by parents who are fluent signers (Gale, deVilliers, deVilliers, & Pyers, 1996; Petersen & Siegal, 1995, 1997). Language delays are a common feature in autism, and play a role in the social and self-awareness deficits observed in the condition.

Harry Continued

Harry came to the clinic to see his psychiatrist. His parents had reported concerns with his behavior in school and his ability to make friends. They thought he was not adjusting well, and that the environment might be difficult for him. Harry, on the other hand, said that he was adjusting better in school. He had begun fourth grade, and said he had a lot of problems in the beginning.

His parents had initially home schooled Harry, recognizing some of his difficulties with learning. By third grade, his mother felt that she could not handle his rigid behavior and that the school setting might help him develop more flexibility. Harry told the therapist that he was making more friends, but his parents disagreed.

Harry admitted he could not understand when the other children in his class and his teacher would suddenly burst out laughing. One day, they had Joke Hour in his class. He mentioned a story that was told in class, and reported he was the only one who did not laugh. The story was about three friends who were marooned on an island and found a lamp.

The lamp had a genie in it. The genie gave them three wishes. The first person asked to go home with a million dollars, and went. The second one wanted a million dollars, a million dollar house, and to go home. His wish was granted. The third person thought for sometime and then said he was getting lonely and wished that they would come back. The whole class laughed, but he just looked at them and did not understand what happened.

Autistic children's verbal communication is limited to labeling and expressing actions; they do not talk about mental states, or their intentions when taking actions. Their conversation is concrete. They commonly make pronoun reversal errors (Tager-Flusberg, 1996) indicating confusion in assigning identity roles.

Autistic children have difficulty with more complex configurations of language, like irony or sarcasm. They take the meaning of statements literally, and do not understand jokes. Ordinary language is processed at the level of content and the underlying intent of the speaker. Autistic children can understand the content adequately, but not the intent, particularly if it is inconsistent with literal content, as in jokes, irony, and sarcasm (Baron-Cohen, 1997). The better language development is in autism the better overall functional outcome in the future.

"KNOWING ME, KNOWING YOU" AND LANGUAGE
Language is a vehicle with which to develop a concept of self. Autistic children reverse the pronouns *you* and *me*, reflecting their limited sense of self and the boundaries between individuals. They also have trouble *knowing you*, missing the second level of conversation and focusing on the surface only. The concept of "knowing what you think of me" is limited by the difficulty in conceptualizing self and others.

Content of Thought, Autism, and Self-Awareness

There are significant differences between the thought content of autism/Asperger's children and that of normals.

Harry Continued

Harry's parents could not understand why he had so much difficulty in school. They thought he was a very bright child, and cited an example of how they had gone to see a relative after they had not visited in 4 years and had lost their way. Harry had rescued them by remembering exactly the right turns to take, as though he had a picture of the roads in his head and was looking at it and giving directions. The parents boasted that they never took maps when Harry rode with them—he was so good at directions.

Adults with Asperger's think in visual terms and describe their inner thoughts as pictures in their heads. They report perception and action as their only inner experience, with no reference to thought, emotion, or inner speech. In contrast, control adults report a complex mixture of inner speech, emotional reaction, mental images, and "pure thought." Autistic individuals think primarily in visual terms (Hulbert, Happe, & Frith, 1994)

In *Thinking in Pictures: And Other Reports From My Life with Autism* (1995), Temple Grandin, a high-functioning autistic adult, described her ability to visualize equipment that she may have encountered, and to modify it to fit immediate needs. She wrote: "I think in pictures. Words are like a second language to me. I translate both spoken and written words to full-color movies, complete with sound, which run like a VCR tape in my head. When someone speaks to me, his words are instantly translated into pictures" (1995, p. 19).

Based on evidence that autistic individuals are visual thinkers, investigators studied whether autistic children could process tasks requiring them to imagine someone else's mental state if pictures were used. High-functioning autistic children could perform the false belief tasks using comic striplike illustrations depicting thoughts (McGregor, Whiten, & Blackburn, 1998) in bubbles above an individual's head.

Autistic individuals think in parts rather than wholes. They are superior to controls in finding Waldo, performing embedded figure tasks, and block design subtests. They do not look at the design as a whole, but at parts of the whole, and are able to put it together. They are also good at putting together puzzles, looking at the shape of the pieces instead of the pattern or picture. Autistics are also better at remembering a series of unrelated words. They do not need a central theme to assist recall as nonautistic individuals do. They have been described as having a weak central coherence (Shah & Frith, 1993). However, the ability of individuals with autism and Asperger's syndrome to think visually and in parts rather than whole units may represent a unique strength.

"KNOWING ME, KNOWING YOU" AND CONTENT OF THOUGHT
Interventions based on visual thought patterns have been utilized to strengthen the sense of self in autistic/Asperger's patients. The assumption

has been that the sense of self and others is strongly visual as well and that pictures and pictoral representations would help promote and understanding that other people have thoughts and feelings.

Harry Continued

Harry continued to have social difficulties in school. He frequently reacted without understanding a situation. Harry enjoyed some repetitive games, and liked to play with others as long as they followed his lead. If the other children refused to play then there was conflict.

The school used a Polaroid camera to record the conflict situations, and used the pictures to help Harry understand how he could modify his behavior to reduce conflict. This technique was much more successful than his regular meetings with the counselor to discuss his role in promoting conflict.

Neuroanatomy, Imaging, Autism, and Self-Awareness

Autism is a biologically based disorder involving many areas of the brain. Histological, imaging, and animal studies have all provided evidence of abnormal function in the condition.

Harry Continued

Harry's parents experienced a great deal of guilt when they recognized that Harry was very different from the other children they met. They wondered if they had somehow caused him to be this way, if their parenting style had been wrong, and if they should have sought help sooner or paid more attention to his diet, and so on. They were reassured that the condition was biologically based and not associated with errors in parenting techniques.

NEUROANATOMY

There are few postmortem brain studies in this group because autistic children and young autistic adults rarely die in sudden catastrophic events. One such study described here used matched control brains. Many brain abnormalities were noted. There was increased cell packing density in the hippocampus, a slightly smaller mamillary body, medial septal nucleus, and atrophy of the neocerebellar cortex with a loss of Purkinje cells. Central, medial, and cortical nuclei of the amygdala were also involved. These findings are characteristic of an immature brain (Bauman & Kemper, 1985).

NEUROIMAGING STUDIES AND INJURY REPORTS
Neuroimaging studies have suggested deficits in several areas of the brain associated with autism. There is comparative information from patients with brain injuries, strokes, and psychosurgery. Evidence has pointed toward abnormalities or involvement of orbitofrontal cortex, left medial frontal cortex, amygdala, and cerebellum.

ORBITOFRONTAL CORTEX
Changes in the orbitofrontal cortex have been implicated in autism. Damage to the orbitofrontal and ventromedial cortex leads to changes in social behavior, such as inappropriate verbalizations, poor choices in personal relationships, and difficulty in conversation (Saver & Damasio, 1991). When the orbitofrontal lobe is damaged, the affected individual tends not to monitor whether a listener is interested in a conversation or not. He or she is insensitive to social cues (Alexander, Benson, & Stuss, 1989) in the manner seen among autistic patients.

Individuals with physiologic insults to the orbitofrontal area show an impaired ability to recognize when social errors have occurred, but they can identify basic facial expressions. They demonstrate difficulty reading the expression in another's eyes, and getting information about another's mental state (Stone, Baron-Cohen, & Knight, 1998a).

In a SPECT scan study, Brodmann areas 10 to 14 of the orbitofrontal cortex were activated when the subjects listened to psychologically oriented words like *know, want, think, imagine,* and *remember.* No such activation was noted when they heard words naming body parts like *hand, shoulder,* or *tooth* in a SPECT scan study (Baron-Cohen et al., 1994). Psychological words are difficult for autistic individuals to conceptualize, but not words indicating concrete objects. Results from both lesion and imaging studies point to the possibility that the orbitofrontal cortex is implicated in the pathology of autism.

LEFT MEDIAL FRONTAL CORTEX
The left medial frontal cortex also shows a variant pattern of activation in autism and Asperger's syndrome. Brodmann areas 8 and 9 are activated when nonautistic persons try to understand stories with psychological state inferences (stories of misunderstanding) and not when stories have physical or factual conclusions (Fletcher et al., 1995). In contrast, individuals with Asperger's did not activate areas 8 and 9, instead utilizing other areas of the brain for psychological stories (Happe et al., 1996).

Brodmann area 9 was also activated when the subject was made to look at an idea from the perspective of another person (put yourself in another person's shoes). In this particular group the participants were thinking of Columbus and how he would have reacted to different situations (Goel, Grafman, Sadato, & Hallett, 1995).

Imaging studies have shown that the areas of brain used to make factual inferences are used by autistic individuals to make abstract inferences also. This may explain the demonstrated weakness of the group in this area.

AMYGDALA

The amygdala is a small almond shaped structure, anterior to the hippocampus. It has been traditionally associated with the fear and autonomic responses. This was supported by the findings of a functional magnetic resonance imaging (fMRI) study showing amygdala activation in response to frightening facial expression (Morris et al., 1996). Monkeys show similar amygdala activation in response to facial expressions of threat, predator warning vocalizations, and infants' vocalizations when separated from their mothers (Brothers & Ring, 1992).

Emery, Lorencz, Perrett, Oram, and Baker (1998) associated amygdala lesions in rhesus macaques with social isolation, failure to initiate social contact, and low response to social gestures. If lesions in the amygdala are produced in infant rhesus monkeys, then the social–emotional deficits of isolation-diminished responsiveness persist into adulthood (Thompson & Towfighi, 1976). Bachevalier (1991) reported that lesions made in infant rhesus monkeys in the medial temporal lobe (amygdala, periamygdaloid cortex, hippocampus, entorhinal, and perirhinal cortices) resulted in long-standing social deficits. If the lesion was limited to the amygdala, the deficits were similar but less intense (Bachevalier, 1994).

Structural MRI scans of autistic adults have shown increased left amygdala volume compared to controls (Abell et al., 1999). On SPECT scan, the autistics patients showed reduced temporal blood flow (George et al., 1992).

The ability to check another person's gaze and to read their intent in their eyes is an important threat assessment technique, and amygdala function is significant in both these functions. In humans, bilateral amygdalotomy impairs the ability to judge the gaze direction, and eye contact in particular. It is not known if the deficit is of a cognitive–geometric nature or is a failure to interpret emotional information from the eye contact. The ability to recognize and respond to another's *looking at me* is an important social function of the amygdala (Young et al., 1995). Lesions of the amygdala in humans have been called acquired autism (Stone, 2000). fMRI conducted on individuals while they performed the Reading the Mind in the Eyes task to estimate another's mental state, showed activation of the amygdala. When the same test was performed on individuals with Asperger's, amygdala activation was not seen, and this group is known to have poor accuracy at this task. Amygdala function does appear to have a role in drawing emotional inferences from the expression seen in another's eyes (Baron-Cohen, Ring et al., 1999).

Similar findings were reported in 2 patients with bilateral amygdala damage, functional deficits in understanding another's eye expression, and inability to recognize a social faux pas (Stone, Baron-Cohen, Young, Calder, & Keane, 1998).

Lesions of the amygdala provide the only animal model of autism. Animals with injured amygdalae are less active than controls when tasks requiring thoughts and mental states are tested. The amygdala may have a major role in the pathogenesis of autism.

CEREBELLUM
The cerebellum is a large structure in the back of the brain. Its function affects balance and gait. Anatomical abnormalities are seen in the cerebellum of autistic brains (Bauman & Kemper, 1994; Courchesne et al., 1988). Neuronal pathways have been described that permit information to be exchanged from the cerebellum to the frontal lobes. Through this pathway, the cerebellum could regulate behavior and the accuracy of cognitive processes (Schmahmann, 1994). Cerebellar abnormalities in the early development of autistic children have been reported (Courchesne et al., 2001); in particular, the total volume of the cerebellum and cerebral hemispheres was larger in autistic children (Hardan, Minshew, Harenski, & Keshaven, 2001). Those autistic children who did not explore much were more likely to have hypoplasia of vermal lobules VI–VII on MRI (Pierce & Courchesne, 2001).

"Knowing Me, Knowing You" and Functional Neuroanatomy

Studies have indicated that the neuropathology of autism is widespread and occurs early in development, causing persistent social difficulties. In terms of emotional awareness, there is difficulty judging the gaze of others (amygdala), and difficulty recognizing others' expressions (amygdala and orbitofrontal cortex), elements of the *knowing you* function of understanding others. Decreased exploration (cerebellum, amygdala) affects the *knowing me* function of understanding the self. Interestingly, turn-taking behavior and conversational rules are affected (orbitofrontal cortex), also reducing input from others.

Interventions and Self-Awareness

Early recognition and early intervention are associated with the best clinical results. As early as 18 months one can detect autistic symptoms in limited pretend play, an absence of joint attention, and failure to follow the gaze of others (Baron-Cohen, Allen, & Gillberg, 1992; Baron-Cohen, Cox, et al., 1996).

The aptitude of preschoolers to participate in joint attention correlates positively with later language acquisition, suggesting a linkage between verbal conceptualization and the ability to connect with others (joint or shared attention), both key elements of self-awareness (Sigman & Ruskin, 1999).

The most prominent clinical interventions are applied behavioral analysis (ABA) and Floortime. Behavioral techniques to teach social behavior to autistic children are also frequently used.

APPLIED BEHAVIORAL ANALYSIS

Applied behavioral analysis (ABA) uses behavioral principles of reinforcement and reward to assist the child in learning such skills as language, play, and turn taking that most children pick up without much effort. Teaching is not limited to the time spent in interventions, but is generalized in a structured environment. The intent is to compensate for deficits in receptivity by overlearning with the goal of bringing skills to the level that learning can occur in a natural setting.

ABA is time intensive and breaks down the tasks to be learned into small discrete parts, which are each taught in a hierarchy of reinforcement. Desired behavior is reinforced and the undesired behavior is redirected or ignored. There is constant monitoring of achievements and failures and the program is individually modified to meet each child's needs. This is complemented with behavior management techniques that the parents and caregivers practice every day.

This approach can be started when the child is fairly young, and many clinicians believe that earlier interventions yield better outcomes. About half the children treated early with ABA improve to the point where they can join a regular classroom by age 6.

FLOORTIME

Floortime was developed by Stanley Greenspan and is described in *The Child with Special Needs: Encouraging Intellectual and Emotional growth* (Greenspan, Weider, & Simon, 1998). The method emphasizes setting aside a special playtime on the floor with the child, with unstructured activities that promote connectedness. Play periods may be 20 to 30 minutes long. The therapist lets the child take the lead and fosters his development, teaching the parent by example. Playtime should be scheduled several times a day, and can engage family and friends as well as parents and therapists. The activity will help the child establish links between emotions, behaviors, and eventually words. The child must be active in the process and may occasionally require special encouragement to be active. The goals of the intervention are to promote attention and intimacy, two-way communication, expression of feelings and ideas, and later the development of logical thought and understanding of the world (Greenspan et al., 1998).

Other clinical approaches include but are not limited to musical interaction, intensive interaction for nonverbal autistic patients, and picture exchange communication systems.

Social Stories and Cartoon Social Stories
Collections of social stories help the autistic child learn the rules and norms of daily living. A cartoon version of the social stories further facilitates training of the visual-thinking autistic child.

Computer Programs and the Internet
Programs for interactive learning of social skills and facial expression recognition are available, but their effectiveness has not yet been established. In many cases the Internet has replaced television as the medium of choice among many individuals with Asperger's, because they do not have to read and analyze confusing body language and expressions. Thus, even though they think in visual terms their limitation in reading expressions causes them problems. They have no trouble reading maps.

"Knowing Me, Knowing You" and Interventions
These interventions are designed to help the child learn more about the self (me), and also about other people and the environment. Floortime is more specifically directed toward showing the child how to develop and participate in relationships than the behaviorally based ABA. Social stories and computer programs also promote awareness of self and others, but their success had not been systematically evaluated at the time of writing in 2003.

Outcome and Prognosis

Long-term outcome studies have concentrated on symptom severity. Nordin and Gillberg (1998) reported that only a small proportion of people with classical childhood autism lead independent lives. Most high-functioning autistic and Asperger's patients improve enough to live on their own. If IQ is less than 50, or they do not have useful speech by age 5 to 6 years, then outcome will be poor.

Of all the interventions available and implemented, no one method has been shown to be statistically superior to the others (Howlin, 1998; Kielinen, Linna, & Moilanen, 2002). One follow-up study of ABA claimed that the gains were maintained several years after the intervention (McEachin, Smith, & Lovaas, 1993). Preschoolers who responded best to intensive treatment were those with a higher developmental intelligence at the onset of the treatment. No other factor correlated with improvement (Gabriels, Hill, Pierce, Rogers, & Wehner, 2001).

Summary

Autism and Asperger's are biologically based inherited disorders with a deficit in communication, socialization, and imagination. There are distinct developmental differences between children with these disorders and normally developing children. The deficits are apparent early; diagnosis before 18 months of age and early interventions are beneficial. An increased frequency of reports suggests a growing incidence of autism and Asperger's. It is as yet uncertain whether actual prevalence or merely awareness of these conditions has expanded.

Several sections of the brain have been implicated in the pathogenesis of autism. The parts affected include the orbitofrontal cortex, left medial frontal cortex, amygdala, and cerebellum. The disturbance seems to be generalized.

Self-awareness is among the major deficits observed. It manifests in the child's development and persists in adulthood, with some moderation of severity. A variety of clinical measures and interventions have been proposed and implemented. Improvement has been observed but no treatment has been proven to be either curative or clearly superior in controlling symptoms.

References

Abell F, Krams M, Ashburner J, et al. The neuroanatomy of autism: a volex-based structural analysis of whole brain scans. *Cog Neurosci.* 1999; 10:1647–1651.

Alexander MP, Benson DF, Stuss DT. Frontal lobes and language. *Brain & Lang.* 1989; 37:656–691.

American Psychiatric Association. *Diagnostic and Statistical Manual of Mental Disorders.* 4th ed. Text Revision. American Psychiatric Press: 2000.

Asperger H. Die "Autistichan Psychopathen" im Kindersalter. *Archive fur Psychiatrie und Nervenkrankheiten.* 1944; 117:76–136.

Bachevalier J. An animal model for childhood autism: memory loss and socioemotional disturbances following neonatal damage to the limbic system in monkeys. In Tamminga C, Schulz S, eds. *Advances in Neuropsychiatry and Psychopharmacology*, Vol. 1. New York: Raven Press; 1991:129–140.

Bachevalier J. Medial temporal lobe structures and autism: a review of clinical and experimental findings. *Neuropsychologia.*, 1994; 32:627–648.

Baron-Cohen S. Are autistic children behaviorists? an examination of their mental–physical and appearance–reality distinctions. *J Autism & Dev Dis.* 1989; 19:579–600.

Baron-Cohen S. Hey! It was just a joke! Understanding prepositional attitudes by normally developing children, and children with autism. *Israel J Psychiatry.* 1997; 34:174–178.

Baron-Cohen S, Allen J, Gillberg C. Can autism be detected at age eighteen months? the needle, the haystack and CHAT. *Br J Psychiatry.* 1992; 161:839–843.

Baron-Cohen S, Bolton P, Wheelwright S, et al. Autism occurs more often in families of physicists, engineers, and mathematicians. *Autism.* 1998; 2:296–301.

Baron-Cohen S, Campbell R, Karmiloff-Smith A, Grant J. Are children with autism blind to the mentalistic significance of the eyes? *Br J Dev Psychol.* 1995; 13:379–398.

Baron-Cohen S, Cox A, Baird G, et al. Psychological markers of autism at eighteen months of age in a large population. *Br J Psychiatry.* 1996; 168:158–163.

Baron-Cohen S, Cross P. Reading the eyes: evidence for the role of perception in the development of a theory of mind. *Mind & Lang.* 1992; 6:173–186.

Baron-Cohen S, Goodhart F. The "seeing leads to knowing" deficit in autism: the Pratt and Bryant probe. *Br J Dev Psychol.* 1994; 12:397–402.

Baron-Cohen S, Hammer J. Parents of children with Asperger's syndrome: what is the cognitive phenotype? *J Cog Neurosci.* 1997; 9:548–554.

Baron-Cohen S, Ring H, Moriarty J, Schmitz B, Costa D, Ell P. The brain basis of the theory of mind: the role of orbitofrontal region. *Br J Psychiatry.* 1994; 165:640–649.

Baron-Cohen S, Ring H, Wheelwright S, et al. Social intelligence in the normal and autistic brain: an fMRI study. *Eur J Neurosci.* 1999; 11:1891–1898.

Baron-Cohen S, Spitz A, Cross P. Can children with autism recognize surprise? *Cog & Emotion.* 1993; 7:507–516.

Baron-Cohen S, Wheelwright S, Jolliffe T. Is there a "language of the eyes"? Evidence from normal adults with autism and Asperger's syndrome. *Vis Cog.* 1997; 4:311–331.

Baron-Cohen S, Wheelwright S, Scott C, Bolton P, Goodyer I. Is there a link between engineering and autism? *Autism.* 1997; 1:53–163.

Baron-Cohen S, Wheelwright S, Stone V, Rutherford M. A mathematician, a physicist, and a computer scientist with Asperger's syndrome: performance on folk psychology and folk physics tests. *Neurocase.* 1999; 5:457–483.

Bauman M, Kemper TL. Histanatomic observations of the brain in early infantile autism. *Neurology.* 1985; 35:866–874.

Bauman M, Kemper TL. Neuroanatomic observations of the brain in autism. In Bauman ML, Kemper TL, eds. *The Neurobiology of Autism.* Baltimore, Md: John Hopkins University Press; 1994: 119–145.

Brothers L, Ring B. A neuroethological framework for the representation of minds. *J Cog Neurosci.* 1992; 4(2):107–118.

Courchesne E, Karns CM, Davis HR, et al. Unusual brain growth patterns in early life in patients with autistic disorder: an MRI study. *Neurology.* 2001; 57:245–254.

Courchesne E, Yeung-Courchesne R, Press GA, Hesselink JR, Jernigan TL. Hypoplasia of cerebellar vermal lobules VI and VII in autism. *N Engl J Med.* 1988; 318(21):1349–1354.

Dawson G, McKissick FC. Self-recognition in autistic children. *J Autism & Dev Dis.* 1984; 9:247–260.

Dawson G, Metzloff AN, Osterling J, Renaldi J. Children with autism fail to orient to naturally occurring social stimuli. *J Autism & Dev Dis.* 1998; 28:479–485.

Emery NJ, Lorencz EN, Perrett DI, Oram MW, Baker CI. Gaze following and joint attention in rhesus monkeys (Macaca mulatta). *J Compar Psychol.* 1997; 111:1–8.

Fletcher PA, Happe F, Frith U, et al. Other minds in the brain: a functional imaging study of the "theory of mind." *Cognition.* 1995; 57:109–128.

Gabriels RL, Hill DE, Pierce RA, Rogers SJ, Wehner B. Predictors of treatment outcome in young children with autism: a retrospective study. *Autism.* 2001; 5:407–429.

Gale E, deVilliers P, deVilliers J, Pyers J. Language and theory of mind in oral deaf children. Paper presented at: Boston University Conference on Language Development, Boston; Nov. 1996.

George MS, Costa DC, Kouris K, Ring HA, Ell PJ. Cerebral blood flow abnormalities in adults with infantile autism *J Nerv Ment Dis.* 1992; 180:413–417.

Goel V, Grafman J, Sadato N, Hallett M. Modeling other minds. *NeuroRep.* 1995; 6: 1741–1746.

Grandin T. *Thinking in Pictures: And Other Reports from my Life with Autism.* New York: Vintage Books; 1995.

Greenspan S, Weider S. *The Child with Special Needs: Intellectual and Emotional Growth.* New York: Perseus Publishing; 1998.

Happe F, Ehlers S, Fletcher P, et al. "Theory of mind" in the brain. Evidence from a PET scan study of Asperger syndrome. *NeuroReport.* 1996; 8:197–201.

Hardan AY, Minshew NJ, Harenski K, Keshavan MS. Posterior fossa magnetic resonance imaging in autism. *J Am Acad Child & Adol Psychiatry.* 2001; 40:666–672.

Harris P, Johnson CN, Hutton D, Andrews G, Cooke T. Young children's theory of mind and emotion. *Cog & Emotion.* 1989; 3:379–400.

Howlin P. Prognosis in autism: do specialist treatment affect long-term outcome? *Eur Child & Adol Psychiatry.* 7:119–121.

Hulbert R, Happe F, Frith U. Sampling the inner experience of autism: a preliminary report. *Psychol Med.* 1994; 24:385–395.

Johnson MH, Morton J. *Biology and Cognitive Development: The Case of Facial Recognition.* Oxford, U.K.: Basil Blackwell; 1991.

Kanner L. Autistic disturbances of affective contact. In: Kanner L, ed. *Childhood Psychosis: Initial Studies and New Insights.* Washington DC: V.H. Winston; 1973: 217–250.

Kanner L, Eisenberg L. Early infantile autism 1943–1955. *Am J Orthopsychiatry.* 1956; 26:55–65.

Kielinen M, Linna SL, Moilanen I. Some aspects of treatment and habilitation of children and adolescents with autistic disorder in Northern Finland. *Int J Circumpolar Health.* 2002; 61:69–70.

McEachin JJ, Smith T, Lovaas OI. Long term outcome for children with autism who received early intensive behavioral treatment. *Am J Ment Retard.* 1993; 97:359–372 [discussion 373–391]

McGregor E, Whiten A, Blackburn P. Teaching theory of mind by highlighting intention and illustrating thoughts. *Br J Dev Psychol.* 1998; 16:281–300.

Meltzoff AN, Moore MK. Newborn infants imitate adult facial gestures. *Child Dev.* 1983; 54:702–719.

Meltzoff AN, Moore MK. Explaining facial imitation: a theoretical model. *Early Dev & Parenting.* 1997; 6:179–192.

Mitchell P. Background of autism. In: *Introduction to Theory of Mind: Children, Autism and Apes.* New York: Oxford University Press; 1997: 57–71.

Morris JS, Frith CD, Perrett, DI, et al. A differential neural response in the human amygdala to fearful and happy facial expressions. *Nature.* 1996; 383:812–815.

Mundy P, Sigman M. The theoretical implications of joint attention deficits in autism. *Dev & Psychopathol.* 1989; 1:173–184.

Nordin V, Gillberg C. The long term course of autistic disorders: update on follow-up studies. *Acta Psychiatrica Scand.* 1998; 97:99–108.

Perner J, Frith U, Leslie AM, Leekam SR. Exploration of the autistic child's theory of mind: knowledge, belief and communication. *Child Dev.* 1989; 60:689–700.

Petersen CC, Siegal M. Deafness, conversation and theory of mind. *J Child Psychol & Psychiatry.* 1995; 36:450–474.

Petersen CC, Siegal M. Domain specificity and everyday biological, physical and psychological thinking in normal, autistic and deaf children. *New Dir Child Dev.* 1997; 75: 55–70.

Philips W, Baron-Cohen S, Rutter M. Understanding intention in normal development and in autism. *Br J Dev Psychol.* 1998; 16:337–348.

Pierce K, Courchesne E. Evidence for a cerebellar role in reduced exploration and stereotyped behavior in autism. *Biol Psychiatry.* 2001; 49:655–664.

Piven J, Folstein S. The genetics of autism. In: Bauman ML, Kemper TL, eds. *The Neurobiology of Autism.*, Baltimore, Md: John Hopkins University Press; 1994: 18–44.

Pratt C, Bryant P. Young children understand that looking leads to knowing (so long as they are looking into a single barrel). *Child Dev.* 1990; 61:973–983.

Repacholi BM. Infants' use of attentional cues to identify the referent of another person's emotional expression. *Dev Psychol.* 1998; 34:1017–1025.

Repacholi BM, Gopnik A. Early reasoning about desires: evidence from 14 and 18 months old. *Dev Psychol.* 1997; 33:12–21.

Saver JL, Damasio AR. Preserved access and processing and social knowledge in a patient with acquired sociopathy due to ventromedial frontal damage. *Neuropsychologica.* 1991; 29:1241–1249.

Schmahmann JD. The cerebellum in autism: clinical and anatomic perspectives. In Bauman ML, Kemper TL, eds. *The Neurobiology of Autism.*, Baltimore, Md: John Hopkins University Press; 1994: 195–226.

Shah A, Frith U. Why do autistic individuals show superior performance on the Block Design task? *J Child Psychol Psychiatry.* 1993; 24:613–620.

Sigman M, Ruskin E. Social competence in children with autism, Down's syndrome and developmental delays: a longitudinal study. *Monogr Soc Res Child Dev.* 1999; 64:Serial number 256.

Sorce JF, Emde RN, Campos JJ, Klinert ND. Maternal emotional signaling: its effects on the visual cliff behavior of 1 year olds. *Dev Psychol.* 1985; 20:195–200.

Stone VE. The role of frontal lobes and the amygdala in theory of mind. In *Understanding Other Minds: Perspectives from autism and developmental cognitive neuroscience.* S. Baron-Cohen, M Tager Flusberg and D Cohen eds. New York: Oxford University Press; 2000: 253–273.

Stone VE, Baron-Cohen S, Knight RT. Frontal lobe contributions to theory of mind. *J Cog Neurosci.* 1998; 10(5):640–656.

Stone VE, Baron-Cohen S, Young AW, Calder A, Keane J. Impairments in social cognition following orbitofrontal or amygdala damage. *Soc Neurosci Abstr.* 1998; 24:1176.

Tager-Flusberg H. Current theory and research on language and communication in autism. *J Autism & Dev Dis.* 1996; 26:169–172.

Thompson CI, Towfighi JT. Social behavior of juvenile rhesus monkeys after amygdalectomy. *Physiol & Beh.* 1976; 17:831–836.

Vinden PG. Junin Quechua children's understanding of the mind. *Child Dev.* 1996; 67: 1701–1716.

Watson JK, Gelman SA, Wellman HM. Young children's understanding of the non-physical nature of thoughts and the physical nature of the brain. *Br J Dev Psychol.* 1998; 16:321–335.

Wellman H, Estes D. Early understanding of mental entities: a reexamination of childhood realism. *Child Dev.* 1986; 57:910–923.

Wing L, Gould J. Severe impairments of social interaction and associated abnormalities in children: epidemiology and classification. *J Autism & Dev Dis.* 1979; 9:11–29.

Young AW, Aggleton JP, Hellawell DJ, et al. Face processing impairments after amygdalotomy. *Brain.* 1995; 118:15–24.

6

Alcoholic Denial

Self-Awareness and Beyond

Kenneth J. Sher
Amee Jo Epler

CLINICIANS ARE REGULARLY puzzled and frustrated by the failure of many alcoholics to recognize the extent to which alcohol use has affected their lives and the lives of those around them. There is, nevertheless, remarkably little agreement in the scientific and clinical literature about the specific character of denial and how best to explain its many manifestations. In this chapter, we review research and theory that may help to elucidate the nature of denial as well as the factors that influence its occurrence. We will take a broad approach, ranging from clinical observation and theory to social psychology and on to neuropsychology. Consistent with the other chapters in this book, we concentrate upon the phenomena and processes that relate alcohol abuse and dependence, alcohol use disorders (AUDs); deficits in self-awareness; and the several distinct processes that contribute to the clinical phenomenon of denial.

During most of the 20th century, denial was considered a central feature of alcoholism, and alcoholism itself was seen as a somewhat homogeneous disorder. As a result of that unitary approach, any failure to either recognize the need for change or desire the standard treatment regimen in the presence of alcohol-related problems was de facto evidence of denial (Edwards, 2000).

Supported by grants: R37 AA7231, R01 AA13987, P50 AA11998, T32 AA13526-01. National Institute on Alcohol Abuse & Alcoholism, Division of National Institute of Health

These views were beginning to change at the turn of the century. Today, AUDs are seen as a heterogeneous group of disorders (Cloninger, 1987; Zucker, 1987; Babor, 1996). Moreover, there is increasing acceptance of the idea that different treatments are needed for individuals with different types of alcohol-related problems (Institute of Medicine, 1990), although research based on this idea has not yet strongly validated the concept of patient–treatment matching (Project MATCH, 1998). This change in perspective is accompanied by an emerging skepticism about the importance of denial as a clinical feature or even a helpful concept in AUDs. The changing view of denial probably stems from a number of factors, including challenges to closely related beliefs such as the need for intrinsic motivation to change. Several studies suggest that coerced treatment outcomes can be as good as noncoerced ones (W. R. Miller, 1985). Perhaps even more critically, some recently developed alternative views of denial-like phenomena are not based in traditional psychodynamic theory that conceptualized lack of awareness as ego defense motivated.

The clinical literature characterizes denial in a variety of ways. In the context of defense mechanisms, "denial is a highly problematic term, sometimes distinguished from, sometimes equated with repression" (Erdelyi, 1985, p. 222). There is a general usage that suggests that denial is a specific variant of repression that is focused on the external world (as opposed to internal events). As typically used (Erdelyi, 1985; Freud, 1920; Horowitz, 1988; Sandler & Freud, 1985), denial refers to the interpretation of external events ("insight"), but sometimes to the actual perception of the event ("sight").

With respect to alcoholic denial, we see an even broader array of definitions and meanings than in the general usage of the term. Consistent with its psychodynamic usage, alcoholic denial has been described as an unconscious ego defense mechanism (George, 1990). It has also been used to refer to a deliberate distortion of facts (Fewell & Bissell, 1978); inaccurate recall of details about drinking episodes (Duffy, 1995); unwillingness to admit the inability to control drinking (Amodeo & Liftik, 1990); a refusal to acknowledge that consequences are related to drinking (Wing, 1996); and many more shades of meaning. As noted by Wing, "there are many aspects of alcoholic denial, including denial of drinking, denial of the amount consumed, denial of the consequences of drinking, and denial that the consequences have any significant relevance" (1996, p. 54). The proposed mechanisms underlying alcoholic denial range from ego defense to social comparison to neuropsychological deficit. We do not wish to argue with the legitimacy of any of these usages because each reflects clinical concerns if not clinical reality. We believe, however, that these various applications can be organized along multiple dimensions simultaneously and are complementary, not contradictory. In Table 6.1 we illustrate how various usages can be organized along five dimensions: Awareness (Is the individual aware of the distortion?), Motivation (Is the motivation primarily to defend against external influences or internal states?), Focus (What is the content domain that is being distorted?), Intentionality (Is the distortion deliberate or unintentional?), and Theory (What is the explanatory mechanism that best describes the underlying process). We use the acronym AMFIT as a mnemonic for these several dimensions of alcoholic denial.

For illustrative purposes, we offer five events that clinicians might consider as examples of denial (broadly construed), and try to place them within the AMFIT scheme to facilitate their understanding. We distinguish awareness and intentionality because we interpret them as phenomenologically and conceptually distinct. Cognitive scientists view intentionality and awareness as "independent features of cognitive processes" (Newman, 2001). We also view awareness, motivation, and intentionality as true dimensions, and thus phenomena can vary in degree along these dimensions; that is, individuals can be partially aware of distortions, some motives can be responses to both internal and external threats, and some behaviors can include a small intentional component. Nevertheless, we believe that this way of conceptualizing the clinical literature is heuristic and helps to parse the specific meanings of the term *denial* as it is used by various clinical writers and by laypersons. We will refer to it as we explore questions of self-awareness in the context of alcoholic denial.

The Validity of Alcoholics' Self-Report: Do Alcoholics Tell the Truth about Their Drinking?

Can and will alcoholics accurately report their alcohol consumption and related behaviors and consequences? Most clinicians believe that alcoholics will minimize both the extent of their drinking and the consequences it has on themselves and on others (e.g., friends, family members, coworkers). Contrary to this widely held perspective, the majority of empirical studies on the validity of self-reported alcohol use indicate that drinkers in general and alcoholics in particular do not systematically underreport their alcohol use and associated behaviors (Babor, Stephens, & Marlatt, 1987; Del Boca & Noll, 2000). This is not to say that systematic distortions, both underreporting and overreporting, cannot and do not occur. Distortions clearly

TABLE 6.1
A Framework for Examining Alcoholic Denial and Related Concepts

EXAMPLE	AWARE-NESS*	MOTIV.†	FOCUS§	INTENT	THEORY
Patient deliberately underreports alcohol use	CS	External	Amount	Yes	Self-report bias
Patient reports drinking heavily but says it is not a problem because friends drink a lot more	CS	Internal	Severity/ need to change	NO	Social comparison
Patient reports drinking heavily and experiencing marital conflict, but does not see the two as related	UCS	Internal	Problems/ cause and effect relationship	NO	Neurological deficits
Patient admits drinking causes problems, but feels he or she is "in control"	UCS	Internal	Severity/ perception of control	NO	Ego defense
Patient endorses hangover and legal consequences due to drinking, but does not feel it is a "problem"	CS	Internal	Severity/ need to change	NO	Problem recognition

* "intentionality and awareness are independent features of cognitive processes" (Newman, 2001, p. 760).

† "The denial may be an attempt to avoid the negative stereotypic stigma attached to the alcoholic label" (Dean & Poremba, 1983, p. 749); Denial is an effort to protect oneself, "from the loss of self-esteem that would occur with the admission of drinking problems" (Rugel & Barry, 1990, p. 46)

§ "There are many aspects of alcoholic denial, including denial of drinking, denial of the amount consumed, denial of the consequences of drinking, and denial that the consequences have any significant relevance" (Wing, 1996, p. 54).

do occur in some cases and appear to be related to several characteristics of the individual drinker; for example, personality, intelligence level, state of sobriety, psychological mood state; the context (e.g., purpose of assessment, extent of confidentiality implied; Del Boca & Noll, 2000); and mode of assessment (Babor et al., 1987; Del Boca & Noll, 2000; Midanik, 1989). Cognitive limitations such as impaired attention, comprehension, retrieval, and integration can contribute significantly to under- or overreporting, and may be related to both premorbid risk factors and neurological consequences of alcohol dependence. Psychological variables such as fear of embarrassment and traits related to social desirability can also play a role.

Variables associated with the assessment itself can influence both systematic and nonsystematic inaccuracies in reporting (Del Boca & Noll, 2000). These task variables, such as how questions are phrased (e.g., number and range of response options available); purpose of assessment (e.g., are there punitive consequences for truthful responses); extent of implied confidentiality (e.g., will information be shared with courts or employers); likelihood of verification (e.g., informants or biomarkers); complexity of questions; and interviewer characteristics (e.g., judgmental versus nonjudgmental) may have more influence on the accuracy of the information sought than the individual characteristics of the drinker (Babor et al., 1987; Del Boca & Noll, 2000). From this perspective, "denial" is a complex interplay between the individual and the assessment context rather than a specific "symptom" of alcoholism (Del Boca & Noll, 2000). A study by Babor, Steinberg, Anton, and Del Boca (2000) indicated that, under ideal data collection conditions, most individuals can and will accurately report their drinking behaviors. Reliability estimates across a number of population groups in alcohol research indicate good test–retest reliability overall (Babor et al., 1987). For example, outpatient alcoholics' reliabilities ranged from .79 for days abstinent to .98 for alcohol-related arrests and convictions (Babor et al., 1987). In collateral–informant studies, validity also appears to be good for a number of alcohol measures (Babor et al., 1987). Across a variety of population groups, correlations with collateral reports on amount consumed, and on alcohol-related symptoms and consequences, ranged from .41 to .92, and from .50 to .79, respectively (Babor et al., 1987).

Research findings on the validity of alcoholics' self-reports thus suggest a picture very different from clinical lore. The main points raised by these studies are that alcoholics do not always minimize or deny the extent of their drinking, and its results, and that standard clinical assessment measures do not always encourage accurate histories. Underreporting and minimization can be related to cognitive variables like attention and memory, that are in turn closely related to several conceptions of awareness. Presumably, the same types of procedures that promote accurate responses in general would be helpful to alcoholics whose underreporting may reflect impaired cognition (e.g., timeline follow-back techniques).

Although the validity of alcoholic self-reports is an important question in its own right, denial (at least in its most common sense) usually refers to a different and more complex psychological event than what is reflected in studies of self-report validity. As noted, earlier interpretations saw denial in psychoanalytic terms, and as a direct response to ego threat.

Traditional Views of Denial

Within the psychodynamic tradition of therapy, denial is often used in discussions of the ego defense mechanisms introduced by Sigmund Freud (1920). As defined by Anna Freud (1936/1966), denial refers to an ego defense against external threats. This is slightly different from the traditional group of defense mechanisms, which protected the ego from internal conflicts (Sandler & Freud, 1985). Given the various internal (e.g., view of oneself as an autonomous and efficacious adult) and external ego threats (e.g., to important interpersonal relationships, health, social status, employment) that can be occasioned by alcohol dependence, it would seem reasonable that a variety of defense mechanisms might be mobilized by the personal and social reverberations of an alcohol use disorder. Indeed, alcoholics have been described by clinicians as using rationalization, projection (Bean, 1981), and avoidance to prevent acknowledgement of reality and emotional discomfort (Amodeo & Liftik, 1990). Rationalization of the cause and effect pattern of events surrounding drinking is also believed to be common among problem drinkers, contributing to differences in how patients and clinicians perceive the effects of alcohol (Addis, 1979).

Although alcoholics have been described in the clinical literature as employing several different characteristic ego defense mechanisms, some have postulated that denial is by far the most pervasive among heavy, problem drinkers (George, 1990). George hypothesized that the reason denial is so common among substance abusers, and that the other defense mechanisms are more rarely observed, is that denial renders additional defense mechanisms unnecessary. The use of ego defenses is argued to be mostly unconscious and distinct from lying and evasiveness. This view holds that the purpose of denial is to preserve the integrity of the ego by permitting continued substance use, warding off feelings of hopelessness and helplessness about the inability to control substance abuse, and blocking accurate appraisal of the consequences of continued abuse (George, 1990).

More recent theorists have extended the notion of denial beyond basic ego defense mechanisms to include other information-processing biases relating to ego or self-functioning. For example, Greenwald (1980) expanded on the theory of ego defense and defines several cognitive biases that serve to defend the ego: egocentricity (i.e., the tendency to organize knowledge around the self and perceive the self as central to events); beneffectance (i.e., "the tendency to take credit for success while denying responsibility for failure"); and cognitive conservatism (i.e., "the desire to maintain and preserve beliefs that have already been established"). He argued that these three biases contribute to the construction of a personal history that serves to protect the ego in ways that are often not reflective of current reality. Thus, the alcoholic individual might bias the processing of information about the self in such a way as to maintain a self-perception of being in control despite mounting evidence to the contrary. Within this context, we can see that self-awareness contributes to the maintenance of denial at two levels: (1) the person selectively screens out threatening information so that it never enters awareness, and (2) the individual is not aware of the fact that he or she is not accurately perceiving reality.

Related to the concept of psychological defense but decidedly more behavioral in emphasis is the notion of self-handicapping, or the idea that "alcohol's performance-inhibiting reputation can be exploited in social and evaluative interactions . . . [to] avoid the negative implications of failure and enhance the positive impact of success" (Berglas, 1987, p. 306; Berglas & Jones, 1978). This concept suggests that drinking can be a strategic maneuver to provide an "excuse" for failure, and that once alcohol has been consumed, the drinker has "nothing to lose." Although the personal repercussions of alcoholic behavior can be huge, the attribution to an external cause (e.g., "demon rum") can protect the ego in much the same way that psychological defense mechanisms are traditionally presumed to operate. A prerequisite of this model is that the individual has at least some self-image, however fragile, needing protection. There is some empirical support for the idea that self-handicapping is an often used (but maladaptive) coping strategy among alcoholics and nonalcoholics alike. Self-handicapping strategies can include a range of behaviors that can explain or excuse failure, like illness or overcommitment.

More important for the present purposes, studies show that when uncertain of their own ability to successfully perform a desired task, some individuals will self-handicap using alcohol (Berglas, 1987). It is nevertheless unclear how prevalent or significant a role self-handicapping plays in the etiology of alcohol dependence; the phenomenon has not been widely studied. In the context of denial, however, it is an important concept because it implies that, as a self-protective function, AUDs may be very difficult to change. Abstinence implies the loss of a treasured and hard to replace coping strategy, and it may be difficult for the individual to objectively assess the effects of drinking on his well-being ("his" is used intentionally here, as self-handicapping appears to be largely a male strategy; Berglas, 1987). It is not clear how aware individuals are when they are self-handicapping, but considerable research on well-learned active avoidance strategies (and self-handicapping can be so construed) suggests that they tend to be automatic and not involve much awareness or effortful processing.

Although not using the term *denial*, several recent approaches to understanding the course and treatment of substance use, abuse, and dependence employ constructs that share common features with at least some definitions of denial. We next consider a few of the most influential of these current models, focusing on those that are most relevant to the broad construct of self-awareness.

PROBLEM RECOGNITION

In some of the research literature, the phenomenon of denial has been addressed by its converse problem *recognition* (Nye, Agostinelli, & Smith, 1999). Problem recognition, or the absence of denial in this context, is defined as acknowledgement of a behavior's negative health and social consequences. Nye and colleagues (1999) further defined problem recognition as awareness of a discrepancy between one's perceived behavior and an external or internal standard of behavior. Within this framework, it is hypothesized that by promoting self-focus on personal behavior and providing normative information as a behavioral standard, therapy may raise awareness of discrepancies among heavy drinking students and thereby improve problem recognition. Indeed, in a study of college students, therapists provided either normative drinking information or encouraged self-focus on drinking (but in this particular study, not both), resulting in better problem recognition (Nye et al., 1999). A similar study demonstrated that accurate normative information and self-focus reduced rates of alcohol abuse among college students (Agostinelli, Brown, & Miller, 1995). Many clinicians believe that problem recognition is an essential step in successful treatment of addictive disorders. Indeed, the first step of the Alcoholic Anonymous Program is, "We admitted we were powerless over alcohol—that our lives had become unmanageable" (Bill W., 1976).

There is little question that some form of problem recognition is important for most individuals who recover from serious substance dependence. The epidemiology of heavy drinking and AUDs in the general population, showing peak prevalence in the early 20s with a rapid decline before age 30 (Grant, 1997; Sher & Slutske, 2003), suggests, however, that many individuals (presumably those with less severe dependency) discontinue heavy alcohol consumption before identifying their behavior as *problematic*. How might such *change without awareness* occur? The *maturing out* effect associated with developmentally limited (Zucker, 1987; Zucker, Fitzgerald, & Moses, 1995) forms of alcoholism appears to be strongly associated with changes in the drinker's life circumstances, particularly to newly adopted roles as wage earners, mates, and parents which are poorly compatible with a heavy drinking lifestyle (Bachman et al., 2002; Sher & Gotham, 1999; Watson & Sher, 1998). Individuals may thus lack awareness of the nature and extent of alcohol problems, or of the significant role of alcohol in their lives, and even enjoy a heavily alcohol-involved lifestyle, and still find motivation to change behaviors that incorporate heavy drinking.

Even for individuals who become involved in formal treatment efforts, problem recognition is not always a necessary "first step" (although presumably it becomes important during the process of change). Voluntary treatment and coerced treatment (e.g., by courts, significant others, employers) have been shown in some studies to have comparable success rates (W. R. Miller, 1985).

In the following sections, we discuss various social–cognitive processes related to problem recognition. These processes are utilized in public health efforts to raise awareness among alcoholics (and those close to them) of alcohol's impact on their lives, and in treatment programs promoting self-awareness among patients who have not yet seen their drinking as a problem requiring change. Indeed, much recent work has attempted to understand behavior change processes, even in the stages preceding problem recognition.

THE TRANSTHEORETICAL MODEL

The transtheoretical model is a currently influential behavioral paradigm that is pertinent to self-awareness and problem recognition (Prochaska & Norcross, 2003). The model was developed from a systematic comparison of the major systems of psychotherapy to build upon the best that each had to offer about behavior change (Prochaska & Norcross, 2003). Several criteria were used to guide the development process including an emphasis on empiricism, the goal of generalizability across a range of human problems, and the ability to account for change in the context of psychotherapy, as well as natural recovery or self-change. Underlying the model is the idea that behavior change requires the use of multiple processes that are uniquely effective at a variety of time points (DiClemente, 1993). The best known component of the model is the stages of change, including precontempla-tion, contemplation, preparation, action, and maintenance, with each stage representing a unique combination of specific attitudes, intentions, and be-haviors that are commonly exhibited by persons as they progress through the course of change (Prochaska & Norcross, 2003). Each stage is associated with specific, change-related processes that mediate movement across stages. Such processes include "the covert or overt activities that people engage in to alter emotion, thinking, behavior, or relationships related to particular problems or patterns of living" (Prochaska & Norcross, 2003, p. 516).

Individuals in the precontemplation stage are not intending to change their behavior in the near or intermediate future; contemplators are consider-ing changing their problem behavior in the near future but have not yet initiated change. Individuals in the preparation stage have committed to change and have formulated or are formulating a plan of action. People who recently changed problem behavior are in the action stage. The maintenance stage occurs when the individual has met some criteria of behavior change for an extended period of time (Grimley, Prochaska, Velicer, Blais, & DiClemente, 1994). The precontemplation and, to some extent, the contem-plation stage are the most relevant to the construct of denial.

Precontemplation is characterized by at least one of the following: (1) a lack of problem recognition; (2) a lack of awareness of the problem; and (3) a lack of recognition of the need for change. Some sample statements from the Stages of Change scale (one of several that classify individuals into their current stage of change to demonstrate the absent awareness character-istic of precontemplation) include: "As far as I am concerned, I don't have any problems that need changing," and "I'm not the problem one. It doesn't make much sense for me to be here" (DiClemente & Hughes, 1990, p. 222). DiClemente (1991) described four reasons why a person might be a pre-contemplator: reluctance, rebellion, resignation, and rationalization. Reluc-tant precontemplators do not want to consider change at all. Rebellious precontemplators are invested in the problem behavior and in making their own decisions; they are extremely resistant to suggestions and direction. Rationalizing precontemplators have elaborate reasons why the problem is not really a problem, or how the problem can be a problem for others but not for them. Resigned precontemplators often have experienced multiple failed attempts to quit drinking and have given up the possibility of change; they are overwhelmed by the problem and lack the energy and investment needed to change (DiClemente, 1991). Notably, the characterization of three of these four precontemplation prototypes imply that lack of awareness of a problem or of a problem's severity is central to the construct of precontemplation; only *resigned* precontemplation does not, by definition, rely to some extent on problem awareness. DiClemente's typology also stresses that individuals can be aware of their problems, but still not be contemplating change. Some of the prototypes in DiClemente's (1991) typology are also consistent with some traditional concepts of denial. Rationalization can be viewed as a defensive maneuver, for example, and reluctance implies conflict surrounding loss of an important activity.

The transtheoretical model attempts to describe processes that are associated with moving from precontemplation to contemplation, and therefore how one moves from limited awareness of a problem or need for change to a fuller awareness of these issues. According to Prochaska, DiClemente, and Norcross (1992), consciousness raising (i.e., increasing information about self and the problem); dramatic relief (i.e., experiencing and expressing feelings about one's problems and solutions); and environmental reevaluation (i.e., assessing how one's problems affect the personal and physical environment; DiClemente, 1993) are some of the processes involved in moving from precontemplation to contemplation. Processes associated with movement from contemplation to preparation include (Prochaska et al., 1992) the same processes just cited as well as self-reevaluation (i.e., assessing how one feels and thinks about oneself with respect to the problem behavior), and self-liberation (i.e., choosing and committing to act or believing in ability to change; DiClemente, 1993).

The transtheoretical model also incorporates several intervening variables. These variables involve *decisional balance* (see following section), and include the risks and benefits of change, self-efficacy, and temptation. Research on decisional balance across a number of problem behaviors has revealed a variety of patterns (Prochaska et al., 1994). For example, benefits outweigh the risks of reducing fat and exercising throughout precontemplation and contemplation stages, while the benefits outweigh the risks only in the precontemplation stage for smoking and condom use behavior areas (Prochaska et al., 1994). Overall, risks outweigh benefits throughout the action stage, and the salience of both benefits and risks declines through maintenance with risks consistently outweighing benefits (Grimley et al., 1994). Second, self-efficacy is defined as a person's confidence in his or her ability to carry out some task or goal. Self-efficacy has been shown to be predictive of change (Grimley et al., 1994). Finally, temptation is measured by assessing the level of desire to engage in a behavior in a particular environment or situation. Self-efficacy and temptation are often considered together when viewed in the context of the transtheoretical model. As self-efficacy measures up, temptation is likely to diminish (Grimley et al., 1994). In general, the gap tends to be widest in precontemplators, for whom temptation is much greater than self-efficacy. The gap narrows among contemplators, and crosses somewhere in the preparation or action stages when self-efficacy becomes greater than temptation (Grimley et al., 1994).

The transtheoretical model is useful to the study of denial because it identifies specific approaches to denial among alcoholics. Traditional notions, such as the idea that *hitting bottom* can be an important goad to action are readily incorporated into the model (e.g., the balance of benefits and risks is altered, enrollment in self-help groups with recovering alcoholics who model difficult change can change self-efficacy expectations). Perhaps more important, this model stresses how achieving the contemplative stage is a significant proximal goal of interventions (i.e., increasing awareness of the need for change), while recognizing that such awareness alone is not sufficient to accomplish behavior change.

DECISIONAL BALANCE

Although the notion of decisional balance is closely tied to the transtheoretical approach, it is a basic concept that is incorporated into several cognitive approaches to the treatment of addiction and warrants some additional discussion. As currently conceived by treatment theorists and researchers, decisional balance theory is based on the decision-making model developed by Janis and Mann in the 1970s (Prochaska et al., 1994). The original model theorized that there were 8 factors that individuals took into consideration when making a decision: utilitarian losses or gains for oneself, utilitarian losses and gains for others, self-approval or disapproval, and approval or disapproval from significant others (Migneault, Velicer, Prochaska, & Stevenson, 1999). Research on these constructs has reduced them to 2 factors: benefits and risks of changing a behavior (Migneault et al., 1999). Most clinicians use this simpler approach. In regard to alcohol, benefits of alcohol use show a positive relation with drinking frequency, quantity, intoxication, and problems, while risks of alcohol use show a negative relation with these variables (Noar, LaForge, Maddock, & Wood, 2003). Most of the current research utilizing the decisional balance model has been associated with the transtheoretical model's stages of change. Specifically, risks of maintaining the current behavior are typically lower in precontemplators and higher among individuals in the action stage of change, and benefits of maintaining the behavior are higher in precontemplators and lower among individuals in the action stage of change (Noar et al., 2003). When decisional balance measures were studied across 12 different problem behaviors, the results were consistent. Not only were precontemplators high in the benefits of maintaining the behavior and low in the risks, but crossover from benefits outweighing risks to risks outweighing benefits occurred during the contemplation and preparation stages, resulting in risks of maintaining the behavior high and benefits low in the action stage of change (Prochaska et al., 1994). Finally, Prochaska (1994), demonstrated two quantitative relations between decisional balance measures and stages of change. The first, called the strong principle, states that a large increase (operationalized as one standard deviation) in the risks of maintaining a behavior is associated with movement from the precontemplation to the contemplation stage of change. The second, called the weak principle, states that a moderate decrease (operationalized as half a standard deviation) in the benefits of maintaining a behavior is also associated with moving from precontemplation to contemplation (Migneault et al., 1999). Thus, it seems that an intervention could concentrate on either increasing the risks of behavior maintenance, or decreasing the benefits of behavior maintenance to alter the decisional balance structure and encourage behavior change, but it is likely that simultaneous efforts toward both goals would improve the clinical outcome.

HEALTH BELIEF MODEL

The Health Belief Model (HBM) attempts to explain factors leading an individual to change addictive behaviors. It is closely related to decisional balance. The HBM was developed to explain why some people avoid screening or reject prevention services. It has been expanded to include decisions people make about treatment once they have been diagnosed (Rees, 1985). The theory includes four beliefs that influence decisions about whether or not to change: severity, susceptibility, benefits of change, and costs of change (Ronis, 1992). Severity is defined as the individual's beliefs about the extent of personal threat associated with the risk behavior, including mortality and morbidity (Clarke, Lovegrove, Williams, & Machperson, 2000). Susceptibility is the perceived likelihood of developing the risk behavior and is often associated with unrealistic optimism (Clarke et al., 2000). The benefits of change are the perceived advantages of changing the risk behavior, and are influenced by beliefs about severity (Clarke et al., 2000). The costs of change are best described as barriers, including actual cost of treatment, inconvenience, and loss of pleasure (Clarke et al., 2000). Each of these considerations is measured as perceived by the individual and not as indicated by objective standards. Thus, two people could have very different perceptions even if the four considerations would actually be the same for both individuals. According to this model, high severity, high susceptibility, high benefit, and low cost would be most predictive of a decision to change a behavior (Ronis, 1992). Self-efficacy is sometimes included in the HBM as a fifth variable referring to the perceived ability to successfully change the behavior. This factor is especially important when considering behavior changes that require special skills or resources (Clarke et al., 2000).

The HBM has been shown to predict compliance in a number of areas, including alcohol treatment (Rees, 1985). Recent research is finding additional uses of the model. In one study, the HBM was used to determine differences among health care professionals and elderly persons at high risk for substance abuse problems (Beisecker, 1991). This study found that health care professionals were more likely to have realistic expectations regarding the benefits of change, but lacked realistic expectations about their personal susceptibility, whereas elderly persons had realistic expectations about susceptibility and severity, but lacked information about the benefits and costs of change (Beisecker, 1991). Thus, the HBM may be useful in identifying areas of focus for intervening with different populations of alcoholics who show diminished awareness of their current state and of the benefits of behavior change.

COMMENT ON COGNITIVE BEHAVIORAL MODELS OF CHANGE
Implicit in the transtheoretical model, the Health Belief Model, and other cognitive approaches that involve decisional balance is the notion that problem recognition and awareness of the need for change are largely rational processes, with the individual engaging in a somewhat objective, deliberate process regarding the nature of alcohol abuse and the need to change. Although empirical work has generated data showing some utility to this approach, it is also clear that there are additional determinants of behavior reflecting either bias in conscious cognitive processes or automatic processes that operate outside conscious awareness. A complete understanding of denial-related phenomena requires more consideration of these nonrational processes.

Addiction, Rationality, and Awareness

To varying degrees, cognitive models of health risk and behavior change portray the individual as a rational person, capable of evaluating the costs and benefits of using intoxicants even when doing so poses threats to physical and psychological health, economic well-being, and status in the community. Although these cognitive models have proven useful from both preventive and treatment perspectives, it is clear that many actions and beliefs of alcoholics seem decidedly irrational, at least superficially. In this section we discuss those factors that might lead the heavy drinker, alcohol abuser, or alcoholic to view their drinking as nonproblematic despite evidence to the contrary.

SOCIAL MISPERCEPTIONS (PLURALISTIC IGNORANCE AND FALSE CONSENSUS)

The term *pluralistic ignorance* was coined in the early 20th century by social psychologist Floyd H. Allport (O'Gorman, 1986). The term refers to how some perceived norms, though widely accepted, are nevertheless inaccurate and influence individuals' attitudes and behaviors accordingly. The construct has also been defined as the tendency of individuals to believe that their own private attitudes are different from those of most other people, when in fact they are highly similar (Prentice & Miller, 1993). In a study of heavy drinking among college students, Prentice and Miller (1993) showed that although students are exposed to many negative consequences of drinking, and thus hold private beliefs that alcohol consumption has deleterious effects, individual students will express the belief that most students think alcohol is a normal part of social contexts and is not a matter for concern. This concept of pluralistic ignorance has been studied within the context of numerous attitudes, beliefs, and opinions because of its purported role as an inhibitor of social change (Isenberg, 1980). Isenberg (1980) explained that, because individuals believe that their private beliefs are not consistent with the beliefs of the majority, they tend to avoid discussing their personal beliefs with others, allowing the false majority belief to remain unchallenged and thus perpetuating the pluralistic ignorance. Furthermore, pluralistic ignorance coercively influences individuals to modify their private beliefs to conform to the perceived majority beliefs (Prentice & Miller, 1993).

While individuals who engage in pluralistic ignorance are not exhibiting denial in most senses of the word, it is plausible that pluralistic ignorance could stimulate denial as a regression to the "perceived" mean. An individual whose belief system is consistent with the wrongly perceived majority attitude (i.e., that excessive drinking is not a cause for concern), will thereby not experience a sense of peer pressure to control excessive alcohol intake. This type of false perception has been considered a significant contributor to excessive drinking among college students (Baer, Stacy, & Larimer, 1991), a segment of the United States population associated with heavy alcohol consumption. In a pair of studies, Baer and colleagues found that college students invariably reported that their peers consumed more alcohol than they did. When intact living groups (e.g., individual dormitories, fraternity/sorority houses) were studied, the estimated level of group alcohol intake was significantly higher than the actual amount consumed, which was computed by averaging individual self-reports. This finding was very robust and was observed regardless of the individual's own level of drinking, gender, and alternate modes of assessment. The students appeared to be influenced by an inaccurately perceived norm. Such widely held false perceptions could stimulate minimization or denial of an individual's or peer group's alcohol-related difficulty.

A similar process of erroneous perception associated with a number of perception behaviors, including some forms of substance use, is the *false consensus effect* (Ross, Greene, & House, 1977). In its simplest form, false consensus refers to individuals' tendency to see other individuals as more similar to themselves than they really are. For example, a Republican is more likely to estimate a higher percentage of Republicans in the general population than a Democrat would. Similarly, heavy drinkers tend to see heavy drinking as more normative than it actually is, and thus less likely to be deviant or a cause for concern.

The false consensus effect was first described by Ross, Greene, and House (1977) as the tendency of people to project their own beliefs, attitudes, and behaviors onto others. It is a robust and well-documented explanation of social judgment biases (Bauman & Geher, 2002). Evidence for the role of false consensus in alcohol-related behaviors has been demonstrated by Suls, Wan, and Sanders (1988), who found that male undergraduates who drank four or more days a week or had three or more drinks per occasion tended to overestimate the incidence of these behaviors among their peers. Study subjects who did not engage in these behaviors underestimated the drinking frequency and intake volume of peers (Suls et al., 1988), further consistent with the false consensus effect.

Ross and colleagues (1977) proposed four mechanisms that may underlie the false consensus effect: *selective exposure* (i.e., people believe that the majority of others share their beliefs because they tend to socialize with people who do have similar beliefs); *salience* (i.e., people's own beliefs are more salient and available to them which can promote overestimation of beliefs in others); *information processing* (i.e., if people attribute their beliefs to situational factors rather than individual characteristics, they are more likely to believe that others in similar situations will share their beliefs); and *motivation* (i.e., people overestimate the similarity of others' beliefs in order to justify their own) (Whitley, 1998). These latter two mechanisms, selective exposure and motivation, may offer some insight into alcoholic denial.

Wolfson (2000) argued that both the motivational and selective exposure components of false consensus may be especially relevant to people who are alcohol dependent. People who engage in deviant behavior are more likely to do so in the company of others engaging in similar behaviors (selective exposure), thus promoting a perception that the behavior is more common than it really is. The person who believes that "everyone does it," is less likely to seriously consider changing his or her own behavior. Furthermore, the person who recognizes his own behavior as deviant will believe that others are behaving similarly to preserve his self-esteem (Wolfson, 2000). The comment, "I don't drink more than most of my friends," often cited as evidence of denial, can be explained as an expression of the false consensus process through the mechanism of either selective exposure or motivation.

The concept of false consensus shares a number of features with the psychodynamic concept of projection, in which personal characteristics are projected onto others. It is different, however, because it is not necessarily related to ego threat or undesirable or negative personal characteristics. As with projection, the individual is likely not aware of his or her biased cognitive processing.

False consensus and pluralistic ignorance effects are both relevant to denial because they could act alone or together to validate excessive drinking from a normative perspective, even in the presence of clear consequences. Perceived norms are powerful predictors of health-related behaviors (Sheeran, Conner, & Norman, 2001), and these common biases represent a challenge to accurate self-perceptions of one's behavior. The "social marketing campaigns" of many modern alcohol prevention programs use objective normative drinking information to confront pluralistic ignorance or false consensus (Agostinelli et al., 1995; Nye et al., 1999). One prevention approach uses mass media to disseminate objective facts about drinking norms to counter distortions about deviant drinking. The issue is not to tell the alcoholic that he or she is drinking too much, but rather to provide information about how much others are drinking. The type of awareness deficit suggested by these social cognitive perspectives is a lack of awareness of what is normative, not what one does oneself.

The Effect of Acute Alcohol Intoxication on Cognition and Self-Awareness, and Why it Matters

Hull (1981, 1987) has argued that one of the most important psychopharmacological effects of alcohol is a reduction in one's state of self-awareness. This argument is based on extensive basic laboratory studies of the effects of alcohol on cognition that consistently show information storage processes impaired by alcohol. This impairment is probably due to a number of factors, including the effects of alcohol on the use of organizational and elaboration strategies that are necessary for encoding information as self-relevant, the cognitive foundation for self-awareness (Hull, 1981). Alcohol disrupts cognition in such a way as to impede the individual from organizing information with respect to the self. This self-awareness model, makes four key assumptions:

1. Alcohol decreases self-awareness.
2. It does so by inhibiting higher order cognitive information processing with respect to its self-relevance.
3. By inhibiting these encoding processes and thus decreasing the individual's sensitivity to self-relevant information, alcohol consumption has the opposite affective and behavioral consequences of manipulations that increase self-awareness. It therefore: (a) decreases the correspondence of behavior with external and internal standards of appropriate conduct, and (b) decreases self-evaluation based on past performances.
4. The fact that alcohol decreases negative self-evaluation following failure [proposition 3(b)] is a sufficient condition to induce and sustain alcohol consumption. (Hull, 1987, p. 275)

This model suggests that individuals drink in order to avoid painful states of self-awareness and are more likely to engage in disinhibited behavior because of alcohol-related decreases in self-awareness. This model can also account for drinking to facilitate desirable behavior that is inhibited by self-awareness (e.g., socializing).

Hull and colleagues (1983) have shown that alcohol appears to reduce behavioral indicators of self-awareness (e.g., intoxicated individuals make fewer self-references than sober individuals when making a self-disclosing speech, even though their overall fluency is comparable to sober counterparts). Perhaps more critically, Hull and Young (1983) found that (nonalcoholic) subjects who were high in dispositional self-awareness (assessed by questionnaire) and received (noncontingent, false) negative feedback on an intelligence test consumed more wine on a sham taste-rating task following the feedback than did subjects who were high in dispositional self-awareness and received positive feedback. Alcohol consumption did not differ as a function of negative–positive feedback in individuals low in dispositional self-awareness. The general pattern of findings in these studies suggests that alcohol reduces self-awareness and that individuals will use alcohol when experiencing painful states of self-awareness (e.g., personal failure). The clinical relevance of these findings was demonstrated in another study (Hull,

Young, & Jouriles, 1986) of relapse in alcoholic patients following detoxification. Relapse was found to be a joint function of high dispositional self-awareness and the experience of life events reflecting failure (i.e., having negative implications for the self).

Hull's self-awareness model of alcoholism suggested that, in contrast to the intuitive notion that alcoholics are low in self-awareness and relatively unaware of the impact of their drinking on themselves and others, they are, in fact, high in self-awareness, *at least when sober.* Indeed, they can be *painfully* self-aware, but because alcohol blunts self-awareness, they are motivated by aversive states of self-awareness to drink (e.g., following personal failure). Thus, in characterizing self-awareness among alcoholics, a crucial variable is whether the alcoholic is currently intoxicated. If so, self-awareness is likely to be low, but Hull's findings suggest that sober alcoholics are most likely characterized by high levels of self-awareness. Because the short-term effects of acute intoxication can inhibit self-awareness, however, the alcoholic may fail to encode the excesses of personal behavior when intoxicated or the effect it is having on others.

Neuropsychological Perspective

Although denial in alcoholics has traditionally been viewed in psychological, especially psychodynamic, terms, 20 years ago Tarter, Alterman, and Edwards boldly proposed that alcoholic denial might be better conceptualized in neuropsychological terms, specifically, as a "developmental defect in the apperception of interoceptive stimuli and in the appraisal of the significance of environmental events" (1984, p. 214). They have hypothesized that the underlying dysfunction leading to difficulty in accurately perceiving and integrating internal and external events is a dysregulated and highly labile arousal system. This dysfunction creates a tendency to focus outwardly and to be minimally attentive to internal states. Tarter and colleagues theorized that the roots of denial precede pathological alcohol involvement, and the neurocognitive deficit associated with denial is a premorbid sign of alcoholism rather than a consequence of it. They reviewed empirical evidence purporting to demonstrate that alcoholics had: (1) disturbed arousal regulation; (2) a variety of cognitive deficits; and (3) a tendency to appraise stressors as being less significant than they actually are. Although it is probably fair to say that the evidence base for each of these assertions was either weak or vague, and there was virtually no evidence to establish the presumed linkages among these deficits, the theory was significant in two respects. First, it suggested that neurological defects could be responsible for ostensibly psychological phenomena like denial. Second, it suggested that such neurological dysfunctions can predate clinical alcoholism.

Although prealcoholic neurological deficits have been demonstrated in people at high risk for alcoholism, like the children of alcoholics (Polich, Pollock, & Bloom, 1994; Sher, 1991), it is now also well-established that with long-term chronic use, brain functioning may be impaired. To some writers, alcohol-related neurocognitive impairment is viewed as a cardinal aspect of alcohol dependence. This view is represented by statements like, "The drinking alcoholic is suffering from an organic brain syndrome and is scarcely available for insight-oriented treatment" (Fewell & Bissell, 1978, p. 8). That is, neurocognitive impairment associated with active alcoholism can preclude the effective application of treatments that rely upon awareness of one's thoughts and motivations. Clearly, neuropsychological impairment in alcoholics exists along a continuum, from undetectable to the profound dementias seen in Korsakoff's psychosis and Wernicke's encephalopathy. It is reasonable to hypothesize that, depending upon the specific nature of the deficit, the neural circuitry underlying self-awareness can be among the compromised processes contributing to various aspects of denial.

In considering cognitive deficits in alcoholics, it is first important to distinguish those that are premorbid from those that are a consequence of alcohol abuse and dependence. The original proposition of Tarter and colleagues (1984) was that some of the deficits observed in alcoholics predated their alcoholism, was largely speculation, because almost all existing research was based on studies of clinical alcoholics (eliminating from evaluation any distinction between premorbid and consequential symptoms). In the ensuing years, evidence has been accumulated that individuals at risk for developing alcoholism differ from their low-risk peers in certain aspects of executive functioning as well as visual–spatial processing (Giancola & Tarter, 1999; Pihl & Peterson, 1991; Sher, 1991). These premorbid neurologic deficits in perceptual and appraisal processes have been hypothesized to play key etiological roles in the development of alcohol dependence. At least some of these premorbid neurological deficits appear to be largely genetic (Almasy et al., 2001; Porjesz et al., 2002), although, they may also be attributable to teratogen exposure (especially alcohol and tobacco) during fetal development (Riley et al., 2001).

Although it is usually assumed that alcohol-related neurological impairment is a direct consequence of the neurotoxic effects of alcohol, it has become increasingly clear that there are multiple etiologies to the various forms of neurocognitive impairment found in alcoholics (Charness, 1993).

These include nutritional deficiencies (Molina et al., 1994), head trauma occasioned by alcohol-related injuries (Solomon & Malloy, 1992), secondary consequences of primary effects, such as hepatic encephalopathy on other organs (McCrea, Cordoba, Vessey, Blei, & Randolph, 1996; Menon, Gores, & Shah, 2001), and neuronal cell death secondary to alcohol withdrawal (al Qatari, Khan, Harris, & Littleton, 2001; Nagy & Laszlo, 2002). These may accompany neuropsychological sequelae of other drug dependencies, which are often comorbid with AUDs (L. Miller, 1985). Importantly, although deficits associated with severe syndromes such as Korsakoff's psychosis appear to persist even after long periods of abstinence, and recent research suggests that alcohol-related impairment incurred during adolescence may be protracted and irreversible (Brown, Tapert, Granholm, & Delis, 2000), much of the neurocognitive loss may be retrievable by extended abstinence (Goldman, 1987).

Duffy (1995) has revisited and elaborated upon the theory of Tarter and associates (1984) in an attempt to cast denial as a neurocognitive deficit caused by alcoholic neurotoxicity. More specifically, he has proposed that chronic alcohol consumption compromises those brain areas necessary for self-awareness, particularly the dorsal convexity and orbitofrontal areas of the frontal lobes and right posterior parietal cortex. He has theorized that "patients with lesions of the anterior heteromodal cortex (i.e., the prefrontal cortex) are unable to monitor their intrapersonal space and, therefore, unaware of their feelings and motivations and lack the ability to develop appropriate strategies" (Duffy, 1995, p. 259). These deficits can lead to poor impulse control (increasing the tendency to begin drinking and lose control of drinking after starting), underestimation of amount consumed, decreased likelihood of using self-regulatory strategies to control drinking, and poor memory for drinking-related consequences.

Although clinical–theoretical analyses like Tarter and colleagues' (1984) and Duffy's (1995) are based on established neuropsychological reasoning, these analyses remain highly speculative because there is a dearth of data relating clinically observed denial to specific indicators of neurological damage or dysfunction (e.g., neuropsychological test data or neuroimaging studies). We have identified only three empirical studies adopting this strategy, and their results are mixed.

The first of these studies was reported by Miller and Barasch (1985), who found a negative correlation between Mini-Mental Status Examination (MMSE) scores and underreporting of alcohol consumption in a sample of 13 inpatient alcoholics. Reporting accuracy was defined as the ratio of the alcoholic's self-report of drinking during the 30 days prior to admission (assessed at two points during hospitalization) to similar estimates provided by two friends or relatives (ratios less than 1.00 thus indicate underreporting). The findings yielded an exceptionally high correlation ($r = .94$) between reporting accuracy and cognitive impairment assessed by the MMSE. Although it seems unlikely that an effect this strong would replicate in other samples, the study does provide preliminary data suggesting a meaningful relationship for later study. Miller and Barasch focused specifically on alcohol consumption rather than alcohol-related problems.

In a more extensive study, Wiseman, Souder, and O'Sullivan (1996) compared the levels of neuropsychological impairment as assessed by the MMSE, the Neurobehavioral Cognitive Status Examination, and WAIS-R block design among three groups of alcoholic patients categorized on the basis of apparent discrepancy between self-rated and psychiatrist-rated alcohol problems. Specifically, deniers' (n = 15) ratings of alcohol-related problems were .5 standard deviations or more lower than that of the psychiatrist; accurate reporters' (n = 16) ratings were within .5 standard deviations of the psychiatrist, and exaggerators' (n = 15) ratings were .5 standard deviations or more greater than that of the psychiatrist. No significant differences among the three groups were observed, although depressive symptomatology was related to less denial.

Rinn, Desai, Rosenblatt, and Gastfriend (2002) rank-ordered 44 alcohol-dependent inpatients referred for neuropsychological evaluation on the basis of clinically observed denial (i.e., the number of denial-related treatment goals that were not achieved by the end of treatment). Correlations between denial score and neuropsychological test performance revealed significant associations on several different tests indicating memory impairment and poorer executive functioning among the participants with fewer denial-related treatment goals met. Indeed, the strongest effect was on the Wisconsin Card Sorting Test, a well-established measure of executive functioning and a sensitive measure of frontal lobe impairment. The results suggest that, "persistent denial was associated with poorer verbal memory, poorer executive functions, poorer visual inference, and mental slowness" (Rinn, Desai, Rosenblatt, & Gastfriend, 2002, p. 55). These findings are consistent with Tarter and colleagues' and Duffy's hypotheses about neurological deficit (either premorbid, acquired, or both) and denial but are far from conclusive. Perhaps most critically, the measurement of denial is both crude and based upon unresolved denial in treatment, not the initial severity of denial. It is possible, therefore, that the results merely show that psychological symptoms of alcohol dependence are less likely to resolve in the presence of significant cognitive impairment. Still, the findings are intriguing and pro-

vide provocative linkages among clinically observed denial and neuropsychological test data, suggesting that deficits in neurological integrity,
including those that may be related to self-awareness processes, may underlie
aspects of denial-related phenomena. Clearly, studies attempting to relate
specific neurological defects to various aspects of denial (e.g., underestimat-
ing amount and level of consumption, and impaired problem recognition) as
articulated in this volume by the Viamontes group, will help to further place
the clinical problem of denial within the context of neurological impairment.
To the extent that conditions commonly comorbid with alcoholism, like
attention deficit hyperactivity and cluster B personality disorders (Sher &
Slutske, 2003), have fairly distinctive associated neurological dysfunctions,
consideration could be given to a range of possible neurologic factors.

Denial: Multiple Phenomena, Multiple Mechanisms

A review of the literature on alcoholic denial yields several important insights. Perhaps most critically, denial remains a loosely defined phenomenon, meaning different things to different professionals. At one extreme, the
term refers to outright dissimulation, deliberate misrepresentation of one's
behavior pattern for the purpose of avoiding some real life consequence like
criticism, incarceration, or treatment referral. At the other extreme, denial
refers to a profound lack of insight occasioned by moderate to severe neurological compromise of processes fundamental to a state of self-awareness and
judgment. Denial is also seen as a motivated but unconscious process, designed to protect one's sense of self-esteem. Beyond these extreme prototypes are additional processes, each individual's normal biases that tend to
make our own behaviors seem "within normal limits."

We propose that a full understanding of denial-related phenomena involves a careful analysis of the possible functions and determinants of denial
in each individual case. Minimization of one's drinking and its consequences
can involve a high degree of deliberate misrepresentation, or it can be an
attempt at accurately relating what one believes, though distorted by factors
affecting self-perception and contextualization. It can occur in high school
students who are not yet alcohol-dependent and neurologically intact, and
in chronic alcoholics suffering from alcohol-related neurological impairment.
Because it has accumulated so many meanings, perhaps the term *denial* should
be jettisoned and replaced with more specific and less value-laden terms. As
noted by McMahon and Jones, "traditional terminology such as 'denial' and
its euphemistic synonym 'resistance' depict the client as being actively (at

worst) or unconsciously (at best) engaged in opposing treatment" (1992, p. 184). For this reason, we next discuss the clinical implications of our review with some ambivalence since perpetuating the use of the term may not be warranted. Less stigmatizing terms, like *precontemplation* or *deficits in problem recognition*, may ultimately be more useful. Perhaps, a taxonomy of denial-related phenomena, based on empirical research, will be referenced to the specific etiologies and functions served by the individual behavior.

Clinical Implications

The conclusions of our review strongly suggest that discussions of denial be qualified by associated motivations and behaviors to understand the immediate meaning of a polymorphous term. In the context of treatment, different varieties of denial call for different therapeutic techniques. If the patient is deliberately misrepresenting a situation to avoid associated consequences, several treatment strategies should be used: (1) the therapist should not facilitate denial by asking close-ended questions; (2) questions should be concrete and should not involve evaluative dimensions; (3) the therapist should advise the patient that self-reports will be validated externally (biomarkers, collaterals); (4) the therapist should remain nonconfrontational to minimize reactance and to support patient self-esteem; and (5) when possible, punitive measures should not follow accurate self-reports. If the patient acknowledges drinking a lot but argues that he is no different from others, it may be more helpful to (1) help the patient accurately assess deviance in his or her peer group; (2) explain false consensus, pluralistic ignorance, and social comparison effects; and (3) provide alternative normative information.

Further, when dealing with motivation to change, there are specific tools that can help move the patient in a direction that avoids the first two types of denial. For example, if the patient acknowledges drinking excessively and experiencing specific problems, but does not see himself or herself as having a problem or needing to change, the general goal will be to increase contemplation and alter decisional balance by (1) reviewing costs and benefits of drinking; (2) using a nonconfrontational style to review with the patient current drinking problems, describe optimal situations, and examine the extent to which alcohol interferes with achieving those goals; and (3) exploiting "teachable moments."

Finally, if neurological impairment appears to be interfering with self-awareness and problem recognition, the clinician should (1) assess and follow neuropsychological functioning; (2) support maintenance and recovery of function either nutritionally, using neuroprotective withdrawal medications, or by treating complicating comorbid conditions. It is also important to understand the time course for recovery of functioning, most of which occurs during the first 2 to 4 weeks. During this time, treatment should be largely supportive, and cognitive treatments that exploit self-awareness, memory, and problem recognition should be postponed until substantial recovery has been achieved.

No single perspective is applicable to all individuals, and many assumptions (e.g., the notion that someone has to "hit bottom" to become meaningfully engaged in treatment), have not been proven valid. Awareness of a problem and motivation to deal with it are malleable states that are available to the therapist for modification and therapeutic exploitation.

References

Addis EA. The alcoholic: "but I haven't got a problem, doctor." *Austral Fam Physician.* 1979; 8(9):976–981.

Agostinelli G, Brown JM, Miller WR. Effects of normative feedback on consumption among heavy drinking college students. *J Drug Ed.* 1995; 25(1):31–40.

Almasy L, Porjesz B, Blangero et al. Genetics of event-related brain potentials in response to a semantic priming paradigm in families with a history of alcoholism. *Am J Hum Gen.* 2001; 68(1):128–135.

al Qatari M, Khan S, Harris B, Littleton J. Acamprosate is neuroprotective against glutamate-induced excitotoxicity when enhanced by ethanol withdrawal in neocortical cultures of fetal rat brain. *Alcoholism: Clin & Exp Res.* 2001; 25(9):1276–1283.

Amodeo M, Liftik J. Working through denial in alcoholism. *Fam in Soc.* 1990; 71(3): 131–135.

Babor TF. The classification of alcoholics: typology theories from the 19th century to the present. *Alcohol Health & Res World.* 1996; 20(1):6–17.

Babor TF, Steinberg K, Anton R, Del Boca F. Talk is cheap: measuring drinking outcomes in clinical trials. *J Stud on Alcohol.* 2000; 61(1):55–63.

Babor TF, Stephens RS, Marlatt GA. Verbal report methods in clinical research on alcoholism: response bias and its minimization. *J Stud on Alcohol.* 1987; 48(5):410–424.

Bachman JG, O'Malley PM, Schulenberg JE, Johnston LD, Bryant AL, Merline AC. *The Decline of Substance Use in Young Adulthood: Changes in Social Activities, Roles, and Beliefs.* Mahwah, NJ: Lawrence Erlbaum; 2002.

Baer JS, Stacy A, Larimer M. Biases in the perception of drinking norms among college students. *J Stud on Alcohol.* 1991; 52(6):580–586.

Bauman KP, Geher G. We think you agree: the detrimental impact of the false consensus effect on behavior. *Curr Psychol: Dev, Learn, Pers, Soc.* 2002; 21(4):293–318.

Bean MH. Denial and the psychological complications of alcoholism. In Bean MH, Zinberg NE, eds. *Dynamic Approaches to the Understanding and Treatment of Alcoholism.* New York: Free Press; 1981: 55–96.

Beisecker AE. Interpersonal communication strategies to prevent drug abuse by health professionals and the elderly: contributions of the health belief model. *Health Commun.* 1991; 3(4):241–250.

Berglas S. Self-handicapping model. In Blane HT, Leonard KE, eds. *Psychological Theories of Drinking and Alcoholism.* New York: Guilford Press; 1987: 305–345.

Berglas S, Jones EE. Drug choice as a self-handicapping strategy in response to non-contingent success. *J Pers & Soc Psychol.* 1978; 36(4):405–417.

Brown SA, Tapert SF, Granholm E, Delis DC. Neurocognitive functioning of adolescents: effects of protracted alcohol use. *Alcoholism: Clin & Exp Res.* 2000; 24(2):164–171.

Charness ME. Brain lesions in alcoholics. *Alcoholism: Clin & Exp Res.* 1993; 17(1):2–11.

Clarke VA, Lovegrove H, Williams A, Machperson M. Unrealistic optimism and the Health Belief Model. *J Beh Med.* 2000; 23(4):367–376.

Cloninger CR. Neurogenetic adaptive mechanisms in alcoholism. *Science.* 1987; 236(4800):410–416.

Dean JC, Poremba GA. The alcoholic stigma and the disease concept. *Int J Addict.* 1983; 18(5):739–751.

Del Boca FK, Noll JA. Truth or consequences: the validity of self-report data in health services research on addictions. *Addiction.* 2000; 95(Suppl 3):S347–S360.

DiClemente CC. Motivational interviewing and the stages of change. In: Miller WR, Rollnick S, eds. *Motivational Interviewing Preparing People to Change Addictive Behavior.* New York: Guildford Press; 1991: 191–202.

DiClemente CC. Changing addictive behaviors: a process perspective. *Curr Dir Psycholog Sci.* 1993; 2(4):101–106.

DiClemente CC, Hughes SO. Stages of change profiles in outpatient alcoholism treatment. *J Sub Abuse.* 1990; 2(2):217–235.

Duffy JD. The neurology of alcoholic denial: implications for assessment and treatment. *Can J Psychiatry—Rev Can de Psychiatrie.* 1995; 40(5):257–263.

Edwards G. *Alcohol: The World's Favorite Drug.* New York: St. Martin's Press; 2000.

Erdelyi MH. *Psychoanalysis: Freud's Cognitive Psychology.* Vol. 15. New York: W.H. Freeman; 1985.

Fewell CH, Bissell L. The alcoholic denial syndrome: an alcohol-focused approach. *Soc Casework.* 1978; 59(1):6–13.

Freud A. *The Ego and the Mechanisms of defense.* New York: International Universities Press; 1936/1966.

Freud S. *A General Introduction to Psycho-Analysis.* New York: Boni & Liveright; 1920.

George RL. *Counseling the Chemically Dependent: Theory and Practice.* Englewood Cliffs, NJ: Prentice-Hall; 1990.

Giancola PR, Tarter RE. Executive cognitive functioning and risk for substance abuse. *Psycholog Sci.* 1999; 10(3):203–205.

Goldman MS. The role of time and practice in recovery of function in alcoholics. In: Parsons OA, Butters N, & Nathan PE, eds. *Neuropsychology of Alcoholism: Implications for Diagnosis and Treatment.* New York: Guilford Press; 1987: 291–321.

Grant BF. Prevalence and correlates of alcohol use and DSM-IV alcohol dependence in the United States: results of the National Longitudinal Alcohol Epidemiologic Survey. *J Stud on Alcohol.* 58(5):464–473.

Greenwald AG. The totalitarian ego: fabrication and revision of personal history. *Am Psychologist.* 1980; 35(7):603–618.

Grimley D, Prochaska JO, Velicer WF, Blais LM, DiClemente CC. The transtheoretical model of change. In: Brinthaupt TM, Lipka RP, eds. *Changing the Self: Philosophies, Techniques, and Experiences.* Vol. 9. Albany: State University of New York Press; 1994: 201–227.

Horowitz MJ. *Introduction to Psychodynamics: A New Synthesis.* New York: Basic Books; 1988.

Hull JG. A self-awareness model of the causes and effects of alcohol consumption. *J Abnorm Psychol.* 1981; 90(6):586–600.

Hull JG. Self-awareness model. In: Blane HT, Leonard KE, eds. *Psychological Theories of Drinking and Alcoholism.* New York: Guilford Press; 1987: 272–304.

Hull JG, Levenson RW, Young RD, Sher KJ. Self-awareness-reducing effects of alcohol consumption. *J Pers & Soc Psychol.* 1983; 44(3):461–473.

Hull JG, Young RD. Self-consciousness, self-esteem, and success-failure as determinants of alcohol consumption in male social drinkers. *J Pers & Soc Psychol.* 1983; 44(6): 1097–1109.

Hull JG, Young RD, Jouriles E. Applications of the self-awareness model of alcohol consumption: predicting patterns of use and abuse. *J Pers & Soc Psychol.* 1986; 51(4): 790–796.

Institute of Medicine. *Broadening the Base of Treatment for Alcohol Problems.* Washington, DC: National Academy Press; 1990.

Isenberg DJ. Levels of analysis of pluralistic ignorance phenomena: the case of receptiveness to interpersonal feedback. *J Appl Soc Psychol.* 1980; 10(6):457–467.

McCrea M, Cordoba J, Vessey G, Blei AT, Randolph C. Neuropsychological characterization and detection of subclinical hepatic encephalopathy. *Arch Neurol.* 1996; 53(8): 758–763.

McMahon J, Jones BT. The change process in alcoholics: client motivation and denial in the treatment of alcoholism within the context of contemporary nursing. *J Adv Nurs.* 1992; 17:173–186.

Menon KV, Gores GJ, Shah VH. Pathogenesis, diagnosis, and treatment of alcoholic liver disease. *Mayo Clin Proc.* 2001; 76(10):1021–1029.

Midanik LT. Perspectives on the validity of self-reported alcohol use. *Br J Add.* 1989; 84(12):1419–1423.

Migneault JP, Velicer WF, Prochaska JO, Stevenson JF. Decisional balance for immoderate drinking in college students. *Sub Use & Misuse.* 1999; 34(10):1325–1346.

Miller F, Barasch A. The under-reporting of alcohol use: the role of organic mental syndromes. *Drug & Alcohol Dep.* 1985; 15(4):347–351.

Miller L. Neuropsychological assessment of substance abusers: review and recommendations. *J Sub Abuse Treat.* 1985; 2(1):5–17.

Miller WR. Motivation for treatment: a review with special emphasis on alcoholism. *Psycholog Bull.* 1985; 98(1):84–107.

Molina JA, Bermejo F, del Ser T et al. Alcoholic cognitive deterioration and nutritional deficiencies. *Acta Neurolog Scand.* 1994; 89(5):384–390.

Nagy J, Laszlo L. Increased sensitivity to NMDA is involved in alcohol-withdrawal induced cytotoxicity observed in primary cultures of cortical neurones chronically pretreated with ethanol. *Neurochem Int.* 2002; 40(7):585–591.

Newman LS. Coping and defense: no clear distinction. *Am Psychologist.* 2001; 56(9): 760–761.

Noar SM, LaForge RG, Maddock JE, Wood MD. Rethinking positive and negative aspects of alcohol use: suggestions from a comparison of alcohol expectancies and decisional balance. *J Stud on Alcohol.* 2003; 64(1):60–69.

Nye EC, Agostinelli G, Smith JE. Enhancing alcohol problem recognition: a self-regulation model for the effects of self-focusing and normative information. *J Stud on Alcohol.* 1999; 60(5):685–693.

O'Gorman HJ. The discovery of pluralistic ignorance: an ironic lesson. *J Hist Beh Sci.* 1986; 22(4):333–347.

Pihl RO, Peterson JB. Attention-deficit hyperactivity disorder, childhood conduct disorder, and alcoholism: is there an association? *Alcohol Health & Res World.* 1991; 15(1): 25–31.

Polich J, Pollock VE, Bloom FE. Meta-analysis of P300 amplitude from males at risk for alcoholism. *Psycholog Bull.* 1994; 115(1):55–73.

Porjesz B, Almasy L, Edenberg HJ et al. Linkage disequilibrium between the beta frequency of the human EEG and a GABAA receptor gene locus. *PNAS.* 2002; 99(6): 3729–3733.

Prentice DA, Miller DT. Pluralistic ignorance and alcohol use on campus: some consequences of misperceiving the social norm. *J Pers & Soc Psychol.* 1993; 64(2):243–256.

Prochaska JO. Strong and weak principles for progressing from precontemplation to action on the basis of twelve problem behaviors. *Health Psychol.* 1994; 13(1):47–51.

Prochaska JO, DiClemente CC, Norcross JC. In search of how people change: applications to addictive behaviors. *Am Psychologist.* 1992; 47(9):1102–1114.

Prochaska JO, Norcross JC. *Systems of Psychotherapy a Transtheoretical Analysis.* 5th ed. Pacific Grove, CA: Brooks/Cole; 2003.

Prochaska JO, Velicier WF, Rossi JS et al. Stages of change and decisional balance for 12 problem behaviors. *Health Psychol.* 1994; 13(1):39–46.

Project MATCH. Matching alcoholism treatments to client heterogeneity: treatment main effects and matching effects on drinking during treatment. *J Stud on Alcohol.* 1998; 59(6):631–639.

Rees DW. Health beliefs and compliance with alcoholism treatment. *J Stud on Alcohol* 1985; 46(6):517–524.

Riley EP, Thomas JD, Goodlett CR, et al. Fetal alcohol effects: mechanisms and treatment. *Alcoholism: Clin & Exp Res.* 2001; 25(suppl 5 ISBRA):110S–116S.

Rinn W, Desai N, Rosenblatt H, Gastfriend DR. Addiction denial and cognitive dysfunction: a preliminary investigation. *J Neuropsychiatry & Clin Neurosci.* 2002; 14(1):52–57.

Ronis DL. Conditional health threats: health beliefs, decisions, and behaviors among adults. *Health Psychol.* 1992; 11(2):127–134.

Ross L, Greene D, House P. The false consensus effect: an egocentric bias in social perception and attribution processes. *J Exp Soc Psychol.* 1977; 13(3):279–301.

Rugel RP, Barry D. Overcoming denial through the group: a test of acceptance theory. *Small Group Res.* 1990; 21(1):45–58.

Sandler J, Freud A. *The Analysis of Defense: The Ego and the Mechanisms of Defense Revisited.* New York: International Universities Press.

Sheeran P, Conner M, Norman P. Can the theory of planned behavior explain patterns of health behavior change? *Health Psychol.* 2001; 20(1):12–19.

Sher KJ. *Children of Alcoholics: A Critical Appraisal of Theory and Research.* Chicago: The University of Chicago Press; 1991.

Sher KJ, Gotham HJ. Pathological alcohol involvement: a developmental disorder of young adulthood. *Dev & Psychopathol.* 1999; 11(4):933–956.

Sher KJ, Slutske WS. Disorders of impulse control. In Stricker G, Widiger TA, eds. *Handbook of Psychology.* Vol. 8. Hoboken, NJ: John Wiley; 2003: 195–228.

Solomon DA, Malloy PF. Alcohol, head injury, and neuropsychological function. *Neuropsychol Rev.* 1992; 3(3):249–280.

Suls J, Wan CK, Sanders GS. False consensus and false uniqueness in estimating the prevalence of health-protective behaviors. *J Appl Soc Psychol.* 1988; 18(1):66–79.

Tarter RE, Alterman AI, Edwards KL. Alcoholic denial: a biopsychological interpretation. *J Stud on Alcohol.* 1984; 45(3):214–218.

W., Bill. *Alcoholics Anonymous: The Story of How Many Thousands of Men and Women Have Recovered from Alcoholism.* 3rd ed. New York: Alcohlics Anonymous World Service; 1976.

Watson AL, Sher KJ. Resolution of alcohol problems without treatment: Methodological issues and future directions of natural recovery research. *Clini Psychol—Sci & Pract.* 1998; 5(1):1–18.

Whitley BE, Jr. False consensus on sexual behavior among college women: comparison of four theoretical explanations. *J Sex Res.* 1998; 35(2):206–214.

Wing DM. A concept analysis of alcoholic denial and cultural accounts. *Adv in Nurs Sci.* 1996; 19(2):54–63.

Wiseman EJ, Souder E, O'Sullivan P. Relation of denial of alcohol problems to neurocognitive impairment and depression. *Psychiatric Serv.* 1996; 47(3):306–308.

Wolfson S. Students' estimates of the prevalence of drug use: evidence for a false consensus effect. *Psychol Add Beh.* 2000; 14(3):295–298.

Zucker RA. The four alcoholisms: a developmental account of the etiologic process. In: Rivers PC, ed. *Alcohol and Addictive Behaviors: Nebraska Symposium on Motivation.* Vol. 34. Lincoln, NE: University of Nebraska Press; 1987; 27–83.

Zucker RA, Fitzgerald HE, Moses HD. Emergence of alcohol problems and the several alcoholisms: a developmental perspective on etiologic theory and life course trajectory. In: Cicchetti D, Cohen DJ, eds. *Developmental Psychopathology.* Vol. 2. New York: Wiley; 1995: 677–711.

7

Reflective Function, Mentalization, and Borderline Personality Disorder

Glen O. Gabbard

BORDERLINE PERSONALITY DISORDER (BPD) is by far the most commonly diagnosed Axis II personality disorder, with a prevalence somewhere between 15% and 25% in clinical populations (Gunderson & Zanarini, 1987). In the general population, the prevalence of BPD is somewhere between 1.8 and 4% (Baron, Gruen, Asnis, & Lord, 1985; Gunderson & Zanarini, 1987; Loranger, Oldham, & Tulis, 1982; Swartz, Blazer, George, & Winfield, 1990). Three-fourths of the patients diagnosed with BPD are female (Gunderson, Zanarini, & Kisiel, 1991), and cultural biases stemming from gender-role stereotypes may contribute to this disproportionate difference (Gabbard, 2000).

The diagnosis is often difficult because comorbidity with Axis I conditions is quite common. Affective disorders, eating disorders, posttraumatic stress disorder (PTSD), and other anxiety disorders are all commonly found in patients with BPD (Gabbard, 2000). These patients also present extraordinary challenges to clinicians. They are typically consumed with establishing exclusive one-to-one relationships that present no risk of abandonment. These relationships are difficult for them to find, and they may pursue them with an air of entitlement that alienates and overwhelms others. When they become close to a clinician or a figure in their personal lives, twin anxieties are frequently activated. On the one hand, they may experience anxiety verging on panic, related to concern that they may be rejected or abandoned at any moment. On the other hand, they also begin to worry that the other person will engulf them and they will lose their own identity in a kind of primitive merger. To deal with the fear of being left alone, BPD patients often create situations from which they must be rescued by the person to whom they are attached, frequently by making suicidal gestures, self-mutilating, or threatening to commit suicide. Cognitive distortions that involve circumscribed losses of reality testing also may occur with patients who suffer from borderline psychopathology. Paranoid perceptions about the treating clinician are a common reaction. These patients may present quite differently from one appointment to the next because of their identity diffusion and shifting presentations of self. They often induce intense countertransference reactions, ranging from feelings of helplessness, rescue fantasies, rage and hatred, terror and anxiety, a wish to transgress professional boundaries to save the patient, or feelings that the patient is particularly special (Gabbard & Wilkinson, 1994).

Neurobiology and Etiology

The etiology of BPD is complex and multifactorial. There is probably a genetic–biological diathesis that is acted upon by certain environmental factors. Figueroa and Silk (1997) suggest that the effects of trauma interact with an underlying predisposition to serotonergic dysfunction. Their hypothesis is based partly on the observation that patients diagnosed with BPD have a significantly decreased level of serotonergic activity. Serotonin has an inhibitory effect on behavior, and the impulsivity characteristic of borderline patients may stem from the altered serotonergic activity (Coccaro et al., 1989; Coccaro & Kavoussi, 1997; Siever & Davis, 1991). The increased vulnerability in these patients associated with lowered serotonin is probably aggravated by trauma, which alters cortisol and catecholimine secretion. Trauma appears to cause hyperreactivity of the hypothalamic–pituitary–adrenocortical axis and has been linked to depression, anxiety, and self-destructive behaviors.

Cloninger, Svrakic, and Pryzbeck (1993) developed the psychobiological model of personality involving four dimensions of temperament and three dimensions of character. Within this model, approximately 50% of personality can be attributed to temperament, which is heavily influenced by genetic variables, and 50% is attributed to character, largely determined by environmental factors (see Figure 7.1).

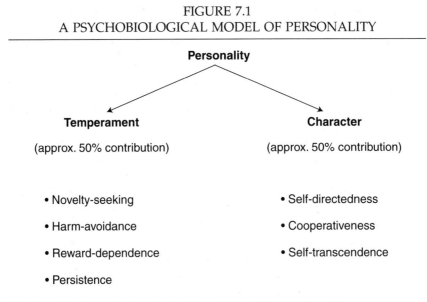

FIGURE 7.1
A PSYCHOBIOLOGICAL MODEL OF PERSONALITY

(Based on Cloninger et al. Arch Gen Psychiatry. 1993; 50:975–990).

The four dimensions of temperament are (1) novelty-seeking, characterized by impulsive decision making, volitility, active avoidance of frustration, and frequent exploratory activity in response to novelty; (2) harm-avoidance, which involves shyness toward strangers, avoidant behavior such as fear of uncertainty, rapid fatigability, and pessimistic worry about the future; (3) reward-dependence, characterized by dependence on approval of others, sentimentality, and social attachment; and (4) persistence, which involves a capacity to pursue a task or goal despite frustration and fatigue.

The three dimensions of character—shaped by social influences, family, trauma, stressors in the environment, and intrapsychic fantasy—are self-directedness, cooperativeness, and self-transcendence. Self-directedness is characterized by resourcefulness, the identification of life goals and purposes, acceptance of self, and acceptance of responsibility for one's choices rather than blaming others. Cooperativeness measures object relatedness and taps into dimensions such as helpfulness, compassion, empathy, and social acceptance. Self-transcendence refers to the individual's identifications beyond the self, altruistic pursuits, and spiritual acceptance.

In a series of investigations, Cloninger and colleagues (1993) found that the character dimensions of self-directedness and cooperativeness are critically important in diagnosing personality disorders. All categories of personality disorder are associated with low cooperativeness and low self-directedness. Certain temperaments are also typical of specific types of personality disorders. Patients with BPD are unique in being high in both novelty-seeking and harm-avoidance. They are impulsive and angry, but also extremely anxious.

In the case of BPD, several environmental factors appear to interact with the genetically based temperament to produce the clinical picture. Zanarini and Frankenburg (1997) have summarized the research findings in this area. Disturbed relationships with both the mother and the father appear to be involved, and borderline patients generally view the maternal relationship as highly conflictual and distant. Neglect may be a more significant etiological factor than overinvolvement. Early losses and separations from parents are also found more frequently in patients with BPD than in control groups of patients. There is also extensive empirical support for the notion that childhood sexual abuse may be an important etiological factor in around 60% of patients with BPD. About 25% of borderline patients have a history of parent–child incest.

In an elegantly designed study, Johnson, Cohen, Brown, Smailes, and Bernstein (1999) examined the relationship between documented neglect and abuse in childhood and personality disorder in adulthood. While physical abuse did not predict BPD, sexual abuse and neglect were both statistically significant predictors of the condition.

Attachment, Mentalization, and Reflective Function

The factors that contribute to the etiology of BPD also affect the child's capacity to attach. Studies of attachment are heavily influenced by Bowlby's seminal works on the subject (1969, 1973, 1980). Attachment is a biologically based bond between the caregiver and the child that ensures the survival and safety of the child. The goal of the child is not the mother itself, as in object relations theory, but the achievement of a physical state of safety in proximity to the caregiver (Fonagy, 2001). Internal working models of relationships are developed and stored as mental schemas, based on integration of past experiences about expectations of others' behavior toward the self.

The attachment strategies are measured in a laboratory scenario known as the Strange Situation (Ainsworth, Blehar, Waters, & Wall, 1978). This situation involves the separation of a toddler from his or her caregiver. One of four behavioral strategies is usually elicited in the child in this laboratory scenario: securely attached (B), anxiously attached avoidant (A), anxiously attached ambivalent-resistant (C), and disorganized-disoriented (D).

Toddlers in the secure category simply sought proximity with a caregiver upon her return, rapidly felt comforted on her arrival, and easily returned to play. The children in the avoidant category seemed less anxious in the absence of mother and snubbed the caregiver when she returned. In fact, they showed no preference for the mother or caregiver over a stranger. The child tries to control the down-regulated emotional arousal because it lacks confidence in the caregiver's ability. Those children in the anxiously attached ambivalent–resistant category showed substantial distress upon separation, and reacted with angry, clinging, intense behavior when the mother returned. They intensify affect in the hope of securing the caregiver's attention. Finally, those in the disorganized–disoriented category tended to seek proximity to the mother in disorienting and strange ways, such as hiding, freezing, or approaching the mother backwards.

There is growing evidence that the categories of attachment style established in childhood have some continuity into adulthood (George, Kaplan, & Main, 1996). The four responses to the Strange Situation correspond roughly to these adult categories of attachment: (1) secure–autonomous individuals who value attachment relationships; (2) insecure–dismissing individuals who deny, denigrate, devalue, or idealize past and current attachments; (3) preoccupied individuals who are confused or overwhelmed by both current and past attachment relationships; and (4) unresolved or disorganized individuals who often have suffered neglect or trauma.

This continuity appears to be related to the representation of relationships. In a secure attachment setting, a working model of relationships is generated, with positive expectations of intimacy and care from others indelibly encoded (Fonagy, 2001). Changes in neural organization may also be related to attachment. Emotion regulation established in early childhood may modify fear-conditioning processes in the amygdala (LeDoux, 1995), or connections between the prefrontal cortex and the limbic system (Schore, 1997). We also have evidence for elevated cortisol secretion and delayed return to baseline in individuals displaying disorganized attachment patterns (Spangler & Schieche, 1998).

Among the most striking features of BPD patients is their obvious insecurity about the availability of significant others in their lives. As one might intuit, research has confirmed a linkage between severe personality disorders and insecure attachment. Stalker and Davies (1995) related the attachment categories to personality disorders that were diagnosed using structured clinical interviews. Seven of eight subjects with a BPD diagnosis were classified as unresolved with respect to either or both trauma or loss. In another study (Alexander et al., 1998), when incest survivors were evaluated, the investigators found that borderline, avoidant, and self-defeating personality disorder scales were elevated consistent with preoccupied and fearful attachment classifications. In a study comparing 12 BPD and 12 dysthymic disorder patients (Patrick, Hobson, Castle, Howard, & Maughan, 1994), all 12 patients with BPD were in the preoccupied category. Furthermore, significantly more borderline than dysthymic patients were rated unresolved with respect to loss or trauma. Specifically, failure to resolve the trauma distinguished the BPD group. Compared with the dysthymic patients, the BPD group showed an incapacity to develop coherent strategies for dealing with thoughts, memories, and feelings connected with early disturbing experiences. They could not formulate a coherent psychological posture that helped them appreciate the significance or implications of traumas.

Fonagy and colleagues (1996) studied these difficulties with processing early trauma and developed a concept of reflective function, which is defined as "the developmental acquisition that permits the child to respond not only to other people's behavior, but to the *conception* of their beliefs, feelings, hopes, pretense, plans, and so on" (Fonagy & Target, 1997, p. 679). Reflective function is dependent on the capacity to *mentalize*. In a normal individual, mentalization takes place nonconsciously and automatically, similar to playing piano or riding a bicycle. It is in the realm of procedural memory and is acquired as the child develops the ability to understand people in terms of their desires, feelings, expectations, and beliefs. Mentalization involves the sense of an internal world that motivates people to behave in certain ways. Mentalization also helps the child to recognize the difference between the perception of events associated with a mental representation and the way events actually are. From a developmental perspective, a child under 3 years of age tends to function in a psychic equivalents mode, in which no distinction is made between how things are perceived and how they actually are. Somewhere between the age of 3 and 6, the child gradually integrates a pretend mode, in which the distinction between representation and reality begins to solidify. For example, a 5-year-old boy may ask his 7-year-old sister to play "mommy and baby" with him. He will then assume the postures of a baby while his older sister cradles him and talks baby talk to him. He knows that his sister is not really his mother and that he is not really a baby. As this developmental example indicates, the capacity to play is intimately related to the ability to mentalize. In the therapeutic situation, this capacity is crucial for the patient to enter a "play space," where there is an "as if" quality to transference (Gabbard, 2000). In other words, patients who mentalize may recognize that their therapist is not actually a father they hate, but the therapeutic situation is "as if" the therapist is the hated father. The distinction is clear to the patient. Patients with BPD often lack the capacity to make this distinction.

Fonagy and associates (1996) found a diagnosis of BPD to be significantly associated with unresolved trauma. These patients were more likely to have a history of abuse, as well as a perception of parents who were less loving and more neglectful than patients without this diagnosis. They were also lower on reflective functioning. The critical distinction the investigators made, however, involved the interaction between reflective functioning, abuse, and BPD. They found that in BPD patients who had minimal reflective functioning, abuse was a key factor. Ninety-seven percent of those with a history of abuse and low reflective functioning met criteria for BPD, while only 17% of abused patients who had high reflective functioning satisfied diagnostic criteria for BPD. Patients who developed BPD appeared to cope with abuse by avoiding reflection on the contents of their caregiver's mind. In particular, they avoided thinking about the caregiver's wish to harm them. The investigators concluded that the inability to mentalize precluded resolution of abuse experiences. In effect, the child defensively shuts down the natural tendency to think and be curious about the parents' behavior. Patients with BPD cope with the intolerable prospect of conceiving of the mental state of their tormentors by defensively disrupting the depiction of feelings and thoughts (Fonagy, 1998). They avoid thinking about thinking.

As one might infer, there is a great deal of evidence that problems with reflective function linked to attachment are intergenerationally transmitted. Secure parents tend to have secure infants. Preoccupied parents tend to have resistant infants. Dismissing parents are likely to have avoidant infants. Finally, unresolved parents are likely to have disorganized infants. Sensitive, responsive caregiving promotes secure attachment, while insecurity is promoted through poorly responsive parenting (Allen, 2001). This intergenerational transmission is heavily influenced by the parents' own internal working models. Expectant parents' mental models of attachment predict subsequent patterns of attachment between infant and mother, and between infant and father (Fonagy et al., 1991). Each parent has an internal working model of relationships that appears to determine that parent's propensity to engender secure—as opposed to insecure—attachments in his or her children. Moreover, the mother's capacity to reflect on the mental state of another human being appears to be a predictor of the evolving relationship between infant and parent. Parents who can appreciate the difference between internal representations and external reality, and can reflect on the role that internal states have on motivating behavior, are three to four times more likely to have secure children than are parents whose reflective capacity is poor. Fonagy and colleagues (1995) demonstrated that the parents' capacity to reflect on mental states serves as a protective factor by decreasing the likelihood of transmitting disturbed attachment across generations. These investigators found that mothers in a highly stressed group had securely attached children if they themselves were highly reflective. Those stressed mothers who lacked reflective functioning did not have securely attached infants.

Instrumental to this model is the idea that a coherent sense of self and other depends upon a reasonably secure attachment bond and the capacity to process and contextualize unpleasant or traumatic experiences. If a mother or caregiver is unresponsive, understanding this behavior as related to the caregiver's disappointment or sadness *independent* of the child may protect the child from inappropriately assuming that the caregiver's reaction is a response to the child's actions. Without that understanding, the child's self-esteem may be severely damaged. Even in the presence of an insensitive caregiver, some children may find a way to establish a relationship with a well-attuned and empathic person who serves the role of an auxiliary attachment bond. Many resilient children are able to do this and grow up with reasonable capacity for mentalization despite traumatic backgrounds.

Case Vignettes

The lack of reflective function or mentalization manifests itself in a variety of ways, including the BPD patient's characteristic way of viewing impulsive behavior. The absence of mentalization causes the patient to view behavior as "coming out of the blue" or "just happening." A sense of agency, an understanding that internal states motivate the behavior, is often absolutely missing . A clinical example will illustrate this pattern:

Ms. A, a 27-year-old BPD patient with an extensive history of physical and sexual abuse by her stepfather, came to a therapy session with her head shaved. The therapist asked her why she had decided to cut off her hair, and the patient responded, "I don't know." The therapist persisted by saying, "Let's try to get beyond 'I don't know.'" Ms. A retorted, "Well, I just don't know. I just did it." The therapist then asked, "When did you cut your hair?" Ms. A explained that she had cut it during the past weekend. The therapist asked her what was going on during the weekend, and Ms. A responded, "Nothing." The therapist then tried to help the patient see the absence of linkage to any internal experience: "You talk about cutting off all your hair as though it just happened, as though it were unrelated to anything going on inside of you or any events around you. Didn't anything happen over the weekend?" Ms. A responded, "I don't think so." The therapist then asked, "Well, what did you actually do on Friday night, Saturday, and Sunday?" The patient thought for a moment and said, "Well, I went to bed with this guy on Friday night that I met at work. I loaned him $200 because he had to spend money on his mother's medical treatment. He said he'd pay me back the next day at work, but he never showed up." The therapist empathized: "That must have felt horrible." Ms. A acknowledged that it did. The therapist then encouraged her to elaborate on her feelings. She said she couldn't really put into words what she was feeling. The therapist then asked her if cutting her hair could be in response to the horrible feelings she had. Ms. A said she didn't think so.

In this vignette the patient's behavior is not attributed to feelings of humiliation or self-loathing connected with the experience with the man. She presents such behavior as being purely unmotivated or "just happening." The borderline patient will often make it seem as if he or she is a leaf buffeted in the wind by forces that don't relate to internal states. In many cases, the main manifestation of the failure of reflective function is the inability to distinguish their transference perceptions of the therapist from the therapist's reality.

Ms. B was a 36-year-old patient with BPD who had grown up in a broken home with a mother who had numerous lovers, some of whom had actually abused Ms. B. She came to her therapy session one day and instead of sitting in the chair as usual, she chose to lie down on the therapist's couch in a prone position. The therapist was startled and asked what she was doing. Ms. B responded that she was lying down on her stomach because she thought her therapist might try to rape her. The therapist asked what made her think that. Ms. B responded, "When I walked in you looked at me in a sexual way." The therapist was a bit taken aback and asked, "You think I was looking at you sexually?" Ms. B, getting increasingly angry, said: "Don't try to deny it. I'm a good judge of human character. I know you were thinking that." The therapist tried to reason with her: "Can you imagine the possibility that the way you perceived me could be different from the way I feel inside?" Ms. B insisted that she was right: "Nice try to get out of it. I know what I saw, and don't try to tell me anything different."

In this vignette the patient's failure of reflective function leads to an almost delusional conviction regarding a transference perception. Circumscribed paranoid psychotic reactions have been prominent in the literature on BPD for many years. Borderline patients are likely to regard their therapist as malevolent if he or she makes a small misstep or if a facial expression is misperceived, as in the case of Ms. B. This conviction that they are correct can be so intense that some therapists begin to doubt themselves and think that maybe the patient is correct. Some treatments are even disrupted because of these kinds of paranoid transferences.

Treatment Considerations

The case of Ms. B illustrates a central problem in the treatment of patients with BPD—namely, that a smoothly functioning therapeutic alliance should not be routinely anticipated. The assumption that a doctor or therapist is there to be helpful is a derivative of secure attachment. Hence patients who have had good attachment relationships in childhood will naturally perceive the therapist's attentions as benevolent and establish a collaborative alliance with the therapist. Research on the therapeutic alliance with borderline patients suggests that it fluctuates wildly throughout the treatment (Horwitz et al., 1996). Special effort must be made to establish consensually held goals with the patient and to help the patient regard therapy as a process that requires collaboration between the two parties. Because so many of these patients have had their personal boundaries violated at home and elsewhere throughout their lives, special attention must also be given to establishing a firm and secure treatment frame. Such details as payment of fees, length of sessions, appointment times, and the confinement of communication to words and not touch must be established from the beginning.

The patient will naturally be skeptical about the idea that the therapist is there to be helpful. Some patients approach the situation by trying to figure out what the therapist wants and then attempting to meet what they believe are the therapist's needs. This scenario is part of an internal working model developed in childhood. A common theme in patients with childhood trauma, especially incest victims, is difficulty in determining *who* is doing *what* for *whom* (Gabbard, 2000). For example, a daughter who has had an incestuous relationship with her father begins to see her role as that of gratifying the father's needs. Her father may rationalize that he is teaching something to his daughter. In addition, the daughter may feel that she is special to her father because he has singled her out as the object of his desire. At the same time, she may be terribly conflicted about such feelings. She expects that parents should look after the needs of their children, but her experience is the reverse of that. She feels like she must attune herself to the needs of her parents.

After careful attention is given to the frame and to the development of a therapeutic alliance, the therapist can then approach specific symptoms of BPD as they relate to impaired reflective functioning (Fonagy 1998). For example, the unstable sense of self is in part related to an absence of mentalization. Similarly, impulsivity is linked to a lack of awareness of one's own emotional states as well as a propensity for action. Some suicidal gestures may be understood as a way of forestalling the possibility of abandonment—a last ditch attempt at reestablishing an attachment relationship through coercion. Even the experience of emptiness can relate to a sense of not having a self or a mind that exists in relationship with other minds. The manifestations of splitting that are so common in borderline patients, particularly the tendency to see other people as all bad or all good, may reflect difficulty in coherently integrating assumed intentions.

The overall thrust of psychotherapy with patients who suffer from BPD is to help them recover reflective function so that they can begin to think about the internal world of themselves and others. Interpretation must be used very judiciously. Many patients experienced parents who denied the reality of their experience. Patients who were abused, for example, often reported abuse to a parent, only to be told that they were lying. Often their internal feeling states have not been validated by parents, like the child who reported to her mother that she was sad and had the mother tell her, "You're not sad, you're hungry. Eat something." For this patient, an interpretation of a hidden or unconscious meaning was perceived as a re-creation of the traumatic experience of childhood, when the child's experience and feelings were invalidated.

In studying audiotaped transcripts of long-term dynamic psychotherapy with borderline patients at the Menninger Clinic, Gabbard, and associates (1994) found that transference interpretations in particular are a "high risk, high gain" intervention. They tend to have greater impact—both positive and negative—than other interventions made with borderline patients. Often they lead to marked deterioration in the patient's therapeutic alliance with the clinician if they are offered without adequate preparation. The study suggested that paving the way for transference interpretation with affirmative appreciation of the patient's internal experience may be crucially important. The psychotherapist should create a holding environment through empathic validation of the patient's experience before offering interpretation of unconscious dynamics.

As a general principle, patients who are unable to mentalize will have a hard time understanding the unconscious meaning of their enactments. It usually is more helpful to simply focus on the patient's elaboration of emotional states that might have triggered an enactment. In the case of Ms. A above, the therapist sought to help her see that she experienced feelings of being exploited by the man who took advantage of her for sex and money.

Some of what the therapist does is based on the developmental model. Children develop a sense of self from seeing themselves in the mother's or caregiver's eye (Fonagy, 2001). Hence a therapist tries to engage in a similar process of observing the patient's moment-to-moment changes in feelings and reflecting those to the patient. Over time, the patient can eventually internalize the therapist's observations of his or her internal state. The therapist might say, for example, "A tear came to your eye as you spoke about your mother. Were you feeling sad?" In this way the therapist encourages internal reflection on feeling states, a first step leading to recognition that behavior is motivated by internal states.

The psychotherapist's task is particularly complicated, though, because patients must understand that their therapist also has an internal world that is separate from them. If we use a developmental model to understand the psychotherapy, we can recognize that parents show their children how their thoughts are both similar to and different from those of the child. When parents reflect back to their children that they recognize a particular feeling state in the child, they are often telling the child that they feel the same way and can thereby understand the child's experience empathically. On the other hand, parents also teach children that they are sometimes mistaken about their parents' feelings and motivations. If a child says, "You hate me because you won't let me stay up late," the parent may need to correct this distortion by stressing how they are enforcing the child's bedtime because they love the child and have his or her best interests in mind.

It is generally useful in the psychotherapy of borderline patients to encourage the patient's fantasy about the therapist's internal state. Gunderson (1996), for example, suggested that when he is called in the middle of the night, he may explore the patient's fantasy in the next session by asking, "How did you think I would feel about your call?" When suicidal patients miss a session, I find it useful to ask them what they imagined I was thinking or feeling as I sat in the office not knowing where they were. Judicious use of self-disclosure may also be helpful in trying to assist the patient in mentalizing the therapist's separate internal subjectivity. There are occasions in therapy when it is useful to clarify what the therapist is actually feeling as opposed to what the patient perceives. Immediate correction of distortions is rarely useful, though, and these moments must be chosen carefully based on the patient's readiness to hear the therapist's internal experience.

Helping patients think through the consequences of self-destructive behavior also may encourage more reflectiveness. Patients often enact such behaviors in the heat of the moment, without having any consideration of the impact they will have on others. Therapists may encourage patients to reflect upon potential adverse consequences of particular behaviors to stimulate a sense of agency about *choosing* what they do or don't do.

When the American Psychiatric Association published its *Practice Guidelines for Treating Patients with Borderline Personality Disorder* (Oldham, Phillips, Gabbard, et al., 2001), the optimal treatment recommended was a combination of psychotherapy (either psychodynamic or dialectical–behavioral) and medication. Using the psychobiological model described by Cloninger and associates (1993), we can postulate that medication may mitigate some of the temperament variables, while psychotherapy may affect aspects of the patient's character. Moreover, agents like selective serotonin reuptake inhibitors (SSRIs) have been shown in double-blind placebo-controlled studies to reduce anger and impulsive verbal aggression (Coccaro & Kavoussi, 1997; Markovitz, 1995; Salzman et al., 1995). Higher doses may be required, up to an equivalent of 80 mg/day of fluoxetine, for maximal therapeutic effect. SSRIs often work synergistically with psychotherapy by reducing the "affective noise" in the patient's mind to facilitate reflection. Intense anger may interfere with the patient's capacity to understand how the therapist's subjectivity is different from the patient's own. When that anger is relieved, the patient is much better able to entertain the possibility and think clearly.

The psychotherapeutic approach based on increasing reflective function has received support from empirical research by Bateman and Fonagy (1999). These investigators compared 38 borderline patients in a psychoanalytically oriented partial hospital program with patients in a control group. The partial hospital regimen consisted of once-weekly individual psychoanalytic psychotherapy, thrice-weekly group psychoanalytic therapy, expressive therapy sessions informed by psychodrama techniques once a week, a weekly community meeting, regular meetings with the case coordinator, and medication review by a resident psychiatrist. The control treatment consisted of regular case review by a senior psychiatrist twice a month, hospitalization as indicated, outpatient and community follow-up, no psychotherapy, and medication similar to that received by the treatment group.

The investigators found a clear reduction in the percentage of active study group patients who made suicide attempts during the previous 6 months, the figure dropping from 95% on admission to 5.3% at 18-month follow-up. The average length of hospitalization increased dramatically in the control group during the last 6 months of the study, while it remained stable in the treatment group, at about 4 days per 6 months. Self-reported state and trait anxiety both decreased substantially in the treatment group, but remained unchanged in the control group. Depression scores also decreased significantly in the treatment group, and there was a statistically significant decrease in severity of symptoms as measured by the Symptom Checklist-90 at 18 months.

The investigators concluded that although improved psychiatric symptoms and fewer suicide attempts were seen after 6 months of treatment, the lower frequency and duration of hospitalization became manifest only during the final 6 months of the study, suggesting a need for longer-term treatment. In a follow-up study, the patients who completed the partial hospital program not only maintained their substantial gains but showed a statistically significant continued improvement on most measures. By contrast, patients treated with standard psychiatric care, showed only limited change during the same period (Bateman & Fonagy, 2001).

Summary

Reflective function and mentalization are closely related concepts referring to a capacity for understanding the representational nature of thought, and the manner in which internal events like thoughts and feelings motivate behavior. In patients with BPD, particularly those who have been seriously abused or neglected in childhood, this capacity becomes disabled as a way to defend against conscious awareness of the trusted abuser's motivations for mistreating the child. As a result, the borderline patient frequently does not have a coherent view of self and other, and does not recognize behavior as motivated by internal states.

Reflective function differs from the conscious variety of self-observation or self-awareness. It is encoded in procedural memory and occurs automatically and outside the realm of consciousness. It guides interpersonal relatedness in the same way that procedural memory of playing the piano guides the hands of the pianist. This deficiency is responsible for much of the symptomatology seen in borderline personality disorder and creates many of the treatment difficulties. Nevertheless, a psychotherapy informed by the developmental model associated with attachment theory and mentalization may be useful in helping the patient to build a greater capacity for reflective function. Medications such as selective serotonin reuptake inhibitors may facilitate the therapy by reducing levels of intense affect and impulsivity.

References

Ainsworth MS, Blehar MC, Waters E, Wall S. *Patterns of Attachment: A Psychological Study of the Strange Situation.* Hillsdale, NJ: Lawrence Erlbaum; 1978.

Alexander PC, Anderson CL, Brand B, Schaffer CM, Grelling BZ, Kretz L. Adult attachment and long-term effects in survivors of incest. *Child Abuse & Neglect.* 1998; 22: 45–61.

Allen JG. *Traumatic Relationships and Serious Mental Disorders.* New York: John Wiley; 2001.

Baron M, Gruen R, Asnis L, Lord S. Familial transmission of schizotypal and borderline personality disorders. *Am J Psychiatry,* 1985; 142:927–934.

Bateman A, Fonagy P. The effectiveness of partial hospitalization in the treatment of borderline personality disorder: a randomized controlled trial. *Am J Psychiatry.* 1999; 156: 1563–1569.

Bateman A, Fonagy P. Treatment of borderline personality disorder with psychoanalytically oriented partial hospitalization: an 18-month follow-up. *Am J Psychiatry.* 2001; 158:36–42.

Bowlby J. *Attachment and Loss.* Vol. 1. London: Hogarth Press/Institute of Psycho-Analysis; 1969.

Bowlby J. *Attachment and Loss.* Vol. 2. London: Hogarth Press/Institute of Psycho-Analysis; 1973.

Bowlby J. *Attachment and Loss.* Vol. 3. London: Hogarth Press/Institute of Psycho-Analysis; 1980.

Cloninger CR, Svrakic DM, Pryzbeck TR. A psychobiological model of temperament and character. *Arch Gen Psychiatry,* 1993; 50:975–990.

Coccaro EF, Kavoussi RJ. Fluoxetine and impulsive aggressive behavior in personality disordered subjects. *Arch Gen Psychiatry,* 1997; 54:1081–1088.

Coccaro EF, Siever LJ, Klar HM, et al. *Arch Gen Psychiatry.* 1989; 46:587–599.

Figueroa E, Silk,KR. Biological implications of childhood sexual abuse in borderline personality disorder. *J Pers Diso.* 1997; 11:71–92.

Fonagy P. An attachment theory approach to treatment of the difficult patient. *Bull Menn Clin.* 1998; 62:147–169.

Fonagy P. *Attachment Theory and Psychoanalysis.* New York: Other Press; 2000.

Fonagy P, Leigh T, Steele M, et al. The relation of attachment status, psychiatric classification, and response to psychotherapy. *J Cons & Clin Psychol.* 1996; 64:22–31.

Fonagy P, Steele H, Moran G, Steele M, Higgitt A. The capacity for understanding mental states: the reflective self in parent and child and its significance for security of attachment. *Inf Ment Health J.* 1991; 13:200–217.

Fonagy P, Steele M, Steele H. et al. Attachment, the reflective self, and borderline states: the predictive specificity of the adult attachment interview and pathological emotional development. In: Goldberg S, Muir R, Kerr J, Eds. *Attachment Theory: Social, Developmental, and Clinical Perspectives* New York: Analytic Press; 1995: 233–278).

Fonagy P. Target M. Attachment and reflective function: their role in self-organization. *Dev Psychopath.* 1997; 9:679–700.

Gabbard GO. *Psychodynamic Psychiatry in Clinical Practice*. 3rd ed. Washington, DC: American Psychiatric Press; 2000.

Gabbard GO, Horwitz L, Allen JG, Transference interpretation in the psychotherapy of borderline patients: a high-risk, high-gain phenomenon. *Harv Rev Psychiatry*. 1994; 2: 59–69.

Gabbard GO, Wilkinson SM. *Management of Countertransference with Borderline Patients*. Washington, DC: American Psychiatric Press; 1994.

George C, Kaplan N, Main M. *The Adult Attachment Interview*. Department of Psychology, University of California, Berkeley; 1996.

Gunderson JG. The borderline patient's intolerance of aloneness: insecure attachments and therapist availability. *Am J Psychiatry*. 1996; 153:752–758.

Gunderson JG, Zanarini MC. Current overview of the borderline diagnosis. *J Clin Psychiatry*. 1987; 48 (Suppl 8):S5–S14.

Gunderson JG, Zanarini MC, Kisiel CL. Borderline personality disorder: a review of data on *DSM-III-R* descriptions. *J Pers Dis*. 1991; 5:340–352.

Horwitz L, Gabbard GO, Allen JG, et al. *Borderline Personality Disorder: Tailoring the Psychotherapy to the Patient*. Washington, DC: American Psychiatric Press; 1996.

Johnson JG, Cohen P, Brown J, Smailes EM, Bernstein DP. Childhood maltreatment increases risk for personality disorders during early adulthood. *Arch Gen Psychiatry*. 1999; 56:600–606.

LeDoux JE. Emotion: clues from the brain. *Ann Rev Psychol*. 1995; 46:209–235.

Loranger AW, Oldham JM, Tulis EH. Familial transmission of DSM–III borderline personality disorder. *Arch Gen Psychiatry*. 1982; 39:795–799.

Markovitz P. Pharmacotherapy of impulsivity, aggression, and related disorders. In: Hollander E, Stein DJ, Zohar J, eds. *Impulsivity and aggression*. New York: John Wiley; 1999:263–287.

Oldham JM, Phillips KA, Gabbard GO, et al. *Practice Guidelines for the Treatment of Patients with Borderline Personality Disorder*. Washington, DC: American Psychiatric Association; 2001.

Patrick M, Hobson RP, Castle D, Howard R, Maughan B. Personality disorder and the mental representation of early experience. *Dev & Psychopath*. 1994; 6:375–388.

Salzman C, Wolfson AN, Schatzberg A. et al. Effect of fluoxetine on anger in symptomatic volunteers with borderline personality disorder. *J Clin Psychopharm*. 1995; 15: 23–29.

Schore AN. Early organization of the nonlinear right brain and development of a predisoposition to psychiatric disorders. *Dev & Psychopath*. 1997; 9:595–631.

Siever LJ, Davis KL. A psychobiological perspective on personality disorders. *Am J Psychiatry*. 1991; 148:647–658.

Spangler G, Schieche M. Emotional and adrenocortical responses of infants to the Strange Situation: the differential function of emotional expression. *Int J Beh Dev*. 1998; 22:681–706.

Stalker CA, Davies F. Attachment organization and adaptation in sexually abused women. *Can J Psychiatry*. 1995; 40:234–240.

Swartz M, Blazer D, George L, Winfield I. Estimating the prevalence of borderline personality disorder in the community. *J Pers Dis*. 1990; 4(3):257–272.

Zanarini MC, Frankenburg FR. Pathways to the development of borderline personality disorder. *J Pers Dis*. 1997; 11:93–104.

8

Attention Deficit/
Hyperactivity Disorder

A Disorder of Self-Awareness

Richard J. Burch

ADHD IS A COMMON, genetically transmitted neurological disorder, with onset in childhood and persistence of symptoms into adulthood. The American Psychiatric Association (2000), in its *Diagnostic and Statistical Manual* (Text Revised), described the disorder as "a persistent pattern of inattention and/or hyperactivity-impulsivity that is more frequently displayed and severe than is typically observed in individuals at a comparable level of development" (p. 85). While this seems like a fairly straightforward description, there is considerable confusion and misunderstanding even among professionals. It is not difficult to understand how the general public can be confused and attach an inappropriate stigma to the disorder.

Much of the confusion, and therefore difficulty with understanding and accepting ADHD as a disorder can probably be traced to the variety of descriptions and diagnostic terms under which it has been chronicled over the past one hundred years. These diagnoses and descriptions have evolved in response to changing theories about the etiology, manifestations, and core deficits of inattention and hyperactivity-impulsivity (Mercugliana, 1999).

Brief Historical Perspective

George Still (1902), a British pediatrician, described the syndrome of symptoms as "a morbid defect of self control that did not respond to punishment." This is an important consideration, which we will discuss later.

It was noticed in the period from the 1930s to the 1950s that some victims of brain insults had symptoms similar to those we see in ADHD. These brain insults included infections, toxins, and head trauma. The term *minimal brain damage* reflected an effort to describe the suspected etiology. In the 1950s and 1960s the designation became *minimal brain dysfunction* (Bax, 1963; Clements, 1966).

Diagnostic and etiologic hypotheses about hyperactivity abounded during the late 1950s, when scientists began to understand the interrelated roles of the cortex, thalamus, and basal ganglia in the regulation of motor behavior. The term *hyperkinetic reaction of childhood* was incorporated in the "New Nomenclature" section of the second edition of the American Psychiatric Association's *Diagnostic and Statistical Manual*, published in 1968.

In 1937, Bradley reported that benzedrine, a psychostimulant, showed some efficacy in the treatment of ADHD symptoms. Methylphenidate, one of the most common pharmacologic treatments of ADHD, was formulated in the 1950s (Bradley 1937,1950). The use of stimulants has become much more widespread in subsequent decades.

In the 1970s, researchers once again began to consider the deficit in sustained attention as predominant rather than secondary. The condition was once again renamed in the third edition of the *DSM* (1980) and now became "Attention Deficit Disorder with and without Hyperactivity."

Current View

The disorder became known as "Attention Deficit / Hyperactivity Disorder" with the publication of the revised *DSM-III* (1987). *DSM-IV* (1994) further classified ADHD by subgroups, "Predominantly Inattentive," "Predominantly Hyperactive-Impulsive," "Combined," "In Partial Remission," and not otherwise specified (NOS). This recategorization also recognized adults with persistent symptoms and impairment.

The reported individual distribution of ADHD types reportedly ranged from 49% to 56% for the predominantly inattentive type, 16% to 22% for the hyperactive–impulsive type, and 23% to 29% for the combined type (Scahill & Schwab-Stone, 2000). Based on several published studies, the best estimate of prevalence of ADHD in children appears to be between 5% and 10% (Anonymous, 1993; Greenhill et al., 1996). The current diagnostic criteria specify that a significant number of symptoms must be present to a degree causing clinically significant functional impairment in social, academic, or occupational settings.

Except for the diagnostic category NOS, *DSM-IV-TR* also requires evidence of some impairment-related symptoms before 7 years of age. Ninety-five percent of the development associated with attention, hyperactivity, and impulse control occurs in most people by 7 years of age. Only 5% of additional development takes place in the next two decades.

Diagnosis of ADHD

In *DSM-IV-TR* criteria are defined by type. The inattentive type includes symptoms of carelessness, difficulty sustaining attention, not listening, not following through, avoiding or disliking tasks requiring sustained mental effort, problems organizing, losing important items, and being easily distractible. All these symptoms share a common theme of inadequate awareness of the self in relation to time, place, situation, or object. These features are all evaluated by means of the basic mental status exam to determine the individual's cognitive status.

Hyperactive type symptoms include squirming and fidgeting, difficulty staying seated, running or climbing excessively (inner restlessness in adolescents or adults), being always "on the go" or "acts as if driven by a motor," and talking excessively. Impulse control deficits include blurting out answers, difficulty awaiting one's turn, and intruding or interrupting others. Again, we see a disconnection related to awareness of self in relation to these basic mental status evaluation parameters.

Poor academic performance is often seen in children with the predominantly inattentive type of ADHD (Baumgaertel, Wolraich, & Dietrich, 1995). Additionally, this type has a lower incidence of comorbidity for oppositional defiant disorder (ODD) and conduct disorder (CD). In girls, the inattentive type of ADHD has a higher prevalence than the other types. Children of the hyperactive–impulsive subtype are more likely to exhibit behavioral rather than academic problems (Lahey et al., 1994). A high proportion (approximately 44%) of these children also meet the ODD/CD criteria. These children are also less likely to develop anxiety or depressive symptoms.

A percentage of children with the combined subtype of ADHD demonstrate both academic (about 55%) and behavioral (about 78%) problems.

This group also has the highest prevalence of comorbid disorders and shows the most profound impairment among the subtypes (Baumgaertel, Wolraich, Dietrich, 1995; Wolraich, Hannah, Baumgaertel et al., 1998; Wolraich, Hannah, Pinnock et al., 1996).

ADHD Over the Life Span

The first major series of challenges to attention and to control of hyperactivity-impulsivity occur in early childhood upon introduction to the school system. Children are typically integrated into society at an age consistent with their developmental ability to cooperate with the structure and authority of the educational system. When development lags or is deficient problems with school performance or disruptive behavior emerge. Teachers in early school grades usually notice these problems first, explaining why ADHD is characterized as a disorder "most commonly diagnosed in childhood."

PRESCHOOL
Preschool children with ADHD demonstrate increased physical activity, aggression, destructive play, and temper tantrums. They may be very noisy, demanding, impatient, and argumentative. Some parents have reported irregular sleeping habits or irregular feeding routines as early as 10 months of age. These youngsters may also show increased curiosity and fearlessness. They often interrupt others, and may be regularly disobedient toward parents or teachers (DuPaul, McGoey, Eckert, & VanBrakle, 2001; Greenhill, 1998).

SCHOOL-AGE CHILDREN
Carelessness in a school-aged child might result in sloppy or incomplete homework with abundant errors. Forgotten or misplaced homework, undone chores, and repeated, unheeded reminders can add to levels of tension in the family. Scolding or punishment, especially for mistakes that have been made many times before, can leave a child with diminished self-esteem and a poor self-image. Difficulties accurately inferring the emotional reactions and states of others contribute to relationship problems and trouble learning social rules and norms. Children with ADHD are poor listeners, and conversational conventions are frequently broken. Completing others' sentences, answering questions before they are complete, and speaking too loudly or in inappropriate settings such as movies or lectures are frequently observed in people with ADHD. They are often teased, ridiculed, ostracized, and

excluded from social activities, and have fewer friends (DuPaul et al., 2001; Greenhill, 1998).

ADOLESCENCE

Although even normal adolescence is fraught with challenges, the ADHD teen experiences them more frequently and intensely. As adolescence approaches, hyperactivity may diminish or evolve into a sense of inner restlessness. Disorganized schoolwork with poor follow-through becomes increasingly prominent as the school systems present more developmentally appropriate challenges. The ability to work independently without enforced scheduling or structure is lacking. The ADHD teen engages in riskier behaviors, has poor self-esteem, poor peer relationships, and difficulties or clashes with authority to a much higher degree than his peers (Hart et al., 1995).

Adolescents with ADHD often report that they don't fit in and have few, if any, friends. Environmental feedback sometimes stimulates insight that their behaviors have contributed to their isolation, but they are unable to identify or control the behaviors as they occur. They aren't fully aware of their situation, or alert to the subtle cues that suggest how others are reacting to us. They misread and misinfer (Cuffe et al., 2001).

Since working memory didn't maintain the stimuli long enough to attach the appropriate signals and file it for future reference, in effect, little was learned from the experience. Adverse results are not expected and therefore the inappropriate behaviors are repeated. Many patients have told me they had problems socially because they "couldn't read between the lines" or "didn't learn from their mistakes."

Adult

Though *DSM-IV* criteria for ADHD were originally formulated for the childhood manifestations of the condition's core deficits, they constitute the basis for the manifestation of the diagnosis as well. The adult descriptors in *DSM-IV-TR* tend not to be as complete or detailed as those specific to ADHD children.

It is of course unusual for adults to run or climb excessively. Moreover, the *DSM-IV-TR* criteria are described in the chapter titled "Disorders Usually First Diagnosed in Infancy, Childhood, or Adolescence." As a result, many adult ADHD individuals go unrecognized and undiagnosed, particularly in the lower socioeconomic groups, experiencing significant morbidity and poor outcomes (Cantwell, 1998).

There are no published epidemiological studies detailing the prevalence of adults with ADHD. Some studies suggest that major symptoms of childhood ADHD persist through adolescence and into adulthood in up to 80% of cases. Prevalence and natural history data suggest that of the 3% to 10% of children diagnosed with ADHD, one- to two-thirds continue to manifest appreciable ADHD symptoms into adult life (Biederman et al., 1996). This calculates to somewhere between 1% and 6% of the general adult population. The most often quoted figure is about 4.6%.

As many as 85% of the possibly 9.5 million adults in the United States may never have been diagnosed (Biederman et al., 1996). Many adult ADHD sufferers are not aware that their symptoms are caused by ADHD. They believe there is something wrong with them, but often attribute it to stress, health problems, anxiety, or depression. They don't know and they don't know that they don't know. Many also suffer from low self-esteem and attribute their problems to poor self-discipline or the inferior quality of their character or personality (Nada-Raja et al., 1997). This is nowhere better expressed than in the title of the 1993 book by Kate Kelly and Peggy Ramundo—*You Mean I'm Not Lazy, Stupid or Crazy?!*

ADHD adults complain that they have family, social, occupational, and relationship problems stemming from ADHD deficits. They have few or no friends. They are easily distractible and restless, with poor memory, difficulty finishing tasks, and low academic and occupational achievement secondary to poor planning and organization. They report emotional distress, frustration, bad temper, and rule-breaking behavior (Offord, 1992; Wender, 2000).

Impulsive ADHD patients are more likely to acquire a sexually transmitted disease or develop a substance abuse disorder. They may suffer from underperformance at work or get fired from or impulsively quit their jobs. They are more likely to have their driver's license suspended, receive speeding citations, and become involved in more frequent and more serious motor vehicle accidents. There are several reports of higher rates of ADHD in populations with antisocial or criminal behaviors (Offord, 1995).

ALAN

Let's use an example of adult with ADHD and describe some of the commonly observed difficulties that stem from the core deficits. Alan is a 38-year-old professional who came to me with a primary complaint of being "depressed again."

He feels his blue mood has been worsening over the past few years as a result of the situation at work. He has been passed over for promotions because of disappointing performance. The quality and timeliness of his work is inconsistent. He misses "details and deadlines." He puts in long hours to try and keep up with his overwhelming workload. He says people seem to like him except for one or two key people in his organization who feel he is overbearing. He worries about his situation to the degree that it leaves him too "keyed up" to be able to fall asleep easily and he often stays up late because of this.

He starts every day in a rush. He hits the snooze 5 or 6 times and has put a large clock in the bathroom because he's found himself standing at the mirror or in the shower daydreaming without being aware of the passage of time until the water gets cold. His wife is kind enough to set out his clothes to keep him on track but everything is gray or blue or black so he will always have the same accessories such as belt and shoes. That way he doesn't get distracted while he looks for these items. He has a small wooden bowl on his dresser he picked up as a souvenir. It has fond memories from his childhood and he's always taken care of it. If his keys, wallet, and pager aren't all there when he's ready to go (and they often aren't because he may have left them in the car or he wore a different coat) he panics.

Moreover, in addition to the stalling of his career, Alan's wife of 7 years complains about his long hours, not listening to her, and not getting things done around the house. She says he "just doesn't get it" and he agrees. He is doing everything to the best of his ability. He has to work long hours to keep up. He tries to listen to her but his mind keeps returning to his job or something he saw on TV, or something he recalls from childhood. The intimacy in his relationship even suffers because he mulls over the hardware store list during lovemaking sessions if there isn't regular variety, or if they have to be quiet so nobody hears.

He knows his home office and garage are a mess but that's because he is a busy man. His projects aren't "incomplete" so much as they are "in progress" (although he has been working on that art-glass window for the front door since they moved in 7 years ago).

As his life history unfolds we discover that he's "always been that way" and he is "just like my dad." In elementary school he was the class clown and barely passed from year to year. His father was extremely impatient with him and he "couldn't even screw up right." He was always getting in trouble at school and at home and he could never figure out why. He was called stupid and lazy. He kept to himself. He couldn't figure out any other way to keep from irritating people.

He was failing language and math classes in fifth grade but got top grades in science and physical education. Alan's father told him that he'd "better turn those damn grades around or you'll be in *big* trouble." The next semester he was failing science and PE and was barely passing language and math! He certainly did "turn those damn grades around!" But for some unexplainable reason he got in trouble anyway. He just couldn't win.

His younger brother was somehow evaluated for some kind of "special thing that meant he got out of classes sometimes" and actually took some medicine for a while. But that all stopped when they moved to a different district again. He never attended two full years in the same school until his last three years in high school.

In high school he had perfect attendance the first year but one of the teachers took a dislike to him and it seemed that he was in the principal's office every day. The second year he met Ike. Ike was older because he was held back a couple of years. He had a car and all of the girls thought he was handsome. Many days on the way to school Ike would pull up in the car while Alan was walking to school and ask him if he want to cut classes with him and "the twins." By the end of high school he was met at each class and escorted to the next by somebody from the office. He doesn't know how many days he missed or how he graduated, but he did.

His friends started getting married and so "I just asked her and she said yes. I knew it was a mistake the first night. I laid there in bed and thought 'what have I done?'" In the third year of marriage his son was born. After 5 years of overdrawn bank accounts, overbalance credit cards, overindulgence in the recreational substances of the times, and overexposure to extramarital experiences they were divorced. He never had more money than he needed to get to the next paycheck.

Throughout his life he felt slightly bewildered and often amazed. He could see what the problems might have been after the fact but almost never as they unfolded. He felt that he needed to do a better job of being a father so he quit smoking, drinking, and carousing. He swore that no matter what he would stay at his next job for at least a year. He went to junior college at night. He finally finished his undergraduate work at age 35 after returning to school every year or so and changing his major from computer systems to business to biology then back to business.

He rationalized that since his parents came from another generation, one was even born in another country, that they didn't understand him, and Alan simply would not accept their declaration that he was a loser. It was their problem, not his. He would "use my intellect" to learn to compensate by religiously keeping lists and reviewing and consolidating them at the end of every day. He also resigned himself to the fact that he could do anything but not everything. He took a time management class and learned to prioritize his life.

He never could understand the concept of religion and deities but he was taken by the Zen Buddhist philosophies of living in the "here and now." He practiced meditation and concentration. He embraced the concepts of the past and future not existing. He forgave himself for being imperfect and redirected himself whenever he noticed he was off course.

His job involved working with different clients over a large area. He loved it. It was fast paced and never the same two days in a row. His second wife was taken by his energy and spontaneity and he was awed with her self-discipline and control. They complemented each other. She handled the checkbook and he made sure life was never boring. When she first met him she thought his reckless driving and impatience were exciting and ambitious.

But when he came to the office for help with depression he had *hit the wall*. That's a term long-distance runners use when they have exhausted all of their energy stores and just cannot keep up the pace as they approach the final stretch in the race. In spite of all of his efforts, compensatory mechanisms, support systems, personal digital assistants, and endurance there was just something that kept him from progressing. He thought if others could do it he must truly be inferior. He was sad and had lost his confidence. He had been depressed as a boy and was "depressed again."

His wife felt he had given up and regressed. She knew he could do any of the things required of him. He just wasn't doing it. She insisted he get help. That's why he was in my office.

He had been promoted from the field to the office because of his outstanding performance. Office work was incredibly mundane and boring for Alan. He saw himself as young and energetic and his coworker as old and stuffy. His organizational skills would be helpful but they eluded him. He could do what was required if he could just stay on task. He also overcommitted early on in his new position. He couldn't get things done because the world around him just didn't move fast enough. He just didn't have a sense of time, timing, and timeliness. Too many tasks, too little time. He spoke impulsively before considering his statements. A deadline in two months made no impression but one in two hours was intense. He had trained himself for the job he came from. This new position was a different culture with different social rules and cues. The subtleties eluded him except in retrospect and rumination. He "couldn't read between the lines."

Alan's ego defense mechanisms, which had served him so well, of suppression, humor, intellectualization, and rationalization had given way to denial, distortion, repression, and regression. Our evaluation revealed that Alan's difficulties were likely related to the ADHD core deficits of inattention and hyperactivity/impulsivity.

Self-Awareness Deficits in ADHD

When people with ADHD know they have the condition, they can attribute repeated difficulties with attention and control of hyperactivity or impulsivity to a genetic predisposition rather than to a flaw in themselves. Their parents and teachers can recognize, understand, and coach them. They can develop habits that accommodate their deficits. They can evolve lifestyles that flourish under the hyperactivity and hyperfocus sometimes seen with ADHD. They can make choices knowing that it would be better to avoid situations that require sustained mental effort at mundane tasks. They can partner with others whose traits complement and augment their own.

If they knew that these core deficits would persist into adulthood they could migrate toward more satisfying and fulfilling careers. They could direct themselves toward careers with a high level of activity. In college they could choose subjects with a sufficient positive emotional charge to keep them focused and on-task.

They would be less likely to self-blame. They might not develop a lifestyle driven by low self-confidence and doubt. They might understand that they are predisposed to speaking too loudly. They could know before the fact rather than after that participating in a conversation or listening in a meeting or lecture requires a deliberate effort or the development of listening skills. Learned early, these skills can be the foundation of a successful education, relationships, or careers. Careers and relationships would be more stable and families would be happier.

With adequate self-awareness of their disorder, people with ADHD might not suffer the physical and mental anguish associated with common comorbid problems such as substance abuse, depression, or anxiety. Motor vehicle accidents and encounters with the legal system might be reduced, resulting in a safer community and less cost to society.

If they were aware that their low frustration tolerance and quick temper were symptoms of ADHD, parents might have more patience and insight into their children's struggles. Insightful parents could see their own ADHD traits in their children and pass on what they have learned about themselves and ADHD. An ADHD child and an ADHD parent without insight often each doubly endure the frustration, hardships, and failures of untreated and uncompensated deficits. Without insight or awareness the root causes are not addressed. The behaviors aren't acknowledged as manifestations of ADHD. They aren't recognized as the results of the underlying core deficits. They are seen as individual flaws and are the source of misunderstandings, anger, and blame.

Self-awareness deficits in ADHD impact social functioning. Hostility has been inversely related to self-awareness by McDowell, Demaree, and Harrison (1994), Epstein and Cluss (1982), and Scheier, (1976). McDowell, Demaree, and Harrison's neuropsychological model of the role of the right cerebrum suggests that diminished awareness of arousal, perceptual, expressive, and integrative processes can increase the potential for hostility. Conduct disorder, oppositional defiant disorder, and antisocial personality disorder have a higher prevalence in ADHD children and adults. Temper outbursts and law-breaking behaviors occur more frequently (Faraone, 2000; Offord, 1992).

ADHD and Comorbidity

Depression, anxiety, and substance abuse are more prevalent in ADHD patients. One in five depressed patients has ADHD. Comorbid psychiatric disorders are often the presenting problems and mask ADHD symptoms. About 75% of patients with ADHD have another psychiatric disorder, and 20% with have two or more additional psychiatric disorders (Offord, 1995).

Comorbid psychiatric disorders with more serious and threatening symptoms including depression and mania, should be addressed with higher priority than ADHD symptoms. Treatments for any of these disorders have the potential to exacerbate the comorbidity. Treatment for ADHD could trigger cycling in bipolar disorder or aggravate anxiety symptoms. The same treatment may serve to improve the mood of a depressed patient.

Problems arise when a comorbid disorder masks ADHD symptoms, or when the ADHD symptoms are attributed to the comorbid disorder. In these cases, ADHD is not addressed, treatment for the presenting complaint does not work, or patients are labeled as *difficult*.

Genetics of ADHD

ADHD runs in families. It is almost as heritable as height and the most heritable psychiatric disorder. The report that "she's just like her dad" is critical diagnostic information in evaluating a patient for possible ADHD (Reeves et al., 1987).

In one study, 55% of families had at least one parent with a lifetime diagnosis of ADHD (Faraone, Biederman, Keenan et al., 1991; Faraone, Biederman, Spencer et al., 2000). The frequency of ADHD in at least one parent was higher in families with an affected girl (63%) than in families with only affected boys (45%). Parents of ADHD children struggle with inattention or cognitive problems, hyperactivity or restlessness, impulsivity, emotional difficulties, and low self-esteem. First degree relatives of ADHD children have a higher prevalence of depression, with an odds ratio of at least 3:2 compared with control children (Biederman, Faraone, Keenan et al., 1990; Frick et al., 1992; Morrison & Stewart, 1971; Schachar & Wachsmuth, 1990).

Neuroimaging in ADHD

Recently, neuroimaging and other technological advances have revealed many insights about the brain regions and neurotransmitter systems as potential mechanisms of ADHD. The specific neurophysiologic mechanism nevertheless remains unknown.

Several areas of ADHD brains reveal structural differences when compared to non-ADHD controls. Frontostriatal regions are strongly implicated. It is suggested that weak or disorganized neurotransmission results in dysregulation of predominantly noradrenergic inhibitory frontocortical executive influences on predominantly dopaminergic striatal structures. Other neurotransmitters, like serotonin, may also be involved. Neuroimaging literature reports differences in caudate, globus pallidus, right frontal lobe, anterior–inferior peribasal ganglia, bilateral retrocallosal, posteriorparietal–occipital regions, and the cerebellum of ADHD patients and controls without ADHD (Bush et al., 1999).

Findings of differences in frontal–striatal functioning were published by Bush and colleagues (1999). Functional MRIs of non-ADHD subjects displayed physiologic activity in the cognitive division of the anterior cingulate gyrus when challenged to process an attention-based task, suggesting that the cognitive division of the anterior cingulate gyrus influences sensory and response selection. It appears to monitor executive functions, competition, complex motor control, motivation, novelty, error detection, working memory, and anticipation. ADHD subjects demonstrated physiologic activity in other areas of the brain believed to be less efficient in these kinds of tasks.

Zametkin's PET scan studies in adults with ADHD revealed lower levels of glucose metabolism in areas involved in the control of attention and motor activity (premotor cortex and the superior prefrontal cortex) (Zametkin et al., 1990).

Several studies using neuropsychological measures in stroke, traumatic brain injuries, and chronic mental illnesses like schizophrenia and dementia, which are associated with decreased cognitive functioning, support the hypothesis that unawareness of illness is related to defective frontal lobe functioning (Young et al., 1998).

Frontal lobe executive function plays a key role in the pathology of ADHD. Dysfunction associated with decreased modulation of attention, hyperactivity, and impulse control, accompanied by unawareness of the disorder's presence, have been strongly related to neurophysiological differences found in ADHD subjects. The severity and frequency of the symptoms correlates with these findings.

Neurotransmitters in ADHD

Although dopamine has long been postulated to be the predominant neurotransmitter substance, ADHD is a polygenic disorder associated with combined dysfunctions in dopamine, norepinephrine, and other neurotransmitter genes such as dopamine DRD2, DRD4, DRD5, dopamine transporter DAT4, norepinephrine, epinephrine, and perhaps serotonin (Comings et al., 2000; Faraone, Doyle et al., 2001).

Transmission of the 7-repeat allele of DRD4 from heterozygous parents to affected offspring may be associated with ADHD (Faraone, 2000; Muglia, 2000).

The interactive role of norepinephrine and dopamine in modulating how the brain processes and responds to stimuli with attention and impulsivity is generally supported in the literature, but the mechanism is not precisely known. We deduce that these neurotransmitters are involved in the pathophysiology of ADHD when we observe relief of symptoms by medications (methylphenidate and dextroamphetamine) known to affect these neurotransmitter systems.

The frontal executive functions of the brain cannot properly perform their inhibitory and integrative functions when neurotransmitter levels (particularly norepinephrine and dopamine) are abnormal. The frontal executive functions of the brain influence activation, focus, effort, emotion, memory, and action. Activation includes organizing and prioritizing work. We must also be able to initiate, sustain, and shift focus appropriately. Regulating alertness, sustaining effort, and adjusting processing speed are essential components of executive functioning. Managing frustration and modulating emotions are also executive tasks. Using working memory, accessing, and recall of information are thought to be the most important executive functions; they are the most commonly reported problem areas for ADHD individuals.

Properly regulated levels of norepinephrine or dopamine receptor stimulation are critical for optimal functioning. Inadequate or excessive norepinephrine or dopamine are associated with substance abuse, fear, anxiety, depression, stress, or ADHD, and can impair executive and cognitive functioning (Mefford & Potter, 1989).

Pliszka and colleagues (1996) suggested that the effect of spontaneous activity of the prefrontal cortex neurons on the posterior attention system is suppressed by norepinephrine, and this may intensify the response to specific input.

Moderate dopaminergic and noradrenergic stimulation of postsynaptic receptors optimizes prefrontal cortex response. In animal studies, dopaminergic and noradrenergic functions are impaired and poorly regulated in the prefrontal cortex in ADHD. This suggests that the imbalance between noradrenergic and dopaminergic systems in the prefrontal cortex is associated with the symptoms of ADHD (Madras et al., 2002; Russell, 2002; Solanto, 2002).

ADHD: "Thinking to a Different Drummer"

Woods and Ploof (1997) postulated that the symptoms of ADHD can be described as the results of behaviors and the associated responses (i.e., reward and punishment). The emotional reinforcement derived from the response is not being appropriately linked and stored for future reference. They refer to this linking of behavior-response-emotion as the "Memory-Feeling-Tone Complex." When this memory-feeling-tone complex is not activated, the initial behavior is repeated without consideration of the consequences.

When a behavior activates a reward, the feedback is met with psychic pleasure. This is mated with the memory of the behavior and its pleasurable response, causing a pleasurable memory-feeling-tone complex. Thus associated, previously neutral stimuli become salient stimuli and the original behavior more readily facilitated. Future behaviors are then selected in the context of this memory-feeling-tone complex (see Figure 8.1).

Conversely, when a behavior results in a punishment, the feedback produces future inhibition of the behavior. The behaviors are modulated by the connection of an unpleasant or painful-feeling-tone complex to previously neutral stimuli.

Studies of neural activity associated with emotion have helped us understand how emotions influence working memory. Dorsolateral prefrontal cor-

FIGURE 8.1
THE MEMORY-FEELING-TONE COMPLEX

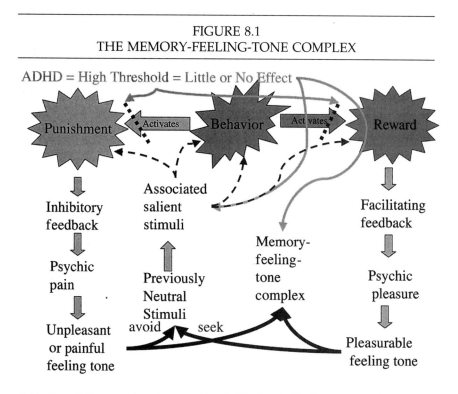

Activation of the reward system provides facilitating feedback to ongoing behavior via psychic pleasure. Activation of the punishment system provides inhibitory feedback to ongoing behavior via psychic pain. These pleasurable feeling-tones are stored together with the behaviors that elicited them in memory as the "Memory-Feeling-Tone Complex." Previously neutral stimuli subsequently become salient stimuli as they are associated with psychic pleasure or pain.

tex activity is influenced by the emotion-evoking qualities of task-relevant stimuli. It is enhanced by pleasant feelings and reduced by unpleasant feelings when compared to neutral stimuli. This was only found when working memory was required. Orbital–frontal cortex was also sensitive to emotional valance but in inverse relationship to dorsolateral prefrontal cortex and when demand for working memory was low. The intrinsic emotional valance, of task-relevant stimuli maintained in working memory modulates dorsolateral prefrontal cortex, activity when active maintenance of stimulus representations in reside working memory (Peristein, Elbert, & Stenger, 2002). The activity of working memory is facilitated by nonneutral emotional valance.

MRI studies of prefrontal cortex activity have also revealed that during processing emotion states can selectively influence cognition related neural activity in the lateral prefrontal cortex. These researchers conclude that during processing, emotion and higher cognition equally contribute to the control of thought and behavior (Gray, Brauer, & Raichle, 2002).

These findings are consistent with Woods and Ploof's model when they suggest that there is an emotional component associated with formation of the memory-feeling-tone complex. Their model suggests that a higher threshold to establish this complex is required in ADHD patients.

These findings are suggestive of the paradoxical hyperfocusing sometimes seen in ADHD patients. The ADHD diagnosis is sometimes resisted because parents will observe that the child can spend hours playing computer games or watching TV or some other activity or function. The enhanced emotional valence associated with the pleasure derived from these activities enables them to reach the threshold at which the memory-feeling-tone complex is formed and reinforced. It helps the stimuli to hold on to working memory and maintain the executive activity.

Memory-feeling-tone complexes are stored and called upon when behavior is contemplated. The *expectancy* of the future reward or punishment is considered. That is, based upon past experiences, the behavior currently being considered is expected to yield a specific result. As this expectancy is fulfilled over and over, the result is codified and responses to salient stimuli become reflexive. Immediate stimuli are screened with reference to future goals. Inner impulses are checked with reference to future punishment. Relevant and appropriate psychic feelings are connected to events, behavior, objects, and people. This process facilitates the ability to identify and empathize with others, and is an essential component of appropriate social functioning.

If, because of inadequate or disorganized signal transmission, the expectancy reflex is not established, then we see diminished screening of immediate stimuli, reduced checking of inner impulses, and consequent inappropriate social functioning. One of the core deficits in ADHD, impulsivity, is the consequence of failing to check impulses with reference to future reward or punishment.

People with ADHD may have a higher threshold for activating the punishment or reward systems, and therefore require more intense responses or multiple iterations of the behavior/reward–punishment system. This higher threshold for activating reward or punishment systems may be attributable to the weaker or disorganized neurotransmission signals. The increase in synaptic dopamine and norepinephrine stimulated by methylphenidate and noradrenergic agents can intensify the neurotransmitter signal and activate the properly adaptive response.

The inability to screen environmental stimuli results in a pathological dominance or inertia of the reflexive orientation, the reflexive orienting toward environmental stimuli, thereby inhibiting sustained focus and attention. This inhibition of reflexive involuntary attention to newly introduced stimuli causes distractibility and the core deficit in ADHD, inattention.

When the meaningful reference point (memory-feeling-tone complex) is weak or missing, each event or environmental stimulus is reacted to as if were a novel experience, whether or not there has been prior exposure to it.

Inability to delay gratification is associated with failure to develop a meaningful concept of future or past (see Figure 8.2). The ADHD patient is

FIGURE 8.2
EXPECTANCY AND THE CONTROL OF IMPULSIVITY

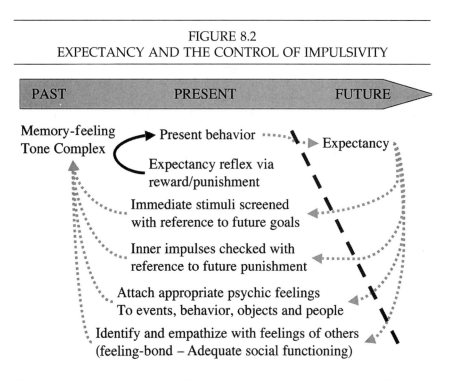

The previously created memory-feeling tone complex is attached to present behaviors facilitating an expectancy of a future outcome. In ADHD the expectancy may not be created or there is a weak association. As a result social functioning and control of impulsivity are impaired.

always in the present. Buddhists strive to live in the here and now in an effort to not miss any of the beauty or harmony of human existence, to focus complete attention on their environment. The person with ADHD does not put his or her observations in context, as if the "desktop" of the brain could not hold more than one page of information at a time. Additionally, with inadequate neurotransmitter modulation, a stimulus is not screened for appropriateness or priority. It is passed on to the "desktop" without constraint, rapidly replacing previously attended to stimuli with the next stimulus encountered.

In a normally functioning system, stimuli are acquired, emotional valence and memories are attached, and the packet is sent to the executive for evaluation. A response is then formulated and memories are updated, with emotional valence reset to an appropriate level: a memory-feeling-tone complex is established. Signals are subsequently sent to other areas of the brain to initiate the response.

With ADHD, a stimulus is received and weak or disorganized signals are inefficiently processed. Insufficient memory association and retrieval may occur and a reflexive, rather than a considered, emotional tone might result. The inadequate modulation of neurotransmitters results in minimal executive functional oversight. Past experiences are not referenced. Impulsive behavioral responses are not checked. The impending potential social environmental impact and associated response is not considered. The product is likely an *impulsive* ill-received, awkward and inappropriate behavioral response.

Even if one has experienced a punishment response to previous behaviors, the emotional charge or *feeling-tone* has not been affixed to the behavior–effect pair in ADHD. The complex is not stored as pointing to a potential punishment. If a punishment is not expected, the disproportionate or undesirable behavior is likely to be repeated. Still's 1902 description of the ADHD syndrome, "does not respond to punishment," remains current after a century of neurophysiologic study.

Reward and punishment establish and maintain the expectation—Pavlovian conditioned reflex. Reward associated with a specific response to stimuli results in activation of the median forebrain bundle. Conversely, punishment produces activation of periventricular system of diencephalon.

Treatments

In most cases, ADHD responds very well to treatment. Often just the diagnosis seems to be a therapeutic intervention with dramatic results. The relief of discovering an explanation for the lifelong inability to "fit in" or "pull out of it" is uplifting for many patients. The diagnosis can be liberating when patients and family learn that the problem is genetic, neurophysiologic, and manageable, rather than characterologic and immutable. A lifetime of guilt and self-doubt begin to dissolve. Families, significant others, and employers can be educated and enlisted to support the patient at home, school, and work. Understanding and acceptance of the patient's abilities are to everyone's advantage.

ESTABLISHMENT OF THE DIAGNOSIS

Appropriate diagnosis and patient education are the first steps to successful treatment and management of this disorder. ADHD is a lifelong condition which first manifests symptoms in early childhood and can remain problematic throughout adulthood. The diagnostic criteria currently require identification of some symptoms or impairment at age 7 or before, but not necessarily a full diagnosis with treatment. Historical reconstruction of events, comments on school evaluations, and interviews or correspondence with parents or others who knew the patient as a young child often provides sufficient information. I often give a list of *DSM-IV* ADHD symptoms to patients and ask them to have their parents rate how they were when they were very young children. I also ask parents to write me a note discussing how they feel about the possibility of this diagnosis for their child.

The responses are revealing. Parents often begin with "I'm so sorry," and are followed by explanations for why diagnosis or treatment were not pursued or school or physician recommendations not followed up. Apologies to their child are common. Regret and guilt are abundant, but acknowledgment of early childhood symptoms are frequently revealed and thereby established.

This effort is best accompanied by an extensive interview using any of a number of various formats or forms provided by Conners. These include an extensive biopsychosocial assessment and an evaluation of symptoms as they are currently and as they have presented since childhood. They help document and support the clinical impression of the provider but do not in themselves establish the diagnosis.

Once symptoms consistent with ADHD that have caused impairment in multiple settings since early childhood have been documented, other disorders that could be causing these symptoms must be ruled out. The differential process can establish multiple diagnoses, such as major depressive disorder and ADHD. It may also eliminate ADHD from consideration if, for example, generalized anxiety disorder were established since childhood.

TREATMENT PLAN

The treatment plan typically includes behavioral therapy and medication. Treatment with medication supported by coaching or individual psychother- apy produces results in days to weeks. The initial response is followed by an ongoing "ah-ha" experience as behaviors like cramming for exams evolve into studying before class, and covering for insufficient checking account funds evolves into financial planning.

Studies suggest that medication with coaching or counseling is the most effective treatment approach to ADHD. The most common, and often success- ful, treatment is medication alone (Anonymous, 1999; Greenhill et al., 1996).

Hypotheses regarding the influence of improper diet or excessive sugar have not been scientifically established. Etiologic theories associated with low birth weight or nongenetic maternal influence have been dismissed.

BEHAVIORAL TREATMENT

There is no oversight group or credentialing body that recommends or has validated psychotherapy, counseling, or behavioral modification guidelines for treatment of ADHD. There are many empirical reports of successful treatment of ADHD symptoms.

Psychoeducation helps the patient and family to understand ADHD and the issues involved in its management. They can understand that it is a genetic, biologic disorder. They are less likely to become frustrated and angry.

Enlisting other important people in the patient's life helps the patient to adapt, respond, cope, and compensate. They can assist in doing the mun- dane, adapting the environment, and reminding the patient of important dates and deadlines. Assistance and advice establishing structure and match- ing tasks to skills and talents is often very helpful.

Structuring the environment can be very helpful. If the keys are placed on the dresser in the same place immediately upon arrival at home, they are more likely to be found the next morning. If the bills are placed in a file to be paid on a certain date it is more likely to be paid on time. Division of chores can get the lawn mowed by the ADHD individual while their partner balances the checkbook.

Time management, organizational skills, and study skills classes, social skills groups, supportive and cognitive therapy groups can all be instrumental in the successful management of ADHD symptoms (Nadeau, 1995).

As core symptoms improve over time the patient must also overcome the learned habits and lifestyle that has evolved as a result of adapting and compensating for ADHD deficits that are now effectively treated. If habits, lifestyle, preferences, and choices are unchanged the newfound potential for improvement may never be challenged or fully realized.

PHARMACOLOGIC TREATMENT

Psychostimulants have repeatedly been shown to effect changes in the core symptoms of attention, hyperactivity, and impulsivity since Bradley first reported improvement in ADHD symptoms using benzedrine in 1937. Several studies demonstrate the effectiveness of stimulants in treating children, adolescents, and adults with ADHD. Appropriate use of stimulants can result in improvement in core symptoms of inattention, impulsivity, and hyperactivity. They also improve aggression, social interactions, and academic productivity and accuracy.

Methylphenidate and dextroamphetamine (and their various formulations) are the most commonly prescribed stimulants used to treat ADHD. Psychostimulants' effects are achieved through modulation of both the dopaminergic and noradrenergic neurotransmitter systems. They have end-effects similar to the sympathetic nervous system effects of dopamine and norepinephrine and are referred to as indirect-acting sympathomimetic amines. The dopaminergic effect possibly improves attention and helps control hyperactivity. The norepinephrine effect tempers impulsive behavior.

Stimulant amines increase the effect of dopamine and norepinephrine by increasing their release at neuronal synapses (see Figure 8.3). They also block their reuptake at the transporter (i.e., reuptake pump). The end result is perpetuation of an increased amount of the neurotransmitter in the interneuronal synaptic junction thereby facilitating neurotransmission. Stimulants exert compensatory effects involving interaction with presynaptic inhibitory autoreceptors.

Preparations of psychostimulants are available in forms that provide varying durations of action. The shorter acting medications have a fairly rapid onset of effect, followed 3–4 hours later by a fairly rapid decline. The extended duration formulations can last 8–12 hours. Individuals can respond differently to these medications, and it is recommended that patients be started at a low dose and be titrated upward until the desired effect is achieved or side effects supervene.

Stimulants promote alert, focused attention and increased motivation, mood, energy, and wakefulness. Stimulants improve executive function. About three quarters of ADHD patients respond to stimulants. The therapeutic effect is more likely to be fully achieved when habits and lifestyle modifications are incorporated into the treatment plan.

Antidepressants thought to be somewhat stimulating have been tried with some effect. Bupropion, tricyclic antidepressants (imipramine, desipramine), and Venlafaxine have all been tried, but reported results have not been impressive.

Alpha-2 agonists such as clonidine and guanfacine are sometimes used as an adjunct to help with hyperactive–impulsive symptoms. Buspirone, an

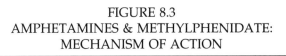

FIGURE 8.3
AMPHETAMINES & METHYLPHENIDATE:
MECHANISM OF ACTION

Pre-synaptic Neuron

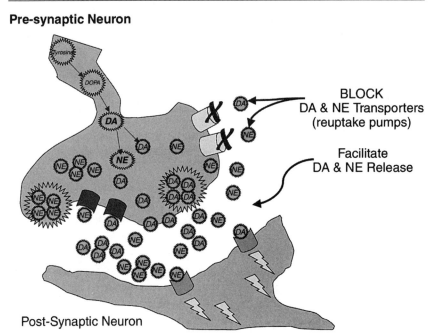

Tyrosine is converted to DOPA and subsequently norepinephirine. These neurotransmitters are released into the neuronal synapse and bind to post-synaptic receptors to facilitae neural transmission. Presynaptic autoreceptors can modulate cellular activity. DA and NE may also be transported back into the presynaptic cells to be released again or broken down. Amphetamines and methylphenidate block DA and NE Transporters (reuptake pumps) and facilitate DA and NE release.

antianxiety medication, has also been tried but largely dismissed as ineffective in ADHD.

Conclusion

ADHD sufferers are out of step with the rest of the world. One patient described having ADHD as being like a car that is out of tune, sometimes sputtering, sometimes racing, never going at the right speed without considerable effort and always idling rough.

ADHD patients appear to have less sensitive neurophysiologic trigger mechanisms than other people for establishing references for executive modulation of attention and behaviors. Their experiences do not accumulate to serve as the basis for learning and adaptive response. Without this accumulation empathy for others and interpersonal interactions are impoverished. Self-esteem is based on negative encounters and the potential within is not achieved.

The oversight and executive management functions of the brain are insufficiently connected to the related stimuli, memories, and emotional valance. The insufficient connections are attributed to weak or disorganized dopaminergic and noradrenergic neurotransmission. The involved systems are predominantly developed early in life. Performance and behavioral deficits are typically first recognized when a child encounters the school system, and this often becomes the initial point of therapeutic intervention. Unfortunately, for a host of reasons, this opportunity is often missed or the problem misunderstood. Though symptoms usually first manifest in childhood, ADHD can remain undiagnosed until failure at a significant educational or occupational juncture is encountered.

Most people respond well to treatment and are pleased with the results. Childhood behaviors and learning improve. Students will likely notice improved attentiveness to classroom lectures, better concentration on homework and tests, and a growing capacity to self-regulate study time and complete projects more efficiently. Occupationally, the patient recognizes more efficient task completion, better communication, and less tardiness or absenteeism. Efforts toward meeting goals and deadlines are more productive. At home listening and interpersonal relationships are enhanced, tensions reduced and financial stressors more controlled.

Our friend Alan (from earlier in this chapter) was amazed at the improvement in his life after he started treatment. The first thing he realized was that the myriad problems he was fraught with boiled down to deficits in attention and impulsivity. He joined a national ADHD advocacy group and read a couple of helpful books. He identified areas to focus on and he set priorities. He also added one small capsule to his vitamins and juice routine in the morning. He viewed it as "just something I have to be aware of and manage."

On a follow-up visit he reported that a few weeks after our initial visit "I went into work one day and I knew what I had to do. What a wonderful feeling!"

References

American Psychiatric Association. *Diagnostic and Statistical Manual of Mental Disorders.* 2nd ed. TR. Washington, DC: American Psychiatric Association; 1968.

American Psychiatric Association. *Diagnostic and Statistical Manual of Mental Disorders*. 3rd ed. TR. Washington, DC: American Psychiatric Association; 1980.

American Psychiatric Association. *Diagnostic and Statistical Manual of Mental Disorders*. 3rd ed., Rev. Washington, DC: American Psychiatric Press, 1987.

American Psychiatric Association. *Diagnostic and Statistical Manual of Mental Disorders*. 4th ed. Washington, DC: American Psychiatric Association; 1994.

American Psychiatric Association. *Diagnostic and Statistical Manual of Mental Disorders*. 4th ed. TR. Washington, DC: American Psychiatric Association; 2000.

Anonymous. A 14-month randomized clinical trial of treatment strategies for attention-deficit/hyperactivity disorder. The MTA Cooperative Group. Multimodal Treatment Study of Children with ADHD [see comment]. *Arch Gen Psychiatry*. 1999; 56(12):1073–1086.

Barkley RA. Attention-deficit hyperactivity disorder. *Child Psychopath*. 1996; New York: Guilford Press; 63–112.

Baumgaertel A, Wolraich ML, Dietrich M. Attention deficit disorders in a German elementary school-aged sample. *J Am Acad Child Adol Psychiatry*. 1995; 34:629–638.

Biederman J, Faraone SV, Keenan K, et al. Family-genetic and psychosocial risk factors in DSM-III attention deficit disorder. *J Am Acad Child Adol Psychiatry*. 1990; 29:526–533.

Biederman J, Faraone S, Milberger S, et al. Predictors of persistence and remission of ADHD into adolescence: Results from a four-year prospective follow-up study. *J Am Acad Child Adol Psychiatry*. 1996; 35:343–351.

Bradley C. The behavior of children receiving benzedrine. *Am J Psychiatry*. 1937; 94: 577–585.

Bradley C. Benzedrine and dexedrine in the treatment of children's behavior disorders. *Pediatrics*. 1950; 5:24–37.

Bush G, Frazier JA, Rauch SL, Seidman LJ, Whalen PJ, Jenike MA, Rosen BR, Biederman J. Anterior cingulate cortex dysfunction in attention-deficit/hyperactivity disorder revealed by fMRI and the Counting Stroop. *Biol Psychiatry*. 1999; 45(12):1542–1552.

Cantwell DP. Psychiatric illness in the families of hyperactive children. *Arch Gen Psychiatry*. 1972; 27:414–7.

Cantwell DP. ADHD through the life span: the role of bupropion in treatment. *J Clin Psychiatry*. 1998;59(suppl 4):92–94.

Clements SD. The child with minimal brain dysfunction. A multidisciplinary catalyst. *Lancet*. 1966; 86:121–123.

Comings DE, Gade-Andavolu R, Gonzalez N, et al. Comparison of the role of dopamine, serotonin, and noradrenaline genes in ADHD, ODD and conduct disorder: Multivariate regression analysis of 20 genes. *Clin Genet*. 2000; 57:178–196.

Conners CK, Erhardt D, Sparrow E. *Conners Adult ADHD Rating Scales*. North Tonawanda, NY: Multi-Health Systems; 1999.

Cuffe SP, McKeown RE, Jackson KL et al. Prevalence of attention-deficit/hyperactivity disorder in a community sample of older adolescents. *J Am Acad Child Adol Psychiatry*. 2001; 40:1037–1044.

DuPaul GJ, McGoey KE, Eckert TL, VanBrakle J. Preschool children with attention-deficit/hyperactivity disorder: Impairments in behavioral, social, and school functioning. *J Am Acad Child Adol Psychiatry*. 2001; 40:508–515.

Epstein LH, Cluss PA. A behavioral medicine perspective on adherence to long-term medical regimens. *J Consult Clin Psychology*. 1982; 50(6):950–971.

Faraone SV. Genetics of childhood disorders: XX. ADHD, Part 4: Is ADHD genetically heterogeneous? *J Am Acad Child Adol Psychiatry*. 2000; 39:1455–1457.

Faraone SV, Biederman J, Keenan K et al. Separation of DSM-III attention deficit disorder and conduct disorder: Evidence from a family-genetic study of American child psychiatric patients. *Psychol Med.* 1991; 21:109–121.

Faraone SV, Biederman J, Spencer T et al. Attention-deficit/hyperactivity disorder in adults: An overview. *Biol Psychiatry.* 2000; 48:9–20.

Faraone SV, Doyle AE, Meck E et al. Meta-analysis of the association between the 7-repeat allele of the dopamine D(4) receptor gene and attention deficit hyperactivity disorder. *Am J Psychiatry.* 2001; 158:1052–1057.

Frick PJ, Lahey BB, Loeber R et al. Familial risk factors to oppositional defiant disorder and conduct disorder: Parental psychopathology and maternal parenting. *J Consult Clin Psychol.* 1992; 60:49–55.

Goldman LS, Genel M, Bezman RJ, et al. Diagnosis and treatment of attention-deficit/hyperactivity disorder in children and adolescents. Council on Scientific Affairs, American Medical Association. *JAMA.* 1998; 279:1100–1107.

Gray JR, Braver TS, Raichle ME. Integration of emotion and cognition in the lateral prefrontal cortex. *Proceedings of the National Academy of Sciences of the United States of America.* 2000; 99(6):4115–4120.

Greenhill LL. Diagnosing attention-deficit/hyperactivity disorder in children. *J Clin Psychiatry.* 1998; 59(suppl 7):31–41.

Greenhill LL, Abikoff HB, Arnold LE, et al. Medication treatment strategies in the MTA study: Relevance to clinicians and researchers. *J Am Acad Child Adol Psychiatry.* 1996; 35:1304–1313.

Hart EL, Lahey BB, Loeber R et al. Developmental change in attention-deficit hyperactivity disorder in boys: A four-year longitudinal study. *J Abnorm Child Psychol.* 1995; 23:729–749.

Kahn RL, Cohen LH. Organic drivenness: A brain stem syndrome and an experience. *N Eng J Med.* 1934; 210:748–756.

Kelly, KM, Ramundo, P. *You Mean I'm Not Lazy, Stupid or Crazy?!* Cincinnati, Ohio: Tyrell & Jerem Press, 1993.

Lahey BB, Applegate B, McBurnett K et al. DSM-IV field trials for attention deficit hyperactivity disorder in children and adolescents. *Am J Psychiatry.* 1994; 151:1673–1685.

Madras BK, Miller GM, Fischman AJ et al. The dopamine transporter: Relevance to attention deficit hyperactivity disorder (ADHD) [Review]. *Behav Brain Res.* 2002; 130:57–63.

Mann HB, Greenspan SI. The identification and treatment of adult brain dysfunction. *Am J Psychiatry.* 1976; 133:1013–1017.

Mash EJ, Barkley RA, eds. *Child Psychopathology.* New York: Guilford Press; 1996.

McDowell CL, Harrison DW, Demaree HA. Is hemispheric decline a function of aging? *Int J Neurosci.* 1994; 79(1):1–11.

Mefford IN, Potter WZ. A neuroanatomical and biochemical basis for attention deficit disorder with hyperactivity in children: A defect in tonic adrenaline mediated inhibition of locus coeruleus stimulation. *Med Hypotheses.* 1989; 29:33–42.

Mercugliana M. What is attention-deficit/hyperactivity disorder? *Pediatr Clin N Am.* 1999; 46(5):831–843.

Morrison JR, Stewart MA. A family study of the hyperactive child syndrome. *Biol Psychiatry.* 1971; 3:189–195.

Muglia P, Jain U, Macciardi F, et al. Adult attention deficit hyperactivity disorder and the dopamine D4 receptor gene. *Am J Med Genet.* 2000; 96:273–277.

Nada-Raja S, Langley JD, McGee R, et al. Inattentive and hyperactive behaviors and driving offenses in adolescence. *J Am Acad Child Adol Psychiatry.* 1997; 36:515–522.

Nadeau KG, ed. *A Comprehensive Guide to Attention Deficit Disorder in Adults: Research, Diagnosis, and Treatment.* New York: Brunner/Mazel; 1995.

Offord DR, Boyle MH, Racine YA et al. Outcome, prognosis, and risk in a longitudinal follow-up study. *J Am Acad Child Adolesc Psychiatry.* 1992; 31:916–923.

Peristein WM, Elbert T, Stenger VA. "Dissociation in human prefrontal cortex of affective influences on working memory-related activity. *Proceedings of the National Academy of Sciences of the United States of America.* 2002; 99(3):1736–1741.

Pliszka SR, McCracker JT, Maas JW et al. Catecholamines in attention-deficit hyperactivity disorder: Current perspectives *J Am Acad Child Adol Psychiatry.* 1996; 35:264–272.

Reeves JC, Werry JS, Elkind GS et al. Attention deficit, conduct, oppositional, and anxiety disorders in children: II. Clinical characteristics. *J Am Acad Child Adol Psychiatry.* 1987; 26:144–155.

Russell VA. Hypodopaminergic and hypernoradrenergic activity in prefrontal cortex slices of an animal model for attention-deficit hyperactivity disorder—the spontaneously hypertensive rat. *Behav Brain Res.* 2002; 130:191–196.

Scahill L, Schwab-Stone M. Epidemiology of ADHD in school-age children. *Child Adol Psychiatry Clin N Am.* 2000; 9:541–555.

Schachar R, Wachsmuth R. Hyperactivity and parental psychopathology. *J Child Psychiatry.* 1990; 31:381–392.

Scheier MF. Self-awareness, self-consciousness, and angry aggression. *J Personality.* 1976; 44(4):627–644.

Solanto MV. Dopamine dysfunction in AD/HD: Integrating clinical and basic neuroscience research. *Behav Brain Res.* 2002; 130:65–71.

Still GF. Some abnormal psychical conditions in children (The Goulstonian lectures). *Lancet.* 1902; 1:1008–1012, 1077–1082, 1163–1168.

Stubbe DE. Attention-deficit/hyperactivity disorder overview. Historical perspective, current controversies, and future directions. *Child Adol Psychiatric Clin N Am.* 2000; 9: 469–479.

Wender PH. Adult manifestations of attention-deficit/hyperactivity disorders. In: Kaplan HI, Sadock BJ, eds. Vol 2. 7th ed. *Kaplan and Sadock's Comprehensive Textbook of Psychiatry.* Philadelphia, PA: Lippincott, Williams & Wilkins; 2000.

Wolraich ML, Hannah JN, Baumgaertel A, Feurer ID. Examination of DSM-IV criteria for attention-deficit/hyperactivity disorder in a county-wide sample. *J Dev Behav Pediatr.* 1998; 19:162–8.

Wolraich ML, Hannah JN, Pinnock TY et al. Comparison of diagnostic criteria for attention deficit hyperactivity disorder in a county-wide sample. *J Am Acad Child Adol Psychiatry.* 1996; 35:319–323.

Woods, SK, Ploof WH. Understanding ADHD: Attention deficit hyperactivity disorder and the feeling brain. Thousand Oaks, CA: Sage; 1997.

Young D, Zakzanis KK, Bailey C et al. Further parameters of insight and neuropsychological deficit in schizophrenia and other chronic mental disease. *J Nerv & Men Dis.* 1998; 186:44–50.

Zametkin AJ, Nordahl TE, Gross M et al. Cerebral glucose metabolism in adults with hyperactivity of childhood onset. *N Eng J Med.* 1990; 323:1361–1366.

9

Anosognosia and Denial of Illness Following Stroke

Robert G. Robinson

IN 1914, BABINSKI reported that some patients with severe hemiplegia appeared to be unaware of their deficit. He called this absence of awareness *anosognosia*, a term derived from the Greek *a* (without), *noso* (disease), and *gnosis* (knowledge). The medical literature of the late 19th and early 20th century went on to report a variety of similar failures of awareness respecting one's own deficits or diseases, including Anton's syndrome of cortical blindness (Anton, 1896), and the absence of awareness of hemianopsia, amnesia, dementia, aphasia (particularly nonfluent aphasia), and mental illnesses like schizophrenia or dementia.

Because they are unaware of their disease, patients with anosognosia may be less likely to seek treatment and be compliant with prescribed medications regimens. They also tend to engage in potentially dangerous activities, and often get lost when they are alone, or believe themselves capable of driving an automobile when they are not (Heilman & Valenstein, 1993). Anosognosia can therefore have grave consequences, and clinicians should monitor their patients' awareness of their own limitations.

Illness denial is similar in the way patients fail to acknowledge their illness or the deficits associated with it. Denial of illness has been reported among patients with brain injury and other disorders (Weinstein & Kahn, 1955).

This work was supported in part by the following NIH grants: MH52879, MH53592 and MH63405. I would also like to thank Teresa Kopel and Stephanie Rosazza for collecting much of this data and Todd Kosier for help with the statistical analysis.

When stroke patients deny their hemiplegia, the distinction between denial and anosognosia appears to be negligible, and the two conditions may be manifestations of the same underlying mechanism. On the other hand, when patients who do not have brain injury deny an obvious impairment or even the existence of a major medical condition like myocardial infarction (Hackett & Cassem, 1974), we may be seeing a different process than the one associated with brain injury. The nature of a brain injury may create cognitive or sensory impairments which contribute to deficits in awareness of impairment, but similar unawareness in patients who have not sustained organic brain injuries probably represents a psychological response to impairment.

The third related phenomenon, found in patients with brain injury, is the indifference reaction. First described by Hecaen and Denny Brown (Denny-Brown, Meyer, & Horenstein, 1952; Hecaen, deAjuriaguerra, & Massonet, 1951) patients with the indifference reaction do not deny the existence of impairment, but their unconcern seems clearly inappropriate to the severity or implications of the illness or impairments. Although somewhat different from denial and anosognosia, this phenomenon appears to share some features of those disorders, including its inaccessibility to empathic understanding of the patient's emotional or cognitive state.

The *alien hand syndrome* is a similar and potentially related condition, characterized by the patient's inability to recognize that a hand, usually the left, is his own. Patients may try to throw the hand out of bed or strike it with their right hand as though it was an interloper invading their personal space. Alien hand behavior may include buttoning a shirt with the right hand while the left hand follows, undoing the work of the right hand. Although relatively unusual, this is among the most striking examples of failed awareness of some part or deficit of one's own body. When they appear as manifestations of injury to the brain, it is usually, but not exclusively, the right hemisphere that has sustained the insult (Heilman & Valensgein, 1993; Starkstein, Fedoroff, Price, Leiguarda, & Robinson, 1992).

There have been many attempts to explain these multiple variations of failed self-awareness. Weinstein and Kahn (1955) proposed psychological etiologies, suggesting that denial is a psychological defense mechanism which attenuates the emotional impact of a catastrophic event such as hemiplegia. Alternatively, it has also been proposed that anosognosia is a confusional state induced by the medical illness or its treatment (Hecaen et al. 1951). Others (Levine, Calvanio, & Rinn, 1991) have suggested that anosognosia may occur when patients do not receive sufficient sensory feedback to communicate to their brains that their limb is weak or that their proprioceptive system is impaired, and they consequently do not sense an absence of motor activity. Hemispatial neglect has also been proposed as a contributory mechanism. If patients neglect left visual field stimuli, they might be unaware that there is no movement in their left arm. Still others have hypothesized phantom movement, a sense that the arm has moved when it has not. Disconnection between the right and left hemisphere has also been proposed to explain anosognosia (Geschwind, 1965a, 1965b), with areas in the right hemisphere that create associations disconnected from language centers in the left hemisphere, and consequent unawareness of impairment. None of these several hypotheses, however, has been shown to explain all cases of anosognosia or denial of illness.

Empirical Studies of Anosognosia and Denial of Illness

We have conducted two studies of anosognosia and denial of illness with two entirely different patient populations. We will examine the results of both studies here, determine whether findings of the first study were confirmed by the second, and will assess whether the two studies lend empirical support to any of the proposed mechanisms for anosognosia or denial of illness following stroke.

First Study

Our first study involved a consecutive series of 80 patients with acute stroke who were assessed using a battery of psychiatric and neuropsychological tests for the presence, severity, and clinical correlates of anosognosia (Starkstein et al., 1992). The demographic characteristics for the 80 patients involved in this study are shown in Table 9.1. There were no significant differences in the background characteristics of the patients. They were predominantly African American, from lower socioeconomic classes, in their late 50s or 60s, and were examined within the first 2 weeks following stroke.

Patients were classified as having mild anosognosia if they denied the existence of a motor deficit but acknowledged it when they were told they had a motor deficit. The severity of anosognosia was considered moderate if the patient denied any motor impairment, even when told one existed, but did acknowledge the impairment when they were shown their paretic arm within their intact visual field. Severe anosognosia was diagnosed when the patient would not acknowledge a motor impairment even after a visual demonstration (Table 9.2).

Patients were given a series of neuropsychological examinations, including sensory neglect using 10 double simultaneous stimulations, intermixed

TABLE 9.1
Stroke Patients with Anosognosia (n = 80)

	NONE n = 53	MILD n = 8	MODERATE n = 9	SEVERE n = 10
Age	56 ± 11	62 ± 11	69 ± 13	62 ± 11
Education	11 ± 4	9 ± 3	11 ± 4	10 ± 3
Gender (n male)	29	5	5	6
Race (n Black)	33	6	6	6
Left handedness	3	0	2	1
N married	16	2	5	2
Hollingshead class IV–V	30	7	3	8
Fam hx psych disorder	9	0	2	1
Personal hx psych disorder	8	0	1	1
Past hx psych disorder	13	0	2	1
Days since stroke	5.7 ± 3.9	7.1 ± 4.9	6.74 ± 4.8	5.6 ± 3.5

Reprinted with permission from Robinson RG, *Neuropsychiatry of Stroke*; 1998, Cambridge University Press.

with 20 single stimulations. They were then asked to identify the site of stimulation. All patients were able to recognize unilateral stimulation of both the right and left side, indicating that hemisensory deficits did not interfere with this testing. Patents were also tested for hemispatial neglect by asking them to copy a complex figure with 10 lines to the left of the midline and 10 lines to the right. Personal neglect was assessed by asking the patients to touch the hand contralateral to the lesion with the hand ipsilateral to the lesion. Motor neglect was tested by asking patients to open and close both hands 20 times. Patients with severe motor deficits were not administered this test. Motor impersistence was tested by asking patients to keep their eyes closed for 30 seconds. Recognition of facial emotion was tested by

TABLE 9.2
Frequency of Motor and Visual Anosognosia in Patients with Mild, Moderate, and Severe Disorders

	MOTOR IMPAIRMENT # ANOSOGNOSIA/ TOTAL WITH IMPAIRMENT	VISUAL FIELD IMPAIRMENT # ANOSOGNOSIA/ TOTAL WITH IMPAIRMENT
Mild	8/8	0/3
Moderate	9/9	0/4
Severe	10/10	2/5

asking the patients to identify the expression on a face included in a series of 20 faces taken from the Eckman and Friesen series.

All patients underwent CT scans using a General Electric 9900 CT scanner with 5 mm thick slices obtained parallel to the canthomeatal line. Damaged areas were localized in specific brain regions using Levine and Grek's procedure (Levine & Grek, 1984). The lesion volume was approximated by dividing the largest lesion area by the area of the brain slice that included the body of the lateral ventricle. This procedure was previously demonstrated to have high reliability and correlation with other methods of determining lesion volume.

The results of the assessment of hemineglect are shown in Figure 9.1. Hemineglect on double simultaneous stimulation was present only on the left side of the body, and was significantly more common among patients with anosognosia than in those patients without. Similarly, left visual field

FIGURE 9.1
ASSOCIATION OF ANOSOGNOSIA WITH NEGLECT
AND VISUAL FIELD DEFECT

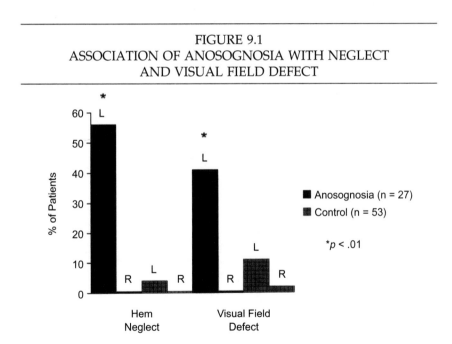

The association of anosognosia with left-sided neglect to double simultaneous stimulation and visual field defect. More than half of the patients with anosognosia showed left-sided hemineglect and L visual field defect significantly more frequently than stroke patients without anosognosia. (Reprinted with permission from Robinson RG, Neuropsychiatry of Stroke, 1998, Cambridge University Press.)

hemianopsia was significantly more frequent in patients with anosognosia than in those without. However, although all 25 patients with hemiparesis and anosognosia were unaware of their motor deficits, only 2 of the 12 patients with visual field deficits and anosognosia had unawareness of their visual field deficit ($\chi^2 = 28.5$, df = 1, $p < .001$) (Table 9.2). Thus, the existence of anosognosia for motor deficits was significantly more frequent than other deficits, and denial of one kind of impairment did not necessarily predict that other types of sensory impairment would also be denied.

Diagnoses of depression among patients with anosognosia are shown in Figure 9.2. There were no significant differences between the groups in the frequency of major depression or the severity of depression or anxiety symptoms as measured by the Hamilton Depression or Hamilton Anxiety Scales. The patients with mild anosognosia, however, had a significantly higher frequency of minor depression than the other three groups ($\chi^2 = 13.9$, df = 6,

---

FIGURE 9.2
FREQUENCY OF DEPRESSION BASED ON THE EXISTENCE
AND SEVERITY OF ANOSOGNOSIA

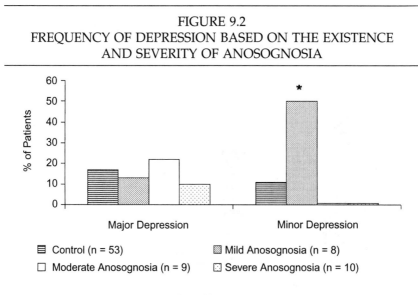

*p = .004

The frequency of major and minor depression by severity of anosognosia. Major depression was equally as common in stroke patients with anosognosia as stroke patients without anosognosia. This indicates that unawareness of physical impairment does not lead to unawareness of mood disorder. (Reprinted with permission from Robinson RG, Neuropsychiatry of Stroke, 1998, Cambridge University Press.)

FIGURE 9.3
DEPRESSION AND IMPAIRMENT SEVERITY RELATED
TO THE EXISTENCE AND SEVERITY OF ANOSOGNOSIA

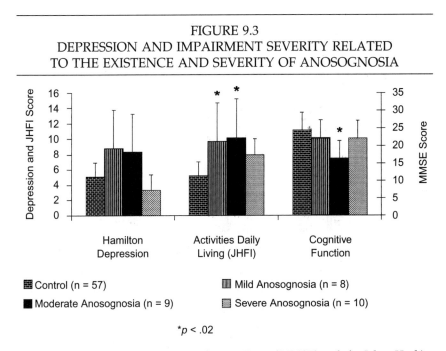

*p < .02

Impairment scores on the Mini Mental State Exam (MMSE) and the Johns Hopkins Functioning Inventory (JHFI) as well as severity of depression scores on the Hamilton Depression scale. Note that patients with anosognosia had greater severity of impairment than patients without anosognosia. (Reprinted with permission from Robinson RG, Neuropsychiatry of Stroke, 1998, Cambridge University Press.)

$p < .05$). Thus, the patient's recognition of depressive symptoms was not significantly influenced by the presence of anosognosia for motor impairment.

The severity of cognitive impairment was not significantly different between patients with and without anosognosia, except that patients with moderate anosognosia had significantly lower Mini Mental scores than patients with no anosognosia (f3, 76 = 3.5, $p < .02$) (Figure 9.3). Furthermore, there was a significant association between impairment in activities of daily living and the presence of anosognosia. Patients with mild or moderate anosognosia were significantly more impaired than the nonanosognosia patients (f3, 76-4.01, $p < .01$).

Results of the neuropsychological examination appear in Figure 9.4. Patients with anosognosia had significantly greater frequency and severity of tactile and visual extinction contralateral to the lesion on double simultaneous stimulation than patients without anosognosia. Those with anosognosia

FIGURE 9.4
THE FREQUENCY OF SENSORY AND SPECIAL NEGLECT
BASED ON THE EXISTENCE AND SEVERITY OF ANOSOGNOSIA

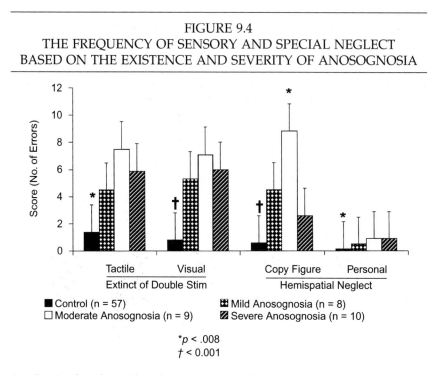

$*p < .008$
$\dagger < 0.001$

Tactile, visual, and spatial neglect in patients with anosognosia and controls. Patients with all severities of anosognosia had significantly more severe neglect in all modalities tested than stroke patients without anosognosia. (Reprinted with permission from Robinson RG, Neuropsychiatry of Stroke, *1998, Cambridge University Press.)*

also showed hemispatial neglect when asked to copy a figure and point to the hemiparetic hand. Patients with anosognosia also showed more motor impersistence when instructed to keep their eyes closed, and could only do so for a significantly shorter period than patients without anosognosia. Patients with anosognosia performed significantly worse than those without the condition in recognizing facial emotion and the emotional content of sentences. Finally, detailed neuropsychological testing using a previously described and validated method was done on 8 patients with anosognosia and 8 matched nonanosognosia patients to assess severity of motor impairment, and lesion location and volume (Starkstein et al. 1993a). Patients with anosognosia were significantly more impaired than control patients on the frontal lobe tasks of verbal fluency ($t = 2.63$ $p < .02$) and Trails B ($t = 7.45$, $p < .001$; Figure 9.5). There were no differences, however, in Block Design from the WAIS, the Rey Auditory Learning task, digit span, or the Benton Visual Retention task (Figure 9.5; Starkstein et al. 1993a). These neuropsychological testing results suggest that anosognosia is specifically associated with frontal lobe dysfunction, even when other neuropsychological deficits due to stroke are controlled.

Of the 80 patients included in this study, 66 had CT scans showing an ischemic lesion. The findings from the CT scan analysis are shown in Figures 9.6 and 9.7. As expected, patients with anosognosia had a significantly higher frequency of right hemisphere lesions than patients without anosognosia ($\chi^2 = 10.3$, df = 3, $p < .015$). Patients with mild or severe anosognosia had a significantly higher frequency of temporal, parietal, and thalamic lesions than patients without anosognosia. Patients with moderate anosog-

FIGURE 9.5
NEUROPSYCHOLOGICAL TEST PERFORMANCE IN PATIENTS
WITH AND WITHOUT ANOSOGNOSIA

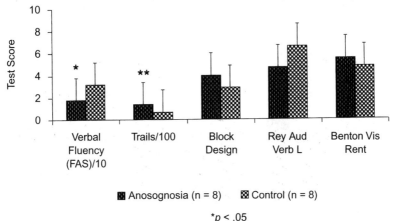

*$p < .05$
**$p < 0.01$

Performance of patients with and without anosognosia who were matched for lesion location on several neuropsychological examinations. Patients with anosognosia were significantly more impaired than controls on verbal fluency (FAS) and Trails A and B but not on any of the other construction, attention, learning or memory tasks. These findings suggest that anosognosia is associated with frontal lobe dysfunction (data taken from Starkstein et al. 1993). Rey aud verb L=Rey auditory verbal learning test; Benton vis rent = Benton visual retention test. (Reprinted with permission from Robinson RG, Neuropsychiatry of Stroke, *1998, Cambridge University Press.)*

nosia, however, had a significantly higher frequency of lesions involving the basal ganglia (Figure 9.6). Brain atrophy was measured in 51 patients. Patients with brain stem, cerebellar, or bilateral lesions were excluded. The results of these measurements are shown in Figure 9.7. All severities of anosognosia were combined into a single group, because only 18 patients were available for analysis. Patients with anosognosia had significantly larger ratios of frontal horn, lateral ventricle, and third ventricle to brain compared to the patients without anosognosia. The patients with anosognosia also had larger lesion volumes, but this was not statistically significant. The width of

FIGURE 9.6
LESION LOCATIONS ASSOCIATED WITH ANOSOGNOSIA

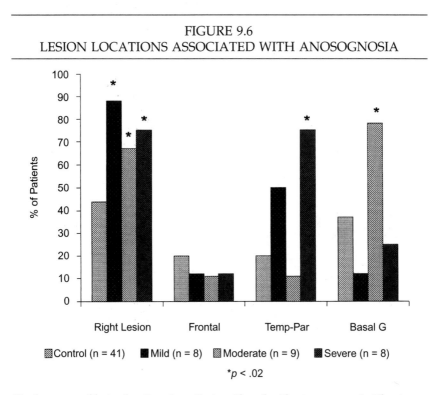

*p < .02

The frequency of lesion locations in patients with and without anosognosia. The strongest association was between anosognosia and right hemisphere lesions. Patients with severe anosognosia were more likely to have temporoparietal (Temp-Par) lesions than any other group, while moderate to severe anosognosia was associated with basal ganglia (Basal G) lesions. Note that frontal lesions were not associated with the existence of anosognosia in this population. (Reprinted with permission from Robinson RG, Neuropsychiatry of Stroke, *1998, Cambridge University Press.)*

FIGURE 9.7
VENTRICLE-TO-BRAIN RATIOS AMONG PATIENTS
WITH AND WITHOUT ANOSOGNOSIA

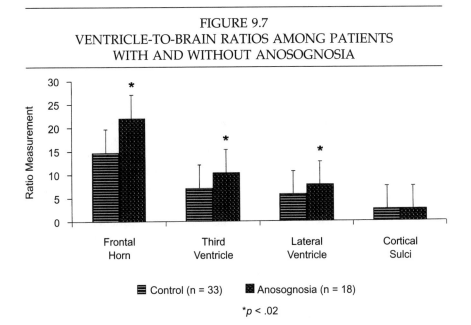

Ventricle to brain size ratios for patients with anosognosia were significantly larger than those for patients without anosognosia. The cortical measures were not different between groups indicating that patients with unawareness of their physical impairment following a stroke have more subcortical brain atrophy (which probably preceded the stroke). Compromised subcortical function in the right hemisphere may mediate this phenomenon of anosognosia. (Reprinted with permission from Robinson RG, Neuropsychiatry of Stroke, *1998, Cambridge University Press.)*

cortical sulci were not significantly different, suggesting that subcortical, but not cortical, atrophy is associated with anosognosia.

A stepwise regression analysis was used to examine the relative importance of each of the factors associated with anosognosia. Diagnosis of anosognosia (i.e., none, mild, moderate, or severe) was the dependent variable, and neglect on double simultaneous stimulation, hemispatial neglect on drawing, recognition of facial emotion, recognition of emotional intonation in sentences, subcortical atrophy, right hemispheric lesion location, and impairments in activities of daily living were independent variables. Two variables were found to be significant and independently associated with the presence of anosognosia. These were the frontal horn ratio, ($r^2 = .49$, $f = 21.0$, $p < .01$) and right hemispheric lesion location ($r^2 = .75$, $f = 4.03$, $p < .05$).

In summary, our first study found anosognosia was significantly associated with a higher frequency of visual, tactile, and spatial neglect, frontal lobe dysfunction, right hemisphere lesions (particularly temporal, parietal, basal ganglia, and thalamus), and subcortical atrophy.

SECOND STUDY

Forty-four patients completed our second study, a double-blind comparative evaluation of nortriptyline, fluoxetine, or placebo in the treatment of both depressed and nondepressed patients following stroke. All patients who completed the Denial of Illness Scale before and after the 3-month treatment period, as well as 2 years later, were included in this study. Patients were considered to have denial of illness if their score on the 10-item Denial of Illness Scale (DIS) was 5 or greater. The items which patients with denial of illness endorsed more frequently than the nondenial patients appear in Figure 9.8. In our first study, we had examined the relationship between scores on the DIS and the severity of anosognosia (Starkstein et al., 1993b).

FIGURE 9.8
FREQUENCY OF DENIAL SYMPTOMS

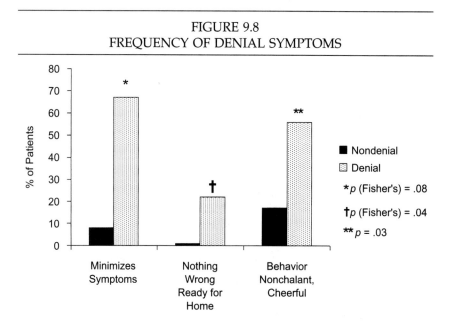

The percent of patients who demonstrated specific behaviors on the Denial of Illness Scale (DIS). These symptoms were significantly more frequent among patients (n = 9) who scored 5 or greater on the DIS compared to those with scores less than 5 on the DIS (n = 35).

FIGURE 9.9
SEVERITY OF ANOSOGNOSIA-RELATED SEVERITY
OF DENIAL OF ILLNESS

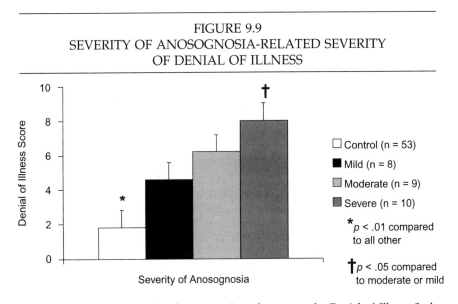

Relationship between severity of anosognosia and score on the Denial of Illness Scale (DIS). Patients with DIS scores of 5 or greater had at least mild severity of anosognosia. (Reprinted with permission from Robinson RG, Neuropsychiatry of Stroke, 1998, Cambridge University Press.)

The relationship between the score on the Denial of Illness Scale and the severity of anosognosia for the 80 patients in our first study is shown in Figure 9.9. Patients scoring 5 or more on the denial scale had at least a mild form of anosognosia. Thus, although patient selection in the second study was based on response to the DIS, they all had at least a mild degree of anosognosia (Starkstein et al., 1993b).

The background characteristics of 9 patients who fulfilled the criteria for denial were compared with 35 patients who did not. There are no significant differences between the patient groups in background characteristics, including prior personal or family history of psychiatric disorder (Table 9.3).

The severity of impairments appear in Table 9.4. Patients who denied impairment were not significantly different from those who did not, in the severity of impairment in conducting activities of daily living (JHFI and FIM), cognition (MMSE), or social functioning (SFE and STC).

On neurologic examination, 91% of the control patients and 78% of the denial patients had ischemic infarcts. The volume of all visible lesions in the control group was 6.5 ± 8.7 SD % of whole brain volume, while the

TABLE 9.3
Demographic Characteristics

CHARACTERISTIC	NONDENIAL (n = 35)		DENIAL (n = 9)	
	Mean	*SD*	*Mean*	*SD*
Age (years)	69.6	10.3	65.3	14.3
Education (yrs)	11.9	2.3	12.2	2.5
	N	*%*	*N*	*%*
Male	19	54.3	5	55.6
Caucasian	33	94.3	9	100.0
Married	16	47.7	7	77.8
Socioeconomic status	12	34.3	5	55.6
Hollingshead class IV or V				
Right handedness	35	100.0	9	100.0
Prior psychiatric history	4	11.4	1	11.1
Family psychiatric history	4	11.4	2	22.2

lesion volume was 3.5 ± 3.6 SD % of whole brain volume in the denial patients. These lesion volumes were not significantly different ($p = .43$). On the other hand, the lesion location was significantly different between the two groups of patients (Figure 9.10). Eighty-eight percent of the denial patients had a right hemisphere lesion, compared with only 45% of the control patients (Fisher's exact, $p = .05$).

When intrahemisphere lesion location was examined, 50% of the patients with denial had a basal ganglia lesion of the right hemisphere, compared with 8% of the controls (Figure 9.11). Similarly, patients with denial tended to have a greater frequency of insular lesions in the right hemisphere than control patients.

TABLE 9.4
Psychiatric Variables

CHARACTERISTIC	NONDENIAL (n = 35)		DENIAL (n = 9)		SIGNIFICANCE
	Mean	*SD*	*Mean*	*SD*	
MMSE	26.2	5.1	24.6	5.5	.3939
JHFI	6.5	3.3	8.0	5.4	.3140
FIM	48.6	9.7	46.5	12.4	.5818
SFE	0.12	0.15	0.14	0.25	.7427
STC	3.5	1.9	2.4	1.3	.1249

FIGURE 9.10
HEMISPHERIC LESION LOCATION AND
THE EXISTENCE OF DENIAL

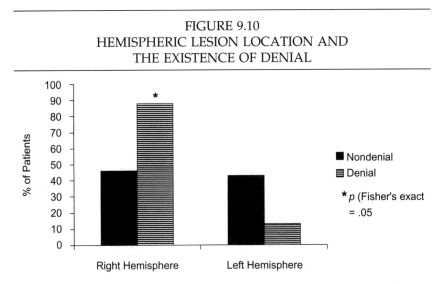

Hemispheric lesion location among patients with Denial of Illness Scale (DIS) scores below 5 and 5 or greater (denial scores). Note that denial of illness occurred predominantly among patients with right hemisphere stroke. Although a few left hemisphere lesion patients also showed denial.

FIGURE 9.11
INTRA-HEMISPHERIC LESION LOCATION AND
THE EXISTENCE OF DENIAL

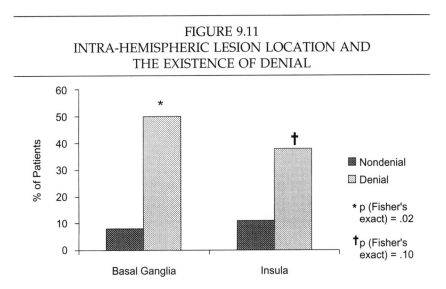

Intrahemispheric lesion location and denial of illness. Both basal ganglia and insular lesions of the right hemisphere were associated with denial of illness (anosognosia).

Relationships between of denial and *DSM-IV* diagnoses of major depression, minor depression, or generalized anxiety disorder are shown in Figure 9.12. There were no significant differences in the frequency of major depression or generalized anxiety disorder. Although the differences were not statistically significant, 23% of the control group and 0% of the denial group had minor depression.

These findings are consistent with our data indicating that the mean severity of neither anxiety nor depressive symptoms on the Hamilton Anxiety and Depression Scales were significantly different for denial and nondenial patients. Hamilton Depression and Hamilton Anxiety scores were both negatively correlated with scores on the denial of illness scale, however (Figures 9.13 & 9.14). Although the strengths of the correlations were statistically significant, they were only moderate, and the severity of denial would explain only about 10% of the variance in Hamilton Depression scores or Hamilton Anxiety scores. These findings suggest, however, that denial impairs recognition of anxious–depressive symptoms or helps to minimize them.

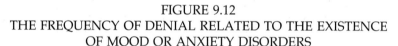

FIGURE 9.12
THE FREQUENCY OF DENIAL RELATED TO THE EXISTENCE
OF MOOD OR ANXIETY DISORDERS

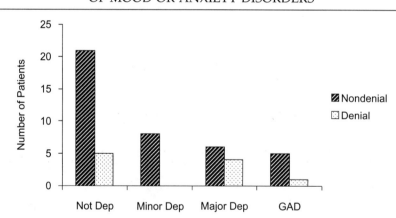

Relationship between denial of illness (anosognosia) and diagnosis of major or minor depression or generalized anxiety disorder (GAD) using DSM-IV diagnostic criteria. Note that depression and GAD were just as common in the denial compared with the nondenial stroke patients.

FIGURE 9.13
CORRELATION BETWEEN SEVERITY OF DEPRESSION
AND SEVERITY OF DENIAL OF ILLNESS

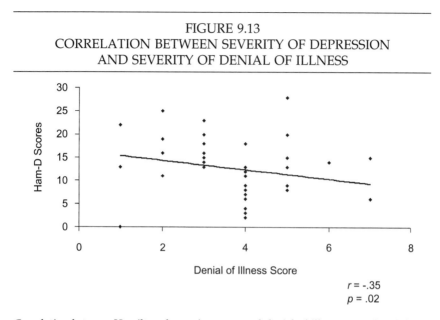

$r = -.35$
$p = .02$

Correlation between Hamilton depression score and denial of illness score (DIS) for 44 patients in this study. Depression scores decreased as DIS scores increased suggesting that denial may have some effect on the report of depression severity.

We were, of course, also able to evaluate whether there were differences in the denial scores among patients who received nortriptyline, fluoxetine, or placebo. There were 12 patients who received nortriptyline or fluoxetine for 12 weeks and 12 patients who received placebo. Although there were not enough patients with denial scores over 5 to analyze, only patients with denial of illness, we matched patients for severity of denial score. The placebo group initially had a mean score of 3.83 ± 1.8 SD, compared to the nortriptyline or fluoxetine group with a mean score of 3.83 ± 1.64 SD. The results of the trial are shown on Figure 9.15. We conducted a repeated measures analysis of variance comparing the active and placebo treated groups. There was a significant time by treatment interaction (f1, 22 = 4.35, $p = .049$). Based on post hoc comparisons, patients who received placebo had significantly higher denial scores at the end of the treatment trial than patients who received active medication. The patients given placebo over the 12-week treatment course increased their denial score; there was no significant change in denial scores among patients treated with active medication. Because the patients were, on average, 2 to 3 months poststroke at

FIGURE 9.14
CORRELATION BETWEEN SEVERITY OF ANXIETY SYMPTOMS
AND SEVERITY OF DENIAL OF ILLNESS

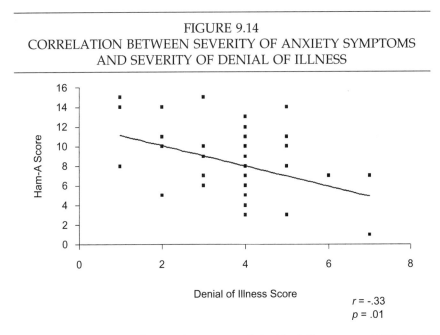

r = -.33
p = .01

Correlation between Hamilton anxiety score and denial of illness score (DIS) for 44 patients in this study. Depression scores decreased as DIS scores increased suggesting that denial may have some effect on the report of depression severity.

the beginning of the treatment trial, these findings suggest that there may be an increased severity of unawareness of illness among some patients over the course of the first 5 to 6 months following stroke. Although treatment with antidepressants did not seem to eliminate or decrease the severity of unawareness of illness, patients receiving active medication did not increase their denial severity. Although this treatment trial cannot be called a success-ful therapeutic intervention, it suggests that intervention may be possible. Stimulants or the new generation of atypical antipsychotic mediations might decrease the severity of anosognosia during the first few months following stroke.

THE MECHANISM OF ANOSOGNOSIA
Some conclusions may be drawn from these two studies about the mecha-nisms which contribute to anosognosia. We were able to identify several consistent findings across two studies which enrolled a very different geo-graphic, racial, and socioeconomic mix of patients. Both studies found that

anosognosia and denial of illness were not associated with prior history of psychiatric disorder, but were strongly associated with right hemisphere lesions, particularly in the basal ganglia and temporal parietal regions. Furthermore, both studies found that the presence of anosognosia and denial of illness were not significantly associated with other psychiatric diagnoses such as major or minor depression or generalized anxiety disorder. The first study found that mild anosognosia was related to more severe impairment in activities of daily living, but the second study found no such association.

The limitations of these studies should also be acknowledged. The first study involved only a single cross-sectional examination of patients who were approximately 1 week poststroke. There was no follow-up of these patients to determine the course of the anosognosia. Second, each study was comprised of a demographically discrete patient population. Participants in the first study were black inner-city residents with low incomes. The second study examined a white middle-class population from the rural Midwest. Given these variations, we don't know whether our findings can be generalized to the entire population of stroke patients. Third, the first study identified patients with anosognosia based on their failure to acknowledge a motor

FIGURE 9.15
THE EFFECT OF ANTIDEPRESSANT TREATMENT
OVER 12 WEEKS ON SEVERITY OF DENIAL

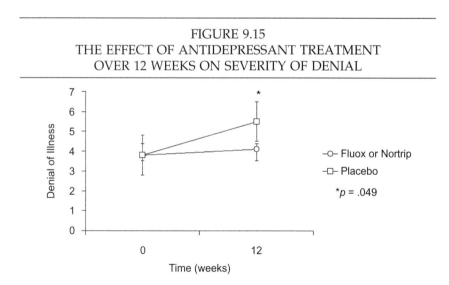

Denial of illness scores (DIS) before and after 12 weeks of double-blind treatment with nortriptyline, fluoxetine, or placebo. There was a statistically significant time by treatment interaction (F1, 22-4.35, p = .049) showing that active treatment was superior to placebo in preventing DIS from increasing over the 3 months of treatment.

impairment. Patients were enrolled in the second study based on their score on a DIS; they scored higher if they minimized symptoms and displayed an unconcerned, nonchalant attitude. Although there was a strong linear relationship between severity of anosognosia and score on the Denial of Illness Scale, subtle variations in the enrollment criteria may have affected the homogeneity of the psychopathology we studied in each experiment.

Given these limitations, how might the findings be construed to illuminate the mechanism of anosognosia? The first conclusion is that the phenomenon of unawareness of impairment appears to be common following stroke. In the first study, 28% of the patients we screened following strokes had at least a mild degree of anosognosia. In the second study, 20% of the patients denied illness. With an overall incidence 20% to 25% of stroke patients who remain unaware of how severely impaired they are, recovery and rehabilitation efforts are significantly affected, as of course is general brain function, in a substantial population. Second, the predominance of injury to the brain's right hemisphere, and particularly to the temporal parietal lobes and basal ganglia, suggests that there is a hemispheric functional asymmetry which allows the right hemisphere to mediate this phenomenon in most patients. It should be noted, however, that 3 patients in the first study and 2 patients in the second study had anosognosia following left hemispheric lesions. Thus, although there may be a reversal of hemisphere specialization in some patients, and perhaps an association between unawareness and left hemisphere lesions, it appears that the mechanisms leading to anosognosia can occur in patients with left as well as right hemisphere lesions. It must be left to subsequent studies to explain how the phenomenon can occur following injury to either hemisphere.

In consideration of the cortical basal ganglia–thalamic loops identified by Alexander, Delong, and Strick (1986), the neurocircuitry mediating anosognosia may involve dysfunction in the pathways extending from the right parietal to the basal ganglia to the thalamus and frontal cortex. An interruption in the right parietal thalamic cortical pathways could impede integration of sensory input, as well as association cortex and higher level integrative processes associated with parietal function. The third finding shared by both studies was that denial of physical impairment does not imply denial of emotional disorder. Patients with and without unawareness of paralysis had the same frequency of major depression, minor depression, and generalized anxiety disorder (GAD). Since we and others have suggested that the pathogenesis of depression involves dysfunction of the frontal–basal–ganglia–thalamic loops in the left (but not right) hemisphere (Cummings, 1993; George et al., 1993; Narushima & Robinson, 2002). This may explain why patients affected by anosognosia can still acknowledge depression: the mechanisms mediating these disorders could be hemisphere specific, and may function independent of one another.

As noted earlier in this discussion, denial has been described as a psychological mechanism for maintaining emotional equilibrium when confronted with the catastrophic loss associated with motor impairment. Our studies resulted in two findings that appear not to support this hypothesis. The first of these is that patients who are anosognostic for motor impairment are not equivalently unaware of visual impairment. Hemianopsia was found in 12 patients with anosognosia, but only 2 of the affected patients denied visual impairment. Second, in both studies, major depression was just as common in patients with anosognosia or denial of illness as it was in patients who were fully aware of and acknowledged their illness. It is uncertain why a patient who characteristically mobilizes denial to protect his conscious awareness from knowledge of catastrophic loss would limit application of the defense mechanism to compromised motor function and not engage it to defend against the emotional trauma of visual impairment or psychological illness (Weinstein & Kahn, 1955). Our finding of depression in these patients certainly does not support this hypothesis.

We have also noted that some investigators cite confusion as the source of anosognosia. We did not detect confusion in any of the patients we enrolled in these two studies, however. In both the first and second studies, the patients with severe anosognosia were not significantly different in their Mini-Mental Status Exam score from patients without anosognosia. It has been further proposed that anosognosia may represent a lack of feedback secondary to spatial neglect. Our first study found that both hemispatial neglect (assessed by the patient's copying a figure or pointing to the contralateral hand), or sensory neglect (demonstrated by unilateral extinction during double simultaneous tactile or visual stimulation) significantly differentiated patients with anosognosia from the controls. There were, however, 12 patients among the 27 with anosognosia who showed no evidence of hemispatial neglect. Hemineglect may indeed be a contributing element to the unawareness phenomenon, but its presence is not a necessary condition for the existence of anosognosia.

Phantom movements and confabulation have also been seen as characteristic precursors of anosognosia. Although these mechanisms are possible, it seems unlikely that phantom sense of movement in the hemiparetic limb would be associated with other features, like acknowledgement of impairment after the patient is shown the hemiparetic arm. Although we did not examine our patients for confabulation, Feinberg and colleagues have tested patients for an association between confabulation and anosognosia, and found no relationship (Feinberg, Roane, Kwan, Schindler, & Haber, 1994). Similarly, both our studies and those of Adair and colleagues (Adair, Schwartz, Na, Fennell, Gilmore, & Heilman, 1997) found that a hypothesized disconnection between the right and left hemispheres was inconsistent with clinical findings that some right-handed people with left hemisphere lesions nevertheless develop anosognosia, despite maintaining left hemisphere dominance for language.

Our studies made two additional associated findings. The first study identified impairment in frontal lobe function, reflected in significantly impaired performance in verbal fluency and Trails B. Although anosognosia patients were impaired in frontal lobe mediated tasks, there were no differences between patients with anosognosia and control patients on block design, the Rey Auditory Verbal Learning Task (RAVLT), and the visual retention task (Figure 9.5). Furthermore, the larger ratios of frontal horn, third ventricle, and lateral ventricle to brain ratios were significantly increased in patients with anosognosia compared to those without the condition. This finding indicates general subcortical, but not cortical, atrophy, which might impair the function of subcortical structures.

Putting all of these findings together, we propose the following hypothesis for unawareness of impairment: Lesions involving the right temporal parietal cortex or basal ganglia would interrupt the normal cortical–basal ganglia–thalamic–frontal circuitry in the right hemisphere. When accompanied by subcortical atrophy, these physiologic insults cause even greater dysfunction of the subcortical pathways in the basal ganglia and thalamus. The disruption of sensory projections from the thalamus to the sensory and association cortex of the right hemisphere precipitates neglect and sensory extinction of input from the left side of the body. Unawareness of hemiplegia could result from impairment of integrative functions mediated by dysfunction of the right frontal lobe and compromised application of sensory data following subcortical afferent disconnection from cortex or remote effects (diachesis) responsible for establishing associations. The characteristic nonchalance and inappropriate affect could reflect disruption of negative emotion associated with right hemisphere lesions or dysfunction (Davidson, Abercrombie, Nitschke, & Putnam, 1999; Davidson & Irwin, 1999). There is a large body of literature supporting the hypothesis that negative emotion and avoidance behavior is mediated by the right hemisphere, and positive emotion and approach behavior by the left (Borod, 1992; Davidson et al. 1999). Thus, emotional dysfunction of the right hemisphere could provide predominance of left hemisphere-mediated positive emotion, with cheerfulness and indifference inappropriate to experience.

Although other explanations might be proposed for anosognosia and denial, the two studies reviewed here show a significant degree of consistency in their findings. Based on the formulation we have proposed, one might wonder why patients with and without anosognosia show about the same incidence of major depression. We have previously proposed that dysfunction within the left hemisphere, produced by either a lesion or a distant effect of a lesion interrupting the left frontal cortical–basal ganglia–thalamic–orbital frontal cortical loop, may mediate depression (Robinson, 1998). Because the left hemisphere is anatomically intact in patients with right hemisphere lesions, it is possible that the depression in these patients could be related to a distant (e.g., left basal ganglia) effect of a lesion in the right hemisphere or that a prior injury to the left hemisphere may provoke an impairment in left hemisphere circuitry that culminates in depression and anosognosia in the same patient.

Summary and Future Directions

This chapter has presented the phenomenon of anosognosia and denial of illness in both its historical and theoretical formulations. Using the results of two studies of different patient populations, we explored the clinical features and potential etiology of anosognosia and denial of illness. The two studies confirmed that anosognosia and denial of illness were associated with right hemisphere lesions involving the temporal parietal cortex or basal ganglia, and with subcortical atrophy. Patients with anosognosia had a significantly higher frequency of unilateral neglect than patients without the condition. Frontal lobe dysfunction is prominent in anosognosia, but patients are normally aware of visual field impairments or emotional disorders such as depression or generalized anxiety disorder. We hypothesized that disruption of the right parietal–temporal–basal ganglia–thalamic loops may lead to decreased sensory output from the thalamus, and therefore unilateral neglect. The sensory neglect may create an unawareness of the impairment, and, combined with frontal lobe dysfunction, may prevent the anosognosia patient from integrating available sensory cues.

Future studies should utilize functional imaging techniques to determine the areas of dysfunction associated with anosognosia. Control patients with similar size and location of the stroke lesion, but without anosognosia, can help to determine which structures may be mediating this phenomenon. Therapeutic intervention, perhaps using stimulant medication or cognitive retraining to help these patients recover their awareness of bilateral stimuli, may improve the prognosis of this clinically significant condition.

References

Adair JC, Schwartz RL, Na DL, Fennell E, Gilmore RL, Heilman KM. Anosognosia: examining the disconnection hypothesis. *J Neurol Neurosurg Psychiatry*. 1997; 63:798–800.

Alexander GE, DeLong MR, Strick PL. Parallel organization of functionally segregated circuits linking basal ganglia and cortex. *Annu Rev Neurosci*. 1986; 9:357–381.

Anton G. Blindheit nach beiderseitiger Gehirnerkrankung mit Verlust der Orientierung in Raume. *Mittherl. Ver. Arzte Steiermark*. 1896; 33:41–46.

Babinski J. Contribution a l'étude des troubles mentaux dans l'hemiplegie organique cerebrale (anosognosie). *Rev Neurol (Paris)*. 1914; 27:845–848.

Borod JC. Interhemispheric and intrahemisphric control of emotion: a focus on unilateral brain damage. *J Con & Clin Psychol*. 1992; 60:339–348.

Cummings J. Frontal–subcortical lesions and human behavior. *Arch Neurol*. 1993; 50: 873–880.

Davidson RJ, Abercrombie H, Nitschke JB, Putnam K. Regional brain function, emotion and disorders of emotion. *Curr Opin Neurobiol*. 1999; 9:228–234.

Davidson RJ, Irwin W. The functional neuroanatomy of emotion and affective style. *Trends Cog Sci*. 1999; 3:11–21.

Denny-Brown D, Meyer JS, Horenstein S. The significance of perceptual rivalry resulting from parietal lesions. *Brain*. 1952; 75:434–471.

Feinberg TE, Roane DM, Kwan PC, Schindler RJ, Haber LD. Anosognosia and visuoverbal confabulation. *Arch Neurol*. 1994; 51:468–473.

George MS, Ketter TA, Gill DS, et al. Brain regions involved in recognizing facial emotion or identity: an oxygen-15 PET study. *J Neuropsychiatry Clin Neurosci*. 1993; 5: 384–394.

Geschwind N. Disconnexion syndromes in animals and man. I. *Brain* 1965a; 88:237–294.

Geschwind N. Disconnexion syndromes in animals and man. II. *Brain*. 1965b; 88: 585–644.

Hackett TP, Cassem NH. Development of a quantitative rating scale to assess denial. *J Psychosom Res*. 1974; 18:93–100.

Hecaen H, deAjuriaguerra J, Massonet J. Les troubles visoconstructifs para lesion parieto occipitale droit. *Encephale*. 1951; 40:122–179.

Heilman KM, Valenstein E. *Clinical Neuropsychology*. 3rd ed. Oxford, UK: Oxford University Press; 1993.

Levine DN, Calvanio R, Rinn WE. The pathogenesis of anosognosia for hemiplegia. *Neurology*. 1991; 41:1770–1781.

Levine DN, Grek A. The anatomic basis of delusions after right cerebral infarction. *Neurology*. 1984; 34:577–582.

Narushima K, Robinson RG. Stroke-related depresssion. *Curr Atheroscl Rep*. 2002; 4: 296–303.

Robinson RG. *The Clinical Neuropsychiatry of Stroke.* Cambridge, UK: Cambridge University Press.

Starkstein SE, Fedoroff JP, Price TR et al. Denial of illness scale. A reliability and validity study. *Neuropsychiatry Neuropsychol Behav Neurol.* 1993; 6(2):93–97.

Starkstein SE, Fedoroff JP, Price TR, Leiguarda R, Robinson RG. Anosognosia in patients with cerebrovascular lesions: a study of causative factors. *Stroke.* 1992; 23:1446–1453.

Starkstein SE, Fedoroff JP, Price TR, Leiguarda R, Robinson RG. Neuropsychological deficits in patients with anosognosia. *Neuropsychiatry Neuropsychol & Beh Neurol.* 1993; 6: 43–48.

Weinstein EA, Kahn RL. *Denial of Illness: Symbolic and Psychological Aspects.* Springfield, IL: C.C. Thomas; 1955.

10

Conversion Disorder

A Disorder of Somatic Self-Awareness

James R. Slaughter
Zac E. Imel

PHYSICIANS OFTEN ENCOUNTER patients who report neurological symptoms that cannot be accounted for by even the most technologically advanced neurologic testing instruments. These patients believe that they suffer from grave physiologic illnesses when they are, in fact, physically healthy. This presentation often meets the criteria for a diagnosis of conversion disorder. Symptoms of hysterical conversion have not historically been specifically described as disorders of self-awareness, but we believe that conceptualizing the condition in the context of self-awareness can help to untangle its many complexities and make it more available to understanding and treatment.

By definition, an individual cannot consciously produce a conversion (hysterical) symptom. If the patient intentionally creates the symptom it is considered factitious or malingering, and may be associated with some manner of secondary gain, such as disability compensation, sympathy, or relief from work or other responsibilities typically afforded people who are sick. Major neurological symptoms such as paralysis, seizures, or anesthesia exist outside the individual's conscious self-awareness. They most often appear as elements of a disease process affecting the central nervous system or following traumatic injury, but they can also occur in response to psychopathology, such as overwhelming anxiety. From a psychological perspective, we might view the hysterical mind as containing a correct view of the body in some "unconscious" location. Neurobiologically, however, we could conceive of a brain dysfunction that results in disordered awareness of the conversion disorder patient's actual state of health. We prefer the latter approach, characterizing the psychological phenomenon as dissociative and the neurobiological phenomenon as a disconnection in the normal neurobiology of self-awareness, which we will shortly describe in more detail.

We intend in this chapter to develop a clear appreciation of conversion disorder by exploring its history, etiology, and treatment in the context of disordered self-awareness. We will review what is currently known of the neurophysiological manifestations of the condition, and suggest some approaches that we think physicians might find helpful in correctly diagnosing and effectively treating conversion disorder.

Conversion and other somatoform disorders are *DSM-IV* diagnostic classifications for the constellation of symptoms once characterized as hysteria. Conversion disorder, somatization disorder, hypochondriasis, pain disorder, and body dysmorphic disorder are all categorized in the *Diagnostic and Statistical Manual of Mental Disorders* (American Psychiatric Association, 1994) as somatoform disorders. They are all characterized by somatic complaints that do not appear to conform to any known pathophysiological mechanism or anatomical abnormality. These somatoform disorders may be further differentiated as monosymptomatic (the patient's focus is on one chief complaint) or polysymptomatic (a multitude of symptoms). Conversion disorder, hypochondriasis, body dysmorphic disorder, and pain disorder are monosymptomatic. The term *somatization disorder* refers to the condition's manifestations in many physical complaints involving multiple organ systems (American Psychiatric Association, 1994). All these disorders involve dysfunctions of physical self-awareness.

Diagnosis of Conversion Disorder

A diagnosis of conversion disorder requires the presence of pseudoneurological symptoms which significantly impair the patient's daily functioning. Psychological factors are inherent to the development of conversion symptoms. The pseudoneurological conversion symptom is temporally related to psychological stress or conflict. Unlike factitious disorder (adoption of the sick role), or malingering (for secondary gain), where no dysfunction of self-awareness is present, patients experiencing hysteria do not intentionally produce these symptoms. "Histrionic" personality features, a persistently exaggerated interpersonal style, may predispose to the development of conversion, but is not a necessary feature of conversion disorder. Individuals with personality disorder diagnoses, notably the histrionic type (5–21%), are nevertheless overrepresented among patients with conversion disorder (American Psychiatric Association, 1994).

Epidemiology

To date, there have been no systematic community epidemiological studies of the incidence of conversion disorder. Estimates in hospitalized patients indicate it may be fairly common in people suffering from medical illnesses. Guze, Woodruf, and Clayton (1971) found that 24% of patients admitted to a general medical service reported having experienced conversion symptoms at some time in their lives. Female to male estimates range from 2:1 to 10:1 (American Psychiatric Association, 1994; Guggenheim & Smith, 1995). The condition is seen with elevated frequency among rural populations, people of lower socioeconomic status, military personnel, people unsophisticated in their knowledge of medical and psychological concepts, and defendants or prisoners within the criminal justice system (APA, 1994; Boffeli & Guze, 1992).

Course

The onset of conversion disorder usually occurs in adolescence or early adulthood. New onset after age 35 is rare (McCahill, 1995; Speed, 1996). Classically, the patient with conversion disorder reports pseudoneurological symptoms, such as pseudoseizures, gait and stance disturbances, paresis-plegia, paresthesia-anesthesia, and dizziness (Kapfhammer, Dobmeier, & Rothenhausler, 1998; Reichlin, Loew, & Joraschky, 1997). Less commonly, patients report blindness, hallucinations, deafness, aphonia, pseudocyesis, a lump sensation in the throat ("globus hystericus"), urinary retention, and syncope.

Comorbid Conditions

Between 30% and 75% of conversion disorder patients have a concomitant Axis I diagnosis (Crimlisk et al., 1998; Tomasson et al., 2001). Depression, anxiety, and somatization are especially common in conversion disorder patients. Of notable concern, between 17% and 70% of conversion disorder patients may have a coexisting neurological disorder, including such major pathology as multiple sclerosis, central nervous system tumors, traumatic brain injury, and seizure disorders (Boffeli & Guze, 1992; Lempert & Schmidt, 1990; Slater & Glithero, 1965; Whitlock, 1967).

Because many conversion disorder patients initially seek help from a primary care physician or a neurologist rather than a psychiatrist, the impact of the condition on the general medical community is substantial (Schurman, 1985). Individuals who express psychological distress through somatic complaints utilize the health care system at a high rate (Katon & Walker, 1998; Rasmussen & Avant, 1989; Spitzer et al., 1994). According to the Primary Care Evaluation of Mental Disorders (PRIME-MD) 1000 study, 14% of primary care patients met DSM-III-R criteria for somatoform disorders (American Psychiatric Association, 1980; Morriss et al., 1998).

History of Hysteria, Pre-Charcot

In 1894, William James lamented;

> Amongst all the many victims of medical ignorance clad in authority, the poor hysteric has hitherto perhaps fared worst; and her gradual rehabilitation and rescue will count amongst the most philanthropic conquests of our generation. At first branded as one inflamed with uterine furor, she was next burned as a witch, and finally treated as so radically perverse and mendacious a jade as to be theatrical even in the hour of death.

Four thousand years of recorded history about hysteria supports James's characterization. Merskey's (1979) review of the early history and evolution of ideas about conversion disorder prior to 1979 provides important insights into how the concept has been both constant and ever-changing in human experience.

Four thousand years ago a description of ailments associated with a "wandering" uterus appeared in the Kahun Papyrus (Griffith, 1897, as cited in Veith, 1965). With few exceptions, Egyptian, Greek, Roman, and European medieval physicians accepted the "fact" that a wandering uterus, moving serendipitously within the body, was the cause of hysterical (Greek *hystereon* = uterus) symptoms. Throughout this time few advances were made in understanding the malady (Merskey, 1979). As late as 1603, Jordan defended witches by arguing that their actions were related to their medical illness. He wrote that hysteria was caused by "the easie passage which [the womb] has to [the braine, heart and liver] by the Vaines, Arteries, and Nerves . . ." (cited in Merskey, 1979, p. 7). While Jordan was the first to note the brain's role in the development of hysterical phenomena, it is clear he considered that the movement of the uterus remained the major etiologic influence in the condition (Veith, 1965).

By the late 17th century, the fantasy of a wandering uterus was replaced by observations that disease and strong emotions sufficed to produce hysterical symptoms (Merskey, 1979). Willis (1684) argued that emotional factors could cause explosions at the base of nerves within the head. Willis contrasted this condition to epilepsy, which affects the middle part of the brain. This early attempt to distinguish epilepsy from hysteroepilepsy presages Charcot's work 200 years later. Sydenham (1697) attributed hysteria to "vehement agitations of the mind by assaults of grief, anger, [and] fear. . . ." (cited in Merskey, 1979, p. 8). Both Willis and Sydenham emphasized dysfunction of the central nervous system resulting from strong emotion. This contention remains a central feature of modern psychiatry's sense of disorder.

In the early 19th century, Brodie (1837) noted that the dysfunction central to hysterical paralysis is not a defect of the muscles but of volition (cited in Merskey, 1979). Carter (1853) acknowledged the role of stress in producing symptoms and introduced a treatment of hysterics that involved removing patients from stressful circumstances and ignoring the symptom. He felt that hysteria was the direct effect of emotions such as terror and sexual passion and noted that men as well as women experienced hysteria (Merskey, 1979). Briquet (1869) observed that hysteria is a "neurosis of brain" affecting behavior. He described the presence of multiple concurrent pseudomedical and psuedoneurological symptoms, which have since been referred to as Briquet's syndrome and somatization disorder (Merskey, 1979). Reynolds (1869) hypothesized that the "ideas" patients entertained might lead to hysterical paralysis and "fits."

The conceptualization and etiology of hysteria evolved significantly from the first written accounts to those published in the late 19th century. Not until the 17th century, thousands of years after the original Egyptian and Greek theory of the wandering uterus, was the brain mentioned in association with the production of hysterical symptoms. During this epoch, hysteria was not considered a disorder of self-awareness. Less than a century later, uterine theories have been thoroughly replaced by acknowledgement that emotional distress is the basis of hysteria. Most striking is that Willis, in the late 17th century, was already postulating the neurobiology of hysteria, moving beyond simply implicating the brain in hysterical phenomenon to highlighting specific locations potentially responsible for symptoms. Charcot further advanced the investigation of the neurobiology of hysteria, also noting that "ideas" can result in hysterical symptoms.

Charcot—Emergence of Modern Neuropsychiatry of Hysteria

Willis, Sydenham, Briquet, and others set the stage for Charcot's work at the Salpêtrière Hospital where he dedicated his professional career to teasing out the tantalizing mystery of hysteria. Charcot (1889) focused on distinguishing the characteristics of *hysteroepilepsy* from those of epilepsy, utilizing the emerging neurological examination to differentiate hysterical fits and paralysis from physiologically based symptoms. At the Salpêtrière, Charcot treated both neurologically ill and "emotionally ill" patients. He observed that hysterics experienced the *arc en cercle* in grand hysteria, or the frequent accompaniment of tunnel or tubular vision and hemianesthesia. He also noted the similarity of the hysteric state to the hypnotic. In experiments conducted on patients, Charcot (1889) tried to determine whether hysteria could influence purely biological events, like the bleeding rate in a hysterically paralyzed and anesthetic arm.

Janet, a pupil of Charcot (1901), built upon the consideration that "ideas" give rise to hysterical symptoms. Charcot and Janet, as well as Freud and Breuer, agreed that ideas influenced the patients' behavior. They strongly influenced the contention that ideas not in conscious awareness result in hysterical symptoms (Merskey, 1979). Breuer and Freud developed the concept of dissociation underlying hysteria. "Subconscious" or "unconscious" conflicts engender dissociative symptoms, which resolve a conflict that is too painful to be consciously experienced. Freud emphasized that sexual or libidinal conflicts are central to the development of hysteria, though the hypothesis that all conflicts be libidinal has of course been strongly challenged. The general model of dissociation inherent in the development of hysterical symptomology nevertheless continues to influence etiologic conceptualizations of conversion disorder (Merskey, 1979). The dissociative process leaves patients unaware that, while experiencing themselves as ill, they continue to be physically healthy.

In the early 20th century, Babinski (1918) treated World War I combat veterans for "shell-shock." He emphasized the "suggestible" nature of shell-

shocked soldiers, and went so far as to suggest that the condition be rela-
beled *pithiatisme* ("suggestible"). Many of Babinski's colleagues had argued
that shell-shock was a direct result of concussion resulting from close proximity to explosions. Babinski and others observed that the emotional trauma
of war was the salient feature, and argued that suggestion led to the conta-
gious nature of the disorder as well as its treatment. Physicians often used
faradic electrical stimulation accompanied by strong suggestion to effect
cures in "shell-shocked" patients (Babinski, 1918). This use of a "physical"
electrical device parallels the modern use of physiologic stimuli like physical therapy (which we will discuss later) to help reverse conversion symptoms.

Kretschmer (1948; cited in Merskey, 1979), writing after the conclusion
of World War II, stressed the importance of the "instinctive survival reflex"
in response to stress. He noted two primitive hysterical patterns of behavior:
(1) immobilization reflex, faint or freeze, and (2) instinctive flurry, wild,
flailing, rapid movements. These descriptions bear a striking resemblance to
the hypokinetic behavior seen in some hysterical patients—paralysis, blindness, deafness, mutism, and dystonia—and the hyperkinetic behaviors displayed by other hysterical patients—hysteroepilepsy, myoclonic jerks, and
tremors. From this perspective, hysteria might be conceptualized as an attempt to dissociate by means of a natural survival reflex. This dissociation
distorts the patient's accurate self-awareness of physical well-being and re-
places it with a sense of physical illness.

Slater and Glithero (1965), as well as Merskey and Buhrich (1975), reminded clinicians that diagnosis of hysteria can be complicated by the presence of occult medical and psychiatric morbidity. Slater and Glithero (1965)
followed a sample of 112 hysteria patients for 9 years. Twenty-four of these
patients were found to have combined hysterical and medical conditions.
An additional 22 were later found to have a comorbid medical illness. Four
patients eventually committed suicide. Merskey and Buhrieh (1975) studied
89 conversion patients and found that 67% had at least one concomitant
medical condition, including seizure, stroke, dementia, and traumatic brain
injury.

Investigators since the time of Charcot have emphasized the importance of an emotional stressor as the initiator of hysterical symptoms. Babinski in particular noted the "suggestibility" of patients with conversion
symptoms, citing this characteristic as central to development and resolution of symptoms. Freud, Breuer, Kretschmer, and others stressed the
dissociative psychological process that confuses the patient's somatic self-
image.

Recent Investigations in Conversion:
Hypnosis and Meditation

Investigations in the late 20th and early 21st century concentrated on comparisons between hysterical states and those induced by hypnosis or meditation, and neurophysiological features of hysterical conditions. Utilizing positron emission tomography (PET) scans, Lou and colleagues (1999) studied meditative states, and found increased regional cerebral blood flow (rCBF) in cortical areas in association with specific yoga experiences. When participants were asked to direct attention to the sensation of their limb's weight, regional cerebral blood flow was increased in the superior frontal (supplementary motor cortex) and parietal cortex. Visual imagery increased activity in the visual associational cortex (though not the primary visual cortex) and parietal lobe. A sense of joy was associated with increased rCBF in the superior temporal and left parietal area. Increased bilateral parietal rCBF was observed in subjects who were instructed to maintain an abstract representation of self. Roelofs, Keijsers, Hoogduin, Naring, and Moene (2002) observed significantly greater cognitive dissociation, somatoform dissociation, and susceptibility to hypnosis among conversion patients compared to normal controls.

Neurophysiology of Conversion:
Nondominant Hemisphere Abnormality

Several investigators have noted that hysterical symptoms are significantly more common on the nondominant side of the body, involving the contralateral right, nondominant hemisphere (Axelrod, Noonan, & Atanacio, 1980; Galin et al., 1977). Seeking to explore whether hysteria patients suffered from parietal lobe dysfunction, Vardi, Finkelstein, and Kesten (1997) used single photon emission computerized tomography (SPECT) to evaluate 12 patients with hysterical symptoms at the time of the scan. They found that 9 of the patients had decreased rCBF in the right parietal area, and 2 patients had decreased rCBF in the left parietal. The Vardi group concluded that conversion disorder is an emotionally dependent sympathetic hyperactivity, originating in the limbic system and then "transmitted asymmetrically from the hypothalamus to the ipsilateral somatosensory integrative parietal cortex" (Vardi et al., 1997, p. 149).

Marshall, Halligan, Fink, Wade, and Frackowiak (1997) used a PET scanner to observe changes in a patient with left leg paralysis while "preparing" to move her limbs and "willing" her leg to move. When preparing to move the affected and nonaffected limb, the patient activated premotor areas bilaterally. When willing her nonparalyzed leg to move, she activated the right primary motor cortex. When willing her left paralyzed leg to move she failed to activate the contralateral primary motor area, however, and activated the contralateral orbitofrontal and anterior cingulate cortices instead. The investigators suggested that these two regions inhibited the premotor cortical effect on the primary motor area, thereby preventing movement. Devinsky, Mesad, and Alper (2001) studied conversion nonepileptic seizures in 79 patients. They found that 76% of these patients demonstrated unilateral cerebral activities, predominantly in the right hemisphere. They found ictal or interictal electroencephalogram (EEG) abnormalities in 78% of conversion patients; 63% of patients showed both neuroimaging and EEG abnormalities; 71% of the 60 study patients with EEG or structural abnormalities showed them in the right hemisphere.

Spence, Crimlisk, Cope, Ron, and Grasby (2000) demonstrated a decrease in rCBF in the left frontal region ipsilateral to the hysterical patient's left-sided sensorimotor paralysis. This ipsilateral finding is inconsistent with contralateral findings previously noted, and reminds us that many hysterical patients are also depressed at the time of their evaluation; left frontal decreased rCBF has been reported in patients experiencing major depressive illness as well.

Neurophysiology of Awareness and Hysteria

In a case study, Tihonen, Kuikka, Viinamaki, Lehtonene, and Partanen (1995) used SPECT imaging to evaluate conversion disorder and found increased perfusion in the frontal lobe and hypoperfusion in the parietal lobe. Tihonen et al. interpreted these findings as a "simultaneous activation of frontal inhibitory areas and inhibition of the somatosensory cortex." Yazici and Kostakoglu (1998) reported similar findings of increased frontal activity and decreased parietal activity.

Lou and associates (1999) identified underlying structures that together subserve the resting state of consciousness and self-awareness, notably the orbital and dorsolateral prefrontal cortex, anterior cingulate gyrus, temporal lobes, inferior parietal lobule, caudate, thalamus, pons, cerebellar vermis, and cerebellar hemispheres. Hysteria likely disrupts this circuit so that stressors are kept from conscious awareness. Psychologically, this diminished level of consciousness has been variously termed the *subconscious* or *unconscious*. We prefer to call the psychological process *dissociation*. The neurobiological basis of this dissociation likely involves disconnection in the circuitry subserving normal consciousness elucidated by Lou and associates (1999).

Vuilleumier and colleagues (2001) studied the effect of vibration when applied to the extremities of patients experiencing hysterical sensorimotor loss. Presuming that an investigator's request would be met with variable effort from one patient to another, the vibration applied to the affected limb was considered a more reliable measure of brain function, since it required no conscious cooperation by the patient. Veuilleumier and colleagues studied 4 patients with psychogenic paralysis using SPECT and found decreased rCBF in the contralateral thalamus and caudate. They concluded that the thalamus and caudate have a role in awareness of illness. In addition, Veuilleumier and colleagues noted the involvement of corticosubcortical circuitry in initiating and inhibiting action and behavior.

There has not yet been a definitive study of the neurobiological etiology of hysterical symptoms. All available information is essentially anecdotal—individual case reports and limited case series involving subjects as their own controls. The nascent state of neurobiological literature on hysteria simply suggests regions of interest for further empirical study. The areas most strongly implicated in the pathology subserve normal resting consciousness, but the manner and degree of their involvement was still highly speculative in the early years of the 21st century.

Treatment

Although significant advances have been made in neurology and psychiatry, treatment of hysterical symptoms still involves interventions introduced over a century ago. In the 19th and early 20th centuries, Charcot (1889) and Babinski (1918) noted the need to perform the appropriate medical–neurological evaluation, then "suggest" (recall *pithiatisme*) the resolution of symptoms. The resolution of this disordered self-awareness involves suggesting how the patients may alternatively perceive their state of good health.

Patients experiencing hysterical symptoms have suffered a stimulus of sufficient intensity to induce dissociation from somatic self-awareness. They are consciously unaware of their healthy somatic state. The therapist reverses this somatic misperception of illness by suggestion of sufficient intensity to reverse the patient's somatic misperception. Once a careful evaluation has established that symptoms are hysterical in etiology, the patient can be confidently reassured of a healthy state. The therapist proceeds to strongly suggest how normal neurological function is to be restored. Slater and Glithero (1965) and Merskey (1979) have reminded us to always utilize great care in concluding that a symptom is conversion.

We find a six-step diagnostic–therapeutic approach to conversion disorder particularly helpful in explaining the condition without embarrassing the patient, establishing a trusting therapeutic alliance, and engaging the patient in therapy:

STEP 1: NEUROLOGICAL FINDINGS SUGGEST HYSTERIA

When conversion disorder is diagnosed, emotional conditions are present that are consistent with the pathogenesis of the condition, while history, signs, laboratory, and radiologic studies rule out neurological disease. Our approach to patients experiencing hysterical symptoms is first to thoroughly examine the patient for medical–neurological causes of the presenting affliction. During the neurological examinations of patients, "la belle indifference," astasia–abesia gait, stocking–glove or nonphysiological sensorimotor loss, and preserved reflexes in paralyzed limbs suggest hysteria. Furthermore, flailing movements during seizures, awakening from sleep in response to loud sound in the "deaf," and optikinetic nystasmus in the "blind" all should raise the titre of suspicion for hysteria, but should not be considered diagnostic in and of themselves. Patients with hysterical symptoms may also be found to experience seizures, strokes, traumatic brain injury, brain tumors, and other serious neurological deficits.

STEP 2: IDENTIFYING PSYCHOSOCIAL STRESSORS

Our review and clinical experience with hysteria suggest that it is essential to understand the circumstances of symptom induction. The patient, perhaps due to the dissociation involved in hysterical symptoms, may not give an accurate history of the events leading to development of the pseudoneurological complaint. When eliciting the history of the present illness, it is important to inquire about what the patient was doing immediately prior to the onset of symptoms. Often the symptom will be recognized as having a direct relationship to current events, like going "blind" when viewing something traumatic. When the history does not confirm a stressor, concerns for neurological illness are heightened. Collateral informants should be utilized when available to provide important details about possible stressors not volunteered by the patient.

STEP 3: INTRODUCE CONVERSION DISCUSSION EARLY

We have often seen patients initially evaluated for serious, even life-threatening conditions such as subarachnoid hemorrhage, seizures, and multiple sclerosis who are dismissed following evaluation, and told, "You don't have anything wrong with your brain. You need to see a psychiatrist." The patient is frequently concerned that the workup was deficient, presenting with comments like, "Just because they couldn't find anything, they want me to see a psychiatrist." We encourage our colleagues to introduce conversion symptoms as a possibility early in treatment: "One possible cause of your paralysis is a reaction to all the stress you have been going through." The patient is thoroughly evaluated, but also prepared to hear that "the examinations are fortunately normal. Your central nervous system is intact like we would want it to be."

STEP 4: LABORATORY EVALUATION

We introduce the laboratory examination to the patient in the following manner: "I believe that what we are dealing with is your body's response to stress, but I would like to see the results of this test to reassure both of us that a medical condition is not causing these symptoms." While the therapist is explaining that symptoms are likely related to stress, the patient should also be assured that they are being taken seriously and genuinely evaluated. Tests should be appropriate to reassure both the patient and the clinician that a thorough and appropriate evaluation has been completed. Avoiding unnecessary laboratory "fishing expeditions" is important, otherwise the patient worries that something has been overlooked. When the clinician is not confident of the diagnosis, however, further testing or referral to a specialist is indicated. When the clinician suspects symptoms are of a hysterical origin, this should be shared with the patient at the earliest available opportunity. The issue can be broached speculatively, without either humiliating or alienating the patient, by framing it something like, "Can you imagine that emotions may be playing a part in your illness?"

STEP 5: STRONG SUGGESTION

When the history, neurological, and psychiatric evaluation, and all relevant laboratory and radiology studies have been completed, the patient should be given a strong and clear suggestion about how the symptom can be resolved. The connection between stress and the symptom is reviewed and the patient is advised that the symptom will improve in a specific way. For example, if there is hysterical paralysis of the legs, the patient is reassured that the "neurological exam is normal, and that the laboratory examination reveals that the neurological system is intact." The suggestion is made that "the legs will begin to move, usually the toes first, the ankles, then the knees. Physical therapy will help fully restore your ability to walk. This process will take about 3 days, at which time you will be walking normally." Strong suggestion is reassuring, and offers the patient a precise chart of what to expect and when. A systematic progression from absent health awareness to clear acceptance of healthy status is strongly encouraged. It will remain important throughout the process to stay attuned to the patient's sensitivity about feeling ridiculed or thinking that his pain and distress are being dismissed as trivial or not real (Table 10.1).

It is very difficult to speculate about how the process of "strong suggestion" affects neurophysiology. Further research will eventually discover how this and other methods of psychotherapy affect brain functioning. Where the process of regaining somatic self-awareness and a return to efficacious expression of the sensorimotor area occurs neurophysiologically remains unclear, but it is probably mediated by frontal lobe function.

STEP 6: EVALUATE AND TREAT COMORBID CONDITIONS
When patients fail to respond to the suggestive method described, or when history, symptoms, and signs point to it, a comorbid psychiatric disorder may be present. Depression is common in patients experiencing hysterical symptoms who develop the conversion symptom. Depression may in fact predispose the patient to a hysterical symptom, as the patient relieves further stress-distress while assuming the sick role. Treatment of the depression un-

---

TABLE 10.1
Treatment of Conversion Disorder

STEP 1: INCONSISTENT NEUROLOGICAL EXAMINATION: Patient presents symptoms and neurological signs that are inconsistent, nonphysiological.

STEP 2: PSYCHOLOGICAL STRESSOR: Examiner identifies psychosocial stressors associated with the onset of symptoms–collateral information is helpful.

STEP 3: EARLY COMMUNICATION REGARDING CONVERSION: The patient is informed early in treatment that an emotional explanation of symptoms is possible, even likely.

STEP 4: LABORATORY EXAMINATION: Laboratory examination appropriate to symptoms (e.g., CT for "stroke," while understanding the likelihood that testing results will be normal).

STEP 5: STRONG SUGGESTION: The patient is given the strong suggestion that the symptoms will resolve, including a description of the pattern of recovery. Physical or other activity therapy is used.

STEP 6: COMORBID CONSIDERATIONS: Is Comorbid Depression or Anxiety present, requiring treatment?

der these circumstances will likely avert the recurrence of hysterical symptoms. Marital, family, or vocational conflicts may be present and directly contribute to hysterical symptoms.

Anxiety often complicates hysterical symptoms. Panic attacks can precipitate conversion symptoms, and it is not uncommon for patients to display hysterical features in response to a first panic attack, so that the panic disorder presents as "pseudoseizures." The conversion symptoms may be the patient's expression of the extreme fear provoked by a panic attack.

Case Example: Bilateral Lower Extremity Paralysis-Anesthesia

STEP 1: INCONSISTENT NEUROLOGICAL SIGNS AND SYMPTOMS

A 35-year-old, never-married woman presented to the emergency room and was subsequently admitted to the neurology service with a chief complaint of sudden loss of motor and sensory function from the waist down. The resident's note read, "Paralyzed from the waist down." Her neurological examination was entirely normal, including 2+ and symmetrical lower extremity reflexes and negative Babinskis except for her subjective complaints of lost motor function and hypoesthesia from the waist down. She displayed an apparent lack of concern about her paralysis. The neurologist noted this as "la belle indifference." He concluded his neurological exam with the notation, "nonphysiological finding."

STEP 2: IDENTIFYING PSYCHOSOCIAL STRESSOR

The patient's history was negative for physical trauma, history of infection, disc disease, or associated conditions, but during the social history the patient reported that she had been markedly obese since adolescence and had not dated until recently. She had recently lost 150 pounds with the help of a commercial diet program, and begun to date her current boyfriend. He had accompanied her to the hospital, and appeared more concerned than she was regarding her paralysis. Just prior to the presenting episode, the boyfriend had suggested that they be sexually intimate, whereupon the patient found herself to be "paralyzed."

STEP 3: EARLY IDENTIFICATION OF EMOTIONS AS CAUSATIVE

The neurologist informed the patient that her neurological examination had showed preserved reflexes, a very good indication of the health of her nervous system. He shared with the patient that emotions can affect neurological functioning, and could account for her present illness. Next he informed the patient he was asking a psychiatrist to consult with him on her care. She accepted this suggestion without apparent concern.

STEP 4: LABORATORY EXAMINATION
The neurologist informed the patient that he was obtaining an MRI of the spine and EMG/NC studies to confirm an intact neurological system. He told her that he expected the results of these exams to be normal, but wanted to confirm his impression that her nervous system was intact.

STEP 5: STRONG SUGGESTION
The attending neurologist and psychiatric consultant concurred that emotions were primary in the patient's paralysis. MRI and EMG/NC were normal. The psychiatric consultant strongly suggested to the patient that the origin of her "paralysis" was very likely an emotional reaction, noting that her neurological examination, MRI scan, and EMG/NC fortunately revealed an intact nervous system. He explained that strong emotions could disrupt the normal functioning of her nervous system, and advised her that once the emotional stress was identified and addressed the paralysis would improve. The psychiatrist proceeded to associate the stressor as the emotional conflict resulting from the desire to please her boyfriend and her reticence about engaging in sex for the first time. Both the patient and the boyfriend accepted this explanation and the need to discuss this important issue. The psychiatrist then strongly suggested to the patient that her paralysis and sensory loss would improve over the next 3 days, suggesting that she would first be able to "wiggle her toes," then move at the ankle, then knee, then hip. He informed the patient that physical therapy ("gait training") would aid a speedy recovery. She started to move her toes during the consultant's visit and proceeded to full recovery in 3 days.

The patient's trust in clinical authority permitted her to accept awareness that her physiologic function remained intact. This new belief in wellness was sufficient to reverse her dissociative state and begin the process of recovery. The neurologist and psychiatrist helped the patient to tell herself, "Even though I still can't move my feet and legs very well, I realize that this is not a physical problem, and if I do what the doctor says I will get over it."

STEP 6: COMORBID CONDITION EVALUATION
The psychiatric consultant explored the patient's history and current mental status for comorbid conditions. She appeared entirely healthy apart from her

conversion disorder. She likely would have met criteria for social anxiety disorder during adolescence, secondary to concern about her obesity. This had resolved with her weight loss.

In this example, the patient is unaware of her healthy condition, believing that she suffers from a serious physiologic abnormality. Strong suggestion prompted awareness of her actual state of somatic health and resolved the disordered self-awareness. From a neurophysiological perspective, disordered self-awareness could represent a disruption at any level of neurological functioning, from the frontal lobe to the somatosensory strip. The precise lesion location(s) for this patient and others are yet to be identified.

Conclusion

Hysteria represents a distorted awareness of physiologic function, a misperception of the health of the nervous system. Psychologically, the patient persists in a dissociative state. The actual neurological mechanisms of hysterical symptoms are being studied with advanced imaging technology like PET, SPECT, and fMRI. The orbitofrontal, parietal, and cingulate cortices, as well as the caudate and thalamus, appear to be the most closely implicated brain structures, and they will be the targets of investigative evaluations of hysteria for the foreseeable future.

Treatment trials involving our recommended "strong suggestion model" and other therapeutic interventions will be further studied. We have only anecdotal experience with hundreds of patients to support the usefulness of this approach. Controlled treatment trials involving suggestion, hypnosis, cognitive–behavioral psychotherapy, sodium amytal, lorazepam, and placebo might further refine effective treatment approaches. Our favored method has the advantages of usually successful outcome without resort to psychoactive medication or hypnosis, while providing direct access to the conscious mind

At the outset of the 21st century, we will paraphrase what William James wrote near the beginning of the 20th: *Poor Hysterics. Viewed as victims, as possessed, as witches, then dissociatives. They are among the most deserving of the progress of human understanding. This is a real disease, a brain disease.*

References

American Psychiatric Association. *Diagnostic and Statistical Manual of Mental Disorders.* 3rd ed. Washington, DC: American Psychiatric Association Press; 1980.

American Psychiatric Association. *Diagnostic and Statistical Manual of Mental Disorders.* 4th ed. Washington, DC: American Psychiatric Association Press; 1994.

Axelrod S, Noonan M, Atanacio B. On the laterality of psychogenic somatic symptoms. *J Ner & Men Dis.* 1980; 168(9):517–525.

Babinski J. *Hysteria or Pithiatism.* Rolleston JD, trans. London: University of London Press; 1918.

Boffeli TJ, Guze SB. The simulation of neurologic disease. *Psychiatric Clin N Am.* 1992; 15:301–310.

Breuer J, Freud S. Studies on hysteria. In: *The Standard Edition of the Complete Psychological Works of Sigmund Freud.* Vol. 2. London: Hogarth Press; 1893–1895/1955.

Briquet P. *Traite clinique et therapeutique de l'hysterie.* Paris: Bailliere; 1859.

Brodie BC. *Lectures Illustrative of Certain Local Nervous Affections.* London; 1837.

Carter RB. *On the Pathology and Treatment of Hysteria.* London: Churchill; 1853.

Charcot JM. *Lectures on Diseases of the Nervous System.* Sigerson G, trans. London: New Sydenham Society; 1889.

Crimlisk HL, Bhatia K, Cope H, David A, Marsend CD, Ron A. Slater revisited: 6 year follow-up study of patients with medically unexplained motor symptoms. *Br Med J.* 1998; 316:582–590.

Devinsky O, Mesad S, Alper K. Nondominant hemisphere lesions and conversion nonepileptic seizures. *J Neuropsychiatry & Clin Neurosci.* 2001; 13:3.

Galin D. Lateral specialization and psychiatric issues: speculations on development and the evolution of consciousness. *Ann NY Acad Sci.* 1977; 299:397–411.

Griffith FI, ed. The Petri Papyri, Heiratic Papyri from Kahun and Gurob: Principally of the Middle Kingdom. In: *Literary, Medical and Mathematical Papyri from Kahun.* Vol. 1. London: Bernard Quaritch; 1897: pp. 5–11.

Guggenheim FG, Smith RS. Somatoform disorders. In: Kaplan HI, Sadock BJ, eds. *Comprehensive Textbook of psychiatry.* 6th ed. Vol. 1. Baltimore, Md: Williams & Wilkins.

Guze SB, Woodruf RA, Clayton PJ. A study of conversion symptoms in psychiatric outpatients. *Am J Psychiatry.* 1971; 128:643–646.

James W. *Psychol Rev.* 1894; 1:195. Review of: P. Janet. *L'etat mental des hysteriques and L'amnesie continue.*

Janet P. *The Mental State of Hystericals.* London: Putnam; 1901.

Jordan E. *A Brief Discourse of a Disease Called the Suffocations of the Mother.* London: John Windet; 1603.

Kapfhammer HP, Dobmeier P, Mayer C, Rothenhausler HB. Conversion syndromes in neurology. A psychopathological and psychodynamic differentiation of conversion disorder, somatization disorder, and factitious disorder. [German] *Psychother, Psychosom, Med Psychologie.* 1998; 48:463–474.

Katon WJ, Walker EA. Medically unexplained symptoms in primary care. *J Clin Psychiatry.* 1998; 59:S15–S21.

Kretschmer E. *Hysterie, reflex, und Instinkt.* 5th ed. [German]. Stuttgart: Georg Thieme; 1948.

Lempert T, Schmidt D. Natural history and outcome of psychogenic seizures: a clinical study of 50 patients. *J Neurology.* 1990; 237:35–38.

Leslie SA. Diagnosis and treatment of hysterical conversion reactions. *Arch Dis Child.* 1988; 63:506–511.

Lou HC, Kjaer TW, Friberg L, Wildschiodtz G, Holm S, Nowak MA. 15O-H2O PET study of meditation and the resting state of normal consciouness. *Hum Brain Mapping.* 1999; 7:98–105.

Marshall JC, Halligan PW, Fink GR, Wade DT, Frackowiak RS. The functional anatomy of a hysterical paralysis. *Cognition.* 1997; 64(1):B1–B8.

McCahill ME. Somatoform and related disorders: delivery of diagnosis as first step. *Am Fam Physician.* 1995; 52:193–203.

Mersky H. *The Analysis of Hysteria.* London: Bailliere Tindall; 1979.

Merskey H, Buhrich NA. Hysteria and organic brain disease. *Br J Med Psychol.* 48(4): 359–366.

Morriss R, Gask L, Ronalds C et al. Cost-effectiveness of a new treatment for somatized mental disorder taught to GPs. *Fam Pract.* 1998; 15:119–125.

Rasmussen NH, Avant RF. Somatization disorder in family practice. *Am Fam Physician.* 1989; 40:206–214.

Reichlin T, Loew TH, Joraschky P. Pseudoseizure "status." *J Psychosom Res.* 1997; 42: 495–498.

Reynolds JR. Remarks on paralysis and other disorders of motion and sensation dependent on idea. *Br Med J.* 1869; ii: 483–485. Discussion, 478–479.

Roelofs K, Keijsers G, Hoogduin K, Naring G, Moene FC. Childhood abuse in patients with conversion disorder. *Am J Psychiatry.* 2002; 159(11):1908–1913.

Schurman RA, Kramer PD, Mitchell JB. The hidden mental health network. *Arch Gen Psychiatry.* 1985; 42:89–94.

Slater ET, Glithero E. A follow-up of patients diagnosed suffering from "hysteria." *J Psychosom Res.* 1965; 9:9–13.

Speed J. Behavioral management of conversion disorder: retrospective study. *Arch Physical & Med Reh.* 1996; 77:147–154.

Spence SA, Crimlisk HL, Cope H, Ron MA, Grasby PM. Discrete neurophysiological correlates in prefrontal cortex during hysterical and feigned disorder of movement. [Controlled clinical trial letter]. *Lancet.* 2000; 355(9211):1243–1244.

Spitzer RL, Williams JB, Kroenke K et al. Utility of a new procedure for diagnosing mental disorders in primary care: the PRIME-MD 1000 study. *JAMA.* 1994; 272:1749–56.

Sydenham T. *Dr. Sydenham's Complete Method of Curing Almost All Diseases, and Description of Their Symptoms to which Are Now Added Five Discourses of the Same Author Concerning the Pleurisy, Gout, Hysterical Passion, Dropsy, and Rheumatism.* 3rd ed. London: Newman & Parker; 1697.

Tihonen J, Kuikka J, Viinamaki H, Lehtonene J, Partanen J. Altered cerebral blood flow during hysterical paresthesia. *Biol Psychiatry.* 1995; 37:134–137.

Tomasson K, Kent D, Coryell W. Somatization and conversion disorder: comorbidity and demographics at presentation. *Acta Psychiatrica Scand.* 2001; 84:288–293.

Vardi J, Finkelstein Y, Kesten M. Parietal lobe dysfunction in hysteria-like behavior. [Abstract]. *J Neuropsychiatry & Clin Neurosci.* 1997; 9:148–149.

Veith I. *Hysteria: The history of a disease.* Chicago: University of Chicago Press; 1965.

Vuilleumier P, Chicherio C, Assal F, Schwartz S, Slosman D, Landis T. Functional neuroanatomical correlates of hysterical sensorimotor loss. *Brain.* 2001; 124(6):1077–1090.

Whitlock FA. The aetiology of hysteria. *Acta Psychiatrica Scand.* 1967; 43:144–162.

Willis T. *An Essay of the Pathology of the Brain and Nervous Shock in which Convulsive Disease are Treated.* Cordage SP, trans. London: Dring, Leigh & Harper; 1684.

Yazici KM, Kostakoglu L. Cerebral blood flow changes in patients with conversion disorder. *Psychiatry Res.* 83(3):163–168.

Index